T0270708

Financial Markets in Central and Eastern Europe

Central and Eastern European countries have built up financial systems adapted to market economies. The stability and efficiency of these systems are essential to their economic development and competitiveness. Many of the countries are also EU accession countries in the process of transforming their legal and institutional infrastructure towards Western European standards. Most of the accession countries are aiming at becoming EMU members and want to replace their currencies with the euro within a few years.

Among the topics analysed in this book are:

- the efficiency of domestic financial institutions in comparison to the efficiency of foreign institutions
- the penetration of foreign banks and the formation of cross-border financial groups
- the implications of financial integration for capital movements and financial stability.

This book contains contributions from high-ranking officials in Central Banks, supervisory institutions, International organisations and academics specialising in the functioning of financial institutions and markets. It provides valuable insights to bankers, politicians and market analysts, as well as to more general readers.

Morten Balling is Professor of Finance at the Aarhus School of Business, Denmark. **Frank Lierman** is Chief Economist at DEXIA Bank, Belgium. **Andy Mullineux** is Professor of Global Finance at the University of Birmingham, UK.

Routledge studies in the European economy

Financial Markets in Central and Eastern Europe

Stability and efficiency perspectives

Edited by Morten Balling,
Frank Lierman and Andy Mullineux

Routledge
Taylor & Francis Group

LONDON AND NEW YORK

First published 2004 by Routledge
2 Park Square, Milton Park, Abingdon, Oxon, OX14 4RN

Simultaneously published in the USA and Canada
by Routledge
711 Third Ave, New York, NY 10017

Routledge is an imprint of the Taylor & Francis Group

© 2004 Selection and editorial matter, SUERF; individual chapters,
the contributors

Typeset in Baskerville by Wearset Ltd, Boldon, Tyne and Wear

British Library Cataloguing in Publication Data
A catalogue record for this book is available from the British Library

Library of Congress Cataloging in Publication Data
A catalog record for this book has been requested

ISBN 0-415-34253-8

Contents

Figures

Tables

Contributors

Morten Balling, Professor, Department of Finance, Aarhus School of Business, Denmark.

Pedro Del Río, Economist, International Economics and International Relations Department, Banco de España, Spain.

Dirk Effenberger, Economist, Financial Markets, Regulation, Economic Research Division, Deutsche Bank, Frankfurt, Germany.

Gerhard Fink, Jean-Monet Professor, Research Institute for European Affairs, Vienna University of Economics and Business Administration, Austria.

Alicia García Herrero, Head of Division, International Economics and International Relations Department, Banco de España, Spain.

Christopher J. Green, Professor of Economics and Finance, Department of Economics, Loughborough University, UK.

Peter Haiss, Lecturer, Institute for European Studies, Vienna University of Economics and Business Administration, Austria.

Zsigmond Járai, President, National Bank of Hungary, Hungary.

Tuuli Koivu, Researcher, Institute for Economies in Transition, Bank of Finland, Finland.

Vahur Kraft, Governor, Central Bank of Estonia, Estonia.

Lelo Liive, Deputy Director, Ministry of Finance, Estonia.

Hans Christian Mantler, Research Fellow, Research Institute for European Affairs, Vienna University of Economics and Business Administration, Austria.

Victor Murinde, Professor of Development Finance, Birmingham Business School, University of Birmingham, UK.

Totka Naneva, Economic Analyst, The World Bank, USA.

Nikolay Nenovsky, Analyst, Bulgarian National Bank, Bulgaria/University of National and World Economy, Sofia, Bulgaria.

Ivaylo Nikolov, Programme Director and Senior Researcher, Centre for Economic Development, Sofia, Bulgaria.

Luigi Passamonti, Senior Advisor and Executive Secretary, The World Bank, USA.

Franz Schardax, Fund Manager, Capital Invest, Vienna, Austria.

Mart Sõrg, Professor of Money and Banking, University of Tartu, Estonia.

Michel Tison, Professor, Financial Law Institute, Ghent University, Belgium.

Mariana Tomova, Assistant Professor, University for National and World Economy, Sofia, Bulgaria.

Janek Uiboupin, Researcher, University of Tartu, Estonia.

Urmas Varblane, Professor of International Business, University of Tartu, Estonia.

Vello Vensel, Professor, Tallinn Technical University, Estonia.

C. Maxwell Watson, Research Fellow, Wolfson College, Oxford, UK.

Peter Zajc, Research Fellow, University of Ljubljana, Slovenia.

Acknowledgements

The editors would like to gratefully acknowledge the excellent support they have received in producing this book from the SUERF Secretariat based at the Austrian National Bank in Vienna, particularly Beatrix Krones and Michael Bailey, and from Jayne Close, Andy Mullineux's secretary of the Department of Accounting and Finance in the Birmingham Business School at the University of Birmingham.

Abbreviations

ABS	Asset backed security
BIS	Bank for International Settlements
BOFIT	Bank of Finland Institute for Economies in Transition
CDO	Collateral debt obligation
CEEC	Central and Eastern European Countries
CEPR	Centre for Economic Policy Research
CEPS	Centre for European Policy Studies
CRENOS	Centro Ricerche Economiche Nord Sud (Centre for North South Economic Research)
DIW	Deutsches Institut für Wirtschaftsforschung (German Institute for Economic Research)
EBRD	European Bank for Reconstruction and Development
ECB	European Central Bank
EU	European Union
EUI	European University Institute
ICT	Information and Communication Technology
IEF	Forschungsinstitut für Europafragen (Research Institute for European Affairs)
IHS	Institut für Höhere Studien (Institute for Advanced Studies)
IMF	International Monetary Fund
IPO	Initial public offering
NBER	National Bureau of Economic Research
OECD	Organisation for Economic Cooperation and Development
OeNB	*Oesterreichische Nationalbank* (The Austrian National Bank)
SUERF	Societé Universitaire Européenne de Recherches Financières (The European Money and Finance Forum)
WIFO	Österreichisches Institut für Wirtschaftsforschung (Austrian Institute of Economic Research)

Introduction

Morten Balling

The chapters in this volume were presented at a Colloquium organized in Tallinn, Estonia 12–14 June 2003 by the Société Universitaire Européenne de Recherches Financières (SUERF) in cooperation with the Bank of Estonia. The theme of the Colloquium was "Stability and Efficiency of Financial Markets in Central and Eastern Europe".

The book is organized according to the key subjects of the Colloquium. The first part contains three chapters of a more general nature presented at plenary sessions. Chapters 4–8 deal with financial efficiency and regulation, Chapters 9–12 deal with foreign and domestic bank strategy, while the remaining chapters concern financial and macro-stability.

In Chapter 1, Luigi Passamonti looks at the coming EU accession of Central and Eastern European countries (CEECs) in the light of the transition which has taken place since 1990. The World Bank and the European Bank for Reconstruction and Development have helped the transition countries with advice and loans and supported financial sector reforms. Much has been accomplished, and the reforms have contributed to the creation of economies based on market principles that are fundamental for EU accession. There are, however, still obstacles to be removed. Citizens in the accession countries want income convergence with citizens in other EU countries. Further development of the financial sector is crucial. It is time to turn the focus away from the local shortfalls and look beyond the national boundaries at what the EU single financial market can provide. The biggest benefit for the new member countries lies, according to the author, in the access for their residents – companies and individuals – to equity investors and the associated institutional investor industry of the single financial market.

Mr Passamonti characterizes the EU Financial Services Action Plan as "fast-moving". The plan has a strong development orientation. If the accession countries want to catch up, they will, for instance, have to improve the effectiveness of their collateral, pledge, foreclosure and bankruptcy procedures. They must look at local credit information and rating systems and the reliability of the accounting and auditing professions. In his concluding remarks, Mr Passamonti includes the very optimistic view that it is quite possible that the new member states may become the main beneficiaries of the EU Financial Services Action Plan.

Chapter 2 is the keynote speech given by Vahur Kraft, Governor, Bank of Estonia. The Governor divides the central bank's direct responsibilities into three large areas: monitoring and analysis of financial system developments; designing and building up financial system safety nets; and banking system regulation. The successful fulfilment of the central bank's functions in relation to monitoring and analysis depends on the quality of information and analysis. The key to vulnerability analysis is successful implementation of, ideally, several analytical tools, including early warning systems and macro-prudential analysis. Estonian banks have become an integral part of major Nordic financial groups. One of the implications is that cross-border supervision has been and will remain an important priority for Estonian supervisors. Estonian financial system safety nets have been developed in compliance with EU practices. The authorities have a current dialogue with market participants. The robustness of the Estonian financial system is strengthened by relatively high reserve requirements and a deposit guarantee scheme. Eesti Bank applies banking regulations as the prior regulatory instrument because the country's financial system is heavily bank-dominated. The bank follows, however, the development in the non-bank part of the financial system. The majority of the work required for the implementation of the *acquis communautaire* has been completed in Estonia and the financial sector is following internationally approved standards and good practices. At the same time, it is – according to the Governor – obvious that, while talking about the creation of an adequate regulatory framework, we are talking of aiming at a moving target.

Chapter 3 is the Marjolin Lecture 2003, given by Zsigmond Járai, President of the National Bank of Hungary. The guiding principle of promoting financial stability is, according to the President, based on a systemic approach. The financial stability objective of the central bank can be defined as the maintenance of a safe and sound financial infrastructure that helps to avoid financial disruptions and promotes a well-functioning real economy. Due to the positive interaction between price stability and financial stability, and the efficiency of monetary policy transmission, central banks have a vested interest in maintaining financial stability. Low and stable inflation is a necessary, but not an adequate, prerequisite for financial stability. In addition to their traditional functions, central banks also carry out special functions that are related to the macro-prudential aspects of financial stability. The difference between macro- and micro-prudential objectives is that the former have as a goal the avoidance of systemic crises and concomitant economic costs, while the latter aim to avoid the bankruptcy of individual institutions, thereby protecting the interests of depositors. In practice, the macro- and micro-prudential aspects cannot be strictly separated. Cooperation and an efficient exchange of information between the central bank and the supervisory authority is required. The increasing use of macro-prudential analysis by central banks is illustrated by the fact that central banks regularly publish financial stability reports. An overview of the contents of the Hungarian Central Bank's semi-annual report on financial stability is presented in the chapter. Potentially, financial stability reports can reduce risks to stability because market participants become better informed. The responsibility of the National Bank of Hungary for the promotion of financial stability was set forth explicitly in the Act on the Magyar Nemzeti Bank by the amendments made in 2001.

The President concludes with a brief account of the stability of the Hungarian financial system. Stress tests conducted by the central bank show that the exposure to market risks is relatively low. By contrast, credit shocks may be a significantly larger source of loss. The banking sector's capital adequacy ratio is relatively high. During the 1990s, foreign bank ownership increased in Hungary partly as a result of a deliberate privatization policy. Today, foreign ownership is close to 70 per cent. The central bank is happy with foreign ownership in the banking sector. The presence of foreign banks has increased competition and efficiency, in the corporate sector in particular. Hungarian membership of the EU from 2004 presents a number of challenges for the financial sector. The banks will need to improve their cost efficiency. EU membership will also present challenges for the authorities. Currently, Hungary does not fulfil the Maastricht criteria and it will take some time to catch up.

In Chapter 4, Tuuli Koivu analyses the relationship between the development of the banking sector and economic growth in 25 transition countries. She measures the qualitative development in the sector with the margin between lending and deposit interest rates. As a measure of the size of the sector, the author applies the amount of credit allocated to the private sector as a share of private sector production. The author finds that the interest rate margin is significantly and negatively related to economic growth. The interpretation is that greater efficiency in the banking sector accelerates economic growth. The relationship between the amount of credit to the private sector and economic growth is less clear. An observed negative link between the lagged amount of credit and growth may reflect banking crises that many transition economies experienced during the research period (1992–2001). According to the author, the results imply that the development of the financial sector cannot be measured solely by its size at least in the transition countries.

Chapter 5 deals with financial sector macro-efficiency. It is written by Hans Christian Mantler, Gerhard Fink and Peter Haiss. The authors aim at giving what they call a decision-oriented review of the growing body of empirical literature that links the financial sector to long-run economic growth. Inspired by Tobin, Merton, Bodie, Levine and others, they specify five main functions that the financial sector should perform: pooling of savings, allocation of resources, exercise of corporate control, diversifying risk and providing a reliable and efficient payment system. They propose to simultaneously consider the macro-economic benefits related to the fulfilment of these five functions and the costs in the financial sector related to carrying out those functions.

In order to give a comprehensive literature review of empirical work dealing with financial sector macro-efficiency, the authors systematically screen 39 top academic journals and 34 working paper series of relevant institutions. They also check literature databases for relevant literature. Among approximately 18,000 articles and working papers, 62 are identified as empirical studies of financial sector macro-efficiency. The authors classify the different financial sector indicators applied in the empirical literature in the following categories: indicators of respectively size, efficiency, structure and "other". Most indicators proxying the size of financial markets focus on stock markets. Stock market capitalization divided by GDP is a very popular measure. With respect to a measure of efficiency, they refer to Koivu's use of the bank interest margin (Chapter 4 in this volume). The ratio of stock market capitalization to credits provided by banks may be used as an indicator for structure. The authors find impressive evidence from broad empirical studies that financial sector size and industry efficiency have an economically important impact on economic growth. Evidence for transition countries indicates that growth enhancing potential lies not so much in financial sector size, but more in financial sector efficiency. Strong evidence supports the conjecture that a country's legal system, its adaptability to changing business conditions and the priority it gives to creditor/investor right protection, law enforcement and the quality of accounting standards drive financial sector development.

In Chapter 6, C. Maxwell Watson defines efficiency of the financial sector as its capacity to allocate capital and to support sustainable growth, including as a conduit and filter for capital flows and as a monetary transmission channel. The accession countries have made major efficiency advances, but in the years to come they will have to have well-focused management strategies in financial institutions, strengthened regulatory and supervisory policies, an appropriate mix of fiscal and monetary policies, and a well-functioning monitoring of broad credit trends, with a macro-prudential frame of reference. Efficiency in allocation is the key both to economic growth and to macro-financial stability. Studies of data from the individual CEECs make it clear that overall financial depth has been improving in recent years.

A decade after transition began, the progress that has been made in strengthening the efficiency of the financial sector is impressive, but it gives no grounds for complacency in terms of the path ahead. Foreign direct investments have up to now played a significant role in terms of capital raising and governance. The domestic financial sector will probably have to assume a more important role in the future. The next few years should also see a growing importance of the interest rate transmission channel for monetary policy. There are still weak outliers among banks, insurance companies and pension funds that may experience financial difficulties in the coming years. Regulatory and supervisory policies will therefore be crucial. Standards of transparency and disclosure, corporate governance and the effectiveness of the judicial system are important for access to the EU and global financial markets. If all of these policy challenges are handled appropriately, the catch-up in living standards towards those of present EU members can be realized.

In Chapter 7, Michel Tison discusses the potential liability of financial supervisors. Claims against the supervisory authority may be based on alleged shortcomings of the latter in adequately discharging its supervisory responsibilities thereby causing losses to the depositors. Alternatively, the supervised institution itself may claim that it has suffered a loss due to a pro-active and harsh intervention by the supervisory authority. Balancing these potential claims creates a dilemma for the supervisor. The present legal situation as regards supervisory liability in the EU member states is characterized by its large diversity. The author gives an overview of supervisory liability of banking supervisors in different EU member states and distinguishes between liability due, respectively, to negligence, gross negligence and bad faith. In an EU perspective, the issue of supervisory liability is still "under construction". Individual member states increasingly tend to limit supervisory liability through statutory immunity regimes, thereby supported by the Basle Committee's Core Principles. On the other hand, depositors more and more put pressure on national courts by relying on EU Law as a legal foundation for supervisory liability.

In Chapter 8, Lelo Liive starts by listing the challenges that efficient financial regulation has to deal with. Globalization, as well as innovation in financial products, structures and technologies belong to the realities that make financial regulation increasingly complex. Regulators should make sure that regulation does not prevent fair competition and innovation. Regulators must respond to the formation of financial conglomerates. According to the author, Estonia has made strong progress to date in developing a private-owned and market-oriented banking sector. With substantial influence in recent years from strong Nordic strategic investors, productivity and efficiency of the financial sector is rapidly approaching Western European standards. The legal infrastructure is currently being updated. The Tallinn Stock Exchange has been integrated with the Helsinki Stock Exchange. In 2001, the Estonian Financial Supervisory Authority was established as an independent institution affiliated with the Bank of Estonia. The Estonian authorities follow very closely the many regulatory initiatives that are related to the EU Commission's Financial Services Action Plan. From the spring of 2003, the accession countries have had the opportunity to take part in the discussions in the system of EU working groups and committees preparing financial regulation.

In Chapter 9, Peter Zajc examines the effect of foreign bank entry on the domestic banking sector in the Czech Republic, Estonia, Hungary, Poland, Slovakia and Slovenia in the 1995–2000 period. The author draws on the BankScope database. Five standard accounting ratios are applied, all defined as fractions of total bank assets: net interest margin, non-interest income, before-tax profit, overhead and loan loss provisions. The statistical analysis shows that an increase in the share of foreign banks in the total number of banks is significantly associated with a reduction of non-interest income and before-tax profit. The foreign bank number is not statistically significantly associated with the net interest margin and loan loss provisions. The impact of foreign bank entry on domestic banks works through increased competition and enhanced efficiency.

In Chapter 10, Christopher J. Green, Victor Murinde and Ivaylo Nikolov model the efficiency of domestic and foreign banks in CEECs in terms of economies of scale and scope. The basis of the empirical analysis is a panel of 273 foreign and domestic banks located in Bulgaria, Croatia, the Czech Republic, Estonia, Hungary, Latvia, Lithuania, Poland and Romania for the period 1995–1999. Again, the data is retrieved from the BankScope database. An interesting result is that foreign banks are not really more efficient than domestic banks in these economies. The analysis seems to challenge the idea that foreign ownership matters with regard to efficiency. Foreign banks are not always more scale efficient than the average domestic bank in the sample European transition economies, neither do foreign banks seem to be ahead of domestic competitors in terms of scope economies.

In Chapter 11, Mariana Tomova, Nikolay Nenovsky and Totka Naneva study the differences and convergence trends in banking system efficiency for nine transition economies in CEE during the period 1993–2001. The authors investigate to what extent banking systems in the CEECs have been successful in the transformation and convergence to the EU as measured by their relative operational efficiency. Data is again retrieved from the BankScope database but also from OECD. They analyse technical efficiency according to two different scenarios: the first is based on the profit-maximizing behaviour of banks, while the second is based on the economic growth-generating objectives of the regulatory authorities. The results of data envelopment analysis are presented in terms of efficiency scores. For the CEE banks, efficiency scores are well below the world average. This implies that banks in the CEECs have to further improve efficiency so as to achieve world and European best practices. Data on time trends indicate that there is convergence in efficiency both in the regional and the European dimension.

In Chapter 12, Mart Sõrg, Janek Uiboupin, Urmas Varblane and Vello Vensel analyse the internationalization of Estonian banks. Foreign banks have intensively entered into the Estonian banking market and currently own more than 86 per cent of the aggregated share capital of Estonian banks. After a comprehensive literature overview, the authors present empirical evidence first on Estonian outward-banking investments and after that on foreign banks' direct investments in Estonia. Estonian outward investments have been in Latvia and Lithuania in particular. Scandinavian banks have been, and still are, very active inward investors in Estonia. In many cases, foreign banks have entered when the local banks were in difficulties. The authors utilize the results of a survey of foreign and domestic banks in Estonia, Lithuania, Poland and Romania. A sample of banks in these countries were asked about their motives for entering new markets. Among the main results are that macroeconomic and political stability of the host country, a good potential for future EU membership and business prospects with existing and potential new clients are considered to be very important factors. The banks were also asked how they evaluated their own prospects for survival as independent institutions. The Estonian banks were, on average, very optimistic and most of them expected to maintain their independence even in the long term. The Polish banks expected, on average, that in the long term they would be involved in a merger with another bank.

In Chapter 13, Franz Schardax presents an early warning model for currency crises. The model applies quarterly data from 12 CEE transition countries. After a brief review of theories and empirical studies of currency crises, the author explains the construction of a multivariate probit model. The author considers such a model to be the most appropriate when information provided in different indicators is to be incorporated at the same time. The predictive power of the model is analysed by means of expectation/prediction tables for different model specifications and by comparing quadratic probability scores. The study lends some support to crisis models which rely on economic fundamentals in explaining currency crises.

In Chapter 14, Dirk Effenberger explores the channels through which institutions can influence a country's vulnerability to currency crises. Certain institutional arrangements can increase the credibility of policymakers' decisions and convince the markets of the stability of an exchange rate. Institutional characteristics like transparency and disclosure requirements, prudential banking and financial supervision and corporate governance rules may reduce information asymmetries. In the empirical analysis both institutional and macroeconomic control variables serve as indicators. The indicators of the quality of the institutional setting in 11 CEECs are retrieved from the EBRD Transition Report. The observed improvement of the institutional setting suggests that institutional reforms have recently contributed to the decline in the number of currency crises in the CEECs. The choice of exchange rate regime matters. The vulnerability of the CEECs to currency crises is reduced significantly with a currency board or a flexible regime. It is the evaluation of the author that ERM II, in which most of the accession countries are expected to participate soon owing to the bilateral intervention obligations, will have much greater credibility than conventional fixed-rate regimes. The quality of the regulatory and supervisory setting and the degree of liberalization also matter. A hybrid model which includes both institutional indicators and macroeconomic variables provide better forecasts than a purely economic model.

Chapter 15 by Alicia García Herrero and Pedro del Río was awarded the Marjolin Prize 2003 for the best contribution to the Colloquium by authors below the age of 40. The authors look at the role that the design of monetary policy may have in fostering financial stability. On the basis of data from 79 countries, they assess empirically whether countries whose central bank focuses narrowly on price stability are less prone to financial instability, when accounting for other factors, and they test which monetary policy strategy, if any, best contributes to financial stability. Historically, there has been a trend towards objectives with a greater focus on price stability. The authors concentrate on banking crises and use existing surveys of crises events to identify periods of systemic and non-systemic crises. The different types of central bank objectives are summarized into an index, which takes a larger value the more narrowly the central bank's statutory objectives focus on price stability. Central bank strategies are classified into exchange rate targeting, monetary targeting and direct inflation targeting.

Countries whose central banks narrowly focus on price stability appear to have a lower probability of suffering from a banking crisis. In addition, higher economic growth and higher real GDP per capita, which is considered to be a proxy for the quality of institutions, significantly reduce the probability of a banking crisis.

1 Financial-sector development as a tool for EU accession

Luigi Passamonti

I am very grateful to SUERF for having invited me to deliver one of the opening addresses of this Colloquium with a reflection on the role of financial-sector development. But the organizers have also saddled me with a task that represents a big intellectual challenge for somebody that does not work in Brussels: to place my reflection in the context of EU accession. I am glad that SUERF pushed me to take this perspective. In making myself familiar with recent EU policy work, I realized how much EU solutions could help realize the full benefits of the reforms the accession countries have started with World Bank and IMF assistance thirteen years ago. I ask for your prior forgiveness if some of my observations regarding EU solutions are off mark.

The transition

Let me start with a quote drawn from a speech at a World Bank conference in 1990 by the Minister of Finance of a transition country:

> We ask ourselves how to unfold the whole process of economic transformation, how to sequence it. That is what we consider the most crucial problem. Then, when the transformation process has already started, as it has in my country, we ask ourselves how not to lose the momentum of the reform; how to build and maintain the necessary political and social consensus; how to maintain credibility of the reform policy; how not to cross the tolerance limit of the population; how to break down the old, unproductive, collectivistic social contract – how to transform it, how to rewrite it; and how to minimize the costs of restructuring in terms of growth, employment, inflation and so on.

These thoughts are indicative of the iron determination with which this Minister was looking at the multiple challenges of transition. He identified many problems. He did not have most solutions. He found them as he went along. He knew he would make mistakes. He did make mistakes.

He and others corrected these mistakes. His country will join the EU in 2004.

Seven additional countries successfully mastered the challenges of transition over the last decade. Two more, Bulgaria and Romania, are on the last mile to accession. Croatia is waiting to be admitted to the official race.

World Bank assistance

The World Bank has helped these countries cope with the transition with advice and loans in an aggregate value of about $15 billion, of which $2 billion have been used to support financial sector reforms through restructuring and privatization of state-owned banks and capacity building of supervisory authorities. EBRD, IFC and MIGA have also supported the transition with several billions of dollars of financial support to companies and financial institutions.

The World Bank's most recent activity has been to conduct thorough assessments of the financial systems of all ten accession countries together with the IMF as part of the Financial Sector Assessment Program. The results have helped the authorities fine-tune their reform strategies. They have also been used extensively by the European Commission to inform their assessment of the performance of financial sector intermediation and financial supervisory arrangements as part of their monitoring of countries' progress towards accession.

Financial sector reform: key to accession process

Without successful financial sector reform, a fundamental criteria for accession – an economy functioning on market principles – would not have been met. This has been a major accomplishment. To establish a proper legal and regulatory framework for financial intermediation activities and, within this framework, to have several hundreds of independent financial institutions mobilize and allocate the nations' savings in a profitable and sustainable way has been a very significant accomplishment – given initial conditions.

But I doubt it would be productive today to look backwards at what these countries have accomplished, even though the accomplishments are truly highly significant, especially if compared to those of other emerging countries at comparable level of GDP or of institutional development. Probably only Mexico can claim to have accomplished a similar overhaul of its financial system over a decade.

Obstacles to be removed

Much should be said, however, on obstacles that still need to be removed. The level of performance and efficiency of the financial sector is far from

EU levels. Eugenio Domingo Solans, a member of the Executive Board of the European Central Bank said recently:

> The traditional role of the financial sector in underpinning investment and realizing growth potential through its intermediation and governance functions is still very limited in most EU accession countries.

There is a long list of 'teething' problems. Private sector credit has not grown much and remains at a low level relative to GDP. SME lending accounts for less than 30 per cent of total loans, even though SMEs represent more than 60 per cent of employment and value added. Stock market capitalization and other measures of market-based finance (mutual funds, pensions, bonds outstanding) are low compared to international levels. Enforcement of laws and regulations is less predictable and less mindful of possible market impact than in the EU-15.

But I do not think either that it would be productive today to look at the further reforms needed with the transition lens – as if the race was soon going to be over. Transition is already over. EU accession is happening. I propose to change the lens of our assessment.

A post-accession perspective

Citizens of new member countries aspire to income convergence with the EU as quickly as possible. What are the pre-conditions for this process to continue? How long will this take? Do any of the strategies and approaches need to be adjusted to reap the benefits of EU membership more rapidly?

Income convergence will occur through the realization of productivity gains. They will be made possible by a range of improvements in how economic activity is organized, supported by sustained high levels of investment and organizational efficiencies gains. At the end of the day, each working citizen of the new member countries will need to produce a multiple unit of output than at present. Financial leverage will help accelerate the build-up of fixed and intangible assets that are necessary to support higher economic activity. It is estimated that less than 20 per cent of SMEs capital needs are now met by bank credit. External finance (i.e., private sector credit), whose stock today in the region amounts to approximately 40 per cent of GDP, will need to converge towards the EU level which is three-and-a-half times bigger, that is 140 per cent of GDP.

Of course, rapid credit expansion could happen in a few years. But the risk of creating a bubble through inadequate credit screening is high. The piercing of the bubble forces abrupt de-leveraging – that is, credit contraction. In this region, the memories of the rapid credit expansion in Finland and Sweden, followed by a sharp credit and output contraction, are still vivid. In Finland the ratio of private credit to GDP moved from 55 per cent in 1985 to 95 per cent in just five years before settling back in 2000 to the level where it started 15 years before. In Sweden, after topping 140 per cent of GDP in 1993, it fell to 110 per cent in 1995 before resuming its upward trend.

Conversely, sluggish credit growth caused by extra-prudent banks sets back potential progress of society towards a higher level of personal welfare. It would be inappropriate for authorities to give the signal that credit risk underwriting standards need to be relaxed. Banks burdened with non-performing loans create many distortions in the financial system.

Even with a strong regulatory framework and supervisory practices, complemented by effective market discipline and supported by strong bank governance, sustainable credit deepening might be elusive.

Indeed there are intrinsic limits to how much capital domestic banks can effectively recycle in the local economy given the deposits they can mobilize, the returns available, the intermediation costs to be incurred, the risk profile of potential borrowers, the loan portfolio concentration risk and the equity base that shareholders are prepared to allocate to that particular business in the country.

What I am referring to is the issue of the size of the domestic financial system. In all accession countries, the individual size is very small. The biggest market is Poland: but the total assets of its 84 banks amount to US$120 billion – the size of the world's seventy-ninth largest bank which is the Commonwealth Bank of Australia. The smallest market is Estonia with US$2.6 billion. The overall size of the banking sector of the ten Central and Southern European accession countries is less than 2 per cent of the EU-15 banking sector. The size of the non-bank financial markets (insurance, pension and mutual funds) and of the equities and bond markets is even smaller relative to GDP.

The constraints of small financial systems

Small financial systems have special challenges. They are penalized by reduced network externalities in the payment and settlement infrastructure. Negative economies of scale apply to both this infrastructure and to the supervisory one. There is a higher cost per euro intermediated to support a small financial system than a larger one. And the policy capacity installed might not be sufficient to deal with emergency situations as it would in bigger markets.

Moving now from the system to individual institutions, the latter try to overcome the small size of the former by pursuing economies of scale in their individual operations. Hence, small systems have higher degrees of concentration than larger systems. But even large banks in small systems operate at sub-optimal scale as their overhead ratios are higher, compensated by higher interest margin spreads. This hampers deposit mobilization. The small equity base constrains their risk appetite. Riskier borrowers are rationed out of the lending market. Loan portfolios are more risky because of a lack of sectoral diversification. Small countries use off-shore deposit facilities more extensively than large countries, thus shifting liquidity abroad. Growth of non-bank finance and market-based finance is more constrained in small markets than in larger markets.

The future of market-based finance in small financial systems is questionable – other than possibly for the riskiest segment of small companies where local investors could have a role. Capital market infrastructure is already subject to international consolidation. Listings and liquidity migrate to few trading centres.

Benefits and beneficiaries of the EU single financial market

I believe EU accession offers a silver lining to the constraints of sub-scale financial systems and sub-scale financial intermediaries. The EU *acquis communautaire* is not a burden to be tolerated for the purpose of being admitted to the European club. The *acquis communautaire*, which is a fast-evolving body of financial sector legislation, could become the fulcrum on which to place the lever of a renewed financial sector development strategy for the new member countries.

The preparation for the EU single financial market, pursuant to the Financial Sector Action Plan, is moving at fast pace. And its implementation is not a matter for regulators. It has the attention of European Heads of State and Government. They are committed to complete it by 2005.

The vision of the single financial market is to create a borderless capital pool, mainly destined for wholesale operators. But the benefits of the economies of scale enjoyed by the operators could accrue to retail investors and small and medium-sized enterprises that have a limited range of choice within national boundaries.

I would like to quote a statement from Alexandre Lamfalussy when he submitted the report of his Wise Men Commission to the European Ministers of Finance:

> We urge governments and European institutions to ensure that there is an appropriate environment for the development of the supply of risk capital for the growing small and medium-sized companies. We believe that if our recommendations are followed and effectively implemented the primary beneficiaries will be those SMEs.

The benefits of a single market will be greatest to the users of those national markets that are the least integrated and the smallest. These are the new member countries.

In the new member countries, much more than in any other EU-15 country, the solution for credit and financial deepening could be found at the level of the EU single financial market – and not within the boundaries of their small financial markets.

It is thus time to turn our sights away from the local shortfalls and start looking beyond the national boundaries at what the EU single financial market can provide. This should be the new lens of our assessment. And then we should go back and examine what each new member country needs to do in order to take advantage of the EU solutions.

We start from a good base: the new member countries have adopted a legislative and regulatory framework that is EU-compatible. And they have achieved a degree of financial sector integration with the EU-15 that is incomparably deeper than the one existing among EU-15 countries. In the Euro area, according to the EU Commission, less than 5 per cent of bank branches are owned by banks from other EU countries. In the new member countries, the percentage is of the order of 70 per cent, controlled by less than a dozen of international banks. In the Czech Republic, Hungary and Poland, the scale of cross-border financial intermediation is, in addition, already quite significant: it represents about 30 per cent of domestic private sector credit intermediation.

The benefits of the single financial market for the new member countries

What will the single financial market allow new member states to achieve? It will foster competition. And it will multiply the options for the provision of financial services. The multi-country presence of foreign investors in the region, combined with their leading position in their home markets, creates a connectivity tissue between the single financial market and the local markets for the benefit of local users – be they companies or individuals.

Local companies will have the option to borrow either from locally-licensed banks or from foreign branches or even from non-resident banks, which will be allowed to sell their services at a distance with a comparable degree of consumer protection.

But the biggest benefit for the new member countries, in my opinion, lies in the access for its residents – companies and individuals – to equity and bond investors and the associated institutional investor industry of the single financial market.

Let me give you some figures: Euro-zone investors hold un-intermediated financial assets worth about €25 trillion, of which €16 trillion are equities. As a comparison, the overall private sector credit of new member countries is €120 billion – a mere 0.5 per cent of the euro-zone asset base. A marginal reallocation of the euro-zone investors asset mix over the medium-term would provide the wherewithal for accelerated economic convergence of the new member countries. These are investors that are used to taking calculated risks as they operate in a very competitive market.

Is this just a dream? Yes, today. But it may become reality over the medium-term. With a single prospectus based on common accounting and disclosure standards and a rapidly converging securities market infrastructure, companies of new member countries will be connected to the diverse universe of investors across the single financial market that have a keener risk appetite and much stronger risk absorption capacity than domestic investors.

The credit risk underwriting considerations for a unit of credit risk in a domestic banking market, like Estonia, where three large banks control 91 per cent of the market with a combined €350 million capital base, are necessarily more restrictive than those applied, to same unit of credit risk, by a large group of investors each with total investable funds in the range of several hundreds of billion euro, even after taking into account the advantages of proximity for credit screening purposes of the domestic banks. The risk tolerance of large investors is bigger than those of small investors for a given unit of risk.

Also, securitization techniques allow the reduction of the risk profile of the unit of credit risk by creating a more diversified loan portfolio on the basis of post-credit approval performance information that the one that can be built *ex ante* on a piece-meal basis by any single bank.

Lastly, within the EU single financial market expanded to ten new member countries, intermediaries will be able to further lower the risk profile by assembling multi-country composite loan portfolios with even smaller credit risk co-variances.

Thus, it may not be far-fetched to think that the solution to SMEs' term borrowing needs in new member countries can be searched in the single financial market. I will speak later of the obstacles to be removed.

Moving now to the investing side, the mutual funds and pension directives will enable local residents, be they companies or individuals, to take advantage of the expertise, economies of scale and risk diversification offered by an industry operating at a global level. The advantage will be faster asset accumulation or lower pension contributions.

How to unlock the benefits? Considerations and obstacles

The benefits of the single financial market for new member countries could be very significant. How to unlock them? There are two background considerations. First, the pre-accession work focused on the adoption of legal and regulatory practices that are largely independent from the broad reform agenda represented by the fast-moving Financial Sector Action Plan. They reflect predominantly *stability* considerations. The main recipients are authorities. Second, the Action Plan has conversely a strong *development* orientation. It involves defining an architecture within which market forces will operate. The main beneficiaries are market participants and users.

And there are two sets of obstacles for the new member countries to reap the benefits of the single market. A first set of obstacles relates to the quality of enforcement of regulatory decisions pursuant to the *acquis* provisions. Lack of a consistent track record in enforcement will influence perceptions of market participants in this respect. Regular monitoring and continuous peer review assistance by the EU-15 will help bridge this perception and reality gap, if national authorities deepen their commitment to strengthening their capacity in this area after accession.

But, and perhaps more importantly, obstacles relate also to matters outside the scope of the core *acquis*. I refer to the effectiveness of the collateral, pledge, foreclosure and bankruptcy procedures. I also refer to the existence of local credit information and rating systems and to the reliability of the accounting and auditing professions.

Shortcomings in the functioning of these key elements of market underpinnings will prevent local borrowers from reaping the benefits of the single financial market. EU-15 investors will be reluctant to buy securities representing a portfolio of claims to small-sized borrowers of new member countries if they doubt the integrity of the prospectus data or if they fear that the servicing agent will face unreasonably protracted judiciary procedures to collect past due amounts. The most recent IMF study on financial globalization indicates that these elements, taken as a whole, enhance the absorption capacity of international capital flows by local financial systems and help recipient countries reap the benefit of financial integration.

These obstacles cannot be removed with the transposition of a new body of EU legislation, as was mainly the case on the way to accession. Their removal requires the identification of local solutions and the active involvement of a complex web of local institutions in their implementation. It is the evolution from law transplantation to institution-building. The former is much quicker than the latter.

A second set of obstacles relates to the fact that the new *acquis* under preparation per the Financial Sector Action Plan prefigures new ways of doing business at the EU scale without particular reference to the situation and the needs of new member countries. And the jury is still out as to who will be the winners and in respect of which strategy. It is, thus, a second evolution: from law transplantation to law-making in an uncertain context.

It falls on the new member countries, therefore, to assess how best to shape their local legislation so as to connect it with the new single market in a way that meets their specific national objectives in a context of strategic flux.

This calls for the formulation of new domestic financial sector development strategies. Where to start from?

A new financial sector strategy in new member countries: preliminary considerations

When launching this strategy exercise, it is important to clearly articulate the over-arching goal of financial sector policy. The main trade-off is between the welfare of the users and the preservation of the stability of the existing financial intermediaries.

Cross-border provision of financial products may benefit users, but it may also threaten local incumbents and shape new entry options in local markets in unexpected ways.

The relative shallowness of the domestic financial systems of new member countries is an opportunity to reflect on how one envisions the progressive deepening in its bank-based and market-based components. While the retail banking business has kept a local market bias, market-based products require the scale that an EU-wide market can provide.

But also on banking there are already indications, as Professor Issing of the European Central Bank has shown, that relationship banking in the euro-area, heretofore the predominant business model, might start to be eroded as a result of overcapacity and product diversification in the commercial banking sector leading to concentration and consolidation.

G-10 countries have looked hard at how the consolidation of financial services is impacting the transmission of monetary policy, the efficiency and competition of financial services delivery and, more particularly, the credit flows to small and medium-sized companies. The January 2001 report, though not conclusive in terms of strong policy recommendations, contains indications that these issues are on the watching brief of central banks.

Consolidation and concentration in small and open national financial systems with a large degree of foreign ownership pose special political challenges. One wonders if one should not pre-empt this concern and design a strategy that might have a lower likelihood of leading to further domestic concentration in small financial systems down the road.

Even in the most sophisticated EU national financial market, as arguably is the UK, there has been a protracted debate on access to financial services by SMEs. The latest Competition Commission report shows that the four largest clearing banks hold a 73 per cent combined market share of this segment. And that their average return on equity of this activity is 36 per cent p.a. – well in excess of their average cost of capital, which is 15 per cent. The annual excess profit is about €1.5 billion, equivalent to four times the capital base of Estonia's banking sector.

Therefore, it will be prudent to undertake a very forward-looking examination as to what options the new single financial market will provide for the new member states in terms of provision of cross-border financial services that will both preserve competition and enhance user's choice.

Full and open consultations

It is thus important in new member countries that the new *developmentally oriented* financial sector strategy and the ensuing new financial sector legislation, including the transposition of new EU directives, be formulated on the basis of full and open consultations – not only with local market participants and users but also with potential new entrants and alternative cross-border providers.

Only in this way will authorities have a comprehensive appreciation of the different vantage points and policy options available to better serve its citizens within the boundaries of the new single financial market.

Tommaso Padoa-Schioppa shed interesting light on the market development process. He said:

> Whoever, as I do, holds the view that freedom and responsibility should pervade the economic life, is inclined to let market forces do as much as they can to transform the structure of the market in an optimal way, not only carry on activities within a given market structure. … But it is crucial to be aware that market-led progress does require co-operation among economic (public and private) agents.

In the EU context, he clarified:

> Further financial integration can only result from an effective interplay between competitive market forces, co-operative efforts among market participants and the action of public authorities. Public authorities should act as both catalyst – fostering co-operation among market participants, whenever needed – and as regulators.

Participatory practices are still more the exception than the norm in most accession countries. Law and regulation making is still seen as the undivided privilege of the authorities. Market participants are rarely consulted. When they are consulted it is with little time to provide a response. And the text submitted for consultations is often in final form with an inner logic that cannot accommodate changes without a comprehensive re-drafting. Finally, market participants are not yet organized to be an effective partner of this dialogue with authorities.

In this context I am pleased to announce that EBRD and World Bank are preparing an initiative, called 'Convergence', that aims at assisting authorities in engaging with and harnessing the incentives of market participants to prepare further financial sector reforms. Although its target area of operation will be individual countries in South Eastern Europe, its know-how and experience could be shared with the new member countries.

'Convergence' will aim to replicate the principle and practices of open and full consultations with market participants and users that has become part and parcel of the EU legislative process as recommended by the Lamfalussy Report. 'Convergence' will help prepare draft laws and regulations that meet public policy objectives with a lower likelihood of hampering or distorting market functioning.

Open discussions help establish a consensus on how public policy could best be shaped to meet the challenges of building a financial market. Prior consultations foster ownership by market participants of the solutions retained. And when this public–private collaborative method is well established, authorities could make their convening power available to help market participants find collaborative solutions that enable further market growth – in terms, for instance, of standardizing credit documentation, payment solutions and financial market practices. The European Central Bank has been very innovative in this respect.

Strengthening financial sector stability

Effective financial system integration of the new member countries with the EU requires continuous work to ensure that the financial stability infrastructure is seamless across the single market. Supervisory practices still differ. It is a big challenge to strengthen them as markets, market practices and institutions change so rapidly. This creates challenges even for the most sophisticated supervisory authorities in the EU.

Market discipline can and should complement official supervision. Transparency and disclosures are key. But there are more elements to it. As Andrew Crockett once said:

> For market discipline to be effective, four pre-requisites have to be met: First, market participants need to have sufficient information to reach informed judgments. Second, they need to have the ability to process it correctly. Third, they need to have the right incentives. Finally, they need to have the right mechanisms to exercise discipline.

Too often has market discipline been seen as a proxy for debt holders selling uninsured instruments in response to a perceived worsening financial condition of the issuer. But market discipline can and should also be equity-based. And not only in terms of acting on the price signalling, but also and more importantly on the actions taken by shareholders and boards to protect the viability of the financial institution. I am referring to the issue of 'bank governance'.

More emphasis on bank governance

Supervisory policies and practices tend to under-rate the potential contribution of effective boards to financial stability. Particularly in jurisdictions with a less-than-consolidated pattern of relationship between supervisor and supervisee (as in the new member countries, also because of the significant number of new foreign investors), an effective board can have a vital role in strengthening the checks and balances system. By effective board I mean a board that is clearly the principal locus of accountability for the stability of the financial institution. It means that its membership has to have the capability, motivation and authority to act independently from management. In this region, too few financial institutions have the pre-requisite in place for board effectiveness: non-executive nature, in substance, of its members and a sufficient number of them being independent from majority shareholders. When one combines this situation with the fact that supervisory authorities are unclear as to how to assess the effectiveness of the parent's management oversight and the value of their financial responsibility for the local affiliate, one derives a sense of discomfort for the quantity of new risk and the pace of build-up the system can sustainably cope with.

I believe that it would be important for national supervisors to look for ways to help boards and shareholders take on more oversight responsibility for financial institutions. One could envisage being able to draw on a combination of incentives and enforcements to promote this change of practices. Supervisors could envisage sharing appropriate information with boards and shareholders on the financial condition of the bank, the adequacy of its risk management architecture and practices and an assessment of senior management actions. Similarly, they should keep the boards accountable for their oversight actions or lack thereof.

A last remark: we have observed that where bank supervisors promote bank transparency and thus induce private sector monitoring of banks, credit access conditions improve.

Conclusion

Financial-sector development in new member countries will be key to sustaining rapid convergence of income levels with old member states as much as it has been to enabling EU accession.

In its first progress report on enlargement in 1998, the EU Commission wrote: 'Taking the two criteria together, that is the existence of a market economy and the capacity to withstand competitive pressure and market forces within the Union, it can be said that none of the applicants today fully meets the Copenhagen criteria.' Three years later, one year before the 2002 Copenhagen summit, the Commission stated that the eight first-wave accession countries were functioning market economies. This attests to the vitality of the new member countries.

It is thus possible for the new member countries to become beneficiaries of the EU Financial Sector Action Plan. This would be a somewhat unexpected outcome. When the Plan was launched in June 1998, the enlargement process was still in its infancy and spurred mainly by political considerations.

EU membership, at a time of a rapidly evolving regulatory framework, combined with a freshly re-configured financial system, characterized by significant ownership links with old EU member states, is the platform for a potential leapfrog in financial sector development.

The vision for a new financial sector development strategy in the region could consist of the following:

- to include explicit considerations of the welfare of the citizen and credit access for the SME in the definition of the guiding policy principle for the strategy;
- to develop a policy formulation tool that allows the identification of least-cost provision options from EU providers (this involves launching open EU-wide consultation processes);
- to accelerate the upgrade of domestic legal, corporate governance, accounting and auditing standards and practices so as to ensure the connectivity of local institutions and firms to the single financial market;
- to adopt measures to favour the establishment and the sustainable operations of small community banks to complement financial services provided cross-border for the benefit of the small user.

This is a major exercise. National authorities and the EU will lead it. But it requires the involvement of many players – also, and in particular, of market participants.

As an old City of London adage goes: 'Markets are not created by rules and regulations; they are created by market participants'. In the new member countries, authorities will need to tap into the experience, energy and incentives of all those that have a stake in this process and can contribute to helping define the new rules of the game.

I am sure that the richness of the deliberations of this three-day Colloquium will help to create the momentum for the launch perhaps of a New Members Financial Sector Action Plan!

Thank you very much.

2 Factors influencing the financial system stability-oriented policies of a small country soon to become an EU Member

The Estonian experience

Vahur Kraft

Introduction

Ladies and Gentlemen,
Dear guests,
Esteemed colleagues,

It is an honour and a pleasure for me to deliver one of the keynote speeches at the concluding session of the first ever SUERF Colloquium to be held in Tallinn.

This Colloquium has been dedicated to the issues of financial efficiency and regulation, foreign and domestic bank strategy, financial and macro-stability – that means issues that are certainly topical from the point of view of any EU candidate country.

The efficiency of financial systems is particularly important for Central and Eastern European countries where modern financial systems have been built up almost from scratch over the last ten years. In line with the EU accession process, full integration of Central and Eastern European countries' financial systems to the EMU has increasingly become a priority. The integration and flexibility of financial systems plays an essential role in promoting full convergence and supporting economic stability within the monetary policy framework of the EMU. On the day of a country's accession to the common currency area, its monetary policy transmission channels, via the financial sector, should be very similar to those of present member states. That would ensure effective and full pass-through of ECB monetary policy signals.

One of the developments many Central and East European countries have experienced is the entrance of foreign banks. Foreign capital has generally had a positive impact on the financial sector, increasing competition and making it possible to import a more advanced management culture and professional skills. But there are also some differences between individual countries' experience that make comparisons all the more interesting.

In my presentation today I would like to take a closer look at the factors influencing the financial sector policies of a small country like Estonia, soon to become an EU member, and I would like to do that from the point of view of the central bank who is at the same time the lead regulator of the banking sector in a country where the banking sector forms more than 80 per cent of the whole financial sector.

What is the central bank's role in supporting financial stability?

Directly or indirectly, the primary goal of most central banks is price stability. Regardless of the exact monetary policy regime under which price stability is targeted, financial systems always have a crucial importance in this process. On the one hand, stable and well-functioning financial systems are, in themselves, promoting price stability via effective resource allocation. On the other hand, monetary policy can be successfully implemented only through effective and well-functioning financial systems.

Monetary transmission cannot be efficient if a weak financial system distorts interest rate signals by increasing margins, or if financial markets have ceased to function for the reason that some of the participants do not trust other players. The causality can also run in the opposite direction. Over the past decade we have, once and again, in many countries, witnessed a weak financial system causing a currency crisis that results in capital flight, devaluation and deep recession. This particular threat is especially relevant to fixed exchange rate systems where financial sector assets and liabilities usually tend to have a currency mismatch. And finally, central banks are interested in financial stability, as they often have to take the leading role in crisis resolution by providing emergency assistance and working out restructuring plans.

What are the most important responsibilities of a central bank in maintaining financial stability?

A central bank's direct responsibilities in maintaining financial stability, apart from its direct supervisory functions, can be divided into three large areas.

First, central banks are responsible for the monitoring and analysis of financial system developments and have to take note of any early signs of possible financial difficulties. Central banks are well positioned for that task because of their close relations with market participants and because of the analytical skills that provide a natural background for analysing the so-called macro-prudential indicators and performing regular stress testing.

Second, central banks are, by definition, involved in designing and building up financial system safety nets. The so-called 'traditional' central banks are directly responsible for short-term emergency liquidity support to prevent the problems of one institution from developing into a systemic crisis. Even if the ability to provide liquidity assistance is limited like it is in case of a currency board, central banks take – or are supposed to take – a leading role in crisis resolution.

Third, central banks are often responsible for the banking system regulation. That is also the case in Estonia, even after the recent restructuring of the supervisory function. From the central bank's point of view, banking regulation policy goes somewhat beyond the traditional micro-prudential approach that is the basis for the Basel capital accords. For a central bank, really important questions are: to what extent does banking policy depend on the general macroeconomic conditions? And should regulatory changes take into account business cycles or should they be guided solely by concerns on the micro level?

Monitoring and analysis

The successful fulfilment of the central bank's financial-stability supporting functions depends to a great extent on the quality of information and analysis available. A thorough understanding of the functioning of modern complex financial systems is a prerequisite for developing an adequate framework for financial intermediation. The availability of timely and high-quality information on changes in the general operating environment, especially risk exposures and potential contagion channels, would enable a central bank to implement timely and effective counteractive measures to support the stability and sustainability of the system.

The key to vulnerability analysis is successful implementation of, ideally, several analytical tools, including early-warning systems and macro-prudential analysis. As we know, early-warning systems typically try to estimate the impact of external factors on domestic financial systems, i.e. how vulnerable the banking sector is to a decline in exports or to a worsening market sentiment, sudden changes in the exchange or interest rates. Macro-prudential analysis undertakes to broaden that approach to a variety of economic indicators, using stress-testing models. Several international organisations focus on the development of macro-prudential analysis, including the BIS, ECB and the IMF.

There are several prerequisites for the development of a reliable and robust early-warning system and even more so for the development of a meaningful macro-prudential approach. Reliable data and reasonably long time series are a necessity as well as high-quality analysis. Of these prerequisites, long time series of data are in relatively scarce supply in the EU accession countries, with only ten years of independent banking history. However, we have the basic building blocks in place.

It should also be noted that creating early-warning systems in small countries like Estonia with a highly concentrated banking sector is probably very different from setting up the systems in large countries. If you only have seven individual banks to supervise, close individual monitoring of each bank might be more cost effective than building up a sufficiently sophisticated aggregated system. The situation is probably very different for a banking sector including hundreds of individual institutions. Still, it is necessary to have both – individual monitoring and early-warning systems – in each case.

For Estonia, some harsh lessons from the late 1990s have underlined the need for as good an understanding of the key vulnerabilities in the financial system as possible. This need has become even more pressing now, when Estonian banks have become an integral part of major Nordic financial groups. While this development has somewhat lessened our concern for immediate liquidity and capital, the new structure of the financial system is yet to be tested during an economic downturn. Cross-border supervision has been and will remain an important priority for Estonian supervisors. At the present time Estonian supervisors have cooperation agreements with the respective authorities of the Baltic countries, Finland, Sweden, Germany and Denmark. We continue to attach high importance to the development of bilateral cooperation with financial supervisory authorities in countries with companies that have subsidiaries or branches in Estonia.

At the end of 2002, Estonian Financial Supervision Authority launched, with assistance from the Nordic Council of Ministers, a cooperation project with the Norwegian financial supervisory authority. The subject of the project is the application of the stress test in Estonia with respect to the asset and liabilities management of insurance companies. Under the USAID/FSVC programme, an employee of FSA advised the insurance supervision department of the Ministry of Finance of Macedonia on the accounting, legal and reporting aspects of insurance activities.

Eesti Pank has a well-developed and sufficiently sophisticated monitoring system in place, making it possible to observe the developments on the level of the whole banking system, a group of banks, a bank's consolidated group or an individual bank, on a monthly basis or on a daily basis – whatever is necessary. The system has been successfully tested over the last year. Eesti Pank has also dedicated significant resources to improve its analytical skills. Against that background, we plan to pay considerable attention to the further upgrading of our financial system analysis and we are looking forward to cooperating in that field with experts from European institutions as well as international organisations.

Safety nets

Estonian financial system safety nets have been developed in compliance with EU practices. Thus, EU membership would not mean any sweeping changes in this sphere. It must be noted, however, that this is one of the very few financial-sector related issues where Estonia has asked for a transition period to full adoption of an EU directive. Namely, the level of funds to be reimbursed by the deposit guarantee scheme is presently somewhat lower than required in the EU.

I would like to stress the importance of dialogue with market participants. Constructive discussions with bank managers serve two purposes. The commercial bankers know – and in their own way understand – both the market situation and the prevailing trends in the so-called 'real economy'. Thus, these regular discussions are a most welcome complement to the economic analysis produced by the central bank experts. But regular contacts also provide a unique channel for moral suasion, for explaining the central bank's concerns. Obviously, these contacts are easy to arrange in a small country like Estonia. We have made use of that advantage and established a dialogue with our financial sector on financial as well as general economic issues, both on a regular and ad hoc basis. Another essential element for crisis prevention is the pre-emptive involvement of the private sector in crisis resolution.

While the 'soft' policy principles support crisis prevention by providing a relatively stable and transparent environment, the resilience of the system still ultimately depends on the actions of market participants themselves. The task of the authorities is to provide an adequate regulatory framework and effective supervision of the implementation of the regulations.

There is another interesting, albeit still debated issue: to what extent the supervisors should rely on banks' internal risk control models and ratings – a subject that has recently been under the international spotlight in connection with the development of the New Basel Capital Accord. Estonian banking supervisors have taken a relatively forward-looking approach in that respect by increasingly relying on the risk-based approach of supervision. At the same time, and keeping in mind the rapidly developing economy and currency board arrangement, we believe that our banking system should have robust liquidity buffers and sufficient capital to withstand the fluctuation of asset prices. Therefore, we have set a relatively high reserve requirement (13 per cent of the banks' liabilities), half of which the banks can hold in high-quality foreign assets.

Finally, I would like to stress that as an essential element of the safety net, our Guarantee Fund, which is based on the principle of compulsory payments by the market participants, is functioning well and has already proved its usefulness in practice. At the time of the 1998 closure of several smaller banks, the depositors were compensated rapidly and without any problems. In addition to the deposit guarantee scheme, the Fund also includes separate sub-funds to offer investment protection and pension protection schemes.

Regulations

Eesti Pank is responsible for regulating the banking system in Estonia. A detailed description of Estonian banking regulations goes far beyond the scope of this presentation. However, I would just like to point out that one advantage of being a transition economy has been the possibility to draw the legislation from scratch. This has very much facilitated the compliance with good practices and the de facto full adoption of the EU *acquis*.

It is important to note, however, that 'adoption' of the *acquis* means not only issuing new legislation but also ensuring compliance with the regulations. Compliance issues have been a long-term priority for us. We can take pride in the fact that Estonia was among the first countries to participate in the pilot project under the IMF and World Bank Financial System Assessment Program (FSAP) in 1999–2000. The assessment involved implementation of recognised norms in financial sector policies and supervision (banking supervision, insurance supervision and securities market regulation and supervision, payment and settlement policies). The FSAP also assessed the transparency and openness of Estonia's monetary and financial sector policy. The results of the mission showed that Estonia's compliance was already good five years ago.

A real regulatory challenge for the central bank in our case is the question to what extent regulatory measures should be taken into account in a broader financial policy context. There are arguments for designing the regulations with a view to business cycles, especially as it seems that, in the modern world, financial systems have become more pro-cyclical than before. In that case, anticipatory measures may pre-empt the possibly devastating effects of asset price volatility and loan losses once the economy starts to cool down.

This approach has a particular appeal under the currency board as the active use of monetary measures is excluded and reserve requirements are essentially the only available monetary tool. In these circumstances, sound prudential measures have had an important role. It should be underlined that, in a heavily bank-dominated financial system, banking regulations might also serve as an instrument to affect domestic demand more directly than under other circumstances. Indeed, Eesti Pank increased the capital adequacy ratio with a view to promoting resilience against cyclical risks in 1997 at the onset of Asian contagion, before the peak of the cycle.

Having said that, one should take a look at the possible problems of the 'macro-prudential' policy approach. It is obvious that, as the financial markets mature and financial instruments become more complex, the tightening of banking regulations will simply intensify capital flows outside the banking system. In that case, major capital flows will be channelled to less regulated areas that will bring about new risks of potentially systemic nature. The second problem is that the determination of the exact stage of a business cycle is simply not possible. In this regard, devices able to dynamically react on cyclical factors are a great challenge. We have under-stood that we are not the only ones to think about these issues; the topic is also debated in several present EU member states.

Adequate framework is a moving target

I have already mentioned that the majority of work required for the imple-mentation of the *acquis communautaire* has been completed in Estonia and our financial sector is following internationally approved standards and good practices. Still, due to the fast development of the Estonian economy, we have found it necessary to keep our regulations sometimes even tighter than those considered necessary by international authorities – so, what we might see upon Estonia's accession to the EU might very well be more lax regulations in some areas.

At the same time, it is obvious that, while talking about the creation of adequate regulatory framework, we are talking of aiming at a moving target.

Within the EU, the realisation of the Financial Services Action Plan should lead to a complete integration of European financial markets by 2005 and securities markets by 2003. Creating a more fully integrated European financial market would certainly mean some changes in the reg-ulatory environment, the outcome of which should be a more flexible framework and better cooperation between regulators and supervisors. One must also keep in mind that effective supervision is, evidently, an important priority from the point of view of the Monetary Union.

Speaking about broader international standards, Basel II framework-related work offers a good example of the continuous development of prudential frameworks to meet the constantly changing, complex modern challenges. Setting up the new framework might not be easy – and the implications would be different depending on the particular environment and also the size of financial institutions. But, comparing the financial system of 1988 to the present day, it is clearly apparent that regulatory reforms are necessary. We can only welcome the active international debates which have accompanied the process. The process of developing the New Accord has, in itself, served the goal of financial stability by bring-ing various important issues like the problem of potential pro-cyclical effects of various regulatory approaches under the international spotlight and initiating extensive research in this area.

I would like to stress the word *awareness* in relation to the modern approach to safeguarding stability. It is one of the aims of the New Accord to make banks monitor and assess their risks more closely and to increase market discipline through enhanced disclosure. It is of utmost importance that a bank's risk assessment considers the specifics of the risks of the insti-tution. Naturally, a more detailed approach means more complicated cal-culations and manuals and it will also require a more intensive exchange of information between the banks and the supervisory institutions to guarantee that all risks will be adequately evaluated.

In Estonia – and probably in many other accession countries, as well as EU member countries – capital adequacy calculation principles have been recently fine-tuned. It is very clear that these adjustments shall not be last ones. The fast development of the international financial system demands continuous regulatory adjustments – both by international institutions and individual countries.

And that leads me, once again, to the crucial importance of the analysis and research backing up the regulatory decisions in a rapidly changing and increasingly complex environment.

The papers presented

The papers presented here during the last three days have provided a valuable contribution to the discussion about the stability and efficiency of financial markets.

The link between the banking sector and real sector was analysed and found to be significant in many papers. An efficient banking sector accelerates economic growth. Financial deepening and increase of financial sector efficiency have been simultaneous in most Central and Eastern European countries. But there are also risks that should not be ignored. For instance, it is not any level of indebtedness that is sustainable. That has been shown not only in theoretical work but also on a historical basis. That, in its turn, highlights the crucial role of financial regulation and supervision. In the context of globalisation, financial regulation is not a domestic matter any more as the financial markets become more and more integrated both by sectors and nations. Integrated markets need a more unified regulatory framework. The unification of the regulatory framework is one of the major challenges the current and future European Union members have to face.

One of the developments characteristic of many CEEC countries is the entrance of foreign banks. Foreign capital has had a positive impact on the financial sector, increasing competition and making it possible to import management culture and professional skills. It is noticeable that no proof of significant negative effects related to the foreign banks entry has been found. It seems that the foreign banks' credit policies have been less sensitive to local economic downturns and the entrance of foreign banks has not imported instability in any form.

Among the determinants of financial stability, institutional factors have been found significant. The exchange rate regime, the quality of regulatory and supervisory framework and the degree of liberalisation of the economy significantly influence financial stability.

The existence of contagion and the effects of common external shocks have important implications for the candidate countries during their accession to the EMU. The existence of external shocks indicates the need for sufficient flexibility.

With this, I would like to conclude my presentation which was, of course, only a short overview of the wide range of issues discussed in the papers presented during the last few days. I sincerely hope that every participant of this Colloquium has obtained useful new information and found some additional insights into the topics of the present Colloquium. SUERF, rather uniquely, brings together three important groups in its membership: central bankers, academics and private financial market practitioners. That has been instrumental in creating a most stimulating atmosphere for the exchange of ideas and viewpoints.

3 The role of central banks in promoting financial stability

The Hungarian experience[1]

Zsigmond Járai

Ladies and gentlemen, it is indeed a great pleasure to be with you here today. Before this year's Marjolin Award is presented to the most outstanding author, let me say a few words about the person who lent the award his name.

One of the most distinguished figures of his time, Robert Marjolin was an exceptionally versatile man: he was a scholar of law, an economist and a politician in one person.

Over recent decades, Western Europe has experienced an unprecedented economic and social upswing, and achieved a high level of economic and political integration. Robert Marjolin played a major role in this development. He helped to organise the European Programme of Reconstruction, which was to be known as the Marshall Plan all over the world.

Due to the political pressure exerted by the Soviet Union, Eastern European countries were unable to join this Programme.

On 16 April 1948, a total of 16 nations ratified the document founding the Organisation for European Economic Co-operation, or OEEC, in Paris. It was this organisation that formulated a programme for rebuilding Europe. The Council of the Organisation was chaired by Paul Henri Spaak, and Robert Marjolin was appointed as Secretary-General of the Executive Committee.

The loans and goods provided within the framework of the Marshall Plan greatly contributed to the reconstruction and rapid economic modernisation of Western Europe. In contrast to the upswing which followed the First World War, the recovery after the Second World War proved to be lasting and led to the development of what we call the 'welfare state'. This made the differences in development between the two blocs in Europe obvious.

The Marshall Plan was also instrumental in resolving the problems caused by the imbalances of the exchange rate parities fixed in December 1946. As early as 1948 and 1949, the Council of the OEEC, urged by the United States, took steps to establish cooperation on currency policy and transform bilateral cash turnover into multilateral cash turnover. In order to overcome the resistance of Britain, which was intent on protecting the sterling zone, OEEC countries established the European Payments Union (EPU) on 19 September 1950. The Marshall Plan intensified the existing conflict between federalists and so-called 'functionalists' who were interested in protecting the old establishment. Eventually, Italy, France, the Benelux countries and the Federal Republic of Germany, all in favour of federalism, opted for the path of European integration and created the Common Market in 1957.

Today, the birth of European citizenship, the removal of internal barriers, the development of the independent pillar of common foreign and security policy and the concept of 'a Citizens' Europe' all show that we are closer than ever to realising the vision of a truly unified European Union capable of resolving its internal conflicts in a democratic manner and maintaining its splendid cultural diversity.

I believe that the unification and unity of Europe can be attributed to a unique, forward-looking geopolitical strategy and economic rationality.

In 1948, when the OEEC was set up to supervise implementation of the Marshall Plan, Jean Monnet, the spiritual founding father of the European Community, was of the opinion that efforts made on a strictly national basis by the individual countries would not be satisfactory. Moreover, the idea that 16 sovereign countries would be able to cooperate efficiently appeared to be a figment of the imagination.

Robert Marjolin did not share this view and voiced his opinion even after the establishment of the European Community, stating that 'the only answer to the question of why nation states opted for a common life is the realisation that no matter how great their disadvantages from Community membership are, they are better off inside than outside'.

Even today, it remains a fundamental question for most European politicians and organisations as to whether they should reinforce their support for either supra-national decision-making, or cooperation between the governments of the member states, both of which are alternatives that exist side-by-side in the EU.

The European Economic and Monetary Union was not merely the result of economic necessity. Many politicians (first and foremost, François Mitterrand, Helmut Kohl and Jacques Delors) who proposed the idea of a common, or even a single, currency in the 1980s had to struggle with the resistance of the Bundesbank and the Bank of England for a long time.

The strict economic terms and conditions set forth in the Maastricht criteria and the establishment of the European Central Bank, independent of the other organisations of the EU as well as the respective governments of the member states, finally won the support of even conservative, cautious central bankers for this unique monetary adventure.

On 2 January 1999, *The Economist* wrote: 'Scarcely 10 years ago, uniting the national monetary systems of the European Union looked a perfectly lunatic idea', and added 'nobody can claim that it was the *tour de force* of events that imposed the EMU on the governments of Europe'. The introduction of the euro was indeed 'spurred on by an extraordinary ambition'. In the end, it was courage, foresight and the willingness to adopt a long-term perspective that gradually overcame caution and the distrust between the member states.

The role of central banks in promoting financial stability – a general overview

Before attempting to provide an overview of central banks' role in promoting financial stability, it is important to explain what exactly is meant by the term 'financial stability'. Theoreticians and practising central bankers alike have offered numerous definitions. Nevertheless, no widely accepted definitions, which are easy to apply in practice, have been formulated up to now, in contrast for example to a term such as 'price stability'. There are both positive and negative definitions. Furthermore, a distinction can be drawn between these various definitions on the basis of whether they adopt a systemic approach or are linked to the volatility of directly observable financial variables (asset prices, interest rates, etc.).

At the Magyar Nemzeti Bank, the guiding principle of promoting financial stability is based on a systemic approach. According to this concept, the financial stability objective of the central bank can be defined as the maintenance of a safe and sound financial infrastructure that helps to avoid financial disruptions and promotes a well-functioning real economy.

Historically, central banks' responsibility for financial stability can be derived from their capacity as lenders of last resort. Accordingly, promoting financial stability, and (generally as a part of this) banking supervision, used to be an integral part of central banking. Over recent decades, however, a new type of institutional architecture has evolved around the world, in which the primary objective of central banks, with their considerable degree of autonomy, is clearly to deliver and maintain price stability. Prudential supervision, in many countries, has come to be a responsibility of institutions independent of central banks. The trend for supervision to become an independent activity can be traced back to the following factors:

a   potential conflicts of interest between price stability and financial stability objectives;
b   concerns about an excessive concentration of power at central banks with considerable autonomy; and
c   the need to integrate banking, securities and insurance supervision, due to the fact that the distinctions between the individual financial services have blurred and financial conglomerates have evolved.

The following question arises: in this new environment, what justifies the high-profile role that central banks play in safeguarding financial stability? One reason can be found in their aforementioned function of promoting stability (acting as lenders-of-last-resort), as well as their performance of fundamental central bank tasks. Due to the positive interaction between price stability and financial stability and the efficiency of monetary policy transmission, central banks have a vested interest in maintaining financial stability. Recent years have witnessed heated debates in the economic community over whether there is any trade-off between price and financial stability. Although no consensus has been reached on this issue, there seems to be agreement over the fact that low and stable inflation is a necessary, but not adequate, prerequisite for financial stability. Furthermore, central banks' interest in financial stability also manifests itself in the role they play in operating and supervising payment and settlement systems. The Swedish central bank, for example, explicitly derives its role in the promotion of the stability of the financial system from this aspect.

But in addition, central banks also carry out special functions that are related to the macro-prudential aspect of financial stability. Systemic crises of the banking system in the 1980s and 1990s, which on several occasions entailed huge fiscal costs and losses in output, highlighted the importance of the macro-prudential dimension of financial stability.

Macro-prudential analysis focuses on the potential threats to financial stability that can be attributed to either unfavourable macroeconomic or financial market developments (so-called 'common shocks'), or to exposure to systemic risk (i.e. contagion). Thus, the difference between macro- and micro-prudential objectives can also be clearly defined: while the macro-prudential goal is to avoid systemic crises and the concomitant economic costs (output losses), the micro-prudential objective is to avoid the bankruptcy of individual institutions, thereby protecting the interests of depositors. The difference between the macro- and micro-prudential approach is also easy to grasp in risk assessment. The pro-cyclical behaviour of banks is a well-known example: while relaxing (or, in an economic downturn, tightening) lending standards may well be a rational policy choice on the level of the individual institutions, a similar collective response from the majority of banks is likely to produce a socially undesirable outcome (for example, excessive expansion of lending or a credit crunch).

In practice of course, the macro- and micro-prudential aspects of financial stability cannot be strictly segregated. Rather, they are two sides of the same coin, because there is an important synergy between the monitoring of systemic risks and the prudential supervision of individual financial institutions. In order that such synergy can be put to the best possible use, an efficient flow of information and close cooperation is required between the institutions (more often than not, the central bank and the relevant supervisory authority) responsible for financial stability. The increasing need for cooperation is well illustrated by various agreements on cooperation between national central banks and supervisory authorities and an EU-level Memorandum of Understanding effective from March 2003 on the high-level principles of cooperation between the central banks and banking supervisors of EU member states in crisis management situations.

It follows from the nature of macro-prudential analysis that it is mainly central banks that are in charge of monitoring financial system stability, even in countries where supervision is undertaken by a separate institution. And that brings us to a second question: what instrumental framework do central banks have available to achieve the objective of financial stability? After all, the instrumental framework of monetary policy is designed mainly to achieve the primary objective of price stability. By following price stability objectives, central banks employing such instruments also indirectly promote financial stability. An as-yet unresolved issue raised during the ongoing debate over the relationship between price stability and financial stability is whether monetary policy should be actively used so that financial imbalances (e.g. the excessive volatility of asset prices) can be avoided. The following are the instruments that central banks can use directly to promote financial stability: emergency liquidity support in order to avoid systemic problems, coordination of private sector solutions in crisis situations (an excellent example of which is the role that the Federal Reserve played in addressing the LTCM crisis), regulation and oversight of payment systems and, with an eye to prevention, evaluation of financial stability for the broad public.

Analyses adopting a macro-prudential approach to financial stability have gained increasing ground in central banking, which is clearly indicated by the fact that central banks regularly publish their respective evaluations of financial stability (either as independent publications or as part of other central bank publications). Performing the analysis of stability is a central bank responsibility, irrespective of whether the relevant central bank also tends to carry out supervisory tasks or only evaluates and tackles systemic risks (in the latter case, independent publications are more common).

What are the underlying considerations for central banks when they publish their respective evaluation of risks that potentially threaten financial stability? First of all, they can reduce risks to stability by regularly publishing their evaluations. With regularly published evaluations, market participants become better informed on risks inherent in the macroeconomic environment and are offered a picture of the potential collective impact of their individual actions. This is all the more important as private participants are less interested in analysing the spillover effects of their individual moves (on other market participants) and less encouraged to assess systemic risks. But publishing evaluations is far from being a one-way street: it also provides an opportunity for dialogue and discussion of potential systemic risks with representatives of the financial sectors.

The Magyar Nemzeti Bank's role in promoting financial stability

Now that I have provided a thumbnail description of the role that central banks play in financial stability and the instrumental framework at their disposal in general, I would like to elaborate on the Hungarian pattern.

The Magyar Nemzeti Bank's role in the division of labour related to promoting financial stability

In Hungary, three institutions are responsible for promoting financial stability. The Magyar Nemzeti Bank (MNB), the Hungarian Financial Supervisory Authority and the Ministry of Finance are responsible for the containment of systemic risks, micro-prudential supervision and financial legislation, respectively. In line with the prevailing international 'best practice', the Act on the Magyar Nemzeti Bank stipulates that 'the MNB shall promote the stability of the financial system and the development and smooth conduct of policies related to the prudential supervision of the financial system'. This general provision also stipulates the promotion of financial stability as one of the MNB's fundamental tasks. Its responsibility for the promotion of financial stability was set forth explicitly in the Act on the Magyar Nemzeti Bank by the amendments made in 2001. This suggests that legislators, keeping abreast of the relevant European practice, wish to ascribe a role in the macro-prudential supervision of the financial system to the MNB that is more accentuated than previously.

As for financial stability in a broader sense, we should also remember the MNB's tasks related to the operation of payment and settlement systems. It is charged with establishing and regulating domestic payment and settlement systems as well as facilitating the safe and efficient operation of such systems. It follows from the interaction between settlement systems and systemic risks that the oversight of payment and settlement systems is also an integral part of the Bank's responsibility as the facilitator of systemic stability.

In connection with the Bank's responsibility in promoting financial stability, the law also stipulates that the MNB's opinion shall be invited on draft decisions and bills affecting the MNB's tasks and the operation of the financial system. This provides for the possibility that the MNB can actively participate in the formulation of regulations governing the financial and economic environment. In this manner, relying on its specialist expertise, gained through performing its central bank functions, the MNB can add considerable value to regulatory work.

In sum, the MNB's responsibility for, and tasks related to, the stability of the financial system rest on three major pillars:

1   macro-prudential analysis and supervision, monitoring systemic risks (as well as occasional intervention) in connection with both bank and

non-bank intermediaries and analysis of macroeconomic developments from a financial stability perspective;

2   regulation and oversight of payment and securities settlement systems in order to support the efficient and sound operation of these systems; and

3   regulatory policy, participation in financial and capital market legislation, upholding systemic stability and efficiency, in particular.

Responsibility for, and tasks related to, the promotion of financial stability falls on and is assigned to the following departments at the Bank:

• *Financial Stability Department*: analysis of the stability of the financial system (banks and non-bank financial intermediaries, financial groups), ultimate responsibility for the preparation of the *Report on Financial Stability*, establishment of the operational framework of the lender-of-last-resort function;

• *Economics Department*: examination of macroeconomic developments from a financial stability perspective;

• *Regulatory Policy Department*: participation in financial and capital market legislation and carrying out background analyses related to regulatory policy; and

• *Payment Systems Department*: efficient and safe operation of payment and settlement systems, oversight and regulation.

It should also be noted that one Vice President is responsible for the organisational units (Financial Stability Department, Regulatory Policy Department and Payment Systems Department) whose primary responsibility involves financial stability.

Macro-prudential analysis at the MNB

The MNB's stance is that, in the interest of promoting and sustaining financial stability, it is highly important that both market participants and institutions with a vested interest in financial stability have access to comprehensive information on the financial system as a whole, its operational environment and its narrowly and broadly defined set of conditions. With these goals in mind, the MNB launched its *Report on Financial Stability* in August 2000. The target audience of this publication includes:

• domestic institutions sharing responsibility for the promotion of financial stability;

• participants of the domestic financial sector, foreign parent banks and potential investors;

• international organisations and financial institutions (IMF, World Bank, OECD, ECB, BIS, etc.);

- foreign central banks and supervisory authorities;
- credit-rating agencies;
- foreign and national research institutes; and
- specialist journals, dailies and interested members of the public.

The *Report on Financial Stability* is a semi-annual publication. There are marked differences in focus between the spring and autumn issues, due to the cyclical availability of reliable information and the priorities of analyses. The spring report provides a more comprehensive analysis of the financial system, with detailed evaluation of non-bank financial intermediaries, cooperative credit institutions as well as the payment and settlement systems being published only once a year. The special feature of the autumn issue is a more detailed investigation of the financial position of and risks run by non-financial companies. The reason for this is that there is a time lag in the availability of annual corporate balance sheet data.

One key feature of the *Report on Financial Stability* is that it is always issued after publication of the *Quarterly Report on Inflation*. In the latter report, the MNB's analysts prepare comprehensive forecasts for the macroeconomic environment, which can also be used as an input for the financial stability analysis. Issuing the *Report on Financial Stability* after publication of the *Quarterly Report on Inflation* allows us to make analyses of financial sector stability on the basis of the latest information available at the time of writing. Since the autumn 2002 issue, the *Report on Financial Stability* opens with the Monetary Council's statement representing the official standpoint of the MNB.

The governing principle behind the structure of the *Report on Financial Stability* is to provide a comprehensive analysis of the risks facing financial intermediaries and the corporate and household sectors fundamentally influencing their stability, as well as to assess the macroeconomic and financial market developments relevant for financial stability. The structure of the *Report on Financial Stability* has seen several changes in past years. These have reflected both internal analytical requirements and the practices of central banks publishing their own stability reports. Table 3.1 illustrates the current structure of the *Report*.

Aggregated micro-prudential indicators, relating to both banks and non-bank financial intermediaries, and macroeconomic and market indicators comprise the two major groups of indicators the MNB uses for its macro-prudential analysis. Macroeconomic and market indicators include data for the corporate and household sectors as well as price information derived from markets (stock market indices, risk spreads, market yields, bank rates, real property prices, etc.), in addition to aggregate data on the national economy. Structural indicators (the depth and structure of financial intermediation, market concentration, etc.) and qualitative information derivable from ad hoc central bank surveys on banks' risk management practices constitute an important input for macro-prudential

Table 3.1 Structure of the MNB's *Report on Financial Stability*

Section	Content	Main features
Analysis of macroeconomic events and financial markets	Review of global economic activity and international financial developments; domestic financial markets; economic growth and inflation; external equilibrium	• Analyses of macroeconomic events from a stability perspective (may differ from the underlying approach of the *Quarterly Report on Inflation*) • Hungary is a small, open economy. Consequently, indicators of developments in the current account balance and deficit financing are given greater emphasis
Banking sector stability	Structural analyses (depth of intermediation, market structure); risks of non-financial corporations and households; banks' lending risks; portfolio quality; market risks; liquidity; capital position; profitability	• Analyses of non-financial corporations and the banking sector, with varying details in the spring and autumn issues of the *Report* • Detailed analyses of the yearly developments in the banking sector in the spring issue of the *Report*. More detailed analyses of the corporate sector (indebtedness, profitability, liquidity, etc.) in the autumn issue • Analyses of lending risks given the greatest emphasis in assessing banking sector risks
Activities and risks of non-bank financial intermediaries	General overview of non-bank financial intermediation: analyses by types of institution; (investment funds, pension funds, life insurers, financial enterprises)	• Detailed analyses in the spring issue of the *Report* • Short analysis focusing on current risks in the autumn issue
Activities and risks of savings cooperatives	Analyses of lending risks; portfolio quality, profitability; capital position	• Annual frequency (spring issue of the *Report*)
Activities and risks of the interbank payment and settlement systems	Analyses of interbank payment turnover; liquidity position of payment and settlement systems; reliability of the systems' operations	• Annual frequency (spring issue of the *Report*)

(*continued*)

Table 3.1 Continued

Section	Content	Main features
Special topics		• Short analyses focusing on the broad subject of stability • Examples: handling of the speculative capital inflows in January, stress tests, consolidated regulation of financial groups
Articles		• Comprehensive, detailed analyses directly or indirectly linked to financial stability • Examples: risk management at banking groups, risks in housing finance, operational risk management, effects of the foreign exchange liberalisation and band widening

analysis. These surveys have already covered all important types of risk, including credit, exchange rate, interest rate, liquidity, operational and group-level risks.

It is important to note that the MNB's macro-prudential analysis cannot rely exclusively on aggregate sectoral data. The reason for this is that average data may mask a substantial amount of information referring to the sector's vulnerability. For this reason, it is indispensable for us to use measures of dispersion and concentration, in addition to analysing sectoral trends. It is also important to relate these indicators to some kind of benchmark or critical value. In the case of cross-country comparisons, the MNB refers to the banking systems of EU countries and other CEE countries at a similar stage of development.

Stress tests applied to the banking sector play a very important role within the instruments of the stability analysis. They contribute an important, dynamic element to the analysis of macro-prudential indicators, as they help to assess the banking sector's ability to withstand potential future macroeconomic shocks (for example, exchange rate, interest rate and credit shocks).

Assessment of financial stability

Following this overview of the major features of macro-prudential analysis carried out in the MNB, let me now give a brief account of the stability of the Hungarian financial system. I will place special emphasis on the effects of the January 2003 speculative attack aimed at shifting the forint's intervention band.

To start with, measuring the depth of financial intermediation by the balance-sheet-to-GDP ratio, Hungary lags far behind the European Union, just like other countries of Central and Eastern Europe. Positively, though, financial intermediation, as measured by the loans-to-GDP ratio, has deepened in recent years, accompanied by a strong pick-up in lending. Looking at developments in market structure, the earlier process of deconcentration reversed in 2001, owing to two large mergers. And although concentration decreased again in 2002, consolidation is expected to continue over the medium term as a result of intensifying competition, narrowing bank margins and falling profits. The intensity of competition among banks varies in the major market segments: whereas competition has been sharp and margins low in the corporate sector, concentration has been significantly higher and margins relatively large in the household market for several years.

In recent years, the banking sector has shifted its focus towards SMEs and households, which used to play a less significant role in bank lending. The market of large companies is now saturated and assessment of the risks carried by SMEs has improved, due to higher profitability and the government's subsidy system. These explain the considerable increase in outstanding loans to SMEs. Housing loans, encouraged by extensive government subsidies, are the most rapidly developing area of bank lending. Bank lending to households has been rising increasingly robustly, rising by 70 per cent in 2002. This expansion was mainly driven by a 161 per cent increase in residential mortgage lending.

Admittedly, the risks in lending to the corporate and household sectors have developed differently recently. Risks in lending to firms increased in 2001 and 2002, due to the domestic and international economic slowdown and the shift towards SMEs noted earlier. However, the quality of the household loan portfolio has improved, owing to households' improving income position and the government's housing subsidy system. The significant volume effect of the pick-up in housing loans also explains part of this quality improvement, due to the increase in the share of less risky mortgage loans and classification of the large volume of new loans into the problem-free category. But despite the strong demand for home loans, the danger of a price bubble developing is low in Hungary. Apart from these positive trends, the risks of household lending are being increased by lack of a positive-list debtor register system.

Analysing exposure to market risks, potential adverse changes in exchange rates or interest rates carry much lower risks for the banking sector. The stress tests conducted by the MNB show that exposure to market risks is relatively low. By contrast, credit shocks may be a significantly larger source of loss. Since the forint's intervention band was widened in May 2001, banks have kept their exposure to exchange rate risk low. However, interest rate risk exposure increased in 2002, measured by repricing gaps. The widening of the negative repricing gap may be associated with higher volatility of interest income over the short term, if the volatility of interest rates increases. However, assuming that the long-term decline in interest rates continues, it will probably have a positive effect on profitability.

Hungarian banks' profitability improved spectacularly between 2000 and 2002 relative to earlier periods. In this, the volume effect of the brisk expansion of lending and the pick-up in loans to households ensuring higher interest margin definitely played a role. The sector's net interest margin is fairly high in international comparison – it not only exceeds the EU average by 2.7 percentage points (according to 2001 figures), but it is higher than in the CEE countries as well. There has recently been a slight shift within banks' income structure towards non-interest income, due to the dynamic increase in fee and commission income. While the sector's costs-to-total-assets ratio has improved modestly in recent years, domestic banks' cost efficiency still lags considerably behind that of banks operating in developed countries.

Although the banking sector's capital adequacy ratio has been falling, its relatively high level (12.5 per cent) and the favourable composition of the regulatory capital (that is, the relatively high share of Tier 1 capital elements) indicates the sector's solid capital position. Compared to the EU average, Hungarian banks' CAR is higher, while the share of non-performing loans is broadly comparable. Based on these aspects, capital provides adequate cover for the risks facing Hungarian banks.

Institutional investors include investment funds, pension funds and life insurance companies. Year after year, they are further increasing their share of the market in re-channelling household and corporate sector savings. However, the depth of Hungarian non-bank financial intermediation still lags behind that seen in the less-advanced EU countries. Non-bank financial intermediaries represent a relatively low risk for the stability of the financial intermediary system. The very strong pick-up in car purchase finance by financial enterprises deserves special mention, as less stringent prudential regulations apply to these firms than to banks. Most of them are owned by banks. Consequently, the qualification of loans, product development, loan appraisal and provisioning are based on the same principles as those of the parent banks. This lowers risks.

Financial groups have been gaining ground in recent years in Hungary, in line with international trends. This process should be monitored from the perspective of financial stability, due to the potentially higher risks of contagion. As a welcome development, the new regulation allowing the assessment and control of financial conglomerates on a consolidated basis will enter into force in 2004. The new regulations will meet the EU requirements and contribute to increase the transparency and controllability of financial conglomerates' business relations and risk-taking.

Viewed from a stability perspective, the most important events of the recent period are connected with the January 2003 speculative attack. As a result of the attack, in two days the MNB had to intervene in the amount of €5.3 billion near the upper limit of the official exchange rate band. Quick actions were taken in order to defend the exchange rate band, which caused the effective yield to fall five percentage points at the short end, the most sensitive section of the yield curve for speculative money. The temporary changes to our instruments isolated the lasting effects from the transitory ones, consistent with our intentions. The interest rate level effective for speculative capital fell to 3.5 per cent. At the same time, the 6.5 per cent interest rate on the two-week deposit facility remained the major policy rate for longer-term government securities as well as for deposit and lending rates. The MNB managed to curb volatility of interest rates, preventing it from spreading from the interbank market to longer-term government papers, bank deposits and loans.

Afterwards, our strategy was driven by two basic objectives in consolidating the situation in the money and foreign exchange markets – meeting the inflation targets and safeguarding financial stability. These two goals were not in conflict, as they required the same actions – stabilising exchange rate expectations and facilitating the outflow of speculative capital as quickly as possible. In order to achieve these goals, the MNB, using intra-band interventions, provided speculators with the possibility of a continuous and controlled withdrawal of hot money, without risking a substantial increase in long-term yields and exchange rate volatility. As the persistence of low interest rates would have influenced financial stability negatively and would have triggered inflationary pressure as well, the MNB attempted to restore its policy instruments and raised the extremely low level of interest rates as quickly as possible. Consistent with this intention, by selling large amounts of euros, the MNB contributed to more than two-thirds of foreign speculative capital leaving the market by the end of February. With the restoration of the Bank's policy instruments, the first phase of consolidation ended on 24 February. 'Silent' intra-band intervention marked the final phase of consolidation.

Despite the apparent uncertainty in the aftermath of the speculation on appreciation, the attack itself or the subsequent movements in yields and the exchange rate posed no threat whatsoever to the stability of the Hungarian financial sector. The prudential rules of the financial regulatory framework (such as capital requirements assigned by the trading book to individual risks, for example) and banks' internal regulations kept risk exposure at a low level even in the beginning. This prevented the income and liquidity position of the sector from being shaken even in the temporarily more volatile financial environment. While the daily turnover of the Real Time Gross Settlement System was, on certain days, more than four-times that of the previous average, the payment system suffered no interruptions either.

Analysis of the banking sector's activities in 2003 Q1 reveals that the January speculative inflow did not jeopardise the sector's stability, just as the after-effects did not carry significant systemic risks. Examining profitability patterns, banks earned profits from the speculative capital flows over the short term. First, the sector had open positions which translated into both neutral and positive income effects implied by increased exchange rate and interest rate volatility. And although the temporary large decline in money market rates narrowed the interest margin, banks were able to find compensation by increasing the spread between lending and deposit rates.

Future challenges

As my assessment has indicated, over recent years the Hungarian financial system has been characterised by stable, profitable performance. But the sector, judged as mature for EU membership in many respects, still faces significant challenges. Many of these are related to Hungary's impending EU accession. We expect competition in the banking market to intensify after Hungary joins the single European market. This, coupled with the effects of nominal convergence with EMU, which will be reflected in lower inflation and interest rates, foreshadows a narrowing of margins. And although a strong increase in non-interest income may partly offset this, improving cost efficiency will be vital for Hungarian banks, due to rising profitability pressures.

In addition to this, several challenges lie ahead for both the domestic financial sector and the authorities responsible for promoting financial stability, which are mainly related to the EU- and EMU-accession. Now, I would like to highlight one issue out of these, namely the potential problems arising from the relatively shallow depth of domestic financial intermediation. For several reasons, the depth of financial intermediation is highly important from the perspective of financial stability. A financial structure supporting economic growth and efficient monetary transmission mechanisms are the major areas of relevance.

Financial deepening and real economic convergence

As a generalisation, we can say that more developed countries have more developed institutional systems and deeper financial intermediation. In addition, economic growth and the depth of financial intermediation are closely and directly related to each other. Furthermore, the depth of financial intermediation is a good forecasting variable for future economic performance. The relationship between the depth of financial intermediation, economic development and growth is of special importance for the accession countries of Central and Eastern Europe, including Hungary, where the level of financial intermediation is very low compared with developed countries. It is a generally accepted view that accession-country financial sectors have significant growth potential, both in absolute and relative terms, relative to economic growth.

In these countries, economic growth conducive to convergence must be accompanied by a significant deepening of financial intermediation. If this fails, it may significantly hinder long-term economic growth. For this reason, the economic and monetary policy mix, supporting sustainable growth, must promote the further deepening of financial intermediation. A central bank, responsible for safeguarding financial stability, can facilitate this process mainly by conducting stable and predictable monetary policy aimed at contributing to the efficiency and transparency of financial markets and by ensuring a low inflation environment for financial intermediation. Why? Because in a stable economic environment, and with inflation and interest rates at consistently low levels, the private sector's equilibrium indebtedness is allowed to be higher. From a macroprudential perspective, it is important to constantly monitor whether the further deepening of financial intermediation, promoting real economic convergence, proceeds gradually, as needed, and whether or not it is associated with excessive lending expansion, due to the pro-cyclical behaviour of the banking sector.

Depth of financial intermediation and monetary transmission

As is known, Hungary is a small, open economy, where the exchange rate has a much greater role in reducing inflation than interest rates. Accordingly, the exchange rate channel is currently the determinant factor in the transmission mechanism. But after Hungary joins the euro area, the transmission mechanism will have to rely more and more on the interest rate channel. One of the necessary conditions for efficient interest rate transmission is a substantial deepening of financial intermediation. Of course, other conditions must also be met. For example, efficient money markets ensuring the smooth distribution of excess liquidity in the banking sector; adequate competition among banks; and completely market-based pricing.

Finally, let me address the relationship between monetary transmission and financial intermediation. First, it should be noted that a number of factors partly counterbalance the low level of financial intermediation in Hungary. For example, due to the predominance of banks, firms are unable to respond to the drop in the supply of credit induced by a central bank decision to alter interest rates by turning to the capital market. In a similar vein, Hungarian banks mostly lend at variable interest rates and the average maturity of loans is not very long in international comparison. These factors, in turn, strengthen the transmission mechanism. It should also be noted that borrowing from foreign banks represents a significant share within firms' financing profiles. Currently, this weakens transmission.

But it will no longer be relevant after accession to the euro area, as the overwhelming majority of funds borrowed from foreign banks originate from the banking systems of Economic and Monetary Union.

Note

1 I wish to acknowledge the assistance of Csaba Móré and Judit Sipos Molnárné in the preparation of this chapter.

4 Banking sector development and economic growth in transition countries

Tuuli Koivu[1]

Introduction

The numerous empirical studies on determinants of growth in transition economies (e.g. De Melo *et al.* 1996; Havrylyshyn 2001; Havrylyshyn *et al.* 1998, 2000; Berg *et al.* 1999) reflect efforts to explain the sizeable variations in growth performance seen in these countries. The relationship between financial markets and economic growth, however, has largely been ignored in earlier empirical studies. To our knowledge, the only study that empirically tests the relation between financial markets and economic growth in transition countries is Drakos's (2002) paper on the effects of the banking sector's structure on economic performance. No studies specifically assess the roles of the size and efficiency of domestic financial markets on economic growth in a large sample of transition countries. This chapter is a modest attempt to rectify this gap in the literature.

In transition countries, the link between financial-sector development and economic growth seems to be ambiguous at best. Berglöf and Bolton (2002) give the financial sector only a minor role as a factor behind economic development. They argue that the differences in development of the financial sectors do not explain different levels of economic development in transition countries. It is true that most investments in transition countries have been financed from cash flows and foreign direct investment has substituted for domestic financing (Krkoska 2001). Conway (2002), however, builds a model where financial-sector development has been one of the key factors behind GDP growth in transition countries. Conway leans in his arguments on McKinnon's (1973) term of financial repression, where resources of the domestic financial sector are insufficient to enhance economic development.

Over the past decade, considerable interest focused on the link between the financial sector and economic growth. Endogenous growth theory emerged in the late 1980s and paved the way for new theories exploring the link. As Pagano (1993) puts it, there are three ways in which the development of the financial sector might affect economic growth under the basic endogenous growth model. First, it can increase the productivity of investments. Second, an efficient financial sector reduces transaction costs and thus increases the share of savings channelled into productive investments. Third, financial-sector development can either promote or decline savings.

The empirical literature on the finance–growth nexus has grown. Most empirical studies using both cross-country and panel analysis conclude development of the financial sector accelerates economic growth (see surveys by, for example, Levine 1997; Thiel 2001; Wachtel 2001). A few time-series or VAR analyses, however, contradict this finding (Demetriades and Hussein 1996; Arestis and Demetriades 1997; Shan *et al.* 2002). The composition of data seems to have been the reason for different results. Papers that use large bodies of data from both rich and poor countries find a causal relationship running from financial-market development to economic growth. Studies of smaller groups of relatively homogenous countries often do not find the causality. These differing results may be explained by the fact that most studies use the size of the financial sector as a measure of development in the sector. However, size is not an optimal measure for financial-sector development for various reasons. As Rajan and Zingales (1998) state, GDP growth and growth of the financial sector can be driven by a common factor such as the savings rate. Rousseau and Wachtel (2000) argue that the growth of the financial sector (e.g. a rise in the amount of credit or stock market capitalisation) can reflect the anticipations of coming higher economic growth. At worst, an increase in the amount of credit can be due to a rise in non-performing loans. Thus, when financial-sector development is measured solely by the size of the sector, the positive growth–finance nexus is only found when the size correlates with the efficiency of the sector. As it is typical that high-income countries have larger and also more efficient financial sectors than low- or middle-income countries, the size of the financial sector seems to accelerate economic growth when the data contains both high- and low-income countries. If one studies countries with similar income levels, the size of the sector itself tells nothing about differences in qualitative levels between countries. This is the reason why these studies do not find causality running from the financial sector to economic growth.

In this study, we attempt to avoid this problem by linking the empirical test more closely to the qualitative development of the financial sector. Due to a lack of information on the equity and debt markets, we concentrate on banking sector development. Overall, other forms of external finance than bank loans had have only little importance in transition countries. We measure the development in the sector with the margin between lending and deposit interest rates. To our knowledge, this variable has not been used previously to measure the efficiency of the banking sector. Although this variable has its drawbacks, we are convinced that it captures the level of efficiency in the sector. As in many earlier studies, our second variable is related to the size of the sector. The variable is the amount of bank credit allocated to the private sector. Often the amount of credit is measured as a share of GDP. However, when it concerns the transition economies, the small size of the private sector may have restricted its credit growth as a share of GDP. Thus, we measure the amount of credit allocated to the private sector as a share of its production. We analyse the finance–growth nexus using a fixed-effects panel model and unbalanced panel data from 25 transition countries between 1993 and 2001.

Our findings support the view that the presence of an efficient banking sector accelerated economic growth in transition economies. Moreover, the interest rate margin is significantly and negatively related to economic growth – a finding that parallels theories suggesting that greater efficiency in the banking sector accelerates economic growth. Indeed, as banking sector reforms and the interest rate margin are negatively correlated, the result has significant policy implications (see Appendix 4.3). Countries with evolved banking sectors have smaller interest margins and higher economic growth than countries struggling with banking sector reform.

The relationship between the amount of credit to the private sector (the second variable) and economic growth is less clear. A rise in the current amount of credit has accelerated economic growth, but when the amount of credit is lagged with one year, it is negatively linked to GDP growth. This outcome contradicts the general literature, but is actually in line with financial market development in transition countries. A couple of characteristics of transition economies should be noted. First, banking crises rocked the financial sectors of many countries during the first decade of transition when proper laws and institutions of banking supervision were still lacking. Thus, a large amount of credit could have led to significant drops in GDP growth with a delay. Second, our findings probably reflect the soft budget constraints still prevalent in many transition countries. Their existence may have encouraged private sector actors to make counterproductive investments. Also in this case, the growth in the amount of credit was sustainable. Against such a background, it is clear that a large banking sector is in itself not necessarily something that promotes high economic growth and, on the other hand, we can argue that the size of the banking sector is not a good variable to measure the development of effectiveness in the sector in transition countries.

The rest of this chapter is organised as follows. Next is a presentation of the data used in this study, which is followed by a summary of the empirical results. Finally, there is an overall conclusion.

Data

We analyse the link between efficiency and size of the banking sector and economic growth using panel data for 25 transition countries during the period 1993–2001 (see Appendix 4.1 for countries and Appendix 4.2 for data sources). The short time period is unfortunate, but goes with the territory in economies in transition. The lack of information on equity and debt markets means they cannot be analysed here. However, they have yet to become significant channels for financing in transition countries. Thus, the overall picture of the relation between financial sector and economic growth in transition countries should not be seriously disturbed.

We measure economic development in terms of annual real GDP growth. Development of the financial sector is difficult to measure, but we attempt to get beyond earlier studies that only measure development with a variable for the size of the financial sector. As noted earlier, size does not necessarily reflect efficiency, and mere growth of the financial sector may not necessarily indicate development. Thus, we look at both qualitative and quantitative development of the financial sector.

To measure the qualitative effectiveness of the sector, we use the interest rate margin (INT). INT measures the difference between deposit and lending rates in the banking market. The margin is likely a good estimator for efficiency in the banking sector as it describes transaction costs within the sector. If the margin declines due to a decrease in transaction costs, the share of savings going to investments increases. As growth is positively linked to investment, a decrease in transaction costs should accelerate economic growth. This variable is thus linked to the theoretical models of Blackburn and Hung (1998) and Harrison *et al.* (1999). Blackburn and Hung (1998) identify a two-way causal relationship between growth and financial development. In their model, the lack of a financial sector means that every investor must individually monitor projects, so that the costs of monitoring are excessive. With a well-developed financial sector, monitoring tasks are delegated to intermediaries. Transaction costs are reduced and more savings can be allotted to investments that produce new technology. Ultimately, this promotes economic growth. Blackburn and Hung also show how a country might become trapped in a vicious cycle of sluggish economic growth and weak financial development. This situation occurs when the initial level of technical development in the country is very low and the expected flow of new technology remains low. Monitoring costs remain so high that financial intermediation is never organised. As a result, transaction costs remain high and economic growth low. Harrison *et al.* (1999) construct a model in which causality also runs both ways between economic growth and financial-sector development. Basically, they argue, economic growth increases banking activity and profits, which promotes the entry of more banks. The greater availability of banking services reduces the non-physical and physical distance between banks and clients, which, in turn, lowers transaction costs.

Naturally, the interest rate margin also has its shortcomings as a measure for efficiency of the banking sector. Ho and Saunders (1981) listed the factors affecting the margins in their dealership model. The margin may, for example, reflect an improvement in the quality of borrowers in the economy and thus decrease credit risk in the market. However, as those improvements are often linked to favourable economic development, we attempt to eliminate the problem with control variables for economic growth in the regressions. The margin can also be related to the competition in the market or describe the risk aversion of bank managers. In addition, the margins may get smaller when the financial flows get larger. Thus, the margin could reflect the size of the economy. However, many banks in the transition countries are part of foreign concerns and their scale advantages do not depend on the size of the particular economy. Despite its shortcomings, the interest rate margin is the best variable by which we could get data to measure the banking sector efficiency in the macro-level.

Our data for interest rate margins is from the Transition Reports published by the EBRD.[2] Unfortunately our data set is somewhat restricted to CEE and Baltic countries, particularly in the first years of the research period, as the data on some CIS countries is limited.

Our second variable, CREDIT, is derived from the variables used in many earlier studies. CREDIT measures the size of the banking sector by dividing the banks' claims on the private sector by the production of the private sector. In earlier studies, the size of the banking sector has been measured as a share of GDP. However, the share of the private sector was very limited over the first years of transition in some countries. It is thus possible that the low level of development of the private sector limited credit growth as a share of GDP. We have earlier tested the link between financial sector and GDP growth by using the amount of credit to the private sector as a share of GDP as a measure for banking sector development. The results from this study do not vary significantly from the results discussed in this chapter (see BOFIT Discussion Paper 14/2002). The data for CREDIT comes from the IMF's International Financial Statistics and is available for 22 transition countries. Despite the drawbacks of this variable discussed above, CREDIT still appears to be a superior option to the pure ratio of broad money to GDP used in some studies, because it excludes credit by development banks and loans to the government and public enterprises. CREDIT also enables us to compare the results with previous studies. However, we cannot be certain about the quality or productivity of the loans.

To control for other factors that influence economic growth, we use a number of control variables. The reform index (RI) consists of five indices published by the EBRD. These indices measure large-scale and small-scale privatisation, price liberalisation, forex and trade liberalisation, as well as competition policy. For each country, we have taken a simple average of these indices for each year. The bigger the index is for a country, the more advanced it is in regard to the reforms in the five areas. Due to the nature of the reforms, their effects on the economy can be seen with a lag of one or two years. We use a one-year-lagged reform index in this study. Inflation (INF) is measured by using the end-of-period consumer price index. A number of studies have found significant effects of inflation and reforms on economic growth in transition countries (De Melo *et al.* 1996; Havrylyshyn *et al.* 1998; Berg *et al.* 1999; Grogan and Moers 2001). To check the robustness of our results, we use OECD countries' GDP growth rates, governments' expenditure, share of exports and gross domestic investments as control variables for GDP growth.

In addition to macroeconomic variables and variables representing structural reforms, the initial conditions at the beginning of transition also determine later economic development (De Melo *et al.* 1996; Havrylyshyn *et al.* 1998; Havrylyshyn and van Rooden 2000). Here, however, we leave out initial conditions as control variables. In a fixed-effects model, the initial conditions should be contained in the individual dummies. Moreover, our research period starts from 1993, when the effects of initial conditions were already waning. Table 4.1 provides summary statistics of the key variables.

Estimation results

To analyse the finance–growth nexus, we use a fixed-effects panel model. This choice is reasonable as our data consists of almost the entire population of transition economies. Wachtel (2001) criticises the use of a country fixed-effects model to determine causality between financial-sector development and economic growth. In his view, fixed effects dominate the equation since the differences in the level of financial sector are larger between countries than over time. However, in transition economies, this is not the case normally. Banking sectors developed

Table 4.1 Summary statistics 1992–2001

Variable	Period	Mean	Median	Max.	Min.	Std. Dev.	Obs.
INT (%)	1992–2001	32.29	10.8	1,898.4	−15	143.40	206
INT[1] (%)	1992–2001	15.22	10.4	77.9	−0.3	13.46	190
CREDIT (%)	1992–2001	37.05	25.87	506.87	0.57	45.31	198
RI	1992–2000	2.76	3	3.8	1	0.72	225
INF (%)	1992–2001	441.8	19.8	10,896	−7.6	1,432	250
Real GDP growth (%)	1993–2001	0.9	3.3	17.6	−31.2	7.7	225

Sources: EBRD, IMF.

Note
1 16 outliers have been removed from the data (Bulgaria 1996, banking crises; Croatia and FYR Macedonia 1992, profound instability in the area; Azerbaijan 1992–1994; Russia 1995–1996; Tajikistan 1995–1998; Turkmenistan 1992–1995; and Ukraine 1992, probable disturbances in the data).

quickly and the level of financial development changes substantially over time. We thus estimate the following regression:

$$\text{GROWTH}_{i,t} = \beta_{0,i} + \beta_1' \text{ FINANCE} + \beta_2'[\text{CONDITIONINGSET}] + u_{i,t}$$

where the dependent variable, GROWTH, equals real GDP growth, $\beta_{0,i}$ is the individual dummy for each country (constant in time), FINANCE equals either INT or CREDIT and CONDITIONINGSET represents a vector of conditioning information that controls for other factors associated with economic growth. The error term is $u_{i,t}$.

Results from the panel estimations are presented in Table 4.2. Note that a shrinking interest rate margin (measure of efficiency of the financial sector) promotes economic growth. The link between the amount of credit and GDP growth seems to be more complicated. The current amount of credit is positively linked to economic growth but, in contrast to many earlier studies, when lagged with one year, the amount of credit seems to be harmful to economic growth. Among the control variables, the reform index seems to have the expected positive sign in three out of

Table 4.2 Link between the financial sector and growth: fixed-effects panel regressions

Regressors	(1)	(2)	(3)	(4) restricted sample
RI$_{-1}$	1.554	2.453	5.222***	−1.840
	(2.160)	(1.882)	(1.887)	(1.256)
INF	−0.001***	−0.001**	−0.001*	−0.006***
	(0.000)	(0.000)	(0.000)	(0.001)
INF$_{-1}$	−0.002***	−0.002***	−0.001	−0.002***
	(0.000)	(0.000)	(0.001)	(0.000)
INT	−0.062***	−0.052***		−0.212***
	(0.011)	(0.014)		(0.029)
INT$_{-1}$	−0.025**	−0.005***		−0.054
	(0.010)	(0.001)		(0.037)
CREDIT	5.876*		1.313	
	(3.328)		(5.300)	
CREDIT$_{-1}$	−2.190		−2.991**	
	(2.709)		(1.409)	
Number of countries	22	25	22	25
Number of observations	154	180	176	165
R^2	0.56	0.56	0.47	0.63
WALD 1	5,310***	490***	100.6***	2,336***
AR(1)	1.733	2.470**	0.992	1.473

Note
Standard deviations in parentheses. * indicates significance at the 10 per cent level, ** at 5 per cent level and *** at 1 per cent level.

four regressions, but the coefficient is significant only in one case. This result is different from most earlier results which have found the reform index to be significantly related to GDP growth. Our result may be partly due to our data set for the first half of the 1990s. It includes only the CEE and Baltic countries as we do not have financial data for many CIS countries for the first half of the 1990s. In addition, the interest rate margin seems to capture some effect of reform index on economic growth. As expected, inflation affects GDP growth negatively. Inflation is significantly related to the growth in all regressions.

In the first regression, we have both variables for the financial sector with their current and lagged values. Both the current and the lagged interest rate margins are negatively and significantly associated with growth. The result does not change significantly when the credit variable is dropped in the second regression. We also test the link between interest rate margin and GDP growth by leaving out several outliers (regression 4). The margin is still negatively linked with economic growth but, as expected, the coefficients of the margin become higher. The results are in line with the theories arguing that an efficient banking sector leads to higher economic growth. The result also has economic implications. If, for example, Romania's interest margin had averaged 6.1 percentage points, as in Hungary, rather than 20.6 percentage points during the period 1992–2000, Romania's annual GDP growth rate would have been almost one percentage point higher.

The current amount of credit allocated to the private sector is positively associated with economic growth. In stark contrast to earlier studies, the lagged value of CREDIT has a negative coefficient. However, the results are not always statistically significant. In fact, our results are quite in line with our earlier sceptical thoughts about using the size of the financial sector as a measure of financial development, as the size does not relate to the efficiency of the sector. In some transition countries, for example, soft budget constraints are still prevalent and lending to enterprises applying soft budget constraints may have resulted in counterproductive investments and financial losses. According to Mitchell (2001), banks may even make the situation worse by keeping such loans on their balance sheets. Another phenomenon linked to the negative coefficient of CREDIT may be a number of banking crises that transition countries experienced in the 1990s. Unsustainable credit growth precipitated banking crises that hurt transition economies (Tang *et al.* 2002). Thus, large amount of credit may have been harmful as the institutions in the financial sector were not ready to work properly in the market economy circumstances.

We checked the robustness of our results with additional control variables in the regressions. The growth rate in OECD countries has positive and significant impacts on growth in transition countries. Including the OECD growth rate into the model does not affect the coefficient or significance of INT and CREDIT. None of the other control variables –

government expenditure as a percentage of GDP, share of exports as a percentage of GDP, gross domestic investments as a percentage of GDP – have any significant effect on INT or CREDIT.

Next, we examine the direction of causality between the financial sector and economic development using a modified Granger causality test. We test for the causality between interest rate spread and economic growth with the following equations:

$$\sum Y_t = c_i + \alpha \sum Y_{t-1}^{i,j} + \beta \sum_{i=0}^{1} INT_{t-i}^{i,j}$$

$$\sum INT_t = c_i + \alpha \sum INT_{t-1}^{i,j} + \beta \sum_{i=0}^{1} Y_{t-1}^{i,j}$$

To test for causality between credit allocated to the private sector and economic growth, we apply the following equations:

$$\sum Y_t = c_i + \alpha \sum Y_{t-1}^{i,j} + \beta \sum_{i=0}^{1} CREDIT_{t-i}^{i,j}$$

$$\sum CREDIT_t = c_i + \alpha \sum CREDIT_{t-1}^{i,j} + \beta \sum_{i=0}^{1} Y_{t-i}^{i,j}$$

The results of estimations are presented in Table 4.3. The causality runs from banking sector development to GDP growth when we measure the development by the interest rate margin. The hypothesis of two-way-causality is also supported as higher GDP growth leads to smaller interest rate margins. This fits fine with the theoretical models of Blackburn and Hung (1998) and Harrison *et al.* (1999) presented earlier. Also, when banking sector development is measured by the amount of credit allocated to the private sector, the causality seems to run both ways. However, on the basis of this study, it is not possible to know the exact factors behind the two-way causality.

Conclusions

This chapter examined the link between the banking sector and real GDP growth in transition economies. We used a fixed-effects panel model and data from 25 transition countries for the period 1993–2001. We used two variables to measure the level of banking sector development: interest rate margin and the amount of credit allocated to the private sector.

The margin between deposit and interest rates, despite its shortcomings, is hoped to capture the efficiency in the banking sector. Our results support the theories that an efficient banking sector, where interest rate margins are low, accelerates GDP growth. The result has important policy

Table 4.3 OLS causality tests between financial sector and economic growth

Regressors	(1)	(2)	(3)	(4)
	Dependent variables			
	Y	Y	INT	CREDIT
Coefficient	3.126***	2.00***	19.235***	0.144**
	(0.355)	(0.599)	(4.333)	(0.036)
Y			−1.692*	0.003**
			(0.990)	(0.002)
Y_{-1}	0.495***	0.484***	0.281	0.005**
	(0.069)	(0.085)	(0.578)	(0.002)
INT	−0.056***			
	(0.009)			
INT_{-1}	−0.003		0.051	
	(0.005)		(0.070)	
CREDIT		3.365*		
		(1.80)		
$CREDIT_{-1}$		−3.012***		0.411***
		(0.884)		(0.125)
Number of countries	25	22	25	22
Number of observations	170	167	170	167
R^2	0.46	0.38	0.14	0.60
WALD 1	101.7***	111.7***	24.67***	25.89***
AR(1)	−0.07	−0.908	−0.490	2.103**

Note
Standard deviations in parentheses. * Significant at the 10 per cent level, ** significant at the 5 per cent level, *** significant at the 1 per cent level.

implications, as the interest rate margin tends to shrink as reforms in the banking sector are promoted.

Our second variable, the amount of bank credit allocated to the private sector as a share of private sector production, seems to have a more ambiguous effect on economic growth. The higher amount of credit has accelerated simultaneous GDP growth in transition economies, but when the amount of credit is lagged with one year, the credit seems to have been harmful to economic development. In other words, the loan growth has not been sustainable. This result is different from the results of earlier studies and, according to our view, is related to the special characters of transition countries. First, the soft budget constraints have been prevalent in many transition countries and credit to enterprises applying soft budget constraints may lead to considerable losses in the economy when investments turn out to be counterproductive. Second, the negative link between the lagged amount of credit and growth may reflect banking crises that many transition economies experienced during the research period. The increase in credit imposed considerable costs in the wake of the crises in many banking sectors. Thus, as the institutions and laws which are necessary for properly working banking sector have not been in place, the credit growth has been harmful to economic development in transition countries.

This result suggests that the development of the financial sector cannot be measured solely by its size, at least in the transition countries. In addition, the countries should not be encouraged to increase the size of the banking sector without first having properly functioning institutions and market structures in place.

The results from this study thus encourage transition countries to carry out extensive reforms in the banking sector. However, due to the problems related to our variables, one has to be extremely careful when interpreting the outcomes of this single study. The finance–growth nexus certainly needs further clarification and research.

A useful extension of this study would be to include more countries in the data set, since, importantly, the time series are much longer for a broader country set. In addition, better variables to measure financial sector development should be found.

Notes

1 All opinions expressed herein are those of the author and do not necessarily reflect the views of the Bank of Finland. The author is grateful to participants in the SUERF Colloquium in Tallinn in June 2003 and at the BOFIT seminar in Helsinki in May 2002 for their valuable comments.
2 Deposit and lending rates are unavailable for identical periods for each country. The overall size of the margin, however, should not be affected significantly by lending/deposit periods. Moreover, the differences in margins between and within countries are large, so a small error in the margins should not disturb the results. Also the IMF has reported lending and deposit rates, but this information is not available for all transition countries. Using the IMF data where possible, the results correspond to the EBRD data.

Appendix 4.1 List of countries

Albania	Georgia	Russia
Armenia	Hungary	Slovak Republic
Azerbaijan	Kazakhstan	Slovenia
Belarus	Kyrgyzstan	Tajikistan*
Bulgaria	Latvia	Turkmenistan*
Croatia	Lithuania	Ukraine
Czech Republic	Moldova	Uzbekistan*
Estonia	Poland	
FYR Macedonia	Romania	

* Due to a lack of data, Tajikistan, Turkmenistan and Uzbekistan are not included in models using the amount of credit.

Appendix 4.2

Table A4.2 Data sources

Variable	Definition	Source
Growth rate of GDP	Real GDP	*EBRD Transition Reports*
Interest rate margin, INT	Margin between deposit and lending rate	*EBRD Transition Reports*
Credit to private sector, CREDIT	Credit to private sector from deposit banks as a share of private sector production	IFS (line 22d), *EBRD Transition Reports*
Reform index, RI	Arithmetic average of EBRD transition indices (index of price liberalisation, index of forex and trade liberalisation, indices of small-scale and large-scale privatisation, index of competition policy)	*EBRD Transition Reports*
Inflation, INF	Consumer price index	*EBRD Transition Reports*
Investments	Gross domestic investment as a share of GDP	IFS
Exports	Exports as a share of GDP	IFS
Government expenditure	Government expenditure as a share of GDP	*EBRD Transition Reports*
Growth rate of GDP in OECD countries	Real GDP	IFS

Appendix 4.3 EBRD index of banking sector reform and interest rate margins (average of 1999–2001)

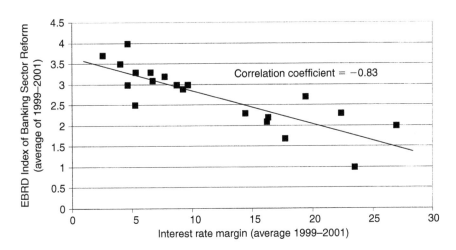

References

Arestis, P. and Demetriades, P. (1997) 'Financial development and economic growth', *Economic Journal*, 107: 783–799.

Berg, A., Borensztein, E., Sahay, R. and Zettelmeyer, J. (1999) 'The evolution of output in transition economies: explaining the differences', Working Paper No. 99/73. Washington, DC: IMF.

Berglöf, E. and Bolton, P. (2002) 'The great divide and beyond – financial architecture in transition', *Journal of Economic Perspectives*, 16: 77–100.

Berglöf, E. and Roland, G. (1995) 'Bank restructuring and soft budget constraints in financial transition', Discussion Paper No. 1250. London: CEPR.

Blackburn, K. and Hung, V.T.Y. (1998) 'A theory of growth, financial development and trade', *Economica*, 65: 107–124.

Conway, P. (2002) 'Bridging the great divide countering financial repression in transition', Working Paper No. 510, William Davidson Institute.

De Melo, M., Denizer, C. and Gelb, A. (1996) 'From plan to market: patterns of transition', Policy Research Working Paper No. 1564. Washington, DC: World Bank.

Demetriades, P.O. and Hussein, K.A. (1996) 'Does financial development cause economic growth? Time–Series Evidence from 16 Countries', *Journal of Development Economics*, 51: 387–411.

Drakos, K. (2002) 'Imperfect competition in banking and macroeconomic performance: evidence from the transition economies', paper presented at BOFIT Workshop in Helsinki, April.

European Bank for Reconstruction and Development, *The EBRD Transition Report*. London: EBRD, various issues.

Grogan, L. and Moers, L. (2001) 'Growth empirics with institutional measures for transition countries', *Economic Systems*, 25: 323–344.

Harrison, P., Sussman, O. and Zeira, J. (1999) 'Finance and growth: theory and new evidence', Discussion Paper No. 35. Washington, DC: Federal Reserve Board.

Havrylyshyn, O. (2001) 'Recovery and growth in transition: a decade of evidence', Staff Papers, vol. 48. Washington, DC: IMF.

Havrylyshyn, O. and van Rooden, R. (2000) 'Institutions matter in transition, but so do policies', Working Paper 00/70. Washington, DC: IMF.

Havrylyshyn, O., Izvorski, I. and van Rooden, R. (1998) 'Recovery and growth in transition economies 1990–1997: a stylized regression analysis', Working Paper No. 98/141. Washington, DC: IMF.

Ho, T.S.Y. and Saunders, A. (1981) 'The determinants of bank interest rate margins: theory and empirical evidence', *The Journal of Financial and Quantitative Analysis*, 16: 581–600.

International Monetary Fund, *International Financial Statistics*. Washington, DC: IMF, various issues.

Krkoska, L. (2001) 'Foreign direct investment financing of capital formation in Central and Eastern Europe', Working Paper No. 67. London: EBRD.

Levine, R. (1997) 'Financial development and economic growth: views and agenda', *Journal of Economic Literature*, 35: 688–726.

McKinnon, R.I. (1973) *Money and Capital in Economic Development*. Washington, DC: The Brookings Institutions.

Mitchell, J. (2001) 'Banks' bad debts: policies, creditor passivity, and soft budget constraints', in Anna Meyendorff and Anjan Thakor (eds), *Designing Financial Systems in Transition Economies*. Cambridge, MA: MIT Press.

Pagano, M. (1993) 'Financial markets and growth: an overview', *European Economic Review*, 37: 613–622.

Rajan, R.G. and Zingales, L. (1998) 'Financial dependence and growth', *The American Economic Review*, 88: 559–586.

Rousseau, P.L. and Wachtel, P. (2000) 'Equity markets and growth: cross-country evidence on timing and outcomes, 1980–1995', *Journal of Banking and Finance*, 24: 1933–1957.

Shan, J.Z., Morris, A.G. and Sun, F. (2002) 'Financial development and economic growth: an egg-and-chicken problem?', *Review of International Economics*, 9: 443–454.

Tang, H., Zoli, E. and Klytchnikova, I. (2002) 'Banking crises in transition countries: fiscal costs and related issues', Policy Research Working Paper No. 1564. Washington, DC: World Bank.

Thiel, M. (2001) 'Finance and economic growth – a review of theory and the available evidence', European Commission Economic Papers No. 158. Brussels: Commission of the European Communities; Directorate-General for Economic and Financial Affairs.

Wachtel, P. (2001) 'Growth and finance – what do we know and how do we know it?', *International Finance*, 4: 335–362.

5 Financial-sector macro-efficiency

Concepts, measurement, theoretical and empirical evidence

Gerhard Fink, Peter Haiss, Hans Christian Mantler

Introduction

Why do countries show different levels of economic development and grow at different rates? Over the centuries, economic literature has offered numerous answers in an attempt to explain cross-country differences: factor accumulation, educational attainment, market distortions, institutional development, legal system effectiveness, international trade and others. Just one decade ago, the financial sector began to attract intensified research efforts.

The suspicion that there may be a relation between the financial sector and economic development had already been suggested by Adam Smith (1776: 297ff). He expressed the view that the high density of banks in Scotland at that time was a crucial factor for the rapid development of the Scottish economy. In the early twentieth century, it was Schumpeter (1911: 140ff) who argued that the creation of credit through the bank system was an essential source of entrepreneurs' capability to drive real growth by finding and employing new combinations of factor use.

More recently, the relationship between financial-sector development and economic growth was analysed in the pioneering work of Goldsmith (1969), McKinnon (1973) and Shaw (1973). These early works, however, shared the weakness that financial intermediation was not modelled explicitly. The existence of financial intermediation was taken for granted (Fry 1997). This weakness carried all the more weight as, at that time, theoretical economic reasoning was strongly committed to the neo-classical assumptions of no information and no transaction costs – epitomised in the Arrow (1964) and Debreu (1959) models. According to this line of thinking, the existence of a financial sector is dispensable. It draws a veil over decision-making in the real sector.

Once the existence of information and transaction costs were accepted in theory building, the perception of the role of the financial sector changed: it plays an active part in ameliorating information and transaction costs in the allocation of financial resources (for example, Merton and Bodie 1995). This laid the foundation for a second generation of predominantly endogenous growth models considering the link between the financial sector and economic growth. Amongst the most prominent ones are Greenwood and Smith (1997), Bencivenga *et al.* (1995), King and Levine (1993b), Bencivenga and Smith (1991) and Greenwood and Jovanovic (1990). Renewed interest in empirical research was stimulated by the seminal papers of King and Levine (1993a, b).

The objective of this chapter is to give a decision-oriented review of the growing body of empirical literature that links the financial sector to long-term economic growth. In contrast to other reviews of the finance–growth nexus (for example, Blum *et al.* 2002; Thiel 2001; Tsuru 2000; Kahn and Senhadji 2000; Levine 1997):

1   we analyse empirical findings from a macroeconomic financial-sector efficiency view, i.e. we ask what properties/framework conditions of the financial sector do promote overall economic development best;
2   we locate relevant articles by systematically screening 39 leading academic journals in finance and economics and 34 working paper series of relevant institutions from 1997 on;
3   we group empirical evidence around four critical dimensions for policymaking: financial-sector size/industry efficiency and economic growth, financial-sector structure and economic growth, the finance–growth nexus in different economic settings and drivers of financial development.

We find that the recent interest in the ties between the real and the financial sector has usually been focused on the bank sector and the stock markets, rather ignoring bond markets and non-bank financial intermediaries as other important sources of external finance. Evidence provided by empirical studies relying on large country samples suggests that financial-sector size and financial-sector industry efficiency have an economically important impact on economic growth. Results for the impact of financial structure are more ambiguous. Evidence for industrialised countries indicates that a relatively high level of financial-sector macro-efficiency may have already been reached. Further increases in financial-sector size/industry efficiency cannot be expected to trigger further growth. Financial structure may have some growth effects by co-determining industry structure and growth. For developing countries, growth-enhancing potential lies mainly in an increase in bank-sector size and industry efficiency. First evidence for transition economies gives higher priority to measures improving bank-sector efficiency than to those fostering financial depth. Legal reforms that encourage the proper functioning of the financial sector and the privatisation of state-owned banks are promising means for tapping the financial sector's growth potential.

This chapter provides a basis for policymakers, market participants and other relevant institutions to be able to tap the financial sector's full growth-enhancing potential. With regard to EU enlargement, this may be of special relevance to candidate countries in securing long-term growth and in speeding up real convergence to the EU.

Additionally, this chapter identifies aspects in the financial-efficiency debate that need more attention than hitherto given:

1 the effect of framework conditions on financial-sector macro-efficiency;
2 the growth impact of bond markets and non-bank financial intermediaries;
3 financial efficiency implications of financial innovations as asset-backed securities, collateral debt obligations and other credit derivatives;
4 the identification of policy measures to promote financial-sector macro-efficiency;
5 the nexus between financial-sector macro-efficiency and macroeconomic volatility.

This chapter progresses as follows: the first section considers different concepts of financial-sector efficiency that form the framework for the subsequent discussion of literature. In the second section, we initially pose the question of how to measure financial-sector efficiency and discuss variables commonly used in empirical work. Subsequently we present empirical evidence on the properties of a macro-efficient financial sector. A concluding section provides policy implications and identifies areas of future research.

How can financial-sector macro-efficiency be defined?

In this section we discuss different concepts of financial-sector macro-efficiency. We ask from a theoretical standpoint how the financial sector is linked to real economic activity and what properties of the financial sector best promote overall economic development. We begin with a functional efficiency concept, i.e. the growth-enhancing effects of different services provided by the financial sector. Next we advance to an efficiency approach that focuses on the industry efficiency of the financial sector. In a third step, we consider a concept that emphasises opportunity costs of real resources diverted to the financial sector. Finally, we integrate the main points of the different concepts to get to a more comprehensive allocative view of financial-sector macro-efficiency.

A functional efficiency concept – the benefits of the financial sector

Tobin's (1984) concept of financial-sector efficiency mainly relates to the economic functions of the financial sector. He originally defined four different types of efficiency:

1   information-arbitrage efficiency;
2   fundamental-valuation efficiency;
3   full-insurance efficiency;
4   functional efficiency.

As the first two concepts focus more on microeconomic aspects of secondary financial markets and the third concept can be seen as a special case of functional efficiency, we chose functional efficiency as a starting point for our considerations. With Merton and Bodie (1995: 12), we see the financial sector's main function in facilitating the allocation and development of economic resources, across space and time in an uncertain environment. This primary function can be broken down into five more specific functions (Levine 1997; Tobin 1984):

a   *pooling savings* – an important function of financial systems is the pooling of savings of individuals by financial intermediaries or financial markets. The agglomeration of savings enables the use of more efficient technologies, that require an initially high level of investment, and of more efficient scales of production (Sirri and Tufano 1995).
b   *allocating resources* – another function of the financial sector is to evaluate and select investment projects. For individual savers, the cost of evaluating a wide range of prospective investment projects may be high, making it unlikely that best use is made of financial resources. Financial intermediaries that specialise in acquiring and evaluating information on investment projects and entrepreneurs may improve resource allocation and thereby enhance economic growth (Greenwood and Jovanovic 1990; King and Levine 1993b). Deep and liquid security markets may also improve resource allocation by providing incentives for the acquisition and dissemination of information about firms (Grossman and Stiglitz 1980; Holstrom and Tirole 1993). This effect, however, is not undisputed. If the market instantly reveals information on good investment opportunities, nobody will have an incentive to collect information (Stiglitz 1985).
c   *exerting corporate control* – the financial sector also monitors investments to reduce the risk that resources are mismanaged. Financial intermediaries avoid the duplication of monitoring costs by monitoring investments for many savers (Diamond 1984). Long-term relationships between financial intermediaries and borrowers (Sharpe 1990), and functional as well as regional specialisation of intermediaries (Harri-

son *et al.* 1999), can further reduce monitoring costs and information asymmetries. Improved corporate control in turn will spur growth by improving the allocation of capital (Bencivenga and Smith 1993). If stock prices efficiently reflect information on firms, stock markets may also exert corporate control by aligning management's and owners' interests via stock-price-based management compensation schemes (for example, Jensen and Murphy 1990; Diamond and Verrecchia 1982) or by facilitating take-overs of poorly managed firms (Scharfstein 1988; Stein 1988). Some authors, however, doubt the ability of stock markets to efficiently exert corporate control (see among others, Bhide 1993; Stiglitz 1985).

d *diversifying risk* – the financial sector protects individual savers and investors against liquidity risks, i.e. the risk that investments need to be liquidated before returns are available. This leads to higher investment in illiquid and more productive projects (Diamond and Dybvig 1983). Productivity gains, in turn, lead to faster economic growth (Bencivenga and Smith 1991). Liquidity risk can also be shared via security markets by selling shares when liquidity is needed (Levine 1991). This, however, requires that transactions on security markets are not too costly (Bencivenga *et al.* 1995). The financial sector also protects individual savers against the idiosyncratic risk that a single investment pays no return. By holding portfolios of investment projects, financial intermediaries can reduce rate-of-return risks (Greenwood and Jovanovic 1990; Levine 1992). Alternatively, individual investors' rate-of-return risks can be directly shared by portfolio diversification on security markets (Levine 1991). Financial systems that ease rate-of-return risks funnel a higher proportion of savings to riskier high-return projects (Saint-Paul 1992; Devereux and Smith 1994; Obstfeld 1994), thereby improving productivity. As King and Levine (1993b) show, this can also affect economic growth by accelerating technological change.

e *providing a payment system* – another contribution of the financial system to growth comes from providing a reliable and efficient payment system, that promotes specialisation and productivity by lowering transaction costs (Greenwood and Smith 1997; Chang 2002).

The quantity and quality of services provided by the financial sector determine how well these five functions are fulfilled. Most researchers assume that the quality of financial services is closely related to the size of the financial system (Andres *et al.* 1999). It is not only the size, however, but also the structure of the financial sector (bank-based versus securities-based) that may determine the provision of financial services, as suggested by a long theoretical debate.[1]

As a by-product, the provision of financial services may also influence the amount that is saved in an economy and thereby affect economic growth. The direction and size of this effect is theoretically ambiguous: the diversification of risks (liquidity risks, rate-of-return risks) may change the saving rate by simultaneously increasing returns and lowering risks. The effect of an increase in returns on saving behaviour depends on income and substitution effects. A decrease in risk may also ambiguously affect savings depending on risk aversion (Devereux and Smith 1994; Levhari and Srinivasan 1969) and precautionary savings (Kimball 1990; Caballero 1990).

Other factors being equal, functional efficiency implies that the financial sector is more macro-efficient when more of the financial services provided:

1   improve the pooling of available financial resources;
2   improve the allocation of these resources to high-productivity projects;
3   improve the exertion of corporate control;
4   improve the diversification of liquidity and rate-of-return risks;
5   improve the specialisation of real production by lowering transaction costs;
6   increase the amount of financial resources available for investment.

Thereby the size and structure of the financial sector may determine the amount and quality of financial services provided.

An industry-efficiency concept – the loss of financial resources

Another concept of financial-sector efficiency (Pagano 1993) stresses the loss of financial resources due to transaction costs of financial intermediaries and security markets when channelling savings to investment. As the provision of financial services is costly, a fraction of savings is absorbed by the financial sector in the form of commission fees, transaction fees, the spread between banks' borrowing and lending rates and so on. Thereby, the amount of financial resources available for investment is lowered.[2] The absorption of financial resources is primarily required for covering costs of resources employed in the financial sector. But it may also reflect X-inefficiencies, burdensome taxes (for example, high reserve requirements and transaction taxes), monopoly rents and so on.

The degree to which financial resources are channelled to investment may be represented by an industry-efficiency measure that relates the amount of financial resources channelled to investment to the amount of savings. In comparison to microeconomic measures of industry efficiency that relate cash flows or profits to factor inputs, this industry-efficiency measure has a more macroeconomic focus: if the financial sector improves its industry efficiency – that is, allocation costs per unit of savings are lowered – the loss of financial resources to the economy is reduced.

Other things being equal, the financial sector is more macro-efficient when the financial-sector industry is more efficient.

An opportunity–cost efficiency concept – the opportunity costs of real resources

Another concept emphasises the diversion of physical capital and labour from the real sector required for producing financial services. This diversion of real resources potentially lowers overall economic output (Santomero and Seater 2000; Deidda 1999): other things being equal, the financial sector is more macro-efficient when less real resources are employed in the financial sector.

Towards a more comprehensive view of financial-sector macro-efficiency

Every concept presented above highlights one important aspect of financial-sector macro-efficiency while holding other things equal. As changes in one efficiency dimension may be related to simultaneous changes in other efficiency dimensions, an exclusive consideration of just one efficiency aspect would result in misleading conclusions. For example, an increase in the provision of financial services may have negative effects, if the additionally employed real resources could have been used more productively in the real sector. Equally, a decrease in financial-industry efficiency may well have positive effects on the real sector, if improved financial services lead to more efficient investment in the real sector.

Following Santomero and Seater (2000) and Deidda (1999), we therefore propose to simultaneously consider the macroeconomic benefits and costs of the financial sector: the financial sector may be termed macro-efficient, if the marginal utility of financial services provided (pooling of savings, allocation of resources, exertion of corporate control, diversification of risk, provision of a payment system) equals marginal costs of the provision of services (loss of financial resources for investment, loss of real resources for real production).

Empirical research on financial-sector macro-efficiency

This section reviews recent empirical literature on financial-sector macro-efficiency from 1997 to 2002. For a review of earlier studies, see Levine (1997).[3] Initially, we describe the process and the results of our systematic literature screening. In a second step we dwell on research strategies to empirically assess financial-sector macro-efficiency. Subsequently, we discuss variables that are used in empirical work as proxies for financial-sector size, industry efficiency, structure and other properties of the financial sector. In a final step, we discuss findings of the empirical literature and group them around four critical dimensions for policymaking:

1   financial-sector size/industry efficiency and economic growth;
2   financial-sector structure and economic growth;
3   the finance–growth nexus in different economic settings;
4   the driving forces of financial-sector development.

Research in 39 top journals and 34 working paper series

To produce a comprehensive literature review of empirical work dealing with financial-sector macro-efficiency, we systematically screened 39 top academic journals in finance and economics and 34 working paper series of relevant institutions. Additionally, we checked literature databases (EconLit, ProQuest) for relevant literature. The list of journals and working paper series, along with the number of identified empirical articles published from 1997 to 2002, is reported in Table 5.1. Articles are considered within the area of financial-sector macro-efficiency if they empirically relate indicators characterising the domestic financial sector to long-term economic growth.[4]

Of the 12,089 articles (editorials not included, book reviews may be included in earlier years, as electronic research did not allow a distinction between regular articles and book reviews) and 5,852 working papers examined, 70 were categorised in the area of financial-sector macro-efficiency. Thereof, eight articles are pure literature reviews,[5] leaving 62 empirical primary studies.

There is an uprising trend in this field of research: 12 articles (17 per cent) were published in 1997–1998. In the following two-year period, it was 19 articles (27 per cent). There were 39 articles (56 per cent) published in 2001–2002. Thus, the topic of financial-sector macro-efficiency clearly gains attention in empirical research.

Strategies to empirically assess financial-sector macro-efficiency

From the theoretical point of view (see p. 67) the apparent solution for assessing financial-sector macro-efficiency would be to directly measure and compare marginal utility and marginal costs of financial services provided. Since marginal utility and marginal costs cannot be directly measured, researchers regress proxies for (1) the size,[6] (2) the structure and (3) industry efficiency of the financial sector on indicators of economic development. As Graff (2000: 199) notes, hardly any empirical model explicitly considers the diversion of real resources to the financial sector. This implies that positive financial-sector growth effects (due to the provision of better financial services, higher industry efficiency and so on) and negative financial-sector growth effects (due to the diversion of real resources to the financial sector) cannot be disentangled in empirical estimation. Thus, from the viewpoint of financial-sector macro-efficiency, an insignificant coefficient for financial variables does not necessarily mean

Table 5.1 Top 39 economic journals, 34 working paper series and the number of empirical articles dealing with aspects of financial-sector macro-efficiency from 1997 to 2000

Journals	Number of studies	Working paper series	Number of studies
American Economic Review	2	BIS – Papers	
Applied Financial Economics	–	BIS – Policy Papers	–
Cambridge Journal of Economics	–	BIS – Working Papers	
Eastern European Economics	–	BOFIT – Discussion Papers	1
Economic Policy	–	CEPS – Working Documents	
Economics of Transition	–	CEPS – Research Reports	–
Empirica	–	CEPR – Discussion Papers	3
European Economic Review	1	CRENOS – Working Papers	2
European Finance Review	–	DIW – Discussion Papers	–
European Journal of Finance	–	EBRD – Working Papers	–
International Economic Review	–	ECB – Working Papers	
International Journal of Finance and Economics	2	ECB – Occasional Papers	–
Journal of Common Market Studies	–	EU – Economic Papers	2
Journal of Banking and Finance	1	EUI – Economics Working Papers	–
Journal of Development Economics	1	EUI – Political and Social Science Working Papers	
Journal of Development Studies	1	IHS – Economics Series	
Journal of Economic Growth	1	IHS – Transition Economics Series	–
Journal of Economic Literature	1	IHS – East European Series	
Journal of Economic Theory	–	IMF – Working Papers	3
Journal of Finance	4	IMF – Staff Papers	
Journal of Financial Economics	4	NBER – International Finance and Macroeconomics Working Papers	
Journal of Financial Intermediation	2	NBER – Economic Fluctuations and Growth Working Papers	5
Journal of Financial Research	–		
Journal of International Money and Finance	–	NBER – Law and Economics Working Papers	
Journal of Macroeconomics	–		
Journal of Monetary Economics	1	OECD – Growth Working Papers	
Journal of Money, Credit, and Banking	3	OECD – Finance and Investment Working Papers	3
Journal of Political Economy	–	OeNB – Working Papers	
Journal of Economic Perspectives	–	OeNB – Focus on Transition	–
Oxford Economic Papers	–	OeNB – Berichte und Studien	
Oxford Review of Economic Policy	3	SUERF – Studies	1
Quarterly Journal of Economics	1	US Federal Reserve Board – Finance and Economics Discussion Papers	–
Review of Economic Studies	–		
Review of Financial Economics	1	WIFO – Working Papers	1

Table 5.1 Continued

Journals	Number of studies	Working paper series	Number of studies
Review of Financial Studies	–	World Bank – International	
Review of International Economics	1	Economics Working Papers	⎫
Review of World Economics	–	World Bank – Macroeconomics	⎬ 6
The Economic Journal	1	and Growth Working Papers	
World Bank Economic Review	–	World Bank – Domestic Finance Working Papers	⎭
Other journals	6	Other working paper series	6
Total	37	Total	33

Source: own research by Fink, Haiss and Mantler (2003).

that the financial sector has no influence on economic growth. For example, in countries with a relatively high level of financial macro-efficiency, marginal utility could equal marginal costs. Thus, regressions show no impact of a variation in financial variables.

With regard to the level of analysis, empirical research divides into three main strands:

1   *country-level research* – the real rate of economic growth, capital accumulation and productivity growth are the most used depending variables. Methodically, most studies apply a cross-country growth regression framework, as proposed by King and Levine (1993a, 1993b).
2   *industry-level research* – growth of industry real value added, growth in the number of firms in an industry, or growth in the average firm size of an industry are the most used depending variables. The methodology applied draws mainly on Rajan and Zingales (1998). Financial variables interacted with measures of industry dependence on external finance, and control variables are regressed on the dependent variable.
3   *firm-level research* – firm sales growth, firm value added or the percentage of firms exceeding their financially constrained growth rate serve as dependent variables. Methodologically, there is no predominant model framework.

Indicators to characterise the financial sector and its segments

Based on the empirical literature reviewed, this sub-section discusses indicators characterising the financial sector and its segments.

We identified 53 different financial-sector indicators. Most indicators used can be assigned to one of the following categories: financial-sector size (25 indicators); financial-sector industry efficiency (11 indicators); and financial-sector structure (nine indicators). Eight indicators relate to

Table 5.2 Financial-sector indicators identified

Category of indicators	Number of indicators identified			
	Financial intermediaries	Financial markets	Aggregate indicators	Total
Financial sector size	10	5	10	25
Financial sector industry efficiency	7	2	2	11
Financial sector structure	5	–	4	9
Other indicators	2	2	4	8
Total	24	9	20	53

Source: own research by Fink, Haiss and Mantler (2003)

other properties (for example, stock market volatility or stock market synchronicity) (see Table 5.2).

Looking at financial-sector segments that are covered, most empirical studies use indicators relating to bank intermediation. Other financial intermediaries, for example, insurance companies and investment funds, are largely neglected, though it has to be acknowledged that there is a certain overlap with the sectors covered. With respect to the financial markets segment, indicators reflecting properties of stock markets are often employed, whereas bond markets are largely neglected.

In the following section, the most important indicators used in the reviewed literature are discussed

Financial-sector size indicators

In proxying the size of bank intermediation, one stream of research relies on a variety of indicators based on money aggregates. Typical measures relate an economy's liquid liabilities to its economic output (i.e. M2 or M3/GDP) (e.g. Loayza and Ranciere 2002; Rousseau and Sylla 1999, 2001; Leahy *et al.* 2001; Levine *et al.* 2000; Levine 1999; Rousseau and Wachtel 2000; Al-Yousif 2002; Evans *et al.* 2002; Arestis and Demetriades 1997). This measure has two limitations:

1 Indicators based on monetary aggregates neither measure whether liabilities are those of monetary authorities, deposit money banks or other financial intermediaries, nor to whom financial resources are allocated in the credit process (Levine and Zervos 1998). Additionally, monetary aggregates also include liabilities of one financial intermediary against another ('double counting').
2 While theoretical considerations mainly relate to the financial sector's services in the allocation of credit, aggregates like M1 or in some cases

M2 reflect more the intermediary sector's ability to provide a reliable store of value and a means of exchange. In some cases, high levels of M1/GDP or M2/GDP may just reflect the lack of more sophisticated financial products for storing and enhancing value, while low levels of this indicator point to high sophistication of financial-sector services (De Gregorio and Giudotti 1995). Measures relating M3 to GDP may be more related to the ability to provide credits to the economy. They, however, still contain M1. Thus, some researchers construct indicators like (M3–M1)/GDP (for example, Andres *et al.* 1999) or (M2–currency)/GDP (for example, Luintel and Kahn 1999).

Alternatively, researchers use credit-based indicators. They are more closely related to the allocation process of resources and allow different types of creditors (monetary authorities, deposit money banks, other financial intermediaries) and debtors (private sector, public sector, financial sector) to be identified. As financial-sector services are thought to enhance growth via private activity, most indicators focus on credit issued to the private sector: credit (all issuers) to the private sector/GDP (for example, Evans *et al.* 2002; Cetorelli and Gambera 2001; Levine 1999; Carlin and Mayer 1999; Claessens and Laeven 2002), credit of deposit money banks to the private sector/GDP (for example Beck and Levine 2001, 2002a; Hahn 2002a; Leahy *et al.* 2001; Bassanini *et al.* 2001) or credit of deposit money banks and other financial intermediaries to the private sector/GDP (for example, Loayza and Ranciere 2002; Hahn 2002c; Gianetti *et al.* 2002; Levine *et al.* 2000; Beck *et al.* 2000b). Only a few studies use ratios including credits of deposit money banks to all sectors or credits of all issuers to all debtors (for example Fisman and Love 2002; Arestis *et al.* 2001; Arestis and Demetriades 1997). Indicators based on the assets of bank intermediaries (for example, domestic assets of deposit money banks/GDP[7]) or the absolute number of banks[8] are rarely used.

Bank-size measures assume a rather 'conservative' definition of products provided by intermediaries. Product innovations such as asset backed securities (ABS) or collateral debt obligations (CDO) are largely neglected. The emergence of ABS in US banking, for example, significantly lowered the aggregate volume of reported bank assets, while inherent risks and costs of financial intermediation remained. If empirical measures applied don't take changes in the product portfolio through which financial services are provided into consideration, empirical research may give a blurred picture.

Most indicators proxying the size of financial markets focus on stock markets. The predominant measure is stock market capitalisation/GDP[9] (for example, Gianetti *et al.* 2002; Hahn 2002a; Rousseau and Wachtel 2000; Cetorelli and Gambera 2001; Demirgüç-Kunt and Levine 1999; Levine and Zervos 1998). As Rajan and Zingales (1998) note, stock market capitalisation not only reflects funding obtained by issuers, but also reflects retained earnings and expected future profits. Higher stock prices in anticipation of future profits would raise the ratio without an increase of capital allocated through stock markets. Thus, a correlation between the capitalisation ratio and economic growth would reflect fulfilled expectations anticipated in stock market prices.[10] To remove price effects, Rousseau and Wachtel (2000) propose a deflation of stock market capitalisation by the stock market index. Levine and Zervos (1998) propose to simultaneously use in regressions another ratio that includes price effects (e.g. value of trades of domestic stocks on domestic exchanges/GDP). If the stock market capitalisation ratio remains significant, the price effect is not dominant. Singh *et al.* (2000) and Rousseau and Sylla (1999) use the number of companies listed on domestic exchanges to proxy for the size of stock markets. To our knowledge, Fink *et al.* (2003), Kahn and Senhadji (2000) and Fink and Haiss (1999) are the only studies also considering the size of bond markets. Fink *et al.* (2003) use the amount of bonds outstanding. Kahn and Senhadji (2000) as well as Fink and Haiss (1999) use indicators based on bond market capitalisation.

In order to proxy the overall size of the financial sector, including financial intermediaries as well as financial markets, researchers construct aggregate measures. Some researchers just sum up the size ratios of single segments (for example: stock market capitalisation/GDP + credits of deposit money banks and other financial institutions to the private sector/GDP) (Beck *et al.* 2000a; Gianetti *et al.* 2002). Other researchers (Levine 2002; Beck and Levine 2000) multiply measures (for example: stock market capitalisation/GDP × credits of deposit money banks and other financial institutions to the private sector/GDP). To avoid problems due to a lack of comparability of some ratios, researchers calculate the first principal component of several size ratios (for example, Beck and Levine 2002b; Leahy *et al.* 2001).

Neusser and Kugler (1998) use the GDP of the financial sector as an overall size indicator, as it covers a broad range of financial-sector activities including, among other items, the deposit and credit business of banks, service charges and commissions related to stock and bond issues and off-balance-sheet activities.

Financial-sector industry efficiency indicators

Size measures can be complemented with some measures reflecting financial-sector industry efficiency. To measure the costs at which bank intermediaries provide financial services, researchers calculate the share of bank overhead costs in total bank assets (for example, Levine 2002; Beck *et al.* 2000a). Regularly, large overhead costs are seen as a sign of a lack of competition and of inefficiency. As Demirgüç-Kunt and Levine (1999) point out, this measure is not unambiguous. Overhead costs of competitive banks may be boosted by large investments that will increase the quality of financial services provided. Therefore low overhead costs may indicate a lack of such investments. Koivu (2002) calculates the bank interest margin (lending rate minus deposit rate in the bank market) to proxy transaction costs within the bank sector. If the margin declines due to a decrease in transaction costs, industry efficiency rises. A smaller interest margin, however, may also reflect a shift to less-risky borrowers in an economy or lower profits for intermediaries due to enhanced competition. Therefore, Drakos (2002), Deidda and Fattouh (2002), Black and Strahan (2002) and Cetorelli and Gambera (2001) refer to the degree of concentration in the bank sector. They relate the total assets of the three or five largest banks to the total assets of the whole bank sector or calculate the Herfindahl index of bank deposits.[11] The underlying assumption is that strong concentration may indicate a lack of competition and high prices for financial services. If economies of scale could be achieved, higher bank concentration may also imply lower prices of financial services (Gianetti *et al.* 2002). Analysing the effects of bank concentration and industry efficiency in US states, Black and Strahan (2002) use dummy variables reflecting restrictions of bank expansion within and across US states as proxy. Andres *et al.* (1999) calculate a reserve requirement ratio to capture the influence of overly high reserve requirements on industry efficiency. This ratio equals the claims of bank institutions on monetary authorities divided by demand deposits and other deposits of bank institutions.

To measure the costs of stock market services, researchers rely on two indicators: value traded (for example, Hahn 2002a; Rousseau and Wachtel 2000; Levine and Zervos 1998; Harris 1997) and turnover (for example, Beck and Levine 2001, 2002a; Hahn 2002a; Singh *et al.* 2000; Levine and Zervos 1998). Value traded equals the value of the trades of domestic stocks on domestic exchanges divided by GDP. This measure does not directly measure costs. The underlying notion is that high liquidity on capital markets indicates low transaction costs. As this ratio includes a price component, it may be similarly distorted as the stock market capitalisation ratio: if stock market prices rise, value traded rises without an increase in the liquidity of the market. To ameliorate this problem, one could simultaneously include the stock market capitalisation ratio in the regression or turn to the turnover ratio. The turnover ratio equals the value of the trades of domestic stocks of domestic exchanges divided by the value of domestic stocks listed on domestic stock exchanges. As this measure includes stock prices in the numerator as well as in the denominator, the ratio is not influenced by stock prices.

In order to construct an aggregate indicator for the efficiency of financial intermediaries and financial markets, Levine (2002) and Beck *et al.* (2000a) divide the value-traded ratio by the share of bank overhead costs in total bank assets. To capture efficiency differences between bank intermediaries and capital markets, the value traded ratio is multiplied by the share of bank overhead costs in total bank assets (Levine 2002; Beck *et al.* 2000a).

Financial-sector structure indicators

Size indicators may also be combined with indicators reflecting the structure of the financial sector or financial-sector segments. Bank-sector size indicators based on monetary aggregates are often complemented by structure indicators, as monetary aggregates neither allow the distinguishing of who allocates savings (central bank versus deposit money banks) nor to whom they are allocated (private sector versus public sector). The underlying assumptions are that deposit money banks are able to provide better financial services and that financial resources allocated to the private sector have higher potential to accelerate economic growth. Thus, indicators are used that relate commercial bank or deposit money bank assets to commercial bank or deposit money bank assets plus central bank assets (for example La Porta *et al.* 2002; Levine *et al.* 2000; Benhabib and Spiegel 2000; Levine 1999) or that relate credit to the private sector to total domestic credit (excluding credit to the financial sector) (for example Levine 1999). Beck and Levine (2002b) and La Porta *et al.* (2002) use the percentage of assets of the ten largest banks owned by the government. Government-owned banks may allocate financial resources to those projects that primarily serve political and not economic goals. To account for economies of scale in the lending process, Black and Strahan (2002) calculate the share of total assets held by small banks.

Differences in the overall structure of the financial sector (for example bank-based financial sector versus securities-based financial sector) are reflected by aggregate indicators combining size indicators of bank intermediaries and capital markets. Levine (2002) and Beck *et al.* (2000a) use the ratio of stock market capitalisation divided by credits of deposit money banks to the private sector and the ratio of trades of domestic shares on domestic exchanges divided by credits of deposit money banks to the private sector. Beck and Levine (2000, 2002b) construct a conglomerate measure by calculating the first principal component of the two aggregate structure indicators described above. Demirgüç-Kunt and Maksimovic (2000) use dummy variables to distinguish between more bank-based and more securities-based financial regimes.

Other indicators

Some indicators identified in empirical work could not be assigned to the above categories.

Al-Yousif (2002) constructs a proxy for the availability of non-cash transaction methods and the complexity of the domestic financial sector by dividing cash held outside the bank system by the narrow money stock

(M1). Guiso *et al.* (2002) construct an indicator from household data to measure the probability for an individual to get access to credit.

Arestis *et al.* (2001), Levine and Zervos (1998) and Arestis and Demetriades (1997) use the standard deviation of changes in stock market prices to investigate the effects of stock market volatility on economic growth. Wurgler (2000) constructs a measure of stock market synchronicity[12] in order to proxy the stock markets' function to provide public signals of investment opportunities. Low synchronicity is associated with more firm-specific information impounded in stock prices.

Tadesse (2002), Black and Strahan (2002), Levine (2002) and Beck *et al.* (2000a) construct a conglomerate measure of financial-sector development by computing the first principal component of various aggregate size, structure and efficiency indicators discussed in previous sections.

Empirical evidence on the link between the financial sector and economic growth

Based on the empirical literature analysed, this sub-section discusses findings of empirical studies. We group studies around four critical dimensions for policymaking (see Figure 5.1):[13]

1   *financial-sector size/industry efficiency and economic growth* – research question: is there an interdependence between financial-sector size/industry efficiency and economic growth? These studies typically rely on large country samples, including all development levels.
2   *financial-sector structure and economic growth* – research question: is there an interdependence between financial-sector structure and economic growth? These studies also rely on large country samples.
3   *the finance–growth nexus in different economic settings* – research question: what are the differences in the finance–growth nexus between different groups of countries? Studies focus on industrialised countries, transition countries or developing countries.
4   *driving forces of financial-sector development* – research question: what forces determine the development of financial-sector size, industry efficiency and structure?

We find impressive evidence that financial-sector size and industry efficiency have an economically important impact on economic growth. For the most part, recent work suggests that the degree to which a country's financial architecture is bank-based or securities-based is not associated with economic growth. Some evidence points to an influence of financial architecture depending on industry composition, the stage of economic development and firm-size distribution. Looking exclusively at industrialised countries, empirical evidence indicates that the link between financial indicators and growth is rather fragile. This may be interpreted as a

Critical dimension	Sub-topic	Study's focus	Study
		Stock market efficiency	Harris 1997 (C)
Financial sector size / industry efficiency and economic growth		Banks, stock markets & economic growth, capital accumulation, productivity improvements, saving rates	Levine and Zervos 1998 (C)
		Financial sector size, industry dependence on external finance & growth	Rajan and Zingales 1998 (I)
		Financial sector size, external financing and firm growth	Demirguc-Kunt and Maksimovic 1998 (F)
		Heterogeneity of finance-growth nexus	Ram 1999 (C)
		Direction of causality	Luintel and Kahn 1999 (C)
		Bank intermediation & economic growth, productivity growth, capital accumulation, saving rates	Beck et al. 2000b (C)
		Size of financial sector (including bond markets) & economic growth	Kahn and Senhadji 2000 (C)
		Bank intermediation & economic growth, productivity growth, capital accumulation	Benhabib and Spiegel 2000 (C)
		Size of financial sector & efficiency of capital accumulation	Wurgler 2000 (C)
		Direction of causality	Rousseau and Wachtel 2000 (C)
		Independent impact of stock markets/banks on growth	Beck and Levine 2001 (C)
		Bank concentration, industry dependence on external finance & growth	Cetorelli and Gambera 2001 (I)
		Bank intermediation & economic growth, productivity growth, capital accumulation	Spiegel 2001 (C)
		Heterogeneity of finance–growth nexus	Deidda and Fattouh 2001 (C)
		Independent impact of stock markets/banks on growth	Beck and Levine 2002a (C)
		Bank intermediation, financing constraints & growth of small, medium and large firms	Beck et al. 2002b (F)
		Financial sector size, industry dependence on external finance & growth	Giannetti et al. 2002 (I,F)
		Human capital and financial development in growth	Evans et al. 2002 (C)
		Finance–growth nexus in presence of financial crises	Loayza and Ranciere 2002 (C)
		Government ownership of banks & economic growth, productivity growth, factor accumulation	La Porta et al. 2002 (C)
		Financial sector size, global growth opportunities & growth	Fisman and Love 2002 (I)
Financial sector structure and economic growth		Financial structure & firms' access to external finance	Demirguc-Kunt and Maksimovic 2000 (F)
		Financial structure & economic growth, industry growth, firms' access to external finance	Beck et al. 2000a (C,I,F)
		Stock markets and the development of information and communication technology	Singh et al. 2000 (I)
		Financial structure & industry growth, new firm formation	Beck and Levine 2000 (I)
		Financial structure & economic growth	Levine 2002 (C)
		Financial structure & industry growth, new firm formation	Beck and Levine 2002b (I)
		Financial structure & firms' access to external finance	Demirguc-Kunt and Maksimovic 2002 (F)
		Financial architecture, firm size & industry growth	Tadesse 2002 (I)

Figure 5.1 Critical dimension and research focus of studies analysed. (Source: Own research by Fink, Haiss and Mantler. (2003).)

Notes

C = country-level analysis; R = regional-level analysis; I = industry-level analysis; F = Firm-level analysis.

Critical dimension	Sub-topic	Study's focus	Study
The finance-growth nexus in different economic settings	Industrialised countries	Direction of finance growth nexus in the US & Germany	Arestis and Demetriades 1997 (C)
		Sweden in early development stages	Hannson and Jonung 1997 (C)
		OECD countries in early development stages	Rousseau and Wachtel 1998 (C)
		Financial development & productivity growth (long-run relationship and causality)	Neusser and Kugler 1998 (C)
		Financial development, inflation & growth	Andres et al. 1999 (C)
		Financial development, industry growth & capital allocation	Carlin and Mayer 1999 (I)
		USA in early development stage	Rousseau and Sylla 1999 (C)
		Direction of causality	Shan et al. 2001 (C)
		Financial development, growth & investment level	Bassanini et al. 2001 (C)
		Financial development & investment level	Leahy et al. 2001 (C)
		Direction of finance growth nexus in five high-income OECD countries	Arestis et al. 2001 (C)
		OECD countries in early development stages	Rousseau and Sylla 2001 (C)
		Dutch Republic, England, Japan and the US in early development stages	Rousseau 2002 (C)
		Stock markets & economic growth in 45 low income and 19 high income countries	Durham 2002 (C)
		Local financial development & growth in an integrated financial market	Guiso et al. 2002 (R)
		Banking concentration & industry growth in low and high income countries	Deidda and Fattouh 2002 (I)
		Financial development & investment level	Hahn 2002a (C)
		Financial development & investment level	Hahn 2002c (C)
		US policy changes fostering bank competition & new firm formation	Black and Strahan 2002 (R)
		Bond markets and economic growth	Fink et al. 2003 (C)
	Transition countries	Bank, stock market, bond market size & economic growth in 10 CEEC transition economies	Fink and Haiss 1999 (C)
		Banking sector size & efficiency in 23 transition economies	Jaffee and Levonian 2001 (C)
		Banking sector size & efficiency in 25 transition economies	Koivu 2002 (C)
		Market power of banks & macroeconomic performance	Drakos 2002 (C)
	Developing countries	Financial intermediation & economic growth in 30 developing countries	Al-Yousif 2002 (C)
		Financial intermediation & economic growth in 26 developing countries	Jalilian and Kirkpatrick 2002 (C)
		Stock markets & economic growth in 45 low income and 19 high income countries	Durham 2002 (C)
		Banking concentration & industry growth in low and high income countries	Deidda and Fattouh 2002 (I)

Figure 5.1 continued

Critical dimension	Sub-topic	Study's focus	Study
Driving forces of financial sector development	Legal framework conditions	Creditor rights, law enforcement, legal origin & banking sector size	Levine 1998 (C)
		Creditor rights, law enforcement, accounting standards, legal origin & banking sector size	Levine 1999 (C)
		Creditor rights, law enforcement, accounting standards, legal origin & banking sector size	Levine et al. 2000 (C)
		Creditor rights, shareholder rights, law enforcement & financial sector development	Beck et al. 2000a (C,I,F)
		Legal system adaptability & financial development	Beck et al. 2002a (C)
		Property rights protection & financial development	Claessens and Laeven 2002 (I)
	Other factors	Pension system reforms	Holzmann 1997 (C)
		State ownership of banks	Barth et al. 2000 (C)
		State ownership of banks	La Porta et al. 2002 (C)

Figure 5.1 continued

sign of relatively macro-efficient financial sectors. Historical studies for industrialised countries detect a strong relation between financial-sector size indicators and economic growth, indicating that, in early development stages, an expansion of the financial sector has growth-enhancing potential. Studies for developing countries support this view. Bank-sector concentration harms growth. First evidence for transition countries indicates that the growth-enhancing potential lies not so much in financial-sector size, but more in financial-sector efficiency.

Strong evidence supports the conjecture that a country's legal background and the priority it gives to creditor/investor rights protection, the enforcement of laws and the quality of accounting standards drives financial-sector development. State ownership of banks retards financial development.

Financial-sector size/industry efficiency and economic growth

This sub-section discusses empirical findings on the relationship between financial-sector size/industry efficiency on the one hand and economic growth on the other hand. With regard to the level of aggregation, we distinguish between country-level, industry-level and firm-level studies.

Studies on the country level mainly expand on the seminal and inspiring articles of King and Levine (1993a, b). Levine and Zervos (1998) explore the nexus between the size/industry efficiency of the bank sector and stock markets on the one hand and economic growth, productivity growth, capital accumulation and saving rates on the other hand. They find that bank-sector size and stock market efficiency are positively correlated with contemporaneous and future rates of economic growth, productivity growth and capital accumulation. Results on the influence on saving rates are ambiguous. Pure stock market size does not affect growth variables significantly. By contrast, Harris (1997) finds just a weakly significant, positive correlation between stock market efficiency and economic growth.

As those results from pure cross-section studies may be subject to endogeneity problems, Beck *et al.* (2000b) re-examine findings on the growth effect of bank-sector size by using panel data techniques. Results confirm the positive effect of bank-sector size on economic growth and productivity growth, but show ambiguous effects on capital accumulation and saving rates. Benhabib and Spiegel (2000) come to similar conclusions.

Evans *et al.* (2002) estimate a translog production function augmented with human capital and bank-sector size variables. They find human capital and bank-sector size to be complements, suggesting that the productivity-enhancing potential of human capital can only be exploited in the presence of a developed bank system. This suggests that the growth-enhancing effect of the bank sector mainly runs through growth in productivity. La Porta *et al.* (2002) find that government ownership of banks is associated with lower economic growth, especially lower productivity growth. Loayza and Ranciere (2002) show that even in countries that have faced financial crises, the growth-enhancing effect of bank-sector size is positive, but smaller than in other countries.

Beck and Levine (2001, 2002a) complement findings by estimating the effect of both stock market efficiency and bank-sector size on economic growth using panel data techniques. Bank-sector size as well as stock market efficiency have an independent, significantly positive effect on economic growth. Kahn and Senhadji (2000) construct aggregate financial-sector size measures including bank intermediation, stock markets and bond markets. The positive finance–growth link is confirmed. Spiegel (2001) finds some evidence that the positive relationship found in these studies may be partially driven by broader national characteristics that are correlated with financial-sector indicators.

Deidda and Fattouh (2001) as well as Ram (1999) point out that in the large cross-country panels used in most studies, there may be huge parametric heterogeneity across countries. Statements on the basis of full-sample estimates do not necessarily hold for subgroups of countries. For a discussion of results based on more homogenous country samples (industrialised countries, transition countries, developing countries) see pages 83–86.

The question of whether causality runs from finance to economic growth or vice versa is explicitly analysed by Rousseau and Wachtel (2000) using a panel of 47 countries. They find support for the notion that bank-sector size and stock market efficiency cause economic growth. The effect of stock market size is weak at best. Luintel and Kahn (1999) reach more ambiguous results with single-country time-series methodology. They find bi-directional causality between bank-sector size and economic growth in each of the ten sample countries.

To shed light on the mechanism by which financial-sector size and industry efficiency affect economic growth, a more recent strand of empirical studies relies on industry-level data.

In their seminal article, Rajan and Zingales (1998) start with the assumption that different industries have a different inherent need for external finance. A better developed financial sector will be able to allocate more resources to those industry sectors strongly depending on external finance and will thereby foster industry growth. The empirical analysis confirms their theoretical conjecture: financial-sector size facilitates the growth of industry sectors relatively dependent on external financial resources. According to Rajan and Zingales (1998), this finding may also help to explain industrial specialisation patterns across countries. Gianetti *et al.* (2002) verify the results of Rajan and Zingales (1998) relying on a larger sample of countries. Cetorelli and Gambera (2001) extend the work of Rajan and Zingales (1998) by exploring whether, for a given financial-sector size, the competition of the bank sector (reflecting its efficiency) has relevance for industry growth. Evidence is mixed: on the one hand, results indicate that there is a negative effect of bank concentration on overall economic growth. On the other hand, there is evidence that bank concentration promotes growth of industries strongly depending on external finance, especially younger firms. Depending on the context, the second effect may become strong enough to outweigh the negative overall effect.

Fisman and Love (2002) argue that Rajan and Zingales' (1998) assumption of a global, industry-inherent need of external finance is too strong. They assume that there are global, industry-specific shocks to growth opportunities. By comparing inter-sectoral growth rates, they find that bank-sector size enhances economic growth by allowing industries to efficiently exploit common shocks to their growth opportunities. Wurgler (2000) shows that the more developed a country's financial sector is in terms of size, the more investment is channelled to growing industries and the less goes to declining ones.

In accordance with country- and industry-level evidence, Demirgüç-Kunt and Maksimovic (1998) find, on the firm level, that the size of the bank sector and the industry efficiency of stock markets is important for facilitating firm growth. Firms in countries with a large bank sector and efficient stock markets can obtain external funds easier and grow faster. Beck *et al.* (2002b) further deepen the understanding. The larger the bank sector, the less firm-growth is negatively affected by financing constraints as collateral requirements, bank paperwork and bureaucracy, high interest rates and so on. This is especially true for small firms.

Financial-sector structure and economic growth

This sub-section discusses empirical findings on the relationship between financial-sector structure and economic growth. With regard to the level of aggregation, we again distinguish between country-level, industry-level and firm-level studies.

To give first empirical, country-level insight into the question of whether countries with bank-based or securities-based financial systems grow faster, Beck *et al.* (2000a) and Levine (2002) use cross-country methodology. They apply a variety of aggregate indicators that reflect overall financial-sector development and structure indicators that compare the size/industry efficiency of financial intermediation and stock markets. Both studies find that the degree to which financial structure is bank-based or securities-based is not associated with economic growth, while overall financial development is clearly associated with economic growth.

On the industry-level, results are more ambiguous. Beck and Levine (2000, 2002b) and Beck *et al.* (2000a) find that industries that heavily depend on external finance do not grow faster in bank-based or securities-based financial systems. The creation of new firms does not depend on financial structure, either. In examining the link between stock markets and the development of information and communication technology (ICT), Singh *et al.* (2000) provide additional evidence: financial structure does not determine the development of ICT. Both the United States, with its flourishing stock markets, and Northern European countries, where stock markets and IPOs play no central role, have reached a high level of ICT. The UK, with its active stock market, failed to become ICT leader.

Tadesse (2002) finds that financial structure does matter for economic performance. Bank-based systems induce higher industry growth in economies with relatively under-developed financial systems and in economies dominated by small firms. Securities-based systems are advantageous in economies with highly developed financial systems and economies populated with large firms.

Firm-level evidence suggests that firm growth does not vary with the degree of bank or market orientation of a financial system (Demirgüç-Kunt and Maksimovic 2000, 2002; Beck *et al.* 2000a). Firm-level results, however, may be interpreted with caution, as they rely only on data of the largest publicly traded firms of each country. More research is needed to clarify the effect of financial structure on small and medium-sized companies.

The finance–growth nexus in different economic settings

This sub-section discusses empirical evidence on differences in the finance–growth nexus between different groups of countries as industrialised countries, developing countries and transition economies.

Based on a panel of 21 industrialised countries, Andres *et al.* (1999) find no significant evidence that the size of the bank sector and stock markets is positively related to economic growth. Bassanini *et al.* (2001) find evidence that there is a positive link mainly between stock market size and economic growth. Their results for bank-sector size and growth are more ambiguous. To assess the effects of financial-sector size on investments, they estimate an investment equation. Again they find a positive and robust link between stock market size and investment and a more ambiguous link for bank-sector size. Leahy *et al.* (2001) re-examine the investment-related results of Bassanini *et al.* (2001) using a broader range of estimation techniques. They reach similar results. Hahn (2002a, c) raises the issue that evidence on a positive link between stock market size (measured by the stock market capitalisation ratio) and economic growth may be driven by stock price effects. Evidence may just reflect the forward-looking nature of stock markets. He re-examines the finance–investment link by using stock market efficiency measures (value traded and turnover) that are less sensitive to changes in stock market prices and finds no statistically significant results. Hahn (2002c) also re-examines

Levine and Zervos' (1998) results for a set of 22 OECD countries finding no significant relation between measures of stock market efficiency and economic growth. He concludes that the seemingly strong relationship between stock market size and investment in OECD countries is indeed mainly due to the forward-looking nature of stock markets and, to a much lesser extent, due to a causal linkage. Durham (2002) finds a positive and significant association of stock market efficiency and growth for 19 high-income economies.

Studies focusing on causality issues show ambiguous results for industrialised countries. Arestis and Demetriades (1997) and Arestis *et al.* (2001) find that bank and stock market size have positive effects on output growth in France, Germany and Japan. The link in the United States and United Kingdom is found to be weak, showing tendencies to run from growth to financial development. In a sample of nine OECD countries, Shan *et al.* (2001) find a causal relation running from bank and stock market size to economic growth only in the case of the USA and Italy. For sub-samples of the 1976–1998 period, they find all causality patterns. In a first attempt to analyse the link between bond-market size and economic growth, Fink *et al.* (2003) provide evidence for 13 OECD countries.[14] A causal link running from the bond market to economic growth is indicated for the majority of countries.

Neusser and Kugler (1998) find no significant long-term relation between aggregate financial-sector size and real growth in roughly half of the 13 OECD countries. There are slightly better results for the long-term relation between financial-sector size and productivity growth. A causal relation running from financial-sector size to productivity growth is only found for the United States, Japan and Germany. Some other countries show reverse causality. Causal links turn out to be statistically weaker, especially for smaller countries, which may be rooted in a higher degree of capital mobility.

In summary, these results indicate that the link between the financial sector and growth is rather fragile for industrialised countries, indicating that the positive effect of financial development found in studies that include a broader set of countries (see pages 80–83), may be especially relevant for early stages of the development process.

Historical studies for OECD countries support this conjecture. In examining 17 OECD countries since 1850, Rousseau (2002) and Rousseau and Sylla (2001) detect that there is a robust correlation between the size of financial intermediation and economic growth and that this relation was strongest in the 80 years preceding the Great Depression (1850–1929). In addition, countries with more developed financial systems engaged in more trade and appeared to be better integrated with other economies. In further studies, Rousseau (2002),[15] Rouseau and Sylla (1999)[16] and Rousseau and Wachtel (1998)[17] complement evidence, by finding that the emergence of financial institutions and markets played a central and leading role for long-term economic development. Hansson and Jonung (1997) find similar results for Sweden. Prior to the Second World War, the size of financial intermediation was a driving force of economic growth.

Based on industry-level analysis, Carlin and Mayer (1999) point out that a country's industry composition has to be taken into account when assessing the finance–growth nexus in industrialised countries. Bank-sector size is positively associated with faster growth of industries that rely heavily on equity financing and lower investment in research and development of industries that rely heavily on bank financing. A well-developed stock market is associated with low fixed-capital formation in industries that rely on equity financing. For low-income OECD countries, a well-developed bank sector is associated with faster growth in industries that rely on bank financing.

Analysing the effect of policies fostering bank-sector competition and consolidation on US state level, from 1970 to 1994, Black and Strahan (2002) present evidence that the deregulation of in-state and interstate branching restrictions increased the number of business corporations by spurring regional bank competition and ameliorating the negative effects of regional bank concentration. In contrast to that, Deidda and Fattouh (2002) find no significant interrelation between bank concentration and manufacturing industry growth for a broad sample of high-income countries.

The question of whether the domestic financial sector still matters in an integrated financial market is explored by Guiso *et al.* (2002). They analyse the importance of regional financial industry for growth in Italian provinces. They find that, within an integrated financial market, regional financial development still affects regional economic development. Small firms in a region particularly depend on the local supply of financial services.

In a first attempt to assess growth implications of financial-sector development in ten Central and Eastern European transition countries, Fink and Haiss (1999) estimate cross-section production functions augmented with measures of bank-sector size, stock market size and bond market size. They find evidence of a positive impact of bank-sector size on economic development. Stock markets show a negative impact. Bond market size is insignificantly related to economic growth in most cases. Jaffe and Levonian (2001) confirm the positive impact of bank-sector development on economic growth using a broader sample of 23 transition economies. They find evidence that indicators for bank efficiency are significantly and positively related to economic output, whereas indicators for bank-sector size are, in most cases, positive but insignificant. Koivu (2002) further refines the picture by exploiting the time-series component of a panel of 25 transition economies. Bank efficiency (measured by the net interest margin) shows a significantly positive and causal impact on growth. In contrast, indicators for bank-sector size show a positive, but insignificant, influence on growth with no clear causality pattern. The results of Drakos (2002) point in the same direction: high bank-market concentration is negatively associated with economic growth.

Al-Yousif (2002) and Jalilian and Kirkpatrick (2002) examine the relationship between the size of financial intermediation and economic growth in developing countries. The majority of estimates point to a positive relation between the size of bank intermediation and growth in developing countries. Durham (2002) finds no significant relationship for the nexus between stock market efficiency and economic growth. Results concerning the direction of causality (Al-Yousif 2002) give support for the view that there is a bi-directional link between bank-sector size and economic growth. There is also some weak support for other causality patterns (supply-leading, demand-leading, no relationship). On the industry level, Deidda and Fattouh (2002) present evidence of a negative relation between the bank sector's concentration and industry growth.

Driving forces of financial-sector development

This sub-section discusses empirical findings on factors that determine the development of financial-sector size, structure and industry efficiency.

The influential work of La Porta *et al.* (1998 and 1997) suggests that the size and structure of the financial sector is a product of the legal system and its tradition.[18] Legal systems that give higher priority to the protection of creditor/investor rights and show higher adaptability to changing economic conditions foster the development of financial systems (Beck *et al.* 2002a). Extending on this line of thought, Levine (1998, 1999) and Levine *et al.* (2000) trace the impact of the legal system on the financial sector through to economic growth on the country level. Levine (1998) shows that countries that put more weight on the protection of creditor rights and more efficiently enforce law have a better-developed bank sector, which in turn is positively associated with economic growth, productivity growth and capital accumulation. Levine (1999) and Levine *et al.* (2000) use a wider range of legal-system variables and show that accounting standards, reflecting standardised information disclosure to the public, are strongly correlated with bank development and growth. Results suggest that improvements in the legal environment may induce higher economic growth via higher bank development. Beck *et al.* (2002a) examine the ties between legal-system adaptability and the financial sector. The adaptability of legal systems is a good predictor for cross-country variations in bank-sector and stock market size. On the industry level, Beck *et al.* (2000a) find evidence that industries strongly depending on external finance grow faster and new firms are created more easily if countries show high levels of creditor rights' protection, minority shareholder rights' protection and effective enforcement of law. Claessens and Laeven (2002) confirm these findings and add that better protection of property rights will favour growth of industry sectors that use a high proportion of intangible assets in the production process. Using firm-level data, Beck *et al.* (2000a) present evidence that, in the presence of a large and industry-efficient financial sector, fostered by the protection of creditor rights, minority shareholder rights, and the efficient enforcement of law, firms are more likely to obtain external finance and exhibit higher growth rates.

Another line of research links state ownership of banks to financial-sector development. Barth *et al.* (2000) and La Porta *et al.* (2002) find that state ownership of banks negatively affects bank-sector size/industry efficiency and stock market size. This suggests privatisation of state-owned banks. Andrianova *et al.* (2003) note that high institutional quality is an important prerequisite for the success of privatisation strategies.

Holzmann (1997) traces the effects of pension-system reforms on bank and stock market size through to total factor productivity, capital formation and private savings. Investigating the case of Chile, he finds evidence for the conjecture that pension-system reforms contribute to the development of the financial sector. This, in turn, is linked to higher productivity gains and capital accumulation. The link between bank and stock market size on the one hand, and the private saving rate on the other hand, is found to be negative.

Summary and conclusions

This chapter analyses theoretical and empirical evidence on the interrelation between the financial sector and economic growth from a macro-efficiency view. After discussing different theoretical concepts of financial-sector efficiency that focus on functions, industry efficiency and opportunity costs of the financial sector, we suggest a move to a more comprehensive financial-sector efficiency view: the financial sector may be termed efficient, if the marginal utility of financial services provided (pooling of savings, allocation of resources, exertion of corporate control, diversification of risk, provision of a payment system) equals the marginal cost of the provision of services (loss of financial resources for investment, loss of real resources for real production).

Based on a systematic literature screening for 1997 to 2002 (12,089 articles in 39 leading academic journals in finance and economics and 5,852 working papers of relevant institutions), we locate 62 empirical primary studies that relate financial-sector properties to long-term economic growth.

We discuss country-, industry- and firm-level research strategies to empirically assess financial-sector macro-efficiency. We describe financial-sector indicators used in empirical studies and dwell on their advantages and drawbacks. Most indicators used can be assigned to the following categories: financial-sector size, financial-sector industry efficiency and financial-sector structure. Empirical studies use a wide range of indicators related to bank intermediation. Other financial intermediaries, such as insurance companies and investment funds, are largely neglected, though it has to be acknowledged that there is a certain overlap with most of the sectors covered. Looking at financial markets, indicators reflecting properties of stock markets are often employed, whereas bond markets are rarely covered.

Impressive evidence from empirical studies relying on large country-samples indicates that financial-sector size and financial-sector industry efficiency have an economically important impact on economic growth. By and large, recent work suggests that the degree to which a country's financial architecture is bank-based or securities-based is not necessarily associated with economic growth. Some evidence is found that bank-based financial systems may perform better in financially less-developed countries dominated by small firms. For financially developed economies dominated by large firms, a securities-based financial architecture seems advantageous. Evaluating the finance–growth nexus for more homogenous groups of countries further refines the picture. In industrialised countries, evidence on the nexus is rather fragile, indicating a relatively high level of financial-sector macro-efficiency. Industry-level evidence suggests that financial structure may have some growth effects by co-determining industry structure and industry growth. Studies covering developing countries and industrialised countries in early development stages suggest that bank-sector size/industry efficiency is an important source of economic development. First evidence for transition countries indicates that the growth-enhancing potential lies not so much in bank-sector size, but more in bank-sector efficiency. Strong evidence supports the conjecture that a country's legal system, its adaptability to changing business conditions and the priority it gives to creditor/investor rights protection, law enforcement and the quality of accounting standards drive financial-sector development. State ownership of banks retards financial development.

Policy implications

The empirical evidence available provides a first basis for policymakers. Policy recommendations, however, may be drawn with caution as research on the finance–growth nexus is still in an early stage. More research is needed to fully understand the interrelation between the financial and real sector. The latest results in research motivate the following policy conclusions.

In the case of industrialised nations, policies aiming at increasing financial-sector size/industry efficiency cannot be expected to trigger further growth. Changes in the financial structure may have some growth effects by co-determining industry structure and industry growth. In transition economies, high priority should be given to policies improving bank-sector industry efficiency and reducing bank-sector concentration. With regard to EU enlargement, this may be of special relevance to the CEE-accession countries in securing long-term growth and in speeding up economic convergence. In the case of developing countries a policy mix that aims at deepening bank intermediation and increasing bank-industry efficiency seems to be adequate. Thereby, legal reforms that encourage the proper functioning of the financial sector and the privatisation of state-owned banks are promising means to tapping the financial sector's growth potential.

Areas for future research

The overview of empirical findings points to a number of aspects of the financial-efficiency debate that need more attention than hitherto given:

a   *effect of framework conditions on financial macro-efficiency* – impressive evidence suggests that the financial sector has an economically important impact on economic growth. Extending on first theoretical evidence (for example, Santomero and Seater 2000; Deidda 1999) and empirical evidence (for example, Koivu 2002; Guiso *et al.* 2002; Tadesse 2002) more research is needed to assess optimality conditions of financial-sector size, industry efficiency and structure within special frameworks. In particular, how does the economic setting of transition economies and developing countries change the finance–growth nexus? How does a country's industry composition, its firm size distribution or its financial integration change the nexus?

b   *growth impact of bond markets and non-bank financial intermediaries* – the recent interest in the ties between the real and the financial sector has usually been on the bank sector and the stock markets, rather ignoring non-bank financial intermediaries and the bond markets as other essential sources of financial services. The few previous research efforts on bond markets cover rather short time horizons (De Bondt 2002) and international, rather than domestic, financial markets (Buch 2002; Soto 2000). They dealt with financial crisis situations rather than the whole business cycle (Herring and Chatusripitak 2000; Batten and Kim 2000) or linked GDP growth to the term structure of interest rates in order to forecast recessions (Harvey 1989, 1991; Gamber 1996; Gerlach and Smeths 1997; Ahrens 2002).

c   *financial innovation* – the impact of the spread of financial-sector innovation (mostly asset-backed securities and collateral debt obligations) on financial-sector efficiency and measures applied might also lead to new conclusions compared to the hitherto rather 'conservative' definition of the financial-sector product range. The jumpstart rise of ABS techniques in US banking lowered the aggregate volume of reported on-balance bank assets, while inherent risks and costs of financial intermediation remained. If the measures applied do not take these underlying changes in financial market microstructure into consideration, empirical research may provide a skewed picture. Scholtens and Van Wensveen (2003: 14) recently depicted the important role of banks in these securitised market segments.

d   *policies to support the development of a macro-efficient financial sector* – currently there is only limited knowledge on appropriate policies to promote financial-sector efficiency. Building on the seminal work of La Porta *et al.* (1997; 1998), recent contributions suggest that the legal system particularly determines financial-sector development. But there is more research needed to deepen the understanding on transmission channels running from the legal system to financial development and to identify a broader set of policy levers.

e   *financial-sector macro-efficiency and the business cycle* – it is well known that credit markets characterised by asymmetric information and agency problems can amplify shocks to the macroeconomy (Bernake *et al.* 1999; Bernake and Gertler 1989, 1990). Little, however, is known as to whether financial-sector properties such as financial-sector size, structure and industry efficiency or regulatory actions magnify or smoothen this mechanism.[19] The current change in the Basle II-framework and the US–Sarbanes–Oxley Act of 2002 on disclosure requirements provide examples of issues to deal with.

Acknowledgements

The authors gratefully acknowledge the support granted by the Jubiläumsfonds of the Oesterreichische Nationalbank (project no. 8,868). The opinions expressed are the authors' personal views.

Notes

1 For a comprehensive review of the financial-structure debate, see Allen and Gale (2001).
2 The underlying assumption is that the resources absorbed are entirely spent on private or public consumption.
3 For a review of studies dealing with bank efficiency from a more microeconomic view, see Berger and Humphrey (1997).
4 Therefore, interesting articles linking capital account openness, the amount of foreign direct investment, foreign portfolio investment or foreign bank lending to economic output (such as Durham 2003a, b; Arestis *et al.* 2002; Bekaert *et al.* 2000, 2001; Klein and Olivei 1999) were not included.
5 Blum *et al.* (2002), Thiel (2001), Wachtel (2001), Mayer and Sussman (2001), Rajan and Zingales (2001), Beck *et al.* (2001a), Tsuru (2000), Levine (1997).
6 As noted on page 65, researchers regularly assume that the size of the financial sector is positively related to the overall provision of financial services (Andres *et al.* 1999).

7 For example, Demirgüç-Kunt and Maksimovic (2000), Demirgüç-Kunt and Levine (1999).

8 For example, Rousseau and Sylla (1999).

9 Stock market capitalisation equals the value of domestic stocks listed on domestic stock exchanges.

10 Fama (1990), Schwert (1990) and Darrat and Dickens (1999) found that a large fraction of stock price variation can be explained by subsequent real activity in the USA. Choi *et al.* (1999) confirm findings for all but one G-7 country. Mauro (2000) extended the analysis to eight emerging-market economies and 17 advanced economies, Aylward and Glen (2000) to 23 developed and developing countries. It is found that stock prices generally have predictive ability, but with substantial variation across countries. Binswanger (2000) showed, for the case of the USA, that the predictive ability may also change over time. He finds that stock prices ceased to lead real activity in the early 1980s. According to Löflund and Nummelin (1997), predictive ability also depends on the stage of the business cycle.

11 The Herfindahl index of bank deposits equals the sum of squared market shares of each bank in the deposit market. In the case of atomistic competition, the index would be close to zero. A value of one would indicate that one bank holds all deposits.

12 Stock market synchronicity equals the fraction of stocks that moves in one direction in a given period of time.

13 For the sake of clarity, we tried to avoid assigning one study to more than one dimension. In some exceptional cases this could not be avoided.

14 The few prior research efforts linking bond markets and economic growth dealt with financial crisis situations rather than the whole business cycle (Herring and Chatusripitak 2000; Batten and Kim 2000) or linked GDP growth to the term structure on interest rates in order to forecast recessions (Harvey 1989, 1991; Gamber 1996; Gerlach and Smeths 1997; Ahrens 2002).

15 Rousseau (2002) presents evidence for the Dutch Republic (1600–1794), England (1700–1850), the USA (1790–1850), Japan (1880–1913).

16 Rousseau and Sylla (1999) analyse the case of the US from 1790 to 1850.

17 Rousseau and Wachtel (1998) consider five countries (the USA, Canada, the UK, Norway, Sweden) from 1870 to 1929.

18 We exclusively refer to those articles that have their main focus on the law–finance–growth nexus. Articles that focus on other aspects of the finance–growth nexus, but also employ legal origin dummies, creditor rights indices and so on are discussed in the relevant section. For comprehensive literature reviews, see Beck *et al.* (2001a) as well as Mayer and Sussman (2001).

19 Ferreira da Silva (2002), Llewellyn (2002), Hahn (2002b), Beck *et al.* (2001b), Owen *et al.* (2000), Wagster (1999), Bhattacharya *et al.* (1998) may give an insight into this issue.

References

Ahrens, R.A. (2002) 'Predicting recessions with interest rate spreads: a multicountry regime-switching analysis', *Journal of International Money and Finance*, 21: 519–537.

Al-Yousif, Y. (2002) 'Financial development and economic growth: another look at the evidence from developing countries', *Review of Financial Economics*, 11(2): 131–150.

Allen, F. and Gale, D. (2001) *Comparative Financial Systems: a Survey*, manuscript.

Andres, J., Hernando, I. and Lopez-Salido, J. (1999) 'The role of the financial system in the growth–inflation link', Bank of Spain Working Papers, 9920.

Andrianova, S., Demetriades, P. and Shortland, A. (2003) 'State banks, institutions and financial development', paper presented at the 24th SUERF Colloquium, Tallinn, June.

Arestis, P. and Demetriades, P. (1997) 'Financial development and economic growth: assessing the evidence', *The Economic Journal*, 107: 783–799.

Arestis, P., Demetriades, P. and Luintel, K. (2001) 'Financial development and economic growth: the role of stock markets', *Journal of Money, Credit, and Banking*, 33(1): 16–41.

Arestis, P., Demetriades, P., Fattouh, B. and Mouratidis, K. (2002) 'The impact of financial liberalization policies on financial development: evidence from developing countries', *International Journal of Finance and Economics*, 7(2): 109–121.

Arrow, K. (1964) 'The role of securities in the optimal allocation of risk bearing', *Review of Economic Studies*, April: 91–96.

Aylward, A. and Glen, J. (2000) 'Some international evidence on the stock prices as leading indicators of economic activity', *Applied Financial Economics*, 10: 1–14.

Barth, J., Caprio, G. and Levine, R. (2000) 'Banking systems around the globe: do regulation and ownership affect performance and stability?', World Bank Working Paper, 2325.

Bassanini, A., Scarpetta, S. and Hemmings, P. (2001) 'Economic growth: the role of policies and institutions. Panel data evidence from OECD countries', OECD Economic Department Working Paper, 283.

Batten, J. and Kim, Y. (2000) 'Expanding long-term financing through bond market development: a post crisis policy task', Deakin University School of Accounting and Finance Working Paper, 2000/07.

Beck, T. and Levine, R. (2000) 'New firm formation and industry growth: does having a market- or bank-based system matter?', World Bank Working Paper, 2423.

Beck, T. and Levine, R. (2001) 'Stock markets, banks, and growth: correlation or causality?', World Bank Working Paper, 2670.

Beck, T. and Levine, R. (2002a) 'Stock markets, banks, and growth: panel evidence', NBER Working Paper, w9082.

Beck, T. and Levine, R. (2002b) 'Industry growth and capital allocation: does having a market- or bank-based system matter?', *Journal of Financial Economics*, 64(2): 147–180.

Beck, T., Demirgüç-Kunt, A. and Levine, R. (2001a) 'Legal theories of financial development', *Oxford Review of Economic Policy*, 17: 483–501.

Beck, T., Demirgüç-Kunt, A. and Levine, R. (2002a) 'Law and finance: why does legal origin matter?', NBER Working Paper, 9379.

Beck, T., Demirgüç-Kunt, A., Levine, R. and Maksimovic, V. (2000a) 'Financial structure and economic development: firm, industry, and country evidence', World Bank Working Paper, 2423.

Beck, T., Demirgüç-Kunt, A. and Maksimovic, V. (2002b) 'Financial and legal constraints to firm growth: does size matter?', World Bank Working Paper, 2784.

Beck, T., Levine, R. and Loayza, N. (2000b) 'Finance and the sources of growth', *Journal of Financial Economics*, 58 (1–2): 261–300.

Beck, T., Lundberg, M. and Majnoni, G. (2001b) 'Financial intermediary development and growth volatility: do intermediaries dampen or magnify shocks?', World Bank Working Paper, 2707.

Bekaert, G., Harvey, C. and Lundblad, Ch. (2000) 'Emerging equity markets and economic development', NBER Working Paper, w7763.

Bekaert, G., Harvey, C. and Lundblad, Ch. (2001) 'Does financial liberalization spur growth?', NBER Working Paper, w8245.

Bencivenga, V. and Smith, B. (1991) 'Financial intermediation and endogenous growth', *Review of Economic Studies*, 58(2): 195–209.

Bencivenga, V. and Smith, B. (1993) 'Some consequences of credit rationing in an endogenous growth model', *Journal of Economic Dynamic and Control*, 17(1–2): 97–122.

Bencivenga, V., Smith, B. and Starr, R. (1995) 'Transaction costs, technological choice, and endogenous growth', *Journal of Economic Theory*, 67(1): 153–177.

Benhabib, J. and Spiegel, M. (2000) 'The role of financial development in growth and investment', *Journal of Economic Growth*, 5: 341–360.

Berger, A.N. and Humphrey, D.B. (1997) 'Efficiency of financial institutions: international survey and directions for future research', *European Journal of Operational Research*, 98: 175–212.

Bernake, B. and Gertler, M. (1989) 'Agency costs, net worth, and business fluctuations', *American Economic Review*, 79: 14–31.

Bernake, B. and Gertler, M. (1990) 'Financial fragility and economic performance', *Quarterly Journal of Economics*, 105: 87–114.

Bernake, B., Gertler, M. and Gilchrist, S. (1999) 'The financial accelerator in a quantitative business cycle framework', in J. Taylor and M. Woodford (eds), *Handbook of Macroeconomics*, vol. 1. Amsterdam: Elsevier Science B.V.

Bhattacharya, S., Boot, A. and Thakor, A. (1998) 'The economics of bank regulation', *Journal of Money, Credit and Banking*, 30(4): 745–770.

Bhide, A. (1993) 'The hidden costs of stock market liquidity', *Journal of Financial Economics*, 34(1): 31–51.

Binswanger, M. (2000) 'Stock returns and real activity: is there still a connection?', *Applied Financial Economics*, 10: 379–387.

Black, S. and Strahan, Ph. (2002) 'Entrepreneurship and bank credit availability', *Journal of Finance*, 57(6): 2807–2833.

Blum, D., Federmair, K., Fink, G. and Haiss, P. (2002) 'The financial–real sector nexus – theory and empirical evidence', IEF Working Paper, 43.

Buch, C. (2002) 'Are banks different? Evidence from international data', *International Finance*, 5(1): 97–114.

Caballero, R. (1990) 'Consumption puzzles and precautionary savings', *Journal of Monetary Economics*, 25: 113–136.

Carlin, W. and Mayer, C. (1999) 'Finance, investment and growth', CEPR Discussion Paper, 2233.

Cetorelli, N. and Gambera, M. (2001) 'Banking market structure, financial dependence and growth: international evidence from industry data', *Journal of Finance*, 56(2): 617–648.

Chang, W. (2002) 'Examining the long-run effect of money on economic growth: an alternative view', *Journal of Macroeconomics*, 24: 81–102.

Choi, J.J., Hauser, S. and Kopecky, J.K. (1999) 'Does the stock market predict real activity? Time series evidence from the G-7 countries', *Journal of Banking & Finance*, 23: 1777–1792.

Claessens, S. and Laeven, L. (2002) 'Financial development, property rights and growth', CEPR Discussion Paper, 3295.

Darrat, A.F. and Dickens, R.N. (1999) 'On the interrelationship among real, monetary, and financial variables', *Applied Financial Economics*, 9: 289–293.

De Bondt, G. (2002) 'Euro area corporate debt securities market: first empirical evidence', European Central Bank Working Paper, 164.

De Gregorio, J. and Guidotti, P. (1995) 'Financial development and economic growth', *World Development*, 23(3): 433–448.

Debreu, G. (1959) *Theory of Value*. New York, NY: Wiley.

Deidda, L. (1999) 'Interaction between economic and financial development', CRENOS Working Paper, November.

Deidda, L. and Fattouh, B. (2001) 'Non-linearity between finance and growth', CRENOS Working Paper, March.

Deidda, L. and Fattouh, B. (2002) 'Concentration in the banking industry and economic growth', CRENOS Working Paper, February.

Demirgüç-Kunt, A. and Levine, R. (1999) 'Bank-based and market-based financial systems: cross-country comparisons', World Bank Working Paper, 2143.

Demirgüç-Kunt, A. and Maksimovic, V. (1998) 'Law, finance, and firm growth', *Journal of Finance*, 53(6): 2107–2137.

Demirgüç-Kunt, A. and Maksimovic, V. (2000) 'Funding growth in bank-based and market-based financial systems: evidence from firm-level data', World Bank Working Paper, 2432.

Demirgüç-Kunt, A. and Maksimovic, V. (2002) 'Funding growth in bank-based and market-based financial systems: evidence from firm-level data', *Journal of Financial Economics*, 65(3): 337–363.

Devereux, M and Smith, G. (1994) 'International risk sharing and economic growth', *International Economic Review*, 35(4): 535–550.

Diamond, D. (1984) 'Financial intermediation and delegated monitoring', *Review of Economic Studies*, 51(3): 393–414.

Diamond, D. and Dybvig, P. (1983) 'Bank runs, deposit insurance, and liquidity', *Journal of Political Economy*, 91(3): 401–419.

Diamond, D. and Verrecchia, R. (1982) 'Optimal managerial contracts and equilibrium security prices', *Journal of Finance*, 37: 275–287.

Drakos, K. (2002) 'Imperfect competition in banking and macroeconomic performance: evidence from transition countries', forthcoming.

Durham, B. (2002) 'The effects of stock market development on growth and private investment in lower-income countries', *Emerging Markets Review*, 3: 211–232.

Durham, B. (2003a) 'Foreign portfolio investment, foreign bank lending and economic growth', Board of Governors of the Federal Reserve System – International Finance Discussion Paper, 757.

Durham, B. (2003b) 'Absorptive capacity and the effects of foreign direct investment and equity foreign portfolio investment on economic growth', *European Economic Review*, forthcoming.

Evans, A.D., Green, C.J. and Murinde, V. (2002) 'Human capital and financial development in economic growth: new evidence using the translog production function', *International Journal of Finance and Economics*, 7(2): 123–140.

Fama, E. (1990) 'Stock returns, expected returns, and real activity', *Journal of Finance*, 45: 1089–1108.

Ferreira da Silva, G. (2002) 'The impact of financial system development on business cycles volatility: cross-country evidence', *Journal of Macroeconomics*, 24: 233–253.

Fink, G. and Haiss, P. (1999) 'Central European financial markets from an EU perspective: theoretical aspects and statistical analyses', IEF Working Paper, 34.

Fink, G., Haiss, P. and Hristoforova, S. (2003) 'Bond markets and economic growth', IEF Working Paper, 49.

Fisman, R. and Love, I. (2002) 'Patterns of industrial development revisited: the role of finance', World Bank Working Paper, 2877.

Fry, M. (1997) 'In favour of financial liberalisation', *The Economic Journal*, 107: 754–770.

Gamber, E. (1996) 'The policy content of the yield curve slope', *Review of Financial Economics*, 5(2): 163–179.

Gerlach, S. and Smeths, F. (1997) 'The term structure of Euro-rates: some evidence in support of the expectations hypothesis', *Journal of International Money and Finance*, 16(2): 305–321.

Giannetti, M., Guiso, L., Jappelli, T., Padula, M. and Pagano, M. (2002) 'Financial market integration, corporate financing and economic growth', European Commission Economic Paper, 179.

Goldsmith, R. (1969) *Financial Structure and Development*. New Haven, CT: Yale University Press.

Graff, M. (2000) *Finanzielle Entwicklung und reales Wirtschaftswachstum*. Tübingen: J.C.B. Mohr (Siebeck).

Greenwood, J. and Jovanovic, B. (1990) 'Financial development, growth, and the distribution of income', *Journal of Political Economy*, 98(5): 1076–1107.

Greenwood, J. and Smith, B. (1997) 'Financial markets in development, and the development of financial markets', *Journal of Economic Dynamic and Control*, 21(1): 145–181.

Grossman, S. and Stiglitz, J. (1980) 'On the impossibility of informationally efficient markets', *American Economic Review*, 70(3): 393–408.

Guiso, L., Sapienza, P. and Zingales, L. (2002) 'Does local financial development matter?', CEPR Discussion Paper, 3307.

Hahn, F. (2002a) 'The finance–growth nexus revisited. New evidence from OECD countries', WIFO Working Paper, 176.

Hahn, F. (2002b) 'Financial development and output growth fluctuation. Evidence from OECD countries', WIFO Working Papers, 181.

Hahn, F. (2002c) 'Bedeutung von Aktienmärkten für Wachstum und Wachstumsschwankungen in den OECD-Ländern', *Materialien zu Wirtschaft und Gesellschaft*, 78.

Hansson, P. and Jonung, L. (1997) 'Finance and economic growth: the case of Sweden', *Research in Economics*, 51: 251–301.

Harris, R.D. (1997) 'Stock markets and development: a re-assessment', *European Economic Review*, 41(1): 139–146.

Harrison, P., Sussman, O. and Zeira, J. (1999) 'Finance and growth: theory and new evidence', Federal Reserve Board Finance and Economics Discussion Paper, 1999/35.

Harvey, C.R. (1989) 'Forecasts of economic growth from the bond and stock markets', *Financial Analysts Journal*, September–October: 38–45.

Harvey, C.R. (1991) 'Interest rate based forecasts of German economic growth', *Review of World Economics*, 127(4): 701–718.

Herring, R. and Chatusripitak, N. (2000) 'The case of the missing market: the bond market and why it matters for financial development', Asian Development Bank Institute Working Paper, 11.

Holstrom, B. and Tirole, J. (1993) 'Market liquidity and performance monitoring', *Journal of Political Economy*, 101(4): 678–709.

Holzmann, R. (1997) 'Pension reform, financial market development and economic growth: preliminary evidence from Chile', *IMF Staff Papers*, 44(2): 149–178.

Jaffee, D. and Levonian, M. (2001) 'The structure of banking systems in developed and transition economies', *European Financial Management*, 7(2): 161–181.

Jalilian, H. and Kirkpatrick, C. (2002) 'Financial development and poverty reduction in developing countries', *International Journal of Finance and Economics*, 7(2): 97–108.

Jensen, M. and Murphy, K. (1990) 'Performance pay and top-management incentives', *Journal of Political Economy*, 98(2): 225–264.

Kahn, M. and Senhadji, A. (2000) 'Financial development and economic growth: an overview', IMF Working Paper, 00/209.

Kimball, M. (1990) 'Precautionary saving in the small and in the large', *Econometrica*, 58: 53–73.

King, R. and Levine, R. (1993a) 'Finance and growth: Schumpeter might be right', *Quarterly Journal of Economics*, 108(3): 717–737.

King, R. and Levine, R. (1993b) 'Finance, entrepreneurship, and growth – theory and evidence', *Journal of Monetary Economics*, 32: 513–542.

Klein, M.W. and Olivei, G. (1999) 'Capital account liberalization, financial depth and economic growth', NBER Working Paper, w7384.

Koivu, T. (2002) 'Do efficient banking sectors accelerate economic growth in transition countries?', BOFIT Discussion Paper, 14/2002.

La Porta, R., Lopez-de-Silanes, F. and Schleifer, A. (2002) 'Government ownership of banks', *Journal of Finance*, 57(1): 265–301.

La Porta, R., Lopez-de-Silanes, F., Shleifer, A. and Vishny, R. (1997) 'Legal determinants of external finance', *Journal of Finance*, 52(3): 1131–1150.

Leahy, M., Schich, S., Wehinger, G., Pelgrin, F. and Thorgeirsson, Th. (2001) 'Contributions of financial systems to growth in OECD countries', OECD Working Paper, 280.

Levhari, D. and Srinivasan, T. (1969) 'Optimal savings under uncertainty', *Review of Economic Studies*, 36(1): 153–163.

Levine, R. (1991) 'Stock markets, growth, and tax policy', *Journal of Finance*, 46(6): 1445–1465.

Levine, R. (1997) 'Financial development and economic growth – views and agenda', *Journal of Economic Literature*, 35: 688–726.

Levine, R. (1998) 'The legal environment, banks, and long-run economic growth', *Journal of Money, Credit, and Banking*, 30(2): 596–613.

Levine, R. (1999) 'Law, finance, and economic growth', *Journal of Financial Intermediation*, 8(1–2): 8–35.

Levine, R. (2002): 'Bank-based or market-based financial systems: which is better?', *Journal of Financial Intermediation*, 11: 398–428.

Levine, R. and Zervos, S. (1998) 'Stock markets, banks and economic growth', *American Economic Review*, 88(3): 537–558.

Levine, R., Loayza, N. and Beck, T. (2000) 'Financial intermediation and growth: causality and causes', *Journal of Monetary Economics*, 46(1): 31–77.

Llewellyn, D.T. (2002) 'An analysis of the causes of recent banking crises', *European Journal of Finance*, 8: 152–175.

Loayza, N. and Ranciere, R. (2002) 'Financial development, financial fragility and growth', Central Bank of Chile Working Paper, 145.

Löflund, A. and Nummelin, K. (1997) 'On stocks, bonds and business conditions', *Applied Financial Economics*, 7: 137–146.

Luintel, K.B. and Kahn, M. (1999) 'A quantitative reassessment of the finance–growth nexus: evidence from a multivariate VAR', *Journal of Development Economics*, 60(2): 381–405.

McKinnon, R. (1973) *Money and Capital in Economic Development*, Washington, DC: Brookings Institution.

Mauro, P. (2000) 'Stock returns and output growth in emerging and advanced economies', IMF Working Paper, 00/89.

Mayer, C. and Sussman, O. (2001) 'The assessment: finance, law, and growth', *Oxford Review of Economic Policy*, 17: 457–466.

Merton, R. and Bodie, Z. (1995) 'A conceptual framework for analyzing the financial environment', in B. Dwight (ed.), *The Global Financial System: a Functional Perspective*. Boston, MA: Harvard Business School Press.

Neusser, K. and Kugler, M. (1998) 'Manufacturing growth and financial development: evidence from OECD countries', *Review of Economics and Statistics*, 80(4): 638–646.

Obstfeld, M. (1994) 'Risk-taking, global diversification and growth', *American Economic Review*, 84(5): 10–29.

Owen, A.L., Iyigun, M.F. and Denizer, C. (2000) 'Finance and macroeconomic volatility', World Bank Working Paper, 2487.

Pagano, M. (1993) 'Financial markets and growth: an overview', *European Economic Review*, 37: 613–622.

Rajan, R.G. and Zingales, L. (1998) 'Financial dependence and growth', *American Economic Review*, 88(3): 559–586.

Rajan, R.G. and Zingales, L. (2001) 'Financial systems, industrial structure, and growth', *Oxford Review of Economic Policy*, 17: 467–482.

Ram, R. (1999) 'Financial development and economic growth: additional evidence', *Journal of Development Studies*, 35(4): 164–174.

Rousseau, P. (2002) 'Historical perspectives on financial development and economic growth', NBER Working Paper, 9333.

Rousseau, P. and Sylla, R. (1999) 'Emerging financial markets and early US growth', NBER Working Paper, 7448.

Rousseau, P. and Sylla, R. (2001) 'Financial systems, economic growth and stabilisation', NBER Working Paper, w8323.

Rousseau, P. and Wachtel, P. (1998) 'Financial intermediation and economic performance: historical evidence from five industrialized countries', *Journal of Money, Credit, and Banking*, 30(4): 658–678.

Rousseau, P. and Wachtel, P. (2000) 'Equity markets and growth: cross-country evidence on timing and outcomes, 1980–1995', *Journal of Banking & Finance*, 24(12): 1933–1957.

Saint-Paul, G. (1992) 'Technological choice, financial markets and economic development', *European Economic Review*, 36(4): 763–781.

Santomero, A. and Seater, J. (2000) 'Is there an optimal size for the financial sector?', *Journal of Banking & Finance*, 24: 945–965.

Scharfstein, D. (1988) 'The disciplinary role of take-overs', *Review of Economic Studies*, 55(2): 185–199.

Scholtens, B. and Van Wensveen, D. (2003) 'The theory of financial intermediation', *SUERF Studies*, 1/2003.

Schumpeter, J. (1911 [1952]) *Theorie der wirtschaftlichen Entwicklung*, Berlin: Duncker und Humblot.

Schwert, G.W. (1990) 'Stock returns and real activity: a century of evidence', *Journal of Finance*, 45: 1237–1257.

Shan, J.Z., Morris, A.G. and Sun, F. (2001) 'Financial development and economic growth: a egg-and-chicken problem?', *Review of International Economics*, 9(3): 443–454.

Sharpe, S. (1990) 'Asymmetric information, bank lending, and implicit contracts: a stylized model of customer relationships', *Journal of Finance*, 45(4): 461–488.

Shaw, E. (1973) *Financial Deepening in Economic Development*. New York, NY: Oxford University Press.

Singh, A., Singh, A. and Weisse, B. (2000) 'Information technology, venture capital and the stock market', University of Cambridge Accounting and Finance Discussion Papers, 00/AF47.

Sirri, E. and Tufano, P. (1995) 'The economics of pooling', in B. Dwight (ed.), *The Global Financial System: a Functional Perspective*. Boston, MA: Harvard Business School Press.

Smith, A. (1776 [1979]) *An Inquiry into the Nature and Causes of the Wealth of Nations*, in R.H. Campbell and A.S. Skinner (eds), *The Glasgow Edition of the Works and Correspondence of Adan Smith*. Oxford: Clarendon Press.

Soto, M. (2000) 'Capital flows and growth in developing countries: recent empirical evidence', OECD Technical Paper, 160.

Spiegel, M. (2001) 'Financial development and growth – are APEC nations unique?', Federal Reserve Bank of San Francisco Pacific Working Papers, PB01/04.

Stein, J. (1988) 'Take-over threats and managerial myopia', *Journal of Political Economy*, 96(1): 61–80.

Stiglitz, J. (1985) 'Credit markets and the control of capital', *Journal of Money, Credit, and Banking*, 17(2): 133–152.

Tadesse, S. (2002) 'Financial architecture and economic performance: international evidence', *Journal of Financial Intermediation*, 11(4): 429–454.

Thiel, M. (2001) 'Finance and economic growth – a review of theory and the available evidence', European Commission Economic Paper, 158.

Tobin, J. (1984) 'On the efficiency of the financial system', *Lloyds Bank Review*, 153: 1–15.

Tsuru, K. (2000) 'Finance and growth – some theoretical considerations, and a review of the empirical literature', OECD Economic Department Working Paper, 2000/1.

Wachtel, P. (2001) 'Growth and finance: what do we know and how do we know it?', *International Finance*, 4(3): 335–362.

Wagster, J.D. (1999) 'The Basle Accord of 1988 and the international credit crunch of 1989–1992', *Journal of Financial Services Research*, 15(2): 123–143.

Wurgler, J. (2000) 'Financial markets and allocation of capital', *Journal of Financial Economics*, 58(1–2): 187–214.

6 Financial-sector efficiency

The impact of policy and the road ahead[1]

C. Maxwell Watson

Executive summary

Efficiency in the financial sector is a broader concept than the cost of intermediation or the liquidity and transparency of markets. It encompasses the sector's depth and effectiveness in allocating capital – in other words, its capacity to support sustainable growth, including as a conduit and filter for capital flows and as a monetary transmission channel. In all of these respects, there were major advances in the countries of the Baltic region and Central and Eastern Europe during the 1990s. This was evidenced by lower spreads; action to address quasi-fiscal deficits; rapidly growing credit to the private sector; greater financial depth; and some increase in securities market capitalization. And in all of these economies the resilience of the sector and its capacity for risk management were strengthened. This progress reflected a range of policy initiatives:

- while restructuring approaches were far from uniform, a key priority was to impose hard budget constraints on former state enterprises – which in some cases was a decade-long task;
- the liberalization of interest rates promoted deepening and competition, and openness to FDI jump-started governance and financing while the domestic financial sector was maturing;
- stronger banking regulation and supervision was a key element, with regulatory frameworks advancing – at times prompted by crises – in the direction of Basel standards;
- favorable macroeconomic policies, over time, fostered financial efficiency – expanding the pool of savings, and allowing resources to be allocated in an intelligible price environment.

Even among the leaders, of course, financial depth remains intermediate, private bond markets are very narrow, and active equity trading is confined to a limited number of major issuers. There are still weaknesses in the nexus of bankruptcy laws, collateral enforcement, and judicial process. Systems are robust, but there is a wide dispersion in the strength of individual banks. And while inflation is low, policy mix issues periodically cast a shadow – because of current account pressures or the risk of aggravating short-term inflows. In some countries, hesitation in imposing hard budget constraints on firms seriously slowed transition, although in these cases reforms were relaunched in the late 1990s.

These countries achieved growing efficiency in financing not by avoiding crises but by pursuing, over time, mutually reinforcing reforms. In most cases they bridged the institutional hiatus between new and old systems in part by importing risk capital and governance through a bold opening to direct investment (FDI) – both in business corporations and in the banking system itself, where levels of foreign ownership are very high. The experience of the 1990s underscores the skills of policymakers, and the optimism with which a sizeable group of them can embark on EU membership. But accession brings new demands as well as opportunities. It places a premium on strategies for market integration and risk management, in a setting of intense competition and volatile capital flows. With strong convergence pressures – both market- and policy-driven – four priorities appear critically important:

- *well-focused management strategies in financial institutions.* Priorities include more sophisticated risk management, especially for SME and household credit; further consolidation; cross-border links between capital market institutions; and a prudent handling of capital inflows.
- *strengthened regulatory and prudential policies.* Even in advanced cases, a major agenda remains – including effective implementation of consolidated supervision; strengthened regulatory and supervisory frameworks for non-bank intermediaries – and enhancements of governance and transparency; more efficient judicial systems and collateral enforcement; and a review of incentives facing distressed institutions and those that may be perceived as "too big to fail."
- *fiscal and monetary policies.* These are crucial if the financial sector is to allocate resources efficiently. One concern is to keep current account deficits within safely financeable ranges; and another is to ensure a policy mix that does not worsen vulnerability to short-term capital flows. In addition, financial markets must evolve to enhance the monetary transmission mechanism.
- *the monitoring of broad credit trends, with a macro-prudential frame of reference.* As risk premia decline further, capital flows into asset markets that are still quite narrow, and domestic credit expends, there are risks of inefficiency in the allocation of capital (at the extreme, a boom-and-bust cycle). Inflows will respond to benign policy signals, but will amplify distortions, including implicit guarantees. The monitoring of credit flows and asset prices can help detect danger signs, and prompt the right blend of micro- and macroeconomic responses.

From a policy perspective, the many aspects of financial-sector efficiency will remain closely linked. In early transition, stemming quasi-fiscal deficits increased efficiency in all dimensions, as did the lowering of barriers to competition. In the late 1990s, sustained disinflation typically required currency boards or more flexible exchange regimes – and in addition these regimes helped reduce the risks inherent in volatile capital flows. In the decade ahead, there will be strong complementarities between prudent macroeconomic policies, effective supervision, and the development of broad and diversified financial markets, with efficient links to the euro area.

In such a setting, the financial sector can play a pivotal role in allocating resources efficiently. Critically, as the CEE economies remain a magnet for capital, it can help to ensure a sustainable convergence toward EU living standards – avoiding the major misallocations and lost decades that punctuated growth in too many other emerging market economies. Efficiency in allocation is the key both to economic growth and to macro-financial stability. To help shed light on these issues, the remainder of this chapter discusses, in turn, the various dimensions of efficiency; the impact of past policies; and challenges on the road ahead.

Dimensions of efficiency

On all measures, there has been major progress in enhancing the efficiency of Central and East European (CEE) financial systems since the early 1990s, even though the pace has varied across countries ... This advance is evident in the narrow sense that spreads in financial institutions typically decreased, and that there was an improvement in the liquidity and transparency of markets. There was also progress in financial deepening. And, gradually, the sector began to function more effectively as a transmission channel for monetary policy.

... *But the change is more striking, and economically significant, if conceived in broader terms.* In the decade of transition there was immense progress across the region in strengthening the sector's capacity for allocating capital efficiently, as hard budget constraints were progressively imposed on former state-owned enterprises, containing quasi-fiscal pressures. At the same time, the sector gained a breathing space in its contribution to growth: typically, a bold opening to FDI brought substantial equity and debt financing to business corporations and jump-started corporate governance – both directly and through ripple effects to suppliers. In some cases, of course, such as Hungary, the shift from mono-banking, and to a price environment that allowed improved investment appraisal, had taken place earlier. But, if one allows for differing starting points (in terms of both reform environment and industrial–financial structure), then the CEE region achieved a financial transformation that is exceptional by any historical benchmark.

It is interesting to review the various dimensions of efficiency, which form a broadly consistent picture. The discussion below proceeds from narrower measures of efficiency, such as banking spreads and return on equity, to broader measures that seek to capture the economic efficiency of the sector and its potential to intermediate capital effectively. These latter dimensions include the evolution of bank asset portfolios, the growth of non-bank intermediaries, and a gradual enhancement of market capitalization and financial depth. Some relevant data are presented in Tables 6.1 to 6.4.

As a first approximation, spreads between bank deposit and lending rates have decreased in most CEE economies. Where competition and depth are greatest, nominal spreads have declined to 5 percent or less.[2] With spreads at this level, net interest margins were still significantly higher in nominal terms – but not necessarily in real terms – than in the EU banking systems.

- In Hungary and Poland, nominal spreads still exceeded 5 percent in the mid-1990s, but by the end of the decade they fell to 2–3 percent. In Hungary, competitive pressures remain very strong, and spreads are still low. In Poland, however, a rise in classified loans over the past two to three years is one factor that may explain a reversion of spreads to somewhat higher levels.

- In Estonia, spreads fell from over 8 percent in the late 1990s to low single digits recently. In Latvia and Lithuania, spreads remained over 6 percent during the 1990s, but data on net interest margins also suggests a recent across-the-board decline of spreads in these economies.

- Spreads in Slovenia tended to fluctuate around the 4 percent mark during the 1990s, in part reflecting a somewhat oligopolistic structure in the banking system – and the existence until the late 1990s of controls on foreign borrowing by corporates. Recently, competitive pressures and efficiency have been stimulated by further external liberalization (of direct investment in banks, and foreign borrowing by corporates), as well as discontinuation of the gentlemen's agreement on interest rates – reforms that will further stimulate competitive pressures.

- In Bulgaria spreads have declined recently to below 5 percent, while in Romania, by contrast, they remain more typically in lower double-digits for private-sector borrowers.

- The need for careful interpretation of data on spreads is illustrated in the Czech Republic and Slovak Republic. In the Czech Republic, nominal spreads were as low as 2–3 percent by the mid-1990s. However, this reflected the prevalence of low-interest-rate lending to former state-owned enterprises. Similar factors help explain the fairly low spreads in the Slovak Republic in the late 1990s. (A fuller discussion will be found in Feldman and Watson (2002).)

Table 6.1 Central Europe at the end of the transition decade

Banking Sector	Czech Republic		Hungary		Poland		Slovakia		Slovenia	
	1998	2000	1998	2000	1998	2000	1998	2000	1998	2000
Capital adequacy										
Risk-weighted ratio	12.1	14.9	16.5	13.7	11.7	12.9	6.7	12.5	16.0	13.5
Asset quality										
30 d. o/due, % total loans	26.4	29.5	10.4	7.9	10.5	15.0	31.7	15.2	10.4	12.6
Bank assets and liabilities										
Assets/GDP (excl. Ctrl Bk)	140	145	69	68	58	62	11	95	72	79
Av. lending spread	4.7	3.7	3.1	3.0	6.3	5.8	4.9	6.4	5.6	5.7
For. owned as % assets	15		61	67	17	70	29	61	5	16
Concentration										
C3	52	55	42	44	24	43	42	50	52	50
C5	70	67	55	61	29	52	50	59	64	63

Sources: adapted from Feldman and Watson (2002), and based on data from IMF staff, EBRD Transition Reports, NBP, NBH, Bank of Slovenia.

Table 6.2 Central Europe – equity markets 1994–2000

Market turnover	Percentage of market capitalization (mid-period)			
	1994	*1996*	*1998*	*2000*
Czech Republic	26	50	37	81
Hungary	22	42	112	93
Poland	177	85	54	69
Slovakia	96	134	74	25
Slovenia	68	82	35	22
Germany	98	123	145	167
Portugal	36	59	96	127
United States	70	92	106	141
Market capitalization	Percentage of GDP (mid-period)			
	1994	*1996*	*1998*	*2000*
Czech Republic	14	31	21	25
Hungary	3	12	29	34
Poland	3	6	13	21
Slovak Republic	8	12	5	3
Slovenia	4	4	13	12
Germany	23	27	45	
Portugal	15	24	57	
United States	74	101	151	

Source: adapted from Feldman and Watson 2002 (based on Claessens *et al.*)

Estimates of real spreads – that is, spreads adjusted for inflation and the impact of reserve requirements – confirm this overall picture with some nuances. Riess, Wagenvoort and Zajc (2002) report a decline in real spreads across the region (except recently in Poland), with competitive conditions in Hungary resulting in a steeper decline than elsewhere. Interestingly, though, they note that this shift appears to take spreads to levels, in real terms, below those in the EU – and thus to levels lower than may be consistent at this stage with a healthy and efficiently functioning sector. This leads to the question of whether there are elements in the policy framework that explain why CEE banks did not expand loan portfolios more rapidly in the 1990s, given high real returns potentially available (apart from the obvious factor that FDI equity and loan flows have provided low-cost external financing to blue chip enterprises). This issue is discussed below (p. 124).

A *further conventional benchmark for bank efficiency is the return on bank equity (ROE).* This also needs to be interpreted carefully, given the impact of recent financial stresses in some countries, and the differing impact of competitive pressures. Low earnings in some cases may reflect the combination of recent recapitalization and prudent charge-offs, while high and

Table 6.3 Central Europe – profitability and efficiency 1995–2000

	1995	*1998*	*2000*
Net interest margin			
Czech Republic	3.2	3.1	2.5
Hungary	5.2	3.9	3.6
Poland	5.1	4.7	3.8
Slovak Republic	4.4	2.8	2.9
Slovenia	3.8	4.6	4.1
EU	2.0	1.5	
Return on average equity			
Czech Republic	9.8	−50.4	5.8
Hungary	19.0	0.3	15.6
Poland	59.4	7.3	12.6
Slovak Republic	16.0	−31.5	28.0
Slovenia	13.8	10.8	16.4
EU	9.0	11.3	
Operating cost/income ratio			
Czech Republic	50.6	91.6	62.5
Hungary	71.8	84.8	71.6
Poland	40.3	57.8	61.8
Slovak Republic	45.1	59.6	68.5
Slovenia	63.8	63.4	51.0
EU	66.8	65.8	

Source: adapted from Feldman and Watson (2002) based on BankScope and Bank of Slovenia.

stable returns may in part reflect a still somewhat sheltered market. And such data are inherently difficult to assess without analysis of valuation rules or asset quality.

- Banks in Hungary and Poland have typically shown a nominal percentage return on equity in the mid-teens in recent years.[3] Returns have eased back somewhat in Hungary since the mid-1990s, consistently with an increase in competition.
- In Slovenia, nominal ROE has been at about the same level as in Hungary and Poland. There has been some uptrend over the past three or four years, but this should be seen in the context of fairly gradual liberalization – with the lagged impact of recent measures still to be felt.
- Banks in the Czech and Slovak Republics incurred sizeable losses in 1997–1998. They have subsequently returned to profitability, although earnings remain low in the Slovak Republic.
- In the Baltics, nominal ROE has varied widely – partly as a result of crises. It has recently lain around the 20 percent mark in Estonia and Latvia, but at low levels in Lithuania.
- In the accession countries of South-Eastern Europe, ROE in Bulgaria

Table 6.4 Banking indicators in the Baltics, 1999–2001 (percentages, unless otherwise indicated)

	Estonia			Latvia			Lithuania		
	1999	2000	2001	1999	2000	2001	1999	2000	2001
Capital adequacy									
Capital adequacy – risk-weighted average	16.1	13.2	14.4	16.0	14.0	14.2	17.4	16.3	15.7
Liquidity									
Liquidity ratio	–	–	–	64.1	66.7	65.5	45.4	49.7	48.0
Total reserves/total deposits	28.1	25.4	14.5	18.9	16.3	14.5	14.9	11.3	8.6
Excess reserves/total reserves	43.3	19.0	–	19.8	7.5	4.8	30.2	28.4	16.8
Asset quality									
Non-performing loans (in millions of domestic currency)	–	–	–	58.0	54.0	46.0	709.3	650.8	509.9
Non-performing loans/total loans	1.7	1.0	1.3	6.0	4.6	2.8	12.0	11.0	7.0
Loan-loss provisioning/gross loans	–	–	–	4.0	3.0	1.7	4.5	3.7	2.6
Loan-loss provisioning/non-performing loans	–	–	–	79.3	74.1	80.4	38.0	35.0	34.0
Profitability									
Return on equity	9.2	8.4	20.9	11.0	19.0	19.0	1.1	4.0	−1.1
Return on assets	1.5	1.2	2.7	1.0	2.0	1.5	0.1	0.4	−0.1
Net interest margin	3.8	3.6	3.3	4.9	4.6	3.3	5.3	5.3	3.9
Loans and deposits									
Loans/deposits	100.9	98.5	95.3	65.9	58.3	70.3	79.3	64.5	62.5
Loans/total assets	56.6	59.2	59.5	43.4	40.3	47.3	53.0	46.6	49.9
Non-resident deposits as a share of total deposits	35.1	34.5	31.8	46.9	51.3	51.9	8.9	8.2	12.6
Nominal interest rate spread	4.5	3.9	5.4	9.2	7.5	5.9	8.2	8.3	6.6
Foreign currency deposits as a share of total deposits	31.1	34.0	30.1	48.2	46.8	45.0	48.8	49.5	49.1
Foreign currency loans as a share of total loans	76.1	77.9	78.7	52.3	51.3	56.3	61.6	66.8	60.6

Concentration									
C3	92.0	91.0	91.0	49.8	51.0	52.8	74.1	83.5	81.9
C5	99.0	99.0	99.0	61.3	62.3	66.2	92.4	91.2	92.4
Memorandum items									
(in percentage of GDP)									
Total assets	62.0	68.0	72.0	50.3	62.2	72.9	26.0	29.0	32.0
Deposits (resident)	22.5	26.1	30.1	17.3	20.7	23.7	15.9	18.7	21.2

Sources: Country authorities and IMF staff estimates.

has recently been in the mid-teens, while in Romania it has been in excess of 20 percent. These data should be interpreted, however, in the context of markets that are less mature, overall.

- Estimates of real returns by Riess *et al.* (2002) indicate that, even abstracting from crises, these are tracking below EU levels. Given a favorable trend in non-performing loans, this reflects low levels of net interest income and some quite high operating expenses. As with real spreads, Riess *et al.* suggest that, while operating efficiencies are rising, opportunities to benefit from the high real returns available are not being fully exploited. Of course, the average real return may also obscure a divergence between stronger performing banks under new – often foreign – ownership, and weaker institutions destined for exit or absorption. (Some evidence of such a bimodal distribution, and a discussion of the role of foreign ownership, is presented by Feldman and Watson (2002).)

Earnings data also suggest that an efficient diversification of income is getting underway, with non-interest revenues beginning to advance. For the time being, banks in the region remain fairly dependent on interest income as a source of earnings, but the dynamic is shifting away from this – an important indicator of a maturing sector. In some cases (such as Hungary) this reflects a growth of fee-earning activities in banks. In others (Estonia, for example) non-banks, such as leasing companies, are evolving rapidly within conglomerate groups led by banks. Non-interest income has risen from negligible levels a few years ago to a level that, in the CEE region as a whole, accounts for more than one-quarter of bank earnings (see Riess *et al.* (2002)).

The ratio of operating costs to income is not entirely reassuring in level or trend, particularly as regards personnel expenditures.[4] In most of the CEE economies, the level of operating costs is on the order of 50–60 percent of income, or somewhat below in a few cases. This is broadly comparable with EU levels. However, when measured against average assets, cost performance appears less favorable. This reflects larger loan-loss provisions, and personnel costs that are more than half as high again as in EU banks – and on a rising trend at the end of the 1990s. Indeed, in Hungary, operating costs in the late 1990s were in a range of 70–80 percent of income, and this reflected to a significant degree the impact of high salary costs, as well as strong competition in the banking market. So, while there have been a series of personnel shake-ups following privatizations in the CEE markets, it seems that staffing levels may still be high.

Information on the asset quality of banks clearly indicates rising efficiency. Data presented in Feldman and Watson (2002), and in published FSSAs, indicates that asset quality across the CEE region has improved strikingly since the early/mid-1990s, even in cases where there were delays and setbacks in the process.

- In Hungary and Poland the proportion of loan portfolios accounted for by classified loans fell sharply in the late 1990s – roughly halving from the levels of about 20 percent that prevailed in 1995. Since 1999 there has been a renewed, significant upturn in loan losses in Poland, however, reflecting the impact on borrowers of a worsening economic situation. This secular decline reflected a major policy effort to deal with the remaining structural problems from the command economy period. In Slovenia, NPL ratios on average have fallen to low single digits.

- In the Baltics, there was a major shake-up of bank portfolios and bank ownership in the late 1990s, precipitated by a combination of domestic factors and by the Asian and Russian crises of 1997–1998. These episodes left asset positions that were typically fairly healthy, with NPL ratios typically well down in single digits. Nonetheless, in some individual banks there has been a continuing need to deal actively with remaining non-performing loans.

- The asset situation of Czech banks, after a protracted period of difficulty, was turned around with a decisive clean-up at the end of the 1990s. From 1999, major reforms also got underway in the Slovak Republic – with insolvent banks being closed, most state-owned banks being sold to foreign owners, and non-performing loans being heavily provisioned.

- In Bulgaria, the level of NPLs was sharply reduced by the end of the 1990s; and in Romania, NPLs are now at a level of some 5–6 percent of loans to the non-government sector.

In some of these cases, however, action still needs to be taken to work through the fiscal implications and the real restructuring associated with banking clean-ups. In some countries, the bulk of non-performing loans were transferred to a consolidation bank. In others, loans to troubled borrowers such as steel companies or shipyards have been covered by an explicit governmental guarantee. So efficiency of the banking system has improved, and quasi-fiscal pressures have been addressed, but the full impact on the economy has not been fully felt.

Overall, though, there is a clear pattern across the CEE: bank portfolios, at varying speeds, shifted away from unproductive lending to enterprises owned, or formerly owned, by the state. And in a majority of cases this process is at, or close to, completion. This represents a crucial enhancement in efficiency, both in terms of stocks of assets and of a diminished risk that managers will fall victim to moral hazard and adverse selection as they allocate new flows of savings. It is also a source of comfort that conventional efficiency measures such as ROE and spreads are becoming based on viable streams of income, and a pricing of risk along market lines, so such data are increasingly meaningful.

Turning from the asset problems of the past to the emerging dynamics of the future, credit to the private sector has now begun to grow strongly. This trend is evident in most of the CEE economies, although this is from a low starting point. Even in the most advanced cases, the ratio of private credit to total bank assets is well below the 60 percent mark typical in the EU – where, as discussed below (p. 113), overall financial depth is also significantly higher.[5]

- In most countries, lending to the household sector (including mort-gage lending) has begun to accelerate from a low base, being followed by credit to firms. In some cases, of course, household mortgage lending may include lending to small businesses. The acceleration of credit to household borrowers is now a well-entrenched trend in several economies, including notably Estonia, Hungary, Poland, and Slovenia. In these cases, the stock of credit to the private sector is cur-rently in a range of 40–50 percent of bank assets – on the order of one-third of GDP. While continuing very rapid credit growth in these countries is essentially a healthy sign in terms of efficiency, it deserves monitoring carefully. And it certainly needs no general stimulus from government subsidies, of the kind provided for housing credit in Hungary. There are other cases, such as Latvia and Lithuania, or Romania, where the stock of credit still remains significantly lower – on the order of some 10–20 percent of GDP.
- In the Czech and Slovak Republics, the data appear to portray a slow-down in private credit growth in the late 1990s – but this is somewhat misleading. It largely reflected an ongoing clean-up of poor quality loans to "private" enterprises formerly owned by the state. Again, this is clearly healthy, and should lay the groundwork for a renewed growth of private credit.

The wide evidence of expanding credit to the private sector is a clear signal of growing efficiency – and part and parcel of a maturing economy. A commonly recurring pattern in the region is for banks to move from crisis and recap-italization to a phase of high liquidity and very risk-averse strategies, and then on to a period in which private credit expands at 20–50 percent annually (from a low base) – with household credit, including mortgages, leading the way. Bulgaria and Romania are only the latest examples of such a cycle. This is not to deny that policy-related factors may also have retarded lending, as discussed on page 124, or that lower inter-national interest rates – as well as domestic risk premia – have also played a part.

Non-bank intermediaries are also expanding in many CEE economies. This trend is contributing to efficiency – for example, in the role of leasing companies in the Baltics and Hungary as a channel of corporate credit – although in some cases, such as Slovenia and the Slovak Republic, the development of this sector has yet to get strongly underway. While leasing in industrial countries had its origins partly in tax distortions and credit controls, in the CEE region it is probably mainly a means of overcoming information asymmetries in such sectors as SMEs (since the lender remains the equipment owner and can repossess). Another example of growth in non-bank intermediaries – and a harbinger of future trends – is the emerging role of pension funds and insurance companies as securities investors, and indeed the role of insurance companies as purchasers of credit derivatives in at least one case. There is a question, however, of whether insurance and pension investors are yet well-placed to manage effectively all the risks that they may contemplate taking on – particularly in derivative markets – or effectively supervised. Alongside higher efficiency, through diversification, risks of misallocation exist.

Equity and bond market capitalization data in some of the CEE economies are also beginning to signal a sustainable increase. Equity capitalization is most advanced in Central Europe, and in some countries is now in a range of 20–30 percent of GDP. Here too, though, data need to be interpreted with caution. In cases where voucher privatization schemes were launched, the value of outstanding paper was boosted to quite a high level as a result. But this approach typically did not enhance corporate governance or facilitate the raising of new capital – due to the dispersion of ownership or monitoring weaknesses in private investment funds. So, as a measure of growing efficiency in the financial sector, raw capitalization data need to be interpreted excluding this element. On that basis, Hungary and Poland are certainly examples of progress in equity market development. Bond market capitalization, too, is highest in Central Europe, where it is typically on the order 30 percent of GDP. But in all CEE economies the overwhelming majority of bonds are floated by governments, with corporate issues on domestic markets a rare occurrence still. And quite a high proportion of government bonds is typically held by foreign investors.

Drawing together these institutional developments, it is clear that overall financial depth has been improving. Financial-sector liabilities as a share of GDP have been edging up in most CEE economies – especially where high inflation had earlier eroded the demand for financial assets. The increasing size of the sector is crucial for its role in allocating savings, with the expansion of claims on the private sector particularly important in that regard. The growing financial-sector balance sheet is also beginning to enhance its efficiency as a channel for monetary policy.

At this stage, it is clearly the banking system that exercises the predominant domestic role in corporate monitoring – but it needs to be borne in mind that foreign direct investors play a parallel, and crucial, role. Notwithstanding the growth of non-bank intermediaries, banks accounts still account for some 80–90 percent of financial-sector intermediation in the CEE economies. However, foreign parents are a key source of funding for blue-chip corporations, and they have been playing a critical role in ensuring strong corporate governance. This may be one reason why domestic securities markets have not expanded more rapidly. But it also means that the CEE economies have imported ready-made corporate governance disciplines for larger companies during a period when their own financial systems have been maturing.

While the financial sector has typically been deepening, its resilience has also been enhanced – and the ability to flex under stress is a critically important aspect of efficiency. The progress in reducing vulnerabilities and in establishing basic systemic stability has been evidenced by stress-testing under the IMF-World Bank Financial Sector Assessment Program. Such assessments have been completed in all of the former transition economies that are joining the EU in 2004, as well as Bulgaria; and in Romania an FSAP began in the spring of 2003. Stress-testing typically revealed good systemic stability in the face of major shocks, such as interest rate and exchange rate changes. It is important to note, though, that stress tests may not capture some potential sources of weakness – for example, implicit guarantees, connected lending, and vulnerabilities in non-bank institutions. Moreover, systems that are judged overall to be stable may nonetheless contain some weak members. And quite frequently there have been cautionary judgments to the effect that supervision of small but rapidly growing non-bank sectors, and potentially in some cases bank credit to households, need to be strengthened to avoid systemic vulnerability in the future – issues discussed further below (pp. 123–124).

In sum, progress in strengthening financial-sector efficiency has been impressive – and all the more so if one considers the relative importance of different issues in setting incentives for the future. Little more than a decade after transition began, the challenges that are arguably most critical in terms of incentives for the future have been tackled squarely. Bank asset quality has been purged of most past problems, systems are reasonably resilient to shocks, and declining spreads – together with the growth of non-bank intermediaries – are clear indications that competition has taken root (Box 6.1). Moreover, several of the areas in which development typically has been more gradual are those in which very rapid early progress might have

---

Box 6.1 The state and pace of financial-sector development

Typically advanced	*Expanding rapidly*
Spreads	Non-bank intermediaries
Bank asset quality	Household credit
System resilience	

Improving steadily	*Improving slowly*
Bank RoE	Operating costs
Bank diversification	Money markets
Financial depth	Market capitalization and turnover

been contained significant risks as well as benefits – market capitalization and diversification both being illustrations of this.

This progress, nonetheless, gives no grounds for complacency in terms of the path ahead. Private sector credit, even in economies such as Estonia, Hungary, Poland, and Slovenia, is still only some one-third of the level, relative to GDP, typical of the EU – accounting for a smaller share of bank assets, in a setting where financial depth is itself more limited. With the exception of Hungary and Poland, money markets throughout the region are still relatively narrow. Capital markets remain fairly illiquid – with active equity trading confined to a handful of stocks; private bond markets narrow; and money markets embryonic in most cases. And although banks have been branching out into fee and commission earning activities – directly and via subsidiaries – they remain very dependent on interest income. By EU standards, financial depth typically remains fairly modest – leaving a considerable way to go to ensure that the financial sector functions efficiently and is competitive in the setting of the EU market in financial services.

Five specific notes of caution, moreover, are in order – lest it be thought that progress in enhancing efficiency in the financial sector has everywhere been even, and that no pressing worries remain at the end of the transition decade:

- *first, it is only now that the role of the domestic banking system is truly moving toward centre-stage.* In most cases – and especially with several of the leading performers – FDI flows and retained earnings, and an associated governance injection, were particularly prominent features during the past decade. The domestic financial sector has certainly been starting to play a growing role. But throughout the region, as economic performance improved, the contribution of the domestic sector lay most crucially in its turn-around from a command-economy role of diverting resources to non-productive uses (including firms whose value added was negative). The sector was cleaned up – reducing risks of misallocation – but played second fiddle to FDI in terms of capital raising and governance. Of course, a large portion of FDI did not have an impact on the financial system but was directly channeled to business enterprises in the context of privatization. Given that in many countries privatization is close to completion, the role of the financial system in allocating funds is likely to grow – indeed there is a question as to whether FDI flows may decline significantly as privatization is completed. Against this background, and with the challenge of shifting to a more diversified industrial structure, it is in the present decade that the contribution of the domestic financial sector will assume more of a make-or-break role.
- *second, the still fairly modest depth of the financial system has implications for monetary transmission mechanisms.* A number of studies confirm that under-developed financial systems, together with corporate and bank balance sheet problems, have rendered monetary policy transmission

channels less effective in transition than in mature economies. This is especially true as regards the interest rate channel. Of course, the clean-up of quasi-fiscal deficits and non-performing loans has been a major advance in this respect, since these typically represented interest rate inelastic lending by banks. Nonetheless, the most interest-sensitive components of bank lending – such as business investment and residential construction – are only now expanding as a portion of bank assets. Thus the next few years should see a growing importance of the interest rate transmission channel, in economies where, at present, the exchange rate typically still remains of central importance. (For a discussion, see Schaechter *et al.* 2000; Kuijs 2002.)

- *third, while transition is largely over, bringing exceptionally large efficiency gains by comparison with the former allocation of financial resources, the strengthening of efficiency since the early 1990s has been very gradual in some countries.* Romania is a case in point, although reforms there have also now accelerated, and current financial and economic indicators are encouraging in that regard. Reforms also experienced major setbacks or false dawns in some Central European countries – notably the Czech Republic and Slovakia: but these countries entered a phase of decisive advance at the end of the 1990s. The countries that had ground to make up in the late 1990s exhibited, for all their differences, a crucial point in common: by the mid- and late-1990s, quasi-fiscal distortions were still having seriously damaging effects on efficiency, leaving a major catch-up to be completed in the banking system. That said, it should be noted that, in countries which are well advanced, such as Poland and Slovenia, there are also important steps still to complete in privatizing banks, which should lead to efficiency gains.

- *fourth, the assessments in this chapter generally relate to the performance of a country's banking system taken as a whole – but there is, in most cases, considerable dispersion in efficiency levels among banks.* Impressive averages for profitability and non-performing loan levels, and satisfactory systemic stress-tests, must not obscure the fact that seriously weaker outliers remain among the banks, insurance companies and pension funds, in a number of CEE financial systems.

- *fifth and finally, for bank-by-bank as well as system-wide assessments, it is clear from the foregoing that conventional efficiency measures need to be evaluated with care.* Examples are where financial systems were swollen by directed credit and unserviceable liabilities of state-owned firms; or where voucher privatization enhanced market volumes, but not underlying governance or capital-raising. The test of efficiency lies in the quality of intermediation, and headline numbers are not always a safe gauge of this. So efficiency needs to be assessed in the context of policy reforms and incentive signals from the financial framework – from banking supervision to the exchange regime. This lesson is important in evaluating the past – and will be no less crucial in assessing trends in the decade ahead. Financial-sector efficiency cannot be divorced from the broader policy reform context.

Policy impact: the experience so far

The improvement of efficiency in the CEE financial systems has reflected a range of policy initiatives. To give a sense of the dynamics of change, and the significance of the EU Accession context, it may be helpful to distinguish between two waves of reform. The first, discussed in this section, was the wide range of measures to address the legacy of the command economy and the original mono-banking system. The second, underway now, comprises measures to bring financial frameworks into conformity with EU requirements and with international standards and codes – and that subject is covered on pages 125–127.

The first wave of financial-sector reforms in the CEE economies was one key element in the transition agenda – designed to lay the basis for a market economy in the financial sector. These reforms accompanied macroeconomic stabilization and trade and price liberalization. They included:

1 the passing of basic financial-sector legislation, and the creation of monetary, regulatory, and supervisory authorities;
2 the separation of commercial banking institutions;
3 the imposition of hard budget constraints on borrowing enterprises; and
4 forms of privatization that aimed, with varying degrees of initial success, to enhance governance and attract new capital for enterprises and banks.

This fundamental systemic transformation was an uncharted course, and the success of the CEE region in advancing so rapidly – to the point where eight countries are in a position to join the EU in 2004 – surely rates as one of the most comprehensive policy successes by a group of nations in economic history. As this effort has continued, the prospect of EU membership has increasingly served as a major encouragement to stay the course with these reforms.

In sequencing reforms, and addressing the financial-sector nexus, countries followed varying approaches – but there is a family resemblance among leading cases. These brought together high quality and mutually reinforcing reforms in areas that were critical for efficient financial systems to take root. Estonia, Hungary, and Poland illustrate this similarity in diversity. Hungary, by the mid-1990s, had administered major structural shocks to the financial and corporate sectors, with a heavy reliance on foreign direct investment; it scrupulously serviced the heavy public debt; but much of its macroeconomic adjustment was left until the mid- and late-1990s. Poland, by contrast, adopted a very tough upfront macro therapy, comprehensively rescheduled its debt, and was more gradual in embracing privatization and inward investment. Both countries in turn differed from Estonia, which, by the late-1990s, achieved success through a strictly rule-based macro-policy framework (currency board, balanced budget), a major banking clean-up in the late-1990s – triggered by the Asian and Russian crises; and absolute openness to foreign capital. It is notable that all three found their different ways to a four-point program that comprised of sound macroeconomics; prudent but comprehensive liberalization; hard budget constraints on firms; and sound basic elements of banking regulation and supervision. The quality and complementarity of these policies, over time, accounts for their success.

It is worth highlighting the reasons why each of these four elements was crucial to set the stage for efficiency gains in the financial sector. This still fairly recent experience is a key guide, indeed, for other transition economies following in this path.

- *Strong macroeconomic policies were essential for the financial system to draw on a growing volume of savings, and allocate resources in response to intelligible price signals.* The initial effort to cut fiscal deficits to low levels succeeded in most of the CEE economies by the mid- to late-1990s. Risks of hyperinflation were averted – by no means a foregone conclusion at the outset in Poland or Slovenia, for example. Indeed, by the late 1990s, inflation was down to low double-digit levels, or lower, throughout Central Europe, the Baltics, and Bulgaria. And when disinflation showed signs of stalling in some cases, monetary regimes were adjusted to foster a further fall to low single digits. Fiscal policy, generally, has experienced more obvious tensions. There have been many episodes in which fiscal deficits widened to risky levels, and external current account deficits and/or speculative capital flows sent up warning signals. But macroeconomic policy proved, at a minimum, sufficiently responsive to avoid a loss of market confidence and damage to the financial sector. If there was an Achilles heel, it lay typically in the mix of fiscal and monetary policy: from the Baltics to the Balkans, difficulties in keeping fiscal deficits within prudent bounds increased the burden on monetary policy – and from a financial-sector perspective, this aggravated risks of large and volatile capital inflows.
- *With approaches to bank and enterprise restructuring and privatization varying widely, the litmus test was countries' ability to strengthen governance in former state enterprises, and tap additional capital for healthy firms.* If there is one dimension along which the more and less successful reform efforts space out intelligibly, it is policymakers' success in imposing hard budget constraints on state-owned enterprises, and in stripping public sector activities out of banks. This was crucial for the

health and efficiency of the financial sector – both directly and because it proved crucial for the sustainability of monetary, fiscal, and pricing reforms. In several economies, the corrosive effects of quasi-fiscal deficits were eliminated by the mid-1990s, while in other cases (Czech and Slovak Republics, Bulgaria, Romania) new reforms with this goal were launched by end of the decade. In all of the transition countries joining the EU in 2004, and in Bulgaria, this key phase has been accomplished in terms of financial-sector ramifications – even though, in some countries (such as the Czech Republic), the fiscal implications of this still have to be fully worked through. In Romania, after several setbacks, loans conceded to enterprises in a soft-budget mode have essentially been cleaned out of the banking system, and the adjustment program adopted in 2002 had the sustained containment of quasi-fiscal pressures as a centerpiece.

- *It was in this perspective of enhancing governance and attracting new capital that a bold external liberalization of FDI inflows paid off handsomely.* By the end of the 1990s, a majority of the CEE economies had allowed major injections of foreign capital and expertise into business corporations and banks – as a result of which, levels of foreign ownership of over 70 percent are common. Some countries (Poland, Slovenia, and Romania) have moved down the same path, but more gradually. In the Czech and Slovak Republics and Bulgaria, the policy shift came only in the late 1990s, but was radical when it occurred – some 90 percent of bank assets passing to foreign management. In the banking sector as elsewhere, privatization approaches that leveraged the openness of these economies typically delivered favorable results. The process has not been without problems – the sale of the Czech bank IPB to a foreign investor being one such – but overall the injection of capital and skills has been a crucial stimulus to banking efficiency. This process of external opening in the financial sector is now moving toward completion throughout the region, with landmarks over the past three years including the removal of residual capital controls in Hungary; the sale of the remaining major bank in the Czech Republic; and the liberalization of foreign investment in banks and external borrowing by corporates in Slovenia. Relatively few old-style controls over the financial sector and capital account now remain. One area where progress is still underway is the modernization of portfolio rules for institutional investors such as pension funds and insurance companies – which needs to be flanked by an appropriate strengthening of the supervisory framework.

- *Strengthening banking regulation and supervision – and the overall legal framework of the financial sector – has been a priority in successful cases.* For example, basic regimes for bankruptcy and the enforcement of collateral were essential for private sector lending to get underway – as well as for financial-sector development in a range of areas from repo transactions to payment systems, residential housing expansion, and SME development. This area of bankruptcy and collateral is one in which substantive progress has proved difficult. It is probably still a significant impediment to private sector lending in many cases (and hence currently the subject of many new reform initiatives). Nonetheless, in this and other areas, the early and basic legislation was essential as a stepping stone to more refined approaches. The second-wave reforms in the financial-sector framework now being put into place, on the eve of EU entry, would not have been conceivable without the advances achieved – and the learning experience with – the new institutions and measures of the 1990s.

The foregoing does not imply that progress was smooth, or that policymakers always kept ahead of events. In some cases advances in financial-sector efficiency underwent major setbacks in the course of the 1990s, and reforms did not achieve a critical mass of change until the end of the decade. Across the region – from the Czech Republic to Romania – major setbacks usually had at least one key element in common: hesitation or reversal in tackling quasi-fiscal deficits. Moreover, reforms often lagged until finally triggered by crisis. Again, this was a recurring feature across the region – from the banking crisis in Estonia to the market pressures on exchange rate pegs in Central Europe, or the generalized economic crisis of the mid- to late-1990s in Bulgaria. The banking crises as such were in some cases a direct consequence of misguided strategies to develop the financial system during the early years of transition. (Governments provided licenses to new financial institutions liberally and without adequate prudential requirements and supervision in order to increase competition and reduce lending rates.) After the banking crises, governments have placed more emphasis on the health of the banking system, and this was most credible where – as in the Baltics – the crises were not followed by generalized bail-outs. Overall, the development of the financial sector was certainly not linear.

The CEE countries have thus improved efficiency in financing not by avoiding crises entirely but by persevering with mutually reinforcing reforms. And in most cases they bridged the institutional hiatus between new and old systems in part by importing long-term finance and governance through a radical opening to FDI. Thus they have mostly moved ahead with less serious setbacks than many other emerging markets or former command economies. Their successful experience is an encouragement and incentive to stay the course for those economies in the region that are still working through some aspects of transition experience.

From a policy perspective, this experience underscores an important message for the future, and for other economies: that the many aspects of efficiency are linked, and policy complementarity is key. Early in transition, eliminating quasi-fiscal deficits increased financial-sector efficiency in all dimensions. The same was true of lower barriers to competition and openness to direct investment flows. More recently, sustained disinflation prompted a shift in exchange regimes toward either currency boards or flexible exchange rates, and in turn these monetary arrangements are reducing the financial sector's vulnerability (directly, and through its clients) to distortions that can be associated with strong and variable capital flows.

Policy challenges on the road ahead

Experience over the past decade provides valuable pointers to policies that can enhance efficiency or, in less advanced cases, accelerate catch-up; but EU integration is also posing new opportunities and challenges. With strong convergence pressures – both market and policy driven – and scarce managerial resources, what are the essential priorities to enhance the efficiency of the financial sector and ensure that it can compete effectively in the single market? This question is addressed later in this chapter, but in the perspective of major managerial and policy challenges, rather than an attempt to log progress in terms of EU Negotiation Chapters, Directives, and Regulations. The spirit of the discussion, as in the earlier sections of this chapter, is not that of a laundry list or a league table but rather an attempt to identify common priorities, linkages to overall economic efficiency, and thus areas that may prove critical in assuring progress that is both timely and sustainable.

In this broad perspective, three features of the financial market setting appear crucial when considering the policy challenges ahead. And a number of these challenges, it should be noted, also raise important issues for banks in existing EU members.

- *The structural changes underway in CEE financial markets will intensify competitive pressures – in banking and more generally.* Some factors should increase banks' loan/deposit spreads selectively, for example, as risk assessment is deepened in SME and household lending; but the overall tendency will be pressure on margins. In addition to the lagged impact of liberalization, market factors will contribute – including the growth of non-bank intermediaries. Even where non-banks develop within bank-dominated groups, they will add to pressures on profitability of the banking unit; and banking is still the overwhelmingly preponderant activity in CEE systems. This is a setting in which smaller players may face difficult market situations, and in a future environment of generous deposit insurance, there may be temptations to engage in excessive risk-taking. Also, in general, non-banks – which are growing rapidly in some markets – are typically supervised less, less well, or later, than banks. So this is an overall context that will challenge financial regulators and supervisors – as further discussed below (p. 123).

- *The growing integration of markets and institutions with EU and euro area markets will remain a keynote of this decade.* This will pose a major challenge for both business decisions and the design of policy frameworks: how to arrive at efficient medium-term strategies for institutional and market change. For example: how can bank managements steer between the need for size (in order for institutions to punch their weight in the European and global financial markets) and the pitfalls of an oligopolistic mentality? And in securities markets and clearing institutions, should any pursuit of national efficiency and excellence be tailored to a regional setting – and if so what is a sensible region of reference? Is a Nordic/Baltic financial market nexus desirable, for example; and, if so, as an end-point or a stepping stone? Over time, even smaller companies may benefit most from a broadening system of regional markets for new issuers, while larger companies will tap global markets directly. If this is the shape of the future, then in reforming and enhancing domestic markets it will make sense to focus most strongly on priorities – from clearing and payments systems to corporate governance, accounting, and disclosure requirements – that will ease the integration of markets, rather than assuming national securities markets will remain the endpoint of development.

- *As economic and financial convergence continues, the CEE region will remain a powerful magnet for capital inflows – and these will need to be absorbed in a setting where new privatization offerings are declining, traded markets are narrow, and a rapid expansion of domestic bank credit is also underway.* These flows have the potential to accelerate the catch-up toward EU living standards. But experience so far in the CEE and elsewhere underscores the implications for policy. Large and potentially volatile capital flows, channeled into quite narrow markets, will continue to impose major disciplines on economic and financial management if the financial sector is to play its part in allocating this influx of capital efficiently. This has layers of implications – for the design of fiscal policy, the development of hedging markets, and the vigilant monitoring of credit flows and balance sheet structure in the private sector. In a setting of strong capital flows, the efficiency of the financial sector in its direct management of these flows, and in its assessment of clients' balance sheets, is critical in avoiding major misallocations of savings that would slow growth (and ultimately run risks of crisis). It should be noted that the variability of capital flows fundamentally reflects, to a substantial degree, changes in investors' assessment of domestic risk premia – rather than just exchange rate speculation – and in that deep sense it is not something that adoption of the euro in itself can dispel.

This market setting offers new opportunities and challenges for the managers of financial institutions and for policymakers alike. These strategic options are, of course, over and above the need for finishing the adoption of the *acquis communautaire* in the sector, as well as completing transition-related reforms in cases where there is still ground to be made up. The focus in the remainder of this chapter will be primarily on the broad challenges of the accession setting for bank managements and supervisors. These are the new aspects of the task of shaping the financial sector to be an efficient servant of the economy. A helpful way of considering influences on efficiency in the decade ahead is to consider the challenges facing three groups of actors. These are managements of financial institutions; regulators and supervisors; and policymakers concerned with the economic framework.

Management strategies in the sector

In the market environment of the coming decade, effective management strategies in financial institutions will be critical in ensuring efficiency at all the levels discussed in this chapter. At times, commentaries and official reports read as if the responsibility for efficient and sound banking lies first and foremost in the lap of the supervisory and regulatory bodies. But policymakers and supervisors can at best try to set a reasonable framework of incentives. The overwhelming element determining how effectively CEE financial sectors perform will be the judgment and flair of management in financial groups and institutions, and their influence on firms, as shareholders and creditors, through available governance channels. From this perspective, the priorities for success in managing financial institutions will certainly include the following.

* *Strengthening risk management systems* – especially in sectors such as SMEs and household credit, where information asymmetries are pronounced. SMEs are currently underserved even in cases such as Estonia, Hungary, and Poland; and their financing is particularly important to support broadly-based, and regionally balanced, economic growth. As regards household credit, falling interest rates and rising incomes are causing a rapid expansion to develop across the region. With both SMEs and households, there is a risk of imprudent lending over the medium term as competition intensifies in a low-interest-rate environment. Careful monitoring of loan standards – and of adequate returns on capital – is a central challenge for the management of financial institutions. Associated with these sectors, and much domestic corporate financing, is the need for sound risk assessment regarding real estate collateral – a microcosm of the factors that led to misallocation and later instability in many other emerging economies. Risk management is essential to protect institutions' own financing capacity; but, in addition, the obverse of risk management is the influence of financial institutions in strengthening corporate governance – a key aspect of financial-sector efficiency.

- *Achieving further selective consolidation in the financial sector.* This is a field in which generalization may lead to pitfalls. In a case such as Poland, competitive pressures will doubtless result in further consolidation in most parts of the financial sector. But more typically in the CEE region, there is already a high degree of concentration (bordering on oligopoly) in certain sub-sectors. In most cases, four or five banks account for more than half of banking system assets, while in several economies (including the Czech Republic, Estonia, Hungary, Lithuania, and Slovenia) fewer banks account for an even higher share of the sector balance sheet. These degrees of concentration, however, often co-exist with a large number of small banks, which are probably not viable without mergers or absorption by larger groups. The process of getting to this outcome may pass through a phase of intense competition that erodes earnings and capital in some banks – with risks of inefficiency through adverse credit selection. Among non-bank intermediaries, the need for consolidation also varies. In some cases – Lithuania or Slovenia, for example – there is already a high concentration in insurance; but in Estonia and Poland the reverse is the case. Credit cooperatives are now consolidating in Hungary, while they still need to move in this direction in Poland. So concentration is an issue for competition and efficiency in varying ways across countries and sectors. Low concentration may be associated with unsustainably weak profitability. High concentration – among institutions that may nonetheless be quite small on a European scale – poses difficult issues for supervisors, in terms of incentives for efficiency, and these are discussed further on pages 124–125.
- *Fostering cross-border linkages between capital market institutions, including exchanges.* Efficiency over the next decade will lie not just in improving domestic market structures but in creating conditions to tap the financing sources of an integrated EU securities market. This has technical implications for country authorities – notably in enhancing clearing and settlement systems; but even more profoundly it has implications for enterprises' willingness to submit to high standards of transparency and disclosure – in excess of national standards.
- *Last, but not least, achieving a prudent channeling of capital inflows to the domestic economy.* A key priority will be to arrive at effective hedging strategies, and ensure a careful monitoring of the financing patterns of corporate clients – including through their direct external borrowing. Due care is needed in ensuring that hedging strategies transfer risks to portfolios in ways that achieve true cover and diversification. Passing on foreign exchange risk to borrowers (thus transforming it into credit risk), or selling credit derivatives to unsophisticated non-bank intermediaries in local markets, are not sustainable ways of hedging positions – certainly for the domestic system as a whole, and probably also for the lending institution itself.

Regulation and supervision

In this market setting, regulatory and supervisory policies will clearly be crucial, especially as they buttress and encourage effective risk management. Even in advanced cases, a major reform agenda remains. Immediate challenges are:

- *to ensure consolidated supervision, especially of complex financial groups – with adequate cooperation among supervisory bodies, and more effective enforcement procedures.* With updated banking legislation being put into place in most CEE economies, this issue is increasingly one of implementation rather than law. It goes to the heart of the supervisory challenge in the period ahead. If domestic credit indeed continues to grow strongly, and capital inflows remain large, these flows will rapidly spread from direct cross-border lending and banking to permeate the sector of non-bank intermediaries. Moreover, if prudential standards need to be tightened to ward off the macro-prudential risks of rapid credit expansion, it is "leakages" through the non-bank sector that represent one major threat to such efforts. The question is one of true efficiency in asset allocation: avoiding a build-up of balance sheet positions that take risk insufficiently into account. In a majority of the CEE economies, the effective implementation of risk-based supervision on a consolidated basis is a key area for strengthening, but in an environment where foreign-owned groups predominate, however, it is not a simple affair. This requires close and continuing interaction with home country supervisors, in order to achieve a blending of local market knowledge with an overview of control and risk assessment systems that operate across an international financial group.
- *to strengthen regulatory and supervisory frameworks for non-bank intermediaries – especially in the areas of leasing, insurance, and pensions.* As already discussed, a rapid growth of non-bank intermediaries is emerging across the region – from Estonia and Hungary to Poland – even if, in some cases, such as Slovenia or the Slovak Republic, it is still at an early stage. Leasing, for example, is growing rapidly in economies as different as Estonia and Bulgaria. During the decade ahead, non-bank intermediaries will be a major growth area throughout the CEE region, and this is currently the field in which financial supervision is, with relatively few exceptions, far from prepared for such growth. Pension fund oversight is a frequently recurring weak point, for example. IMF FSSA analyses pick on the regulation and supervision of non-banks more frequently than that of banks – not as posing systemic threats now, but as needing careful monitoring and firm supervision to avoid trouble down the road.
- *to strengthen standards of transparency, disclosure and corporate governance – including such issues as the treatment of minority shareholders.* This is

directly relevant to domestic securities investors such as pension funds and insurance companies – but of course is also crucial to ensure that corporations achieve broadening access to EU and global financial markets. FSSAs and other commentaries have seized on this as an area where the strengthening of national practices would yield great benefits over a short time horizon – again in cases that range from the Baltics to Poland or Bulgaria. Essential priorities in this area, to foster market integrity, include accounting and auditing standards.

- *to apply penalties to firms and groups in an effective and graduated manner, against clear benchmarks of prudence.* This is a frequent difficulty, with examples to be found in the power of the supervisory body itself to issue and revoke licenses; supervisors' ability to directly intervene and wind up distressed institutions; the availability of a ladder of graduated sanctions and penalties for banks and non-banks; and, indeed, the willingness to act early and publicly to deter abuse – including securities market infringements. Benchmarks needing strengthening are frequently the monitoring of connected lending – including to shareholders; the sophistication of loan classification systems; and the rigor of provisioning standards.

- *to enhance the effectiveness of commercial courts and the judicial system, including for the perfection and realization of collateral.* This is critical for, among other things, the operation of payments systems and repo markets, household mortgage credit, and SME, as well as other, corporate, financing. In their analysis of real lending spreads and earnings in the CEE region, Riess *et al.* (2002) are surely right to pick on this as an area where weakness in the financial framework may be inhibiting banks from fully exploiting the high-risk-adjusted returns that are potentially available in domestic markets. Again, some weaknesses are common – from collateral realization in Hungary to the bankruptcy law in Bulgaria, or the broad range of insolvency provisions in the Slovak Republic. And, in the overwhelming majority of cases, judicial systems deliver results only slowly.

- *to keep under review the incentives for financial groups with dominant market position* ... Regulators and supervisors need to ensure a framework that sets the right incentives for competitive behavior and for risk management. To be large enough to compete across borders, a CEE bank may need to expand to a size where it is one of a few elephants in the domestic bath tub. Competition issues that this raises have had to be addressed already in EU economies where (as in the Netherlands, for example) domestic consolidation advanced rapidly, with sound strategic goals. So, effective competition enforcement and policing will be very important. Another prerequisite is to ensure that markets remain open to new entrants – including from abroad: in the CEE, the practical ease of entry to financial markets should help to ensure effective competition even where existing players have large market positions.

- *. . . including where institutions are so large domestically as to feel themselves "too big to fail."* In a highly competitive environment, very large banks could be induced to take on undue risks in a belief that they will inevitably be bailed out by national authorities in the case of bad lending outcomes or adverse market shocks. This could be compounded by the generous levels of deposit insurance (relative to household income levels) that will be introduced as the *acquis communautaire* in this area is implemented. The potentially favorable impact of foreign ownership on expertise and financing capacity needs no underscoring; but there may still be a question of whether, in combination, the domestic size of some banks, the apparent security provided by the foreign parent, and generous deposit insurance, might engender moral hazard – potentially leading local management to allocate resources inefficiently. Foreign owners should be a stimulus for prudence in loan standards – but the history of financial liberalization is rich with examples where parent banks have been blind to "herd instinct" developments in a foreign market that lead to a macroprudential debacle – even where individual loan standards may seem adequate. And, in the event of serious stresses, the support of foreign owners may not be unconditional. The intrinsic limits on foreign owners' willingness to recapitalize have already been illustrated in the Czech Republic (and, indeed, in Croatia). And more broadly, their readiness to stay engaged may also depend on confidence in overall policy management – a point that experience in Argentina has graphically underscored. The extent of concentration and foreign ownership means that supervisors need to keep under review the implications for bank behavior, and for economic and financial policy, of institutions' market positions and incentives.

Reflecting this context, a further wave of financial-sector reforms has been underway in the CEE economies since the end of the 1990s. The stimulus for these reforms, which will set the stage for a further advance in financial-sector efficiency, has arisen from two sources. The first is the commitment to align financial frameworks closely with those in the EU, as countries adopt the financial-sector component of the *acquis communautaire*. The second and complementary stimulus has been the desire to advance toward the highest levels implied by international standards and codes. It is these priorities that led all ten former transition countries that are EU candidates to initiate World Bank-IMF/FSAP programs and Standards Assessments over the past three years, while maintaining their active dialogue with the EU institutions in the framework of the enlargement negotiations. These priorities are pressing – though not more so than remaining steps (where needed) to complete liberalization or fully eliminate quasi-fiscal pressures.

    Policymakers' specific priorities and concerns are well reflected in a new wave of reform initiatives, which typically still has some way to run. The following are characteristic examples of changes recently made or currently underway in financial-sector frameworks.

- Updated *Acts of Parliament governing the banking sector*, to lay a legal basis on which to address supervisory and regulatory gaps. These Acts typically have included provision for the consolidated supervision of banks and complex financial groups. New Acts were introduced in Estonia (1999), the Czech Republic (2002), and Hungary (2001) – which also introduced new central bank, credit, and capital market laws (though the full legal basis for consolidated supervision still needs to be put into place). Slovenia introduced a comprehensive Financial Sector Action Plan in 2002. Poland has been moving to ready new legislation on banking, insurance, and securities business. Romania updated its Banking Act in 2001, and plans a further set of amendments to bring it fully in line with EU Directives in 2003. And since 1999 – in a major catch-up – the Slovak Republic has introduced new laws covering central banking, banking, securities markets, and insurance.

- Initiatives to *coordinate the supervision of different branches* of financial-sector activity, and also deepen links with foreign supervisory authorities. Examples include the creation of unified supervisors in Hungary (2000) and Latvia (2001) – and a movement in this direction in Estonia. Alternatively, in the same spirit, there was a formalization of links between domestic supervisors through Memoranda of Understanding or Protocols (as in Lithuania or Romania); or the setting up of a coordinating committee of supervisors (and the plan for a unified non-bank supervisor) in Bulgaria. Slovakia, in turn, has decided to unify bank and non-bank supervision under the auspices of the central bank by 2005. Supervisory coordination is, again, a key area given the rapid emergence of complex financial groups, and the immense importance of foreign-owned institutions in CEE financial markets. But the creation of unified supervisors is not a guarantee of success in itself: there is a real challenge in merging regulatory cultures and ensuring that supervision standards are leveled up in the process – especially for non-bank intermediaries.

- Legal or regulatory changes to facilitate *the enforcement of collateral.* In some cases this concerned all types of collateral and, in others, specific types of transaction such as repurchase agreements and pledges (as in Hungary). As noted above, satisfactory arrangements for collateral provide indispensable underpinning for quite a wide range of financial-sector activities – from payments systems to repo transactions and SME lending programs.

- The introduction of *Real-Time Gross Settlement*, to replace existing payments systems. Developments here moved ahead rapidly in cases as diverse as Bulgaria, Estonia, and Slovenia, where such systems had not already been introduced in the 1990s. So far, experience has been encouraging – the main concerns relating to transitional arrangements, rather than the efficiency of the planned RTGS systems or their compatibility with international standards and codes. These systems, among their other advantages, are of central importance in the key area of cross-border financial market integration.

- New *Pension Fund Laws*, for example, in Estonia, Lithuania (for a "third pillar" – with a second pillar also under consideration), and Slovenia – following reforms already implemented in Hungary and Poland, among others. The importance of pension fund reforms lies, among other things, in their potential to stimulate capital market activity and hence more efficient financial markets – as well as their links to fiscal reforms that enhance longer run macro-stability. Initiatives in this direction are also under consideration in the Czech and Slovak Republics and Romania.

These reforms typically represent the alignment of regulation and supervision with EU and best international practices. They deserve special attention because of their actuality in many CEE countries, but also because they represent imminent issues for others countries – within and outside the accession group – as they move on to meet comparable challenges. Of course, in these latter cases, the more sophisticated reforms will only take root satisfactorily on the basis of a sustained effort to put residual problems of the transition firmly behind.

The macroeconomic and macro-prudential framework

As noted at the outset of this chapter, for the financial sector to allocate resources efficiently, fiscal and monetary policies must assure a reasonably stable macroeconomic and financial setting. It is worth underlining a few of the considerations that will be key in the period immediately ahead.

- In the fiscal field, the central challenge is to restrain *public sector demands on savings* so as to (1) keep external current account deficits within safely financeable ranges; and (2) arrive at a macroeconomic policy mix that does not trigger avoidable volatility in short-term inflows (which is a particular risk when monetary policy bears too much of the burden of macroeconomic restraint). Given the pressure on CEE budgets, it is not surprising that concerns about the medium-term stance of fiscal policy recur continuously – from the Czech Republic to Hungary and from Poland to Lithuania. Recent trends in a number of countries confirm this to be a very important watchpoint for the future. Also, in an operational market perspective, public debt management can play an important role in setting viable benchmarks for corporate borrowing costs.

- In the *monetary field*, a first priority is to ensure continuing low and fairly stable rates of inflation. A second is to steer money market and central bank instrumentation over time toward euro area norms – although in those countries that have a currency board, of course, the development of money markets as such is likely to be limited for the time being, since commercial banks use the forex window to access liquidity. (In the case of Estonia, for example, banks have access to the forex window at the central bank in real time and at no cost.) More generally, the growing depth of financial systems in all the CEE economies – and especially the growth of lending for business and residential investment – will enhance the impact of interest rates as a transmission channel for monetary policy.

- A further priority, perhaps less easy to implement, is to assure a *vigilant monitoring of credit flows and asset prices*, and thus safeguard against the build-up of macro-prudential vulnerability. This will require an informed exchange between monetary and supervisory authorities, who both have insights to bring to the area of macro-prudential analysis. The publication by central banks of Financial Stability Reports – along the lines of what is already done in Hungary – can play a valuable role in focusing policy attention and also educating markets.

While fiscal and monetary priorities are not addressed here, to avoid overlaps with papers on financial stability, the macro-prudential monitoring of overall credit flows and asset prices deserves comment. This is an area where, in the first instance, the underlying efficiency of allocation by the financial system is directly at issue. Only in a later stage is it a question of threats to financial stability.

Notably, as domestic risk premia decline – and as capital inflows continue into asset markets that are narrow, alongside a rapid growth in domestic credit – there is a concern that capital could be misallocated, slowing economic growth and increasing vulnerability. Monetary authorities and supervisors need to stay ahead of the curve in assessing such risks – with the first signs likely to be lying in problematic patterns in credit flows, or exuberance in asset prices, that suggest distortions in the allocation of savings. The preparation by central banks of regular financial stability reports – in which Hungary was a frontrunner – is one helpful way of focusing official and public attention on such issues.

To try to address such issues proactively, at the stage when they raise concerns about efficiency rather than risks of crisis, two areas deserve particular attention.

- *The role of foreign currency borrowing is a potential source of vulnerability.* Many CEE financial systems are passing on currency risk to corporations or households by lending in euros (or US dollars). But, unless borrowers are formally or naturally hedged, these banks are simply transforming currency risk into credit risk. So the growth of this financing – usually at low interest rates, and to priority sectors – may appear an efficient expansion of intermediation. But when weighted, for risk it may well amount to a misallocation of resources by the lenders. Supervisory authorities can take action to monitor this through banks' prudential returns. And, equally importantly, they or monetary authorities can follow the example of the New Zealand or Israeli authorities in calling for business firms to also submit reports of their unhedged borrowings. In the balance sheet analysis of crises, such borrowings have emerged as a major factor explaining the depth and duration of output decline.

- *In both household and commercial real-estate-related lending, there are potential risks over the medium term, as competition intensifies in narrow markets and in a lower-interest-rate environment.* The same applies to some degree in securities-linked financing. While a careful monitoring of individual loan standards is essential, warning signs may show up first in overall credit flow data, in asset price indices, and in banking or market spreads. So far, developments in securities and real-estate-related lending do not suggest such overlending in the CEE region. But over time a prudent assessment will require both supervisors and monetary officials to take a perspective broader than a loan-by-loan view. They will need to watch attentively for disturbing persistence in credit growth to non-traded-goods sectors; for positive co-variance between portfolio segments that may be linked directly or indirectly to the real estate or securities markets; and for asset price developments out of line with experience in other comparable economies. An unproductive over-extension of credit to real estate may be the single most common source of inefficiency in the allocation of resources in newly liberalized financial markets – with foreign-owned institutions not necessarily more perceptive than others in that connection. More generally, the risk of rapid credit growth, intermediated by bank or non-bank institutions that are not effectively supervised on a consolidated basis, is a key watchpoint for the future flagged throughout the CEE region in the FSSAs undertaken by the IMF.

The risks of misallocation associated with heavy capital inflows and with real estate market activities have the potential to be mutually reinforcing. These linkages have been explored in the recent literature on the role of real estate lending and of corporate balance sheet pressures in financial crises, which focuses *inter alia* on the role of foreign financing in incomplete financial sectors and with narrow real estate markets.[6] But these analyses have a relevance to the role of the financial sector in a broader context than that of financial crises. In particular, they shed light on the risks of growing inefficiency in allocation by the sector, which may impair economic growth even where it does not result in a crisis. Of course, capital inflows remain potentially of great value in accelerating convergence toward advanced economy living standards. The issue is not to impede them, but to contain the impact of market (or indeed policy-induced) distortions, including overshooting and asset price bubbles.

Policy is far from powerless in the face of such market developments, but the response needs to be pre-emptive – and well-orchestrated across a range of macro- and micro economic instruments. Well-balanced restraint through macroeconomic policies can clearly play a key role in reducing risks of a boom and bust cycle developing, but this is at the level of aggregate demand (and the impact of policy mix on capital inflows). The more difficult question conceptually is how microeconomic policies can address underlying capital market or real economy distortions. One obvious area is to remove tax or regulatory incentives that may be contributing to the problem – for example in housing subsidies, overly generous mortgage interest deductions, or zoning restrictions that are limiting the supply of development property. Importantly, however, there is also some evidence – notably from experience during the Asian crisis – that prudential policies can play an effective pre-emptive role. Indeed the varying impact of real estate and balance sheet effects among the countries affected by the Asian crisis appears to have resulted, in part, from the impact of regulation and supervision in containing distortive effects in the financial sector, which was more effective in some Asian economies than others (for a discussion, see Collyns and Benhadji 2002). This is not to argue that prudential instruments should be used for macroeconomic goals. The issue is to identify aggregate credit developments that are increasing the risk inherent in bank assets, and to respond with conventional supervisory instruments – thus flanking macroeconomic policy adjustments that reduce the overall pressure on resources where needed. This concerted approach to macro-prudential risks is likely to be of key importance in ensuring efficient allocation of resources in the CEE economies as they face the opportunities and challenges of full integration with the EU.

Concluding observations

In the period ahead, macroeconomic and financial-sector policies will face new challenges as the CEE region remains a magnet for international capital. These flows can accelerate the catch-up in living standards toward those of present EU members, but only if resources are allocated efficiently, and growth is not punctuated by crisis. In these regards, the financial sector has a pivotal role to play. In allocating resources, it will respond strongly to benign policy signals, but it will also amplify distortions in the economic setting, such as implicit guarantees or deficient tax regimes. The impressive performance of CEE economies in the past decade – a historic example of regional economic success – must not blind one to troubling experience in other emerging markets.

Looking forward, the focus must thus remain on initiatives – from non-bank supervision to sound fiscal policy – that will allow the sector to contribute fully as policymakers chart the road to full EU integration. Efficiency in this broad sense will reflect sound risk management in financial institutions, buttressed by consolidated supervision. But it will also depend on the scale and financing of fiscal and current account deficits; on the development of broad and diversified markets, with efficient linkages to the single capital market of the future; and on the joint vigilance of monetary and supervisory authorities over developments in capital and credit flows.

Notes

1 This chapter draws in particular on analysis contained in Financial System Stability Assessments for a number of CEE economies, which were completed by the IMF in the course of 2001–2002, and are posted on the IMF website at www.imf.org; on the book, *Into the EU – Policy Frameworks in Central Europe* (IMF, June 2002), edited by Robert A. Feldman and the author – and notably on Chapters 4 and 5, by Wagner and Iakova, where the data in Tables 6.1–6.3 was first presented; and on the paper "Practice Makes Perfect: a Review of Banking in Central and Eastern Europe," by Riess, Wagenvoort and Zajc (EIB Papers, Volume 7, No. 1). The chapter has benefited from comments by, among others, Robert Burgess, Paulo Drummond, Philippe Egoume, Robert Feldman, Juan-Jose Fernandez-Ansola, Richard Haas, Karl Habermeier, Russell Kincaid, Juergen Kroeger, Neven Mates, Cristian Popa, Jerald Schiff, Alfred Schipke (to whom the data in Table 6.4 are due), and Istvan Szekely. Remaining errors and omissions are the author's alone.

2 As reported in Feldman and Watson (2002) and in published IMF Financial System Stability Assessments (FSSAs). Unless otherwise indicated, spreads here are defined as the difference between average deposit and lending rates. Broadly similar trends emerge from a comparison based on the ratio of net interest margins to bank assets. Main data sources throughout will be found in footnote 1. There is a full list of references at the end of this chapter.

3 For background data and a fuller discussion, see IMF FSSAs and Feldman and Watson (2003).

4 For data on total operating costs, see Feldman and Watson (2002) and IMF FSSAs; and for a discussion of their components over time and versus EU levels, see Riess *et al.* (2002); and on EU costs as such see Belaisch *et al.* (2001).

5 The growing penetration of ATMs and e-banking in some countries is a further sign of greater efficiency.

6 For a discussion see, for example, Hilbers *et al.* (2001), or Mulder *et al.* (2002).

References

Belaisch, A., Kodres, L., Levy, J. and Ubide, A. (2001) "Euro-area banking at the crossroads," IMF, Working Paper WP/01/28, March.

Collyns, C., and Senhadji, A. (2002) "Lending booms, real estate bubbles and the Asian crisis," IMF Working Paper WP/02/20, January.

Feldman, R.A., and Watson, C.M. (eds) (2002) *Into the EU – Policy Frameworks in Central Europe*, IMF.

Hilbers, P., Lei, Q. and Zacho, L. (2001) "Real estate market developments and financial sector soundness," IMF Working Paper WP/01/129, September.

IMF (2001a) "Czech Republic – Financial System Stability Assessment" (July).

IMF (2001b) "Poland – Financial System Stability Assessment" (June).

IMF (2001c) "Slovenia – Financial System Stability Assessment" (September).

IMF (2002a) "Bulgaria – Financial System Stability Assessment" (August).

IMF (2002b) "Hungary – Financial System Stability Assessment – Follow-up" (June).

IMF (2002c) "Latvia – Financial System Stability Assessment" (March).

IMF (2002d) "Lithuania – Financial System Stability Assessment" (February).

IMF (2002e) "Slovak Republic – Financial System Stability Assessment" (September).

Kuijs, A. (2000) "Monetary policy transmission mechanisms and inflation in the Slovak Republic", IMF Working Paper WP/02/80, May.

Lipschitz, L., Lane, T. and Mourmouras, A. (2002) "Capital flows to transition economies: master or servant?" IMF Working Paper WP/02/11, January.

Mulder, C., Perrelli, R. and Rocha, M. (2002) "The role of corporate, legal and macroeconomic balance sheet indicators in crisis detection and prevention," IMF Working Paper WP/02/59, March.

Riess, A., Wagenvoort, R. and Zajc, P. (2002) "Practice makes perfect: a review of banking in Central and Eastern Europe," EIB Papers, Volume 7, No. 1.

Schaechter, A., Stone, M.R. and Zelmer, M. (2000) "Adopting inflation targeting: practical issues for emerging market countries," IMF Occasional Paper No. 202.

Svennsson, L. (1998) "Open economy inflation targeting," NBER.

Van der Hagen, P. and Thimann, C. (2000) "Monetary policy challenges in transition and toward accession," Joint Vienna Institute and OeNB, November.

7 Challenging the prudential supervisor – liability versus (regulatory) immunity

Lessons from the EU experience for Central and Eastern European countries

Michel Tison

Introduction

Since the early 1990s, bank failures in different EU countries have increasingly led to liability claims being directed against supervisory authorities. These have been for alleged negligence or improper conduct by these authorities in exercising their supervisory responsibilities over credit institutions. In general, these claims are introduced by depositors with the failed banks who, following the bank failure, have not managed to fully recover their deposits, as the latter are often only partially covered by deposit guarantee schemes. More exceptionally, liability claims originate from shareholders of the bank or the bank management itself, alleging unlawful conduct of the supervisory authority.

Several factors can explain the increasing importance of the supervisory liability issue. First, this evolution goes along with the gradual emergence of prudential regulation as a formal body of law in EU countries, mainly as a consequence of the adoption of European directives and the need to implement these directives into formal rules at national level. Up to two decades ago, prudential supervision of banks rested mainly on vague and general rules, the application of which left a large discretion to the authorities responsible for prudential supervision. At present, the supervisory action is much more embedded into formal, often very detailed, rules pertaining to both authorisation requirements and ongoing supervision. The ensuing formalisation of supervision not only substantially reduces the latitude of supervisory authorities, but also makes the supervisory action more open to challenge by different stakeholders. Furthermore, the European directives also stress the need to provide for adequate legal protection to the supervised entities, allowing them, to a large extent, to challenge decisions of the supervisory bodies in court.

Second, the 'emancipation' of the financial consumer in recent years has increased the risk of litigation against the prudential supervisors, and might increasingly induce depositors with a failed bank to attempt to shift their losses onto the supervisory authorities. This situation might also, in part, be caused by the (mis)perception of depositors as to the capacity of prudential authorities to avoid banking failures.

The basic assumption of this chapter is that integrated markets within the European Union, in the near future to include Central and Eastern European countries, should function under more or less similar rules as regards possible supervisory liability. As prudential law in the EU countries is, to a large extent, based on European directives, which intend to create a level playing field between EU member states, there is an argument for promoting more convergence as regards supervisory liability as well. It goes without saying that this issue also bears specific importance for the emerging economies in Central and Eastern European countries, as these countries are also adapting to the *acquis communautaire*.

In the first part of the chapter, we will discuss the sources of supervisory liability, and the policy issues involved for the regulators as regards accepting or limiting liability. After that, we provide an overview of the present legal situation in the EU member states, which will show large disparities as regards the legal framework for supervisory liability. We then attempt to provide a cross-country analysis of possible situations where liability may arise, based on cases brought before the courts in the member states examined.

In the third part of the chapter, we analyse the implications of EU banking integration, and in particular the harmonisation of banking supervisory standards, on supervisory liability. We submit first that home country control in EU banking leads to a shift in liability to the home country supervisor and home country liability laws as well. Further, we will examine how convergence in liability regimes amongst EU member states could be achieved. Specific attention will be devoted to the possible application of the so-called *Francovich*-liability to supervisory liability. Our conclusion will reflect on the prospects for convergence of supervisory liability in the EU and the importance of the issue for the new member states.

Causes and risks of supervisory liability: the supervisor's dilemma and policy issues

In general, liability of the banking supervisor can be conceived in two ways: liability towards third parties, mainly depositors; or liability towards the financial institution subject to supervision. This duality in supervisory liability risk will often confront the supervisory authority with a dilemma, to the extent that the interests of financial institutions and depositors do not necessarily converge. This is particularly the case when a financial institution is in financial distress.

Liability towards depositors

In general, the creditors of a financial institution, in particular depositors, will claim liability of the prudential supervisor following the bankruptcy of the supervised institution, to the extent that they have not managed to fully recover their claims out of the bankruptcy or after reimbursement by the deposit guarantee or investor compensation system. The motives underlying their claim against the supervisory authority are alleged short-comings of the authority to adequately discharge its supervisory responsibilities, thereby causing losses to the depositors. The grievances formulated by the claimants are generally related to negligent passivity or a lack of diligence on the part of the supervisor, faced with indications of financial distress of the supervised institution. For instance, if the supervisor failed to take adequate intervention measures, such as replacing the bank managers or temporarily prohibiting business, although it knew or ought to have knowledge of serious dysfunctions (for example fraud) or financial difficulties of the supervised bank. Less pronounced are the cases in which the supervisory authorities have failed to closely follow and monitor a financially distressed bank through periodical verifications and assessment of the intervention measures it has taken.

Liability towards the supervised financial institutions

The potential cases of supervisory liability towards the supervised institution itself or its shareholders do not relate to alleged passivity or negligence in exercising prudential supervision, but more to the opposite situation of 'overreaction' by the supervisor or unlawful conduct. Indeed, a financial institution bears primary responsibility for the management of its business, and cannot therefore blame the supervisor for having been negligent or too passive in detecting or reacting to its own shortcomings. By contrast, a financial institution could suffer damages following a proactive or harsh intervention by the supervisory authority, which might affect its reputation and frustrate depositors' confidence. For instance, the supervisor might be blamed for having intervened too severely following indications of financial difficulties of the supervised financial institution (for example, prohibition of certain activities or withdrawal of the banking licence in reaction to limited financial difficulties). Furthermore, the supervisor might incur liability for infringing specific prohibitions, such as violation of its professional secrecy obligations.[1]

The supervisor's dilemma

The above-mentioned liability risks are illustrative of the delicate situation the prudential supervisor is faced with in exercising its supervisory duties, in particular when confronted with a financially distressed credit institution. In such a case, the supervisory authority has to find a balance between conflicting interests, which are intrinsically connected with the basic objectives of prudential regulation: on the one hand, maintaining the safety and soundness of financial institutions and the financial system as a whole; on the other hand, protecting the depositors and other creditors of financial institutions. A proactive attitude of the prudential supervisor towards the supervised institution might be beneficial for (prospective) depositors of the individual bank, but may harm the financial institution itself as a consequence of loss of reputation or credibility in the market, and even produce destabilising effects on the financial system as a whole. By contrast, adopting a cautious attitude, though protecting the financial institution, could subsequently expose the supervisory authority to claims from depositors, if, for example, it has enabled the financial institution to further accumulate, under an apparent solvency, losses to the detriment of (prospective) depositors and other creditors.[2] The supervisor's dilemma is very similar to the situation of a credit institution in discharging loans to a business enterprise: when the borrower is in financial distress, the creditor has to find a balance between, on the one hand, the risk of liability towards other creditors of the failing borrower for having created an apparent solvency by maintaining a credit line and, on the other hand, the risk of liability towards the borrower itself for abruptly putting an end to the credit relation.[3]

Supervisory liability: policy issues

The issue of supervisory liability, and whether or not, or to what extent to accept it as a matter of principle, is essential in the design of banking regulation and policy. Exposing supervisory authorities to large liability risks could, in fact, lead to a shift of the cost of banking failures to the state. This would run contrary to the very purpose of prudential regulation in a market economy: the ultimate objective of prudential regulation should not be to avoid banking failures altogether at any cost, but to leave primary risks for banking failures to the shareholders and creditors of the failed banks. Prudential regulation merely constitutes a specific external monitoring device regarding the financial solidity and integrity of financial institutions, which basically does not modify the allocation of risks in case of a banking failure. Hence, prudential regulation is not a substitute to the normal system of risk allocation within a business enterprise, but merely constitutes an additional external controlling mechanism over a bank's management, the existence of which is motivated by the existence of information asymmetries of (small) depositors entrusting their savings to banks.

The same motives underpin the existence of systems of deposit guarantee and investor compensation, which are to be seen as a limited remedy for market failures resulting from the specific risks banks and other financial institutions generate for (small) depositors and investors.

The foregoing does not imply, however, that supervisory liability should be banned altogether. The rationale for prudential regulation, i.e. maintaining depositor confidence through specific integrity and financial control mechanisms, generates a legitimate expectation on the part of depositors and other bank creditors as to the effectiveness of supervision, i.e. diminishing to some extent the likelihood that bank failures occur, without completely eliminating them. Under this approach, bank supervisors are expected to exercise supervision with reasonable care, taking into account the instruments of supervision at their disposal. However, banks cannot be totally prevented from failing, and banking supervisors cannot be expected to prevent fraud or unforeseeable losses within the bank.[4] The supervisor may, however, be expected to react diligently and with reasonable care to problems arising within a supervised financial institution, thereby seeking to conciliate as much as possible the interests of the financial system and those of bank creditors. Submitting prudential supervisors to liability rules, therefore, is not in itself incompatible with the interests pursued by prudential regulation, as it does not automatically shift the cost of banking failures to the state, but only sanctions negligent or unreasonable behaviour from the part of the supervisory authority.

An argument frequently invoked to fend off liability of supervisory authorities is the existence of deposit guarantee systems, which cover the losses incurred by depositors in case of a bank failure. In our view, this argument is flawed. First, deposit guarantee systems generally contain quantitative limits as to coverage, in order to limit moral hazard from the part of depositors and bank management.[5] As a consequence, depositors do not necessarily fully recover their claims from the failed bank. To the extent the bank failure may be (in part) attributed to negligence or shortcomings by the prudential supervisor, there is no reason why the damages suffered by depositors could not be claimed from the authorities that have caused these damages. Second, deposit protection systems nowadays are not generally funded through government funds, but by the financial community itself, based upon the solidarity principle.[6] Consequently, the assertion that the public authorities already offer financial protection through deposit guarantee systems does not hold true.

Finally, submitting prudential authorities to a liability regime might even be regarded as a strength of the financial system, as it will have a disciplining effect on the supervisor itself: granting total immunity from liability creates a moral hazard risk on the part of the prudential authorities, as the accountability for their own actions would be reduced. By contrast, a liability regime which takes due account of the nature of prudential supervision and the need for sufficient discretion in taking supervisory measures, will function as a monitoring mechanism with respect to the exercise of supervision, and eventually benefit the financial system as a whole. The assumption that the stringency of financial regulation can be beneficial for the attractiveness of a country's financial system (paradigm of 'competition for excellence'), may also apply as regards the issue of supervisory liability: granting (regulatory) immunity from liability could be seen as an element of weakness for the supervisory system, while applying a well-balanced liability regime could be indicative of the accountability of the supervisory authorities. This is not to say that liability is presumed whenever a banking failure occurs: the interested parties claiming liability will have to demonstrate the specific shortcomings in the exercise of prudential supervision, taking into account the (limited) resources of supervision.

Overview of liability regimes in different EU countries

The present legal situation as regards supervisory liability in the EU member states is characterised by its large diversity. Different patterns can be identified in this respect. In a first group of countries, no specific liability rules exist with respect to the exercise of prudential supervision, and general tort liability rules apply. Very often, this situation appears not to be the result of a deliberate policy choice, but may be explained by the lack of any precedents in jurisprudence as regards liability claims against supervisory authorities in these countries. By contrast, a second – increasing – group of EU member states has enacted specific rules as regards the limitation of liability that could be incurred by supervisory bodies. Through specific laws, liability is either confined to the situation of gross negligence or bad faith from the part of the supervisory bodies, or even results in total immunity from liability. It is interesting to notice that, very often, the intervention by Parliament to grant (partial) immunity from liability follows specific court decisions where judges have held the supervisory authority liable towards depositors. These immunity regimes are therefore specifically aimed at neutralising possible liability claims in the future. Finally, in a third group of member states, some limitation of liability stems from the general tort law, which to a certain extent protects state bodies from excessive liability claims.

It should be noted, furthermore, that the diversity of general tort law regimes between EU member states further adds to the fragmentation of supervisory liability regimes. Illustrative in this respect is the concept of 'relativity' or 'proximity' that exists in some countries (such as Germany, the United Kingdom and the Netherlands), but not in others (such as Belgium). According to this concept, the breach of a legal rule will only lead to liability towards persons alleging damages as a consequence of this breach if the said rule is intended to protect their interests. In the context of supervisory liability, this implies that liability towards depositors will only come into play if prudential regulation is considered to protect the interests of (individual) depositors, and not (only) the interests of the financial institutions or, more generally, the financial system. We will see that this issue stood at the centre of debates in different jurisdictions.

It goes without saying that prudential supervisors themselves favour some immunity from liability in the exercise of their responsibilities, as appears from the Basle Committee's *Core Principles for Effective Banking Supervision.*[7] Core Principle 1, which lays down the essential preconditions for effective banking supervision, stresses *inter alia* the need to provide for 'legal protection for supervisors'. The explanatory memorandum to Core Principle 1 further specifies in this regard that supervisors should enjoy 'protection [normally in law] from personal and institutional liability for supervisory actions taken in good faith in the course of performing supervisory duties'. The Core Principles are not, however, in any respect to be regarded as legally enforceable rules, but are merely recommendations. Moreover, it should be stressed that the *Core Principles* as adopted by the Basle Committee primarily emanate from the supervisory authorities themselves, who have an evident self-interest in promulgating (partial) immunity from liability as a good standard for prudential regulation.

The next sections will give an overview of the main characteristics of the legal regime as regards supervisory liability. A comparative summary is provided in Table 7.1.

Country-analysis

Germany

THE CASE LAW

Historically, the first EU member state where, to our knowledge, supervisory liability arose in the courts was Germany. The German situation is archetypical for the evolution in several member states, which introduced statutory immunity regimes, as a reaction to case law holding the banking supervisor liable for negligence.

The legal foundation for supervisory liability in German law is §839 *Bürgerliches Gesetzbuch* (BGB), according to which a public servant can be held liable for damages for breach of a professional duty owed to third parties. According to general tort law, however, only those third parties who establish that the duty which allegedly has been breached was instituted not only to protect the general interest, but also the interests of the claimant, are eligible to claim damages (so-called '*Schutznormtheorie*').[8] Hence, in order to base supervisory liability on §839 BGB, the plaintiff must first prove that prudential regulation and supervision not only serves the general interest, but also the individual interests.

The case law with respect to the latter issue showed an interesting evolution. Until the late 1970s, the case law firmly held that the then-applicable banking supervisory law (the *Kreditwesengesetz 1939*) served the public interest only. Private individuals, either the supervised banks or

Table 7.1 Comparative overview of supervisory liability of banking supervisors in different EU member states, compared to the Basle Committee *Core Principles* recommendation

Country	Subject of liability	Liability criteria			Source
		Negligence	Gross negligence	Bad faith	
Basle Committee	Not specified	N	N	Y	Core Principle 1
United Kingdom	Financial Services Authority	N	N	Y	Schedule I, section 19(3) Financial Services and Markets Act
Germany	Bundesanstalt für Finanzdienstleistungsaufsicht	N	N	N	§ 6 III Kreditwesengesetz
France	French state	N	Y	Y	Case law of Conseil d'Etat
Belgium	Banking, Finance and Insurance Commission	N	Y	Y	Art. 68 Law 2 August 2002
The Netherlands	De Nederlandsche Bank	(Y)	(Y)	(Y)	General tort law (subject to relativity requirement)
Luxembourg	Commission de Surveillance du Secteur Financier	N	Y	Y	Art. 20 Law of 23 December 1998
Ireland	Central Bank of Ireland	N	N	Y	Section 25A Central Bank of Ireland Act 1997

bank creditors, could therefore not claim damages for alleged deficient prudential supervision.[9] It was commonly accepted that the same conclusion subsequently applied in application of the 1961 Banking Act.[10] The German Supreme Court (*Bundesgerichtshof*) confirmed this point of view with respect to insurance supervision:[11] the Supreme Court held that prudential supervision realised a *collective* protection of the insured, only indirectly granting protection to individual insured persons as part of the group.

Two judgments of the German Supreme Court delivered in 1979[12] fundamentally reversed the traditional opinion. Based on a detailed analysis of the German Banking Law of 1961 and the purposes of banking supervision under this Act, the Supreme Court held that the Banking Act purported to protect individual bank creditors, who could therefore claim damages from the banking supervisory authority for alleged deficient supervision. Considering prudential supervision as a creditor protection device at the same time implied that neither the supervised bank, its shareholders,[13] nor competitors of the bank[14] could claim damages from the supervisory authority.

These judgments provoked fierce debates amongst scholars.[15] Opponents basically argued that accepting liability would, in the end, lead to a situation of state guarantee for failed banks.[16] Proponents of the judgments welcomed the individualist approach advocated by the Supreme Court, as it would respond to creditors' expectations as to the proper functioning of the supervisory authorities.[17]

In further elaborating the conditions of possible liability, the Supreme Court took into account the necessity of leaving a sufficient margin of discretion to the supervisory authority, within which it should be able to take account of the interests of both the creditors and the supervised credit institution itself. The judge must refrain from assessing the opportunity of decisions or measures taken by the prudential supervisor, but should only investigate whether the supervisor has made an error in judgment given all the elements of the situation at hand. Liability would then be established, without the victim having to prove that the supervisor behaved arbitrarily or abused its powers. In the end, the discretion left to the prudential supervisor will substantially reduce the risk of liability being actually established. In the *Herstatt*-case, the *Oberlandesgericht* to which the case was redirected after the Supreme Court's judgment did not hold the supervisory authority liable, as it considered that the latter did not commit any error in judgment of the situation.[18]

THE REACTION: STATUTORY IMMUNITY

In view of the liability risk generated by the Supreme Court decisions, Parliament amended the *Kreditwesengesetz* in 1984. A new paragraph 3 was added to §6 of the law, which states that the banking supervisor fulfils its statutory tasks exclusively in the general interest. The objective of the law was clearly to fend off liability claims in the future, by indicating that prudential supervision did not serve the protection of individual creditors.[19] Similar provisions were enacted in the field of investment firm supervision and insurance supervision.[20] They have been maintained after the recent reform of the structures of financial supervision.[21] As a result, the supervisor finds itself totally shielded from civil liability.

Several authors questioned the compatibility of this statutory immunity with the German constitution.[22] The (lower) courts that had to judge on liability cases in recent years are not, however, inclined to support this point of view.[23]

The United Kingdom

THE CASE LAW

The United Kingdom witnesses a roughly similar evolution with respect to supervisory liability as Germany, though only very few cases were brought before the courts, which appeared quite reluctant to accept supervisory liability. Parliament subsequently sought to neutralise a possible liability risk by granting partial immunity of liability through law.

The issue of supervisory liability only appeared in the late 1980s in English case law. However, an earlier judgment of the Privy Council, delivered in a case involving the banking law of Hong Kong,[24] constituted an important precedent. The plaintiffs, who were creditors of a failed bank, alleged that the Hong Kong supervisory authority had negligently granted and maintained a banking licence to the failing bank. The Privy Council held that liability could only be conceived when a sufficient proximity existed between the supervisory authorities and the bank creditors, such as to legitimate a duty of care of the former towards the latter. The Privy Council held that this condition was not met under Hong Kong law, given the limited instruments of supervision, which did not allow a continuous monitoring over the bank's daily management, and the consideration that supervision did not intend to offer to individual creditors any guarantee as to the bank's creditworthiness.[25]

The English courts proved to be even more stringent as regards the conditions of supervisory liability. In *Minories Finance Ltd* v. *Arthur Young* and *Johnson Matthey plc* v. *Arthur Young*[26] the Queen's Bench Division added that the existence of a duty of care, the breach of which could give rise to supervisory liability, had to be 'fair and reasonable'. As a consequence, the court held that no supervisory liability could exist towards the supervised bank itself: accepting liability would entail the possibility for banks to shift the costs of bad management to the supervisory authority. Likewise, the court held that no supervisory liability could exist towards the supervised bank's parent company, as the latter possesses ample means to monitor the management of its subsidiary bank.[27] On the contrary, the court did not make a firm statement as to possible liability of the Bank of England as supervisory authority towards bank creditors. This may explain why Parliament amended the Banking Act in 1987.

THE REACTION: STATUTORY IMMUNITY

Parliament reacted to the potential liability risk towards depositors, left open by the courts, by including in the Banking Act 1987 a provision according to which neither the Bank of England nor any of its staff members or board members could be held liable for any act of negligence in discharging the Bank of England's statutory duties, unless it appears that the act or omission was done in bad faith. A similar limitation of liability was granted to the regulatory bodies instituted under the Financial Services Act 1986.[28] At present, the Financial Services and Markets Act 2000, which has unified supervision over financial services providers in the hands of the Financial Services Authority (FSA), provides for a similar immunity regime, safe for one exception: beneath bad faith, liability of the FSA can also be based on a breach of the Human Rights Act.[29] The immunity regime does not exclude the possibility of challenging supervisory acts through judicial review.[30]

Since a statutory immunity regime does not necessarily rule out liability based on common law, it was not clear how the courts would react to the new statutory regime.[31] In the aftermath of the BCCI failure, a number of depositors claimed damages from the Bank of England for alleged improper supervision.[32] Both the Queen's Bench Division in the first instance,[33] and the Court of Appeal in appeal,[34] held that only the tort of misfeasance in public office could give rise to liability under common law. Though the issue was not decided unequivocally, the House of Lords, upon appeal against the judgment of the Court of Appeal, decided that misfeasance in public office required that the supervisor should have knowledge of the fact that its acts would cause damages to depositors.[35] It is submitted that this requirement is similar to the condition of bad faith under statutory law. Hence, the statutory limitation of liability to situations of bad faith cannot be circumvented through a liability claim based on common law.[36]

Ireland

The situation under Irish law is largely similar to the present statutory regime in England. In 1997, the Central Banking Act 1987 was amended by insertion of a new section 25A, which states that:

> [t]he [Central] Bank or any employee of the [Central] Bank or any member of its Board or any authorised person or authorised officer

appointed by the [Central] Bank for the performance of its statutory functions shall not be liable for damages for anything done or omitted in the discharge or purported discharge of any of its statutory functions under this Act unless it is shown that the act or omission was in bad faith.

The provision seems to be inspired by the English statutory immunity, with a view to anticipating possible future liability cases. No reported cases on liability claims directed against supervisory authorities have been found.

Luxembourg

A statutory regime granting partial immunity from liability to the prudential supervisor was introduced in Luxembourg law in the 1990s. Until 1993, the law merely stated that the state did not bear liability for the acts of the Institut Monétaire Luxembourgeois (IML), which then exercised prudential supervision over banks. The law did not, however, exempt the IML from liability. When implementing the EU Second Banking Directive into national law, Parliament has, probably bearing in mind a liability risk following the BCCI-failure,[37] laid down limitations to possible liability of the banking supervisory authority towards the supervised credit institutions and its creditors. This provision has subsequently been copied into the 1998 law shifting banking supervision to the Commission de Surveillance du Secteur Financier (CSSF).[38]

The Law of 23 December 1998 first clarifies, in a way similar to German law and the earlier German case law, the objectives of prudential supervision: supervision exclusively serves the public interest, and does not purport to protect the individual interests of the institutions subject to supervision, their clients or third parties.[39] Second, the same provision lays down the conditions of possible supervisory liability: the supervisory authority can only be held liable towards either a supervised financial institution, its clients or third parties, when it is established that the damage incurred by the victims is caused by a gross negligence in the choice and use of the methods deployed for the exercise by the supervisory authority of its public duty. It may be submitted that gross negligence does not only encompass bad faith, which constitutes the standard for liability under English and Irish law, but more generally refers to a shortcoming which a normal person placed in the same circumstances would never commit. In this regard, the liability regime is largely similar to the situation that at present prevails in France and Belgium (see pages 145–147).

However, it should be stressed that, absent any case law, the scope of the statutory liability regime still remains unclear, as the explanatory memorandum of the law underlined that the statutory regime did not preclude the application of the general rules of law as regards liability of public authorities.[40]

France

The situation in French law as regards supervisory liability is peculiar in several respects. First, contrary to the previous countries analysed, no statutory provision exists as concerns supervisory liability, though there is extensive case law on the matter. The number of cases that specifically involved supervisory liability over banks and investment firms is substantially higher than in other European countries.[41] This may be related to the relatively high number of small-bank failures in France over the last decades compared to its neighbouring countries. By contrast, over more than 40 years of jurisprudence, only two cases are known where the courts effectively held the state liable for deficient supervision.[42] Second, contrary to the other jurisdictions examined, liability under French law rests directly on the state, as the authorities responsible for prudential supervision (Commission Bancaire for credit institutions and Commission des Opérations de Bourse for portfolio managers) are deprived of legal personality.

The principles guiding supervisory liability under French law are to be found in general tort law, as applied by the courts. First, it should be noted that, contrary to German law, French tort law does not apply the 'relativity' rule. It is therefore irrelevant to first examine whether or not the prudential rules are intended to protect the (individual) interests of banks or bank creditors, or merely serve the public interest. In contrast with other civil law countries, however, the French judiciary has traditionally applied less stringent standards with respect to liability of public authorities when, due to the complexity of their duties, these authorities should not be held liable for normal negligence (*faute légère*).[43] In that case, public authorities can only be held liable for their gross negligence (*faute lourde*) in exercising their duties. The Conseil d'Etat, which is in last instance competent to decide on liability claims directed against public authorities,[44] has consistently applied this specific liability standard to prudential authorities, without ever extensively explaining its position.[45] This approach did not meet unanimous consent in legal writing.[46] This specific liability regime as applied by the courts probably explains why Parliament has refrained until now from introducing specific legal provisions limiting supervisory liability.

In recent years, some lower administrative courts have taken a different view on the criteria for supervisory liability, accepting liability even in case of normal negligence (*faute légère*).[47,48] However, in the landmark *Kechichian*-judgment of 30 November 2001,[49] the Conseil d'Etat maintained its traditional jurisprudence, limiting supervisory liability to situations of gross negligence.[50] As far as liability of the Commission des

Opérations de Bourse in its prudential supervision over portfolio managers is concerned, the Paris Court of Appeal equally applies the 'gross negligence'-standard.[51]

It is surprising to note that the Conseil d'Etat, though repeatedly referring to 'gross negligence' as standard for supervisory liability, never gave any definition of it or provided any element to aid in distinguishing between normal and gross negligence. Several authors see the difference as follows: while a normal negligence corresponds to a shortcoming which would not be committed by a 'normal' supervisor placed in the same circumstances, gross negligence refers to those situations of such a flagrancy that even a non-professional would not have committed them. It supposes a manifest deficiency in the functioning of the public service, which leads to apparent mistakes.[52]

Belgium

Belgian law did not, until 2002, have any specific statutory regime as regards supervisory liability, nor did it face supervisory liability claims brought before the courts in the field of banking supervision.[53] In contrast to the situation under French law, it was generally accepted that, under Belgian law, the prudential supervisor could be held liable for negligence according to the normal liability standards of general tort law (article 1382-1383 Code civil).[54] As a consequence, the supervisor could be held to damages for its normal negligence.

This situation has recently changed: the reform of the supervisory system by Act of 2 August 2002 has led to inclusion in the law of a limitation of liability for the Banking and Finance and Commission in the exercise of its statutory tasks. Article 68 Law 2 August 2002 first states, in a way similar to German law, that the Banking, Finance and Insurance Commission (BFIC) fulfils its duties in the general interest only, though the legal significance of this provision is not entirely clear.[55] Further, the law states that the BFIC, its bodies and personnel are not liable for any decision, act or behaviour in the exercise of their statutory tasks,[56] except in the event of fraud or gross negligence. Government explained the inclusion of the provision with reference to the Basle Committee's Core Principles on the one hand, and the circumstance that prudential supervision under a normal liability regime would entail disproportionate financial risks for the supervisory authority.[57]

Liability in case of fraud or gross negligence will be borne by the Banking, Finance and Insurance Commission itself, as it is an independent authority with legal personality.[58] This could be potentially problematic, as the BFIC is funded through contributions made by the institutions supervised by it. This raises the question of what would happen if the BFIC's financial resources are insufficient to pay damages once liability is established: it would be difficult to accept for the supervised institutions to ultimately bear the costs of liability through (increased) contributions to the BFIC. Therefore, it may be submitted that, to the extent the BFIC exercises a task of public interest, a budget deficit of the BFIC following an obligation to pay damages in liability should ultimately be borne by the state.

Possible cases of liability: a cross-country analysis

Notwithstanding the differences outlined already in this chapter between different EU countries as regards the standards for supervisory liability, the situations in which depositors have sought to hold supervisory authorities liable do not substantially differ in fact. A cross-country analysis of the case law illustrates that liability, when it is not totally excluded by law, can occur under different circumstances. This allows us to further refine the possible situations of potential liability in different aspects of supervision over credit institutions.

Supervisory action as regards illicit banking activities

According to the EU Coordinated Banking Directive,[59] all credit institutions should, prior to taking up a banking activity, obtain an authorisation from the competent authority in their home member state. The directive does not oblige member states to entrust supervisory authorities with powers of investigation in order to search for the possible illicit taking-up of banking activities by non-authorised firms. To the extent that supervisory authorities only have supervisory powers as regards duly authorised credit institutions, as is the case, for example, in France,[60] they may not be held liable for losses incurred by creditors of non-authorised firms. By contrast, when individual member states have granted investigative powers to supervisory authorities, as is the case in Belgium[61] and Germany,[62] the existence of such powers may be important for possible liability cases, to the extent that depositors might suffer damages as a result of illicit deposit-taking business by non-authorised enterprises.[63] The precise scope of such investigative powers should be taken into account when assessing supervisory liability: generally, the investigative powers cannot be analysed as a legal obligation to actually prevent any illicit banking business, but more as a duty to duly monitor possible irregular situations. Liability could then, for instance, occur when the supervisory authority, after having been informed of possible illicit activities (for example, advertisements in newspaper, complaints from customers), failed to accurately investigate and follow up the indications it possessed. The supervisor should take all reasonable action in order to put a halt to overt irregular situations, or enquire into situations that cast doubt as to their legality.

The granting, or refusal to grant, a banking licence

As a rule, the decision to grant a banking licence is not discretionary for the banking supervisor: the supervisory authority cannot make its decision dependent on the economic needs of the market,[64] and it is normally obliged to grant a licence to every applicant that satisfies the authorisation conditions laid down by law. This is not to say that the banking supervisor has no leeway at all in deciding how to apply the authorisation requirements: many authorisation requirements are very generally worded, and leave room for discretion to the supervisor (for example, the requirement of adequate internal organisation and internal controls within the credit institution). The Coordinated Banking Directive provides for adequate legal remedies for the applicant when the banking supervisor refuses to grant a banking authorisation (for example, judicial review).[65] The possibility for judicial scrutiny also implies that the banking supervisor should indicate the reasons for its refusal to grant a licence.[66]

Apart from the possibility to quash the supervisor's refusal through a judicial review, a decision to refuse a licence could lead to supervisory liability towards the applicant, to the extent that the refusal has deprived the latter of a commercially profitable opportunity.[67] Equally, the banking supervisor that does improperly consider a bank manager as being not 'fit and proper' runs a liability risk towards the latter.

The reverse situation – the banking supervisor is blamed, mainly by depositors, for having granted a banking licence to a credit institution that did not satisfy the legal requirements for it – also occurs, and has in fact been repeatedly invoked before the courts in different countries.[68] The courts are understandably reluctant to accept liability for these motives,[69] as they have to judge on the facts as they appeared at the moment of granting the authorisation, and should avoid the pitfall of an *a posteriori* assessment of the situation. The court should only examine whether, at the time of applying for a banking licence, the applicant satisfied the legal requirements for it, and whether any indications were present which could possibly justify subjecting the authorisation to certain conditions or even refusing it. If the bank satisfies the legal authorisation requirements at the time of granting the licence, the supervisor has not acted improperly. In reality, most difficulties in financial institutions only appear during their existence, and cannot be reduced to unjustified decisions from the part of the supervisor when granting the licence.

Ongoing prudential supervision and intervention measures

The most frequently occurring cases of supervisory liability are related to the supervisor's 'crisis management' of financially troubled credit institutions: after an occurrence of a banking failure, the supervisor is blamed by third parties, mostly depositors, for not having reacted adequately to indications of financial deterioration or fraud within the supervised financial institution, and consequently to be liable for the accumulation of losses suffered by the plaintiffs. The question of whether the supervisory authority has acted with due care and diligence should be assessed by taking account of the factual situation at the time of the difficulties and of the instruments and means the supervisor generally possesses to intervene towards the troubled financial institution.

In all legal systems examined, it is clear that the supervisory instruments and means created by law do not enable continual supervision through on-site verifications. Supervision is basically exercised on the basis of reporting requirements imposed on credit institutions, by means of either periodic reports or specific reports on certain issues commissioned by the supervisory authority to the credit institution itself or to its auditors. On-site verifications are mainly intended to verify from time to time the data gathered through the reports. When the reports provided to the supervisory authority contain indications of irregularities, inconsistencies or financial difficulties, it may however reasonably be expected that the supervisory authority will adopt a more proactive attitude towards the supervised financial institution. This might, depending on the circumstances, lead to a request for additional information on the part of the bank or even to an on-site verification.[70] The case law indicates that this is considered a critical element in assessing 'reasonable care' by the supervisory authority: it is crucial to adequately follow up and monitor problems which the supervisor has discovered through its normal supervisory activity or through information received from third parties,[71] and to take measures which are adequate to the situation. Moreover, in choosing the intervention measures that the law offers to the supervisor, the latter should act proportionately to the gravity of the situation. For instance, in the case where there are indications of serious fraud within the institution, taking measures towards bank management will be more appropriate than in the case of a deteriorated financial situation that is caused by inadequate internal controls. As supervisory authorities enjoy a large degree of discretion in the choice and use of intervention measures, the judge should refrain from 'taking the supervisor's seat', and substituting its judgment for the supervisor's decision. The judge should merely assess whether the supervisory authority, after having balanced the interests of both the bank itself and its stakeholders, could reasonably decide as it actually did. This implies, for instance, that the mere fact that the banking supervisor did not react to problems discovered within a financial institution does not, in itself, lead to liability.[72] Basically, the courts will have to decide whether, at that time, the supervisor's action was adequate to deal with the situation, taking account of its seriousness,[73] without being too stringent as to unduly frustrate the depositors' confidence.

The case law indicates that liability may in these circumstances occur when the supervisor failed to take any action notwithstanding the knowledge of serious difficulties within the financial institution, or when the measures taken were inadequate in view of the seriousness of the problems (for example, by giving an 'ultimate warning' only, without further action, despite the existence of serious irregularities[74]). Equally, the supervisor should be consistent in its action: liability could arise when the supervisor first ordered a credit institution to recapitalise and take other redress action, but subsequently softened its demands without objective justification.[75] Under these circumstances, the supervisor might be blamed for not having withdrawn the bank's authorisation when it appeared that the depositors' interests were seriously threatened.

Supervisory liability: the EU context

Although the various EU directives aimed at creating an integrated EU banking and financial services market do not directly touch upon supervisory liability, the ongoing process of financial integration nevertheless indirectly influences this issue. Two elements deserve further attention: first, the implications of the system of home-country control for supervisory liability in terms of identification of the supervisory authority which bears responsibility, for the law applicable to liability claims and for the court competent to decide on such claims. Second, the Europeanisation of supervisory law raises the fundamental question of whether supervisory liability could be based directly on EU law. This issue is critical in view of the disparities existing between member states as regards supervisory liability. Founding supervisory liability directly on EU law could allow depositors to circumvent immunity regimes existing in their national laws.

Supervisory liability in a home-country control paradigm

With the creation of a European passport and home-country prudential supervision, the Coordinated Banking Directive not only shifts responsibility for prudential supervision to the country of origin, but also liability: depositors with a branch of a credit institution with its head office in another EU member state will have to direct their liability claims against the home-state supervisory authority. This shift in the subject of liability also has important consequences for the law applicable to a liability claim and the determination of the competent judge to decide on such claims. The rules of private international law with respect to cross-border liability issues will generally lead to the applicability of the home country law.[76] As regards the determination of the territorially competent judge, depositors could theoretically bring an action against the foreign (home-country) supervisory authority before the courts in the host country, by virtue of the applicable European rules.[77] In reality, however, it is most unlikely that a home-state public authority would accept the jurisdiction of a host-state court. According to a commonly accepted principle in international law, sovereign states normally enjoy immunity before foreign jurisdictions. As prudential supervision directly emanates from public authority, this rule could equally apply to supervisory authorities.[78] As a consequence, depositors might in fact be forced to also bring a liability claim against the foreign supervisory authority before the courts of the home country.

It appears from the foregoing that the legal protection depositors enjoy as regards supervisory action may differ according to the competent supervisory authority in a system of home-country control: to the extent the home-state supervisor enjoys (partial) immunity from liability, this regime would also affect depositors of foreign EU branches, while depositors with local banks in the host country could possibly be better protected. However, this risk of inequality is not unique, as it also appears in other aspects connected with home-country rule and mutual recognition, such as a deposit guarantee.[79] Contrary to the latter situation, which is clearly enacted in the EU directives and about which banks should inform their depositors, the implications of home-country control on supervisory liability have hardly been explored until now. Nevertheless, further convergence as regards responsibility for supervision in a home-country control paradigm and the legal effects of it as regards liability, with respect to both applicable law and international jurisdiction, should be welcomed, as they increase, at least from the perspective of the supervisory authority, legal certainty as to the legal framework of supervisory action.

On the other hand, further cross-country convergence as regards supervisory liability would be more consistent with the aim of an integrated market, where decisions to allocate deposits should not be influenced by possibly diverging liability regimes.[80] In this regard, it is of critical importance to find the right balance between the legitimate expectations of depositors as to the quality of prudential supervision, and the need to allocate primary responsibility for bank failures to the banks themselves and their stakeholders. As we have already indicated, we believe that systems which generally eliminate liability or limit it to bad faith on the part of the supervisor do not strike a fair balance between the interests at stake, and might fail to sufficiently discipline supervisory authorities to exercise due care in their tasks. On the other hand, courts should take into account the nature and complexity of prudential supervision in assessing possible liability.

Should further convergence as regards supervisory liability be achieved through European regulation? This would not be necessary to the extent that other means can achieve the same objective. In the following section, we argue that the doctrine of state liability for non-compliance with EU law, as developed by the European Court of Justice, can lead to the desired convergence, and at the same time avoids excesses in the assessment of supervisory liability.

Founding supervisory liability on EU law

The jurisprudential context: Francovich *liability*

Since its landmark *Francovich*-judgment[81] the European Court of Justice has consistently held that a member state could be held liable for non-fulfilment of its obligations under EU law, and that this liability could be legally based on EU law, not on the law of individual member states. The Court considers that the legal protection of individuals against member states could not differ from the protection that is granted to them under Article 228, para. 2 EC against the institutions of the European Union.[82]

Since the obligation to exercise prudential supervision and the minimum requirements attached to it are determined by the various EU banking directives, it could be argued that shortcomings in the exercise of prudential supervision constitute a breach of the member states' obligations under the EU directives, and therefore could form the legal foundation for a liability claim directed against the member state for the acts or omissions of its supervisory authority. However, according to the Court's case law, a number of conditions must be satisfied in order to establish *Francovich*-liability, namely:

1   there should be a breach by the member state of its obligations under EU law;
2   the allegedly breached rule is intended to grant rights to private individuals;
3   there must be a serious breach of Community law;
4   there is a direct causal link between the breach of Community law and the damages suffered by the victims.

These conditions will be further examined in the context of supervisory liability.

Application of Francovich-*liability to deficient prudential supervision*

BREACH OF AN OBLIGATION IMPOSED BY EU LAW

The Court's case law witnesses a flexible approach as regards the first condition for member state liability: both the source of the breached rule (EC Treaty or provision of secondary legislation, such as directives) and the originator of the breach (executive power, independent agency, Parliament or judiciary) are irrelevant in order to establish member state liability. Furthermore, recent case law suggests that liability could arise out of both a normative breach of European law, and individual breaches, for instance in the application of rules of European origin in individual cases.

This leads to a further refinement as regards possible liability cases: on the one hand, state liability could arise when a member state has failed to duly implement EU banking directives into national law, and thus has caused damage to private individuals. This situation is generally considered per se as a serious breach of EU law. An interesting application in the sphere of banking can be found in two German court decisions, which held the German state liable for not having implemented the 1994 Deposit Guarantee Directive on time. The plaintiffs, who were depositors with a German-based bank that went bankrupt, successfully invoked *Francovich*-liability against the German state, which was held to indemnify the depositors for the losses they had incurred as a consequence of the non-existence of a deposit guarantee system in compliance with the directive. Every depositor was awarded an indemnity of up to €20,000, corresponding to the minimum coverage level to be offered by each deposit guarantee system to be instituted under the 1994 directive.[83]

By contrast, supervisory liability is not related to a normative incompatibility of national law with EU law, but concerns the alleged improper application of obligations under national law, which originates in EU law, where the former is compatible with the latter. Although the case law of the European Court of Justice with respect to *Francovich*-liability principally concerned issues of normative breach of EU law, at least one case accepted *Francovich*-liability in a situation of non-normative breach of EU law.[84] As a consequence, the circumstance that supervisory liability is not concerned with a normative breach of EU law does not preclude the application of the *Francovich*-doctrine.[85]

BREACH OF A RULE WHICH IS INTENDED TO GRANT RIGHTS TO PRIVATE
INDIVIDUALS

Critical in applying *Francovich*-liability is the condition that the breached rule, in particular the prudential requirements imposed by the EU directives, are intended to confer rights to private individuals. This requirement in fact incorporates the 'relativity' rule in the *Francovich* doctrine: an analysis of the objectives of the EU prudential rules must indicate their purpose to protect private individuals. The case law of the European Court of Justice, however, witnesses a quite flexible approach as to this requirement: it is not required that the EU rules satisfy the conditions of direct applicability, being worded in a precise and unconditional way such as to allow private individuals to invoke them directly before the courts. The Court is satisfied with the demonstration that the EU rules are intended to protect the *interests* of private individuals.[86]

It is submitted that the prudential rules imposed by the EU banking directives effectively satisfy this condition. It appears clearly, from both the preamble to the Coordinated Banking Directive and from its provisions, which embody the core of prudential rules and the obligation to organise prudential supervision, that the directives aim at protecting both the interests of credit institutions and depositors. It is clear that the prudential rules, which constitute the harmonisation deemed necessary to realise an integrated market,[87] intend to create a climate of confidence amongst member states and for depositors and other bank customers which is a necessary precondition for allowing cross-border banking business. Moreover, the case law of the European Court of Justice in the area of banking has repeatedly stressed the importance of the provisions on banking authorisation and prudential rules in terms of protection of the consumer.[88] The objective of creditor and depositor protection is finally also embodied in Article 4 of the Coordinated Banking Directive, which, as a rule, allows only credit institutions subject to prudential supervision to accept deposits from the public.[89]

Recently, a few cases were decided in national courts, both in England and in Germany, where the plaintiffs invoked *Francovich*-liability for alleged deficient prudential supervision over a troubled bank. First, in the BCCI liability claim introduced against the Bank of England, the Court of Appeal, and subsequently the House of Lords, examined whether all requirements for establishing *Francovich*-liability were met. In the Court of Appeal, two out of the three judges considered that EU prudential regulation was not intended to grant rights to private individuals,[90] but the third judge expressed a thoroughly explained dissenting opinion.[91] Upon appeal, the House of Lords confirmed the Court of Appeal's decision, following the opinion expressed by Lord Hope of Craighead:[92] the latter strongly advocated that the EU directives[93] were intended primarily to harmonise prudential regulation with a view to creating a single banking market, without imposing a general obligation to exercise prudential supervision or conferring rights in this respect to individuals.[94] In his Lordship's view, the protection of depositors was just one element that had been taken into account in the harmonisation process amongst others, such as the establishment of competitive equality between credit institutions. Surprisingly, however, the House of Lords did not deem it necessary to refer this important issue related to the interpretation of the banking directives to the European Court of Justice for a preliminary ruling, arguing that the directives were not open for diverging interpretation (so-called *acte clair*-doctrine). As a consequence, the House of Lord's decision barred the attempt made by the plaintiffs to circumvent the statutory limitation of supervisory liability as contained in the 1987 Banking Act. It may be submitted that the fierce opposition to submit the issue to the Court of Justice might in part be inspired by a desire to keep control over the case in 'national' hands and to preserve the statutory protection against liability granted to the Bank of England.[95]

A similar reluctance as to incorporation of *Francovich*-liability in prudential supervision appeared in a recent German Court of Appeal decision,[96] where the plaintiffs argued that the immunity from supervisory liability existing in German law was incompatible with the European banking directives, to the extent the latter granted rights to individuals. The Court of Appeal dismissed the argument, without extensively explaining it. However, the plaintiffs appealed against the judgment before the German Supreme Court (*Bundesgerichtshof*), and again alleged that the conditions for *Francovich*-liability were met with regard to different EU banking directives, which oblige the member states to exercise prudential supervision over credit institutions. The German Supreme Court, in contrast to the English House of Lords, admitted that this raised questions as to the interpretation of the banking directives, which were far from clear. As a consequence, the Supreme Court made an interim judgment,[97] in which it submitted a series of preliminary questions to the European Court of Justice, which essentially concern the issue of whether various EU banking directives[98] can form the basis for *Francovich*-liability of the German state for alleged deficient prudential supervision. The case is currently pending before the European Court of Justice. Ultimately, a positive answer by the European Court of Justice would lead to incompatibility of the German statutory immunity from liability, or at least enable its circumvention as far as the application of EU-originated prudential rules is concerned. The open attitude from the part of the German Supreme Court should be welcomed. Submitting the issue to the European Court of Justice will contribute to more uniformity in the interpretation of the banking directives as regards *Francovich*-liability.

SERIOUS BREACH OF EU LAW

The requirement of a serious breach of Community law,[99] has important implications in the context of supervisory liability: as already indicated, member states enjoy a certain discretion in applying the often generally worded provisions of EU banking law in day-to-day supervision, both as regards authorisation requirements[100] and for ongoing prudential requirements.[101] This leads to the conclusion that *Francovich*-liability allows to counter the risk of excessive liability claims: it appears from the case law of the European Court of Justice that a 'serious' breach will only occur when the supervisory authority has manifestly and gravely disregarded the limits on the exercise of its discretionary powers.[102] In other words, the concerns that have led some national courts to incorporate the complexity and limited means of supervision into their liability assessment can equally be met when founding liability on *Francovich*. Where, by contrast, prudential requirements in the banking directives prescribe a clear obligation, a 'serious' breach will follow from the mere non-compliance with the obligation (for example, authorisation of a credit institution which does not satisfy the initial capital requirement of €5 million).

CAUSATION

A member state will only be held for damages when there is a direct link of causation between the serious breach of EU law and the damage suffered by private individuals. Applied to the situation of deficiencies in prudential supervision, the requirement of a direct causal link can constitute a further buffer to effectively holding a member state to compensate depositors for deficient prudential supervision: the member state will only be held to compensate the victims for those damages which are directly connected to an alleged shortcoming in exercising prudential supervision.

Conclusion on Francovich-*type liability and prudential supervision*

The analysis of the conditions attached to *Francovich*-type liability as applied to supervisory liability has showed that accepting a basis for liability in EU law should not necessarily lead to excessive liability claims. In fact, the corrective techniques used in different countries aimed at incorporating the complexities of supervision and the primary responsibility of the supervised institution into the liability decision, can also be applied under *Francovich*-liability: *Francovich*-type liability does not only allow the circumstances of fact in which the supervisor's behaviour should be assessed to be fully taken into account, avoiding thereby an *a posteriori* assessment.[103] Moreover, the leeway left to supervisory authorities in the actual exercise of prudential supervision, and the arbitrage to be made between different, sometimes conflicting interests, will also, in *Francovich*-liability, influence the role of the judge: it is not up to the judge to substitute itself to a banking supervisor, but merely to assess whether the supervisory authority, in the given circumstances of time and facts, should reasonably have acted as it has done.

In the end, the conditions attached to *Francovich*-liability are largely similar to the way the courts in different member states have approached supervisory liability under general tort law.[104] However, accepting *Francovich*-liability as regards deficient prudential supervision would offer a substantial additional protection to depositors in those member states that, at present, apply a full or partial immunity from liability. We believe that accepting a *Francovich*-type supervisory liability would be beneficial in two respects: first, given the disciplining effects on the banking supervisor's behaviour, accepting liability would increase the reputation of the system in an international perspective ('competition for excellence'). Second, applying a similar liability regime in a single European market would eliminate potential competitive distortions between member states, and create a level playing field between member states. This is all the more important in view of the system of home-country control, which also shifts liability to the home-country supervisor.

General conclusion

Although supervisory liability has been discussed in several EU member states for quite some time, recent cases show that it appears under a new dimension in the context of the Europeanisation of supervisory law. We have tried to demonstrate that there should be no *a priori* reluctance to allowing EU law to serve as a legal basis for supervisory liability, as it contains all elements to achieve a well-balanced liability regime which takes due account of the complexities of prudential supervision. It will then be up to the courts not to over-protect depositors and to avoid the temptation of the 'deep-pocket syndrome' in allocating liability for bank failures to the state.

However, from an EU perspective, the issue of supervisory liability still is 'under construction', and different orientations have been identified: on the one hand, individual member states increasingly tend to limit supervisory liability through statutory immunity regimes, thereby supported by the Basle Committee's *Core Principles*. On the other hand, depositors increasingly put pressure on national courts by relying on EU law as a legal foundation for supervisory liability in order to circumvent limitations originating in member states' law. We have argued that allowing *Francovich*-liability in the field of prudential supervision allows a fair balance to be found between the legitimate expectations from depositors in the quality of supervision and the risk of systematically shifting the cost of banking failures to government.

With the prospect of accession in 2004, the discussions about supervisory liability will increasingly influence most of the Central and Eastern European Countries (CEECs) as well. As CEECs have incorporated the *acquis communautaire* into their national laws, or are in the process of doing so, most of them already operate under similar prudential standards as the EU member states. However, building a stable and sound banking system requires more than simply 'transplanting' the legal rules.[105] It also requires the setting up of well-staffed supervisory agencies that can effectively ensure high-quality supervision. Supervisory liability could also in this context serve as a disciplining factor. If the outcome of the German case currently pending before the Court of Justice leads to the acceptance of *Francovich*-liability in the field of banking supervision, policymakers both in the EU and the CEECs should be aware of the imperative need to ensure high standards not only in regulation, but also in day-to-day supervision at all times.

Notes

1 See, for instance, in England: *Melton Medes* v. *Securities and Investment Board* [1995] 2 *Weekly Law Reports*, p. 247.
2 J.-W. van der Vossen (1992) 'Supervisory standards and sanctions', in M. van Empel and R. Smits (eds), *Banking and EC Law Commentary*, Amsterdam Financial Series, Deventer: Kluwer, looseleaf, (March), pp. 48–49.
3 There is, however, an important difference between both situations which makes the supervisor's dilemma even more acute: while the bank-borrower relationship stems from a contract, the prudential supervisor embodies the

public interest in discharging its legal duty to supervise. Nevertheless, it should be noted that the existence of lender liability also rests on the assumption that banks are 'special' in relation to other creditors, and sometimes have (wrongfully) been considered as exercising a public interest duty in granting loans.

4　See also R. Smits and R. Luberti (1999) 'Supervisory liability: an introduction to several legal systems and a case study', in M. Giovanoli and G. Heinrich (eds), *International Bank Insolvencies: A Central Bank Perspective*. London: Kluwer Law International, 363, p. 367.

5　In the European Union, the 1994 Deposit Guarantee Directive provides for the creation or recognition by the member states of deposit guarantee systems which should provide a minimum coverage of at least up to €20,000 in the event of a bank failure. Member states may provide for a higher coverage ceiling.

6　Indeed, within the European Union, government funding or support for deposit guarantee systems could be considered a state aid contrary to Article 87 EC.

7　Basle Committee on Banking Supervision (1997) *Core Principles for Effective Banking Supervision*, Basle, September 46 p., http://www.bis.org/pub/bcbs30a.pdf.

8　See, *inter alia*, Bundesgerichtshof 31 March 1960, *Neue Juristische Wochenschrift*, 1960, p. 1005; Bundesgerichtshof 28 April 1960, *Versicherungsrecht*, 1960, p. 979; Bundesgerichtshof 27 May 1963, *Neue Juristische Wochenschrift*, 1963, p. 1821; See also K. Bender (1978) 'Die Amtspflichten des Bundesaufsichtsamtes für das Kreditwesen gegenüber einzelnen Gläubigern eines Kreditinstituts', *Neue Juristische Wochenschrift*, p. 622.

9　Oberlandesgericht Bremen, 13 November 1952, *Neue Juristische Wochenschrift*, 1953, p. 585; Oberlandesgericht Hamburg, 28 June 1957, *Betriebs-Berater*, 1957, p. 950; See also H.Ch. Kopf and H. Bäumler (1979) 'Die neue Rechtsprechung des BGH zur Amtshaftung im bereich der Bankenaufsicht', *Neue Juristische Wochenschrift*, p. 1871.

10　See Oberlandesgericht Köln, 19 September 1977, *Neue Juristische Wochenschrift*, 1977, p. 2213.

11　Bundesgerichtshof 24 January 1972, *Neue Juristische Wochenschrift*, 1972, p. 577; Critically: R. Scholz (1972) 'Versicherungsaufsicht und Amtshaftung', *Neue Juristische Wochenschrift*, pp. 1217–1219. The Supreme Court considered in the same judgment that an identical rule applied for banking supervision, although the banking act was not at stake in the case.

12　Bundesgerichtshof 15 February 1979, (*Wetterstein*), *Neue Juristische Wochenschrift*, 1979, p. 1354; Bundesgerichtshof 12 July 1979, (*Herstatt*), *Neue Juristische Wochenschrift*, 1979, p. 1879, *Juristenzeitung*, 1979, p. 683, *Wertpapier-Mitteilungen*, 1979, p. 632. The latter case, introduced in the aftermath of the *Herstatt* bankruptcy, annulled the judgment of the Oberlandesgericht Köln, 19 September 1977, cited *supra* note 10.

13　See Bundesgerichtshof 15 March 1984, *Neue Juristische Wochenschrift*, 1984, p. 2691; this is similar to the English case law: (see pages 142–143).

14　Compare H.-J. Papier (1986) in K. Rebmann and F.J. Säcker (eds), *Münchener Kommentar zum BGB*. Vol. 3, 2nd edn, München: Beck, §839, para. 216, p. 1942.

15　For a general overview, see E. Habscheid (1988) *Staatshaftung für fehlsame Bankenaufsicht?* Bielefeld: Giese King, p. 42 et seq. and the references cited in Note 1.

16　See, *inter alia*, E. Bleibaum (1982) *Die Rechtsprechung des BGH zur Staatshaftung im Bereich der Bankenaufsicht* Würzburg, p. 22 et seq.; H. Hahn and E.

Bleibaum (1983) 'Bankenaufsicht und Staatshaftung', in H. Hahn (ed.) (1983) *Institutionen des Währungswesens*, Baden-Baden: Nomos, p. 118; T. Niethammer (1990) *Die Ziele der Bankenaufsicht in der Bundesrepublik Deutschland.* Berlin: Duncker & Humblot, p. 153; G. Püttner (1982) 'Von der Bankenaufsicht zur Staatsgarantie für Bankeinlagen?', *Juristenzeitung*, pp. 47–50; E. Schwark (1979) 'Individualansprüche Privater aus wirtschaftsrechtlichen Gesetzen', *Juristenzeitung*, pp. 673–674.

17 H.Ch. Kopf and H. Bäumler, *l.c.*, op cit., *supra* note 9, pp. 1872–1873.

18 A new appeal against this decision before the Supreme Court was unsuccessful: see Bundesgerichtshof 21 October 1982, *Neue Juritische Wochenschrift*, 1983, p. 563.

19 W.M. Waldeck (1985) 'Die Novellierung des Kreditwesengesetzes', *Neue Juristische Wochenschrift*, p. 892; F. Rittner (1987) *Wirtschaftsrecht*, 2nd edn, Heidelberg: C.F. Müller, p. 583; N. Horn and P. Balzer (1995) 'Germany', in *Banking Supervision in the European Community. Institutional Aspects*, Brussels: Editions de l'ULB, p. 142; P. Claussen (1996) *Bank- und Börsenrecht.* München: Beck, pp. 40–41, para. 15.
See, however, M. Brendle (1987) *Amtshaftung für fehlsame Bankenaufsicht?* Darmstadt: S. Toeche-Mittler Verlag, pp. 442 and 565, who considers that §6 III *Kreditwesengesetz* does not touch upon the individually protective aspect of banking supervision.

20 See §1, para. 4 *Börsengesetz*; §4, para. 2 *WertpapierHandelsGesetz*; §81, para. 1, third sentence *Versicherungsaufsichtsgesetz*.

21 §4, para. 4 of the *Finanzdienstleistungsaufsichtsgesetz* (FinDAG) dated 22 April 2002 (*BGBl* I, 2002, p. 1310) states that the integrated supervisor (*Bundesanstalt für Finanzdienstleistungsaufsicht*) may exercise its functions and use its powers solely in the general interest.

22 For an extensive analysis, see E. Habscheid, op. cit., *supra* note 15, p. 85 et seq.; H.-J. Papier, op. cit., *supra* note 14, para. 215. See also, more recently, M. Gratias (1999) *Staatshaftung für fehlerhafte Banken- und Versicherungsaufsicht im Europäischen Binnenmarkt.* Baden-Baden: Nomos, pp. 79–94.

23 See Oberlandesgericht Köln, 11 January 2001, *ZIP – Zeitschrift für Wirtschaftsrecht*, p. 645; *Wertpapier-Mitteilungen*, p. 1372; *Entscheidungen zum Wirtschaftsrecht*, 2001/20, 962, note R. Sethe. An appeal against this judgment has been made before the German Supreme Court (see page 155), in which the incompatibility of §6 III Kreditwesengesetz with the German constitution has also been invoked. No final judgment has been delivered yet by the Supreme Court.

24 *Yuen-Kun-yeu and others* v. *Attorney General of Hong-Kong* [Privy Council], [1987] 2 *The All England Law Reports*, p. 705

25 A similar case was decided with respect to the banking legislation of the Isle of Man: see *Davis* v. *Ratcliffe*, [1990] 1 *Weekly Law Reports*, p. 821.

26 *Minories Finance Ltd* v. *Arthur Young* (a firm) (Bank of England, third party); *Johnson Matthey plc* v. *Arthur Young* (a firm) (Bank of England, third party) [QBD], [1989] 2 *The All England Law Reports*, p. 105.

27 See also *Hall* v. *Bank of England* [CA], 19 April 1995, cited in Ch. Proctor (2002) 'Financial regulators – risks and liabilities', *Butterworths Journal of International Banking and Financial Law*, p. 19, where the shareholders of the deposit-taking company blamed the Bank of England for having instructed the management to proceed to the sale of assets, causing losses to the shareholders.

28 See s. 187 Financial Services Act 1986.

29 See Schedule I, Section 19(3) Financial Services and Markets Act 2000.

30 See G. Penn (1989) *Banking Supervision. Regulation of the UK Banking Sector under the Banking Act 1987*, London: Butterworths, p. 22.

31 Compare E.P. Ellinger and E. Lomnicka (1994) *Modern Banking Law*, 2nd edn, Oxford: Clarendon Press, p. 32, according to whom the statutory provision has eliminated separate actions under common law.

32 See about the claims introduced: A. Jack (1993) 'BCCI depositors sue Bank for failing as regulator', *Financial Times*, 25 May. It appeared that 6,019 depositors introduced the claim against the Bank of England: See *Three Rivers District Council and Others* v. *Governor and Company of the Bank of England* [CA], [1995] 3 *Weekly Law Reports*, p. 650, [1995] 4 *The All England Law Reports*, p. 312.

33 *Three Rivers District Council and others* v. *Bank of England (No. 3)*, [1996] 3 *The All England Law Reports*, p. 558 [QBD].

34 *Three Rivers District Council and others* v. *Bank of England*, [1999] 4 *The All England Law Reports*, p. 800 [CA].

35 *Three Rivers District Council and Others (original appellants and cross-respondents)* v. *Governor and Company of the Bank of England (original respondents and cross-appellants)*, [2000] 2 *Weekly Law Reports*, p. 1220. See also http://www.publications.parliament.uk/pa/ld199900/ldjudgmt/jd000518/rivers-1.htm. Hitherto, no final decision has been made on the facts of the case: see Ch. Proctor (2001) 'BCCI: suing the supervisor', *The Financial Regulator*, No. 6, p. 35 et seq.; Ch. Proctor, 'Financial regulators . . .', op. cit., *supra* note 27, pp. 15–19.

36 See also Ch. Proctor, 'BCCI: suing the supervisor', op. cit., *supra* note 35, p. 37, who assimilates *misfeasance in public office* to *bad faith*. Compare *Three Rivers District Council and others* v. *Bank of England (No. 3)*, [1996] 3 *The All England Law Reports*, (558), p. 596 j, in which the court decides that the existence of misfeasance in public office under *common law* implies the demonstration that the defendant acts in bad faith in the sense of section 1(4) Banking Act 1987.

37 Apparently, a liability claim has also been filed against the banking supervisory authority in the aftermath of the BCCI failure, the holding company of which was established in Luxembourg: see E. de Lhoneux and M. Cromlin (1995) 'Luxembourg', in *Banking Supervision in the European Community*, Brussels: Editions de l'ULB, p. 233. The outcome of that liability claim is unknown.

38 Law of 23 December 1998, 'portant création d'une commission de surveillance du secteur financier', *Mémorial*, A no. 112, 24 December 1998.

39 See Art. 20 Law of 23 December 1998.

40 See A. Elvinger (1994) 'Histoire du droit bancaire et financier luxembourgeois', in *Droit bancaire et financier au Grand-Duché de Luxembourg*. Brussels: Larcier, vol. 1, pp. 44–45, para. 144; E. de Lhoneux and M. Cromlin, op. cit., *supra* note 37, p. 234.

41 This has not changed in recent years. For instance, in the aftermath of the BCCI failure, more than 60 liability claims were brought before the courts in France (see Commission Bancaire, *Rapport 1994*, p. 96). The withdrawal of the authorisation of 'United Banking Corporation' in 1993 provoked more than 80 claims (Commission Bancaire, *Rapport 1993*, p. 90), and led to the landmark 'Kechichian'-judgment of the Conseil d'Etat in 2001 (see footnote 42).

42 See Conseil d'Etat 24 January 1964, *Achard, Juris-Classeur Périodique*, 1965, édition Générale., II, No. 14416, and recently Conseil d'Etat 30 November 2001, *Kechichian, Juris-Classeur Périodique*, 2002, édition Générale, II, No 10042, with note J.-J. Menuret, *Petites Affiches*, 2002, No. 28, p. 7, with opinion of A. Seban.

43 For an overview of the relevant case-law, see F. Moderne, note under Conseil d'Etat 29 December 1978, *Recueil Dalloz*, 1979, I.R., p. 155.

44 See, for the first application of this jurisprudence, Tribunal des Conflits, 8 February 1873, *Recueil Dalloz*, 1873, III, p. 17, which grants to the administrative courts, and not to the civil courts, exclusive competence as regards liability claims directed against public authorities. However, as regards liability of the Commission des Opérations de Bourse, the Cour d'Appel of Paris is considered to be competent, not the administrative courts.

45 See for the first case Conseil d'Etat 12 February 1960 (2 cases), *Banque*, 1960, p. 320, note X. Marin.

46 See, for instance, the criticism voiced by J. Becqué and H. Cabrillac (1960) 'Chronique de législation et de jurisprudence françaises', *Revue trimestrielle de Droit civil*, p. 614. Others found in the approach adopted by the Conseil d'Etat a right balance between the duty to supervise on the one hand and the risk of shifting the cost of all bank failures to the state on the other: see, for instance, F. Moderne, note under Conseil d'Etat 29 December 1978, *Recueil Dalloz*, 1979, I.R. p. 155; M. Waline, note under Conseil d'Etat 13 June 1964, *Revue de droit public*, 1965, p. 82; R. Denoix de Saint-Marc (1986) 'Rapport français', in *La responsabilité du banquier: aspects nouveaux*, Travaux de l'Association Capitant, Vol. XXXV, Paris: Economica, p. 573.

47 See for an analysis D. Fairgrieve and K. Belloir (1999) 'Liability of the French state for negligent supervision of banks', *European Business Law Review*, p. 17; M. Andenas and D. Fairgrieve (2000) 'To supervise or to compensate?', in M. Andenas and D. Fairgrieve (eds), *Liber amicorum Lord Slynn of Hadley: Judicial Review in International Perspective*. London: Kluwer.

48 Interesting in this respect are two judgments delivered by the Cour Administrative d'Appel (TAA) of Paris: TAA Paris 30 March 1999, *El Skikh, La Semaine Juridique*, 2000, Edition Générale., II, No. 10276; TAA Paris 25 January 2000, *Kechichian*. The latter decision was subsequently quashed by the Conseil d'Etat.

49 Conseil d'Etat 30 November 2001, op. cit., *supra* note 42. The judgment is the more important as it was decided in full court, and not merely in one of the Conseil's chambers.

50 Again, the explanation advanced by the court to limit liability to gross negligence was extremely short: the Court merely stressed that supervisory liability could not be a substitute to the primary responsibility of a bank towards its depositors.

51 Cour d'Appel Paris, 6 April 1994, *Bulletin Joly Bourse*, 1994, 259, note J.-M. Desache.

52 See, *inter alia*, opinion of A. Seban in Conseil d'Etat 30 November 2001, *Kechichian, Petites Affiches*, 2002, No. 28, (7), pp. 10–11; J.-J. Menuret, note under Conseil d'Etat 30 November 2001, *La Semaine Juridique*, 2002, Edition Générale., II, No. 10042, p. 502, para. 7.

53 Although one decision has been reported with respect to supervision over securities brokers: see Cour de Cassation 9 October 1975, *Revue critique de jurisprudence belge*, 1976, p. 165, note A. d'Ieteren and R.O. Dalcq.

54 Since the landmark judgment of the Cour de Cassation in the Flandria-case (judgment of 5 November 1920, *Pasicrisie*, 1920, I, p. 193) it is clear that public authorites are subject to the same liability standards as private individuals. Different court decisions have referred to possible liability of the prudential supervisor, without ever accepting it in the facts of the case: see Court of First Instance, Brussels 28 June 1955, *Journal des Tribunaux*, 1956, p. 71; President Commercial Court Bruges 15 January 1982, *Rechtskundig Weekblad*,

1982–1983, column 2784; Court of First Instance Brussels, 24 October 1994, *Bank- en Financier wezen*, 1995/4, p. 232.

55 Indeed, under German law, the rule that supervision only serves the general interest is motivated by the existence of a 'relativity'-requirement in liability law. Belgian law does not, however, require 'relativity' as a precondition for establishing liability.

56 Through reference to the BFIC's statutory tasks in general, the limitation of liability will encompass all functions taken up by the BFIC, including its supervision over public offer prospectuses and take-overs. This clearly exceeds the motivation for partial immunity advanced by Government, which referred only to the BFIC's prudential functions.

57 It is submitted, however, that the inclusion of the statutory limitation of liability was, at least in part, also provoked by the liability claim introduced against the BFIC after the failure of Bank Fisher by a number of former depositors.

58 See Article 44, Act of 2 August 2002.

59 Article 4, Directive 2000/12/EC of the European Parliament and of the Council of 20 March 2000 relating to the taking up and pursuit of the business of credit institutions, *Official Journal of the European Communities* L 126 of 26 May 2000, p. 1.

60 See Ch. Gavalda and J. Stoufflet (1990) *Droit du crédit*, vol. I: *Les institutions*, Paris: Litec, p. 253, para. 366.

61 See Article 78, Law of 2 August 2002.

62 The issue was raised by the plaintiffs before the Supreme Court in the *Wetterstein*-case (see footnote 12), which involved losses incurred by depositors with a non-authorised financial institution. The Supreme Court held that §44 II *Kreditwesengesetz*, which empowers the supervisory authority to investigate whether a person or company qualifies as a credit institution, also serves the interests of the latter's creditors.

63 According to Article 4 of the Coordinated Banking Directive, member states should normally only allow credit institutions to collect deposits or other reimbursable funds from the public or solicit the public with a view to deposit-taking.

64 See Article 9, Coordinated Banking Directive.

65 Article 33, Coordinated Banking Directive.

66 As imposed by Article 10, Coordinated Banking Directive: 'Reasons shall be given whenever an authorisation is refused ...'. The same rule applies when an authorisation is subsequently withdrawn: see Article 14.2, Coordinated Banking Directive.

67 Compare, in France, with respect to the control by the Commission des Opérations de Bourse on financial information for real estate investment companies: Tribunal d'Arrondissement Paris, 5 April 1979, *Recueil Dalloz*, 1980, I.R. 389.

68 See, in the UK, the allegations of depositors in the BCCI case: *Three Rivers District Council and others* v. *Bank of England (No. 3)*, [1996] 3 *The All England Law Reports*, p. 558 [QBD]. Under French law, see: M. Waline, note under Conseil d'Etat 13 June 1964, *Revue de droit public*, 1965, p. 83.

69 See, for instance, in France: Conseil d'Etat 12 February 1960, *Banque*, 1960, p. 321, note Marin; Conseil d'Etat 13 June 1964, *d'André*, *La Semaine Juridique*, 1965, Edition Générale, II, No. 14416; Conseil d'Etat 19 January 1966, *de Waligorski*, *La Semaine Juridique*, 1966, Edition Générale, II, No. 14526.

70 See the allegations of the plaintiffs in the German Supreme Court decision which is currently pending before the European Court of Justice by way of preliminary ruling (see footnote 97): the supervisor is blamed for not having

taken adequate measures, such as promulgating a moratorium on deposits, after having discovered serious financial difficulties in a supervised credit institution. Moreover, the plaintiffs consider that the supervisory authority should have taken adequate prudential measures in order to make sure that the supervised bank would join a deposit guarantee scheme.

71 This was the case in the allegations made by the plaintiffs in the German *Herstatt* case: the plaintiffs considered that the supervisory authority had been informed by third parties of the disproportionate size of speculative foreign exchange transactions undertaken by Herstatt, but had failed to adequately react to this situation, for instance by making an investigation into Herstatt's accounts and consequently by not ordering Herstatt to limit its foreign exchange exposure.

72 Conseil d'Etat 13 June 1964, *d'André, La Semaine Juridique*, 1965, Edition Générale, II, No. 14416, *Revue de droit public*, 1965, p. 84.

73 See also X., note under Conseil d'Etat 13 June 1964, *d'André, La Semaine Juridique*, 1965, Edition Générale, II, No. 14416.

74 Conseil d'Etat 24 January 1964, *Achard, La Semaine Juridique*, 1965, Edition Générale, II, No. 14416, *Revue de droit public*, 1965, p. 43.

75 Conseil d'Etat 30 November 2001, *Kechichian*, op. cit., *supra* note 42.

76 For a detailed analysis, see M. Tison (1999) *De interne markt voor bank- en beleggingsdiensten.* Antwerp: Intersentia, pp. 717–720, para. 1414–1420.

77 Namely the 2001 Brussels II regulation, which decides *inter alia* on international competence for liability claims. According to the case law of the Court of Justice, an action can be brought before the courts of either the country where the acts were committed or the country where the damage was provoked. The latter would allow the depositors, who allegedly have suffered damages in their country of residence, to bring the liability claims before the courts of their country of residence. See also European Court of Justice, 19 September 1995, *Marinari*, case C–364/93, *European Court Reports*, 1995, p. I–2719.

78 See also Ch. Proctor, 'Financial regulators . . .', op. cit., *supra* note 27, p. 78.

79 Indeed, the 1994 Deposit Guarantee Directive also imposes a system of mutual recognition of guarantee systems. As a consequence, depositors of a foreign branch will be protected by the home-state guarantee system, though it may provide for a lower level of coverage than the deposit guarantee system which has been put in place in the country where the branch is established. It should be noted, however, that the risk of 'reverse discriminations' in this context can be eliminated through the 'top-up option', which allows the credit institution to 'top up' the level of deposit guarantee to the (higher) level which exists in the member state of its foreign branch.

80 A similar concern exists as regards deposit guarantee systems: depositors should make their choice as to where to deposit their savings not dependent on the amount of deposit protection, but principally on the financial soundness of the bank and the financial return on their deposits. This explains why the EU Deposit Guarantee Directive limits the possibility for banks to use better deposit guarantee coverage as a competitive device in advertisement or otherwise.

81 European Court of Justice 19 November 1991, *Francovich and Bonifaci*, cases C–6/90 and 9/90, *European Court Reports*, 1991, p. I–5357.

82 European Court of Justice 5 March 1996, *Brasserie du pêcheur/Factortame III*, cases C–46/93 and 48/93, *European Court Reports*, 1996, p. I–1029.

83 Landesgericht Bonn, 16 April 1999, *ZIP – Zeitschrift für Wirtschaftsrecht*, 1999, p. 959, *Entscheidungen im Wirtschaftsrecht*, 2000/5, p. 233. See also Landesgericht

Bonn, 31 March 2000, *not reported* (cited by R. Sethe in *Entscheidungen im Wirtschaftsrecht*, 2001/20, p. 861).

84 European Court of Justice 23 May 1996, *Hedley Lomas*, case C–5/94, *European Court Reports*, 1996, p. I–2604 (the case concerned the refusal by UK authorities to grant an export licence for the export of sheep to Spain).

85 Compare also M.H. Wissink (2002) 'Staatsaansprakelijkheid voor falend banktoezicht; het oordeel van de House of Lords in de Three Rivers-zaak', *Sociaal-Economische Wetgeving*, p. 97.

86 See T. Tridimas (2001) 'Liability for breach of community law: growing up or mellowing down?', *Common Market Law Review*, p. 328. See also M.H. Wissink, op. cit., *supra* note 85, p. 95.

87 And thus realise the fundamental freedoms of services and establishment, as commanded by Article 47.2 EC.

88 See, in particular, European Court of Justice 12 March 1996, *Panagis Pafitis*, case C–441/93, *European Court Reports*, 1996, p. I–1347, para 49; European Court of Justice 9 July 1997, *Parodi*, case C–222/95, *European Court Reports*, 1997, p. I–3899, para. 22; European Court of Justice 11 February 1999, *Romanelli*, case C–366/97, *European Court Reports*, 1999, p. I–862.

89 And if a member state would allow other actors to collect deposits from the public, Article 4 requires them to provide for adequate rules for the protection of depositors.

90 The judges thereby confirmed the decision delivered in the first instance by the Queen's Bench division: see *Three Rivers District Council and others* v. *Bank of England (No. 3)*, [1996] 3 *The All England Law Reports*, pp. 607–608 and 612–615.

91 See the opinion of Lord Justice Auld in *Three Rivers District Council and others* v. *Bank of England*, [1999] 4 *The All England Law Reports*, p. 800 [CA].

92 *Three Rivers District Council and Others (original appellants and cross-respondents)* v. *Governor and Company of the Bank of England (original respondents and cross-appellants)*, [2000] 2 *Weekly Law Reports*, p. 1220 (opinion of Lord Hope of Craighead).

93 It should be noted, however, that the facts of the case were prior to the entry into force of the 1989 Second Banking Directive, several provisions of which are more clearly oriented towards depositor protection than the provisions of the 1977 First Banking Directive.

94 Lord Hope adopted a very narrow approach in this respect, which in fact came down to requiring that a provision of EU law only conferred rights upon individuals when the conditions for direct applicability were met. See also, critically, M. Andenas (2000) 'Liability for supervisors and depositors' rights – the BCCI and the Bank of England in the House of Lords', *Euredia*, 2000/3, p. 407; H.M. Wissink, op. cit., *supra* note 85, p. 94.

95 This attitude of 'legal protectionism' has been highly criticised: see X., (2000) 'European banking law as applied by the House of Lords: overshadowing the *acte clair* doctrine', *Euredia*, 2000/3, pp. 305–306; M.H. Wissink, op. cit., *supra* note 85, p. 96.

96 Oberlandesgericht Köln 11 January 2001, *ZIP – Zeitschrift für Wirtschaftsrecht*, 2001, p. 645, *Wertpapier-Mitteilungen*, 2001, p. 1372, *Entscheidungen in Wirtschaftsrecht*, 2001/20, p. 962, note R. Sethe.

97 Bundesgerichtshof 16 May 2002, III ZR 48/01, *ZIP – Zeitschrift für Wirtschaftsrecht*, 2002, p. 1136.

98 The questions submitted to the Court of Justice are deliberately broadly worded, and concern not only the core prudential directives, but also the 1994 Deposit Guarantee Directive and the 1989 Solvency Ratio Directive.

99 See European Court of Justice 8 October 1996, *Dillenkofer*, cases C–178–179/94, C–188–190/94, *European Court Reports*, 1996, p. I–4867.
100 For example, the requirement of a sound administrative organisation of the credit institution and adequate internal controls.
101 For example, the obligation to take adequate measures with regard to irregularities, without specifying the means or instruments to take action.
102 See *Brasserie du pêcheur/Factortame III*, op. cit., *supra* footnote 82, p. I–1029, para. 55.
103 Compare J.-V. Louis, G. Vandersanden, D. Waelbroeck and M. Waelbroeck (1995) *Commentaire Mégret. Le droit de la CEE*, vol. 10: *La Cour de Justice. Les actes des institutions*, 2nd edn, Brussels: Editions de l'ULB, para. 11, p. 295.
104 See, for instance, the situation in Germany prior to statutory immunity, and the case law in France and in Belgium (the latter prior to the 2002 law).
105 See, for a previous study, focused on deposit guarantee: M. Tison (2002) 'Harmonisation and legal transplantation of EU banking supervisory rules to transitional economies: a legal approach', in D. Green and K. Petrick (eds), *Banking and Financial Stability in Central Europe. Integrating Transition Economies into the European Union.* Cheltenham: Edward Elgar, pp. 37–71.

8 Reforms enhancing the efficiency of the financial sector and the implications of future EU membership

Lelo Liive

Introduction

I welcome the initiative of SUERF to address the questions on efficiency and regulation of the financial sector on the Colloquium and at the same time give thanks for the opportunity of participating in this discussion. The timing is opportune for an accession country where, on one side Estonia is finishing its preparations to attain the legal status of EU member state and when, at the same time, the Financial Services Action Plan is to be finalised. This allows us to have both a newcomer's and still an outsider's view on the reforms taking place in the Union. But this also demands concentration on the new challenges coming from the rights and obligations of the membership. The 1990s were extremely exciting times for Central and Eastern Europe as a market-oriented financial sector was to be built up. The new millennium for the EU will see ten recruits hoping for the best that they will have a voice on European issues.

The financial system is regulated to achieve a wide variety of purposes. It is essential for regulation and regulators to have clearly defined objectives. Everybody should agree that regulation must work first for the interest of financial market clients in order to promote market efficiency, and only after this for the regulators. Regulation must be carefully balanced; competition, in order to enhance growth and renew ideas, must be installed in the appropriate framework of protecting in particular, the private depositors, investors and other retail customers of the financial services.

As referred by Herring and Santomero (1999) actual financial regulation attempts to accomplish several objectives. Besides safeguarding the financial system against systemic risk, at least three broad rationales for financial regulation may be identified: protecting consumers from opportunistic behaviour; enhancing the efficiency of the financial system; and achieving a broad range of social objectives, from increasing home ownership to combating organised crime.

Numerous reports have focused on European issues and specific EU member state cases. Several papers have dealt with global financial markets. This chapter looks for solutions for an accession country searching to find a balance between the rapid development of the financial and economic systems and the promotion of efficient financial regulation.

This chapter focuses on four separate but related questions in relation to financial regulation:

1   is it possible to define an optimal financial regulation?
2   what is the role of regulators in fostering the development of an efficient financial market?
3   how successful has Estonia been in enhancing the efficiency of the financial sector?
4   what are the implications of future EU membership for Estonia?

Each phenomenon is a system of proportions and references. Approaching systematically to the ultimate fundamental of the object – financial regulation – as an organised system, one realises that the globalisation and integration of financial markets and instruments determine its nature, phenomenon, changes and so on. So as to gain an understanding of a phenomenon, we must insulate it into elements to analyse. This chapter includes a variable of particular interest, along with a set of conditioning information. Here economic and legal determinants were researched to help in reaching our conclusions.

The knowledge gained as a member of a number of Estonian working parties, created to analyse and develop a model and the legal acts for the creation of a financial sector, and negotiating with EU commissioners, as well as in taking part in several relevant international conferences, has had a major influence in the writing of this chapter.

Is it possible to define an optimal financial regulation?

Mergers, globalisation, technological changes and conglomeratisation are some of the factors influencing the financial industry world-wide. I must agree with Calomiris *et al.* (2001) that regulators at both the national and international level will have to respond to market-driven changes. Financial institutions delve into a wider range of products and activities, policy-makers have to decide not only on the legal framework for the financial sector but also on the regulatory structure overseeing all types of financial activities.

A country's economic performance is critically determined by a well-functioning financial system facilitating transactions, mobilising savings and allocating capital across time and space. Financial institutions provide payment services and a variety of financial products that enable the corporate sector and households to cope with economic uncertainties by hedging, pooling, sharing and pricing risks. A stable, efficient financial sector reduces the cost and risk of investment as well as of producing and trading goods and services.

The objective that distinguishes financial regulation from other kinds of regulation is that of safeguarding the economy against systemic risk. Concerns regarding systemic risk focus largely on banks, which have traditionally been considered to have a special role in the economy. The safety nets that have been rigged to protect banks from systemic risk have succeeded in preventing banking panics, but at the cost of distorting incentives for risk taking. Financial innovation, and the emergence of new financial markets, have made the risk characteristics of financial firms and the financial system generally more complex. That is why Llewellyn (2001) has said that the systemic dimension to regulation and supervision may no longer be exclusively focused on banking. Banks have lost some of their uniqueness, which has traditionally been the basis of a case for supervision by the central bank.

The increasing internationalisation of financial services and continuing advances in technology have posed a different set of challenges for domestic and international regulation alike. As stated by Calamiris *et al.* (2001), the proliferation of financial instruments, coupled with innovative investing and trading strategies, keep financial institutions several steps ahead of regulators who will inevitably lag in gaining the requisite expertise required to assess the new risks.

Financial markets provide a crucial source of information that helps coordinate decentralised decisions throughout the economy. Rates of return in financial markets guide households in allocating income between consumption and savings, and in allocating their stock of wealth. Firms rely on financial market prices to inform their choices among investment projects and to determine how such projects should be financed.

Rapid technological innovation and an evolving business environment, together with long-term changes in needs and profiles are reshaping the financial system. The system will have a progressively greater array of participants, products and distribution channels that will expand beyond the traditional categories of banking, insurance and financial exchanges. Competition is emerging from new providers of financial services and through the increasing globalisation of financial markets. This generates increasing pressure for improved efficiency and performance.

Technological innovation has been the major force in shaping financial services delivery. Technology has made it easy to access markets and products both domestically and internationally; it has made it possible to analyse and monitor risk more efficiently, to disaggregate it on a broad scale, to price it more accurately and to redistribute it more effectively. This will also facilitate the conduct of financial activities through homes, workplaces and other sites physically remote from service providers, and further reduce entry barriers to new suppliers.

Safeguarding financial markets and institutions from shocks that might pose a systemic risk is the prime objective of financial regulation. Herring and Santomero (1999) defined systemic risk as the risk of a sudden, unanticipated event that would damage the financial system to such an extent that economic activity in the wider economy would suffer. Such shocks may originate inside or outside the financial sector, and may include the sudden failure of a major participant in the financial system, a technological breakdown at a critical stage of settlements or payments systems, or a political shock such as an invasion or the imposition of exchange controls in an important financial centre.

The regulatory framework is itself an important driver of changes in the financial system. The government and regulatory environments profoundly influence the structure and scale of financial services activities. The influence is by no means confined to direct financial regulation. Changes in the role of governments, in particular the departure of government as an owner of financial institutions and associated removal of explicit government guarantees of financial-sector liabilities also has a significant impact, as does national taxation systems on investment choices and the international competitiveness of the national financial systems.

One of the most striking features of the wholesale financial markets is the trend towards international integration as deregulation has moved many of the barriers to cross-border transactions and technology has lowered the costs. As markets have become increasingly global, the volume of cross-boarder financial activities as international bond issues and derivatives trading has increased. The competition in many financial markets occurs globally, rather than at the national level. Advances in the means of achieving secure electronic transactions and critical mass of electronic network coverage are now well within sight. Global retail electronic financial transactions are likely to emerge in the near future and will almost certainly flourish up to 2010 if the regulatory environment is accommodating.

Last but not least, the changes in consumer needs and profiles are gradual but powerful influences in financial-sector development. Demand for financial services is reflected in households increasing both their financial assets holdings and borrowing from the financial sector. This shows the growth of wealth and changing financial needs arising from demographic and life-circle changes (ageing of the population, increasing expectations of higher retirement incomes, greater job mobility, longer periods spent on training and so on).

Better access to information and a weakening of traditional supply relationships are raising consumer awareness of product and supplier value, thereby increasing competitiveness in the market. Greater familiarity with the use of alternative technologies means that more households are pushing lower cost and more convenient means of accessing financial services. Consumers are becoming increasingly sophisticated and effective in demanding value for money.

Although the financial markets remain subject to a wide array of regulations and entry restrictions, recent changes in the regulatory framework in both the EU and candidate countries are aimed at focusing on innovation on the delivery of financial services and creating a more competitive environment in financial markets.

The challenge for efficient regulation lies in facing all the aforesaid changes: innovation in products, structures, technologies and so on. The European Regulated Market is certainly at the heart of these changes. So the regulation must be based on the realities of today, but it must, at the same time, provide for the changes of the future. It must be flexible enough to permit speed, and choice of direction, of change.

What is the role of regulators in fostering the development of an efficient financial market?

Financial innovation and structural change in the financial system have challenged many of the assumptions made at the time current regulations were created. That is why institutional structure and evolution of the structure of the financial system and the business of market participants are directly connected.

Regulators should ensure that regulation does not prevent fair competition and innovation. Any regulatory interference must be properly justified and proportional. Regulators need also to ensure the maintenance of an appropriate regulatory framework that is capable of addressing any new risk or damage to efficiency and investor protection.

The subject of technology and consolidation bring us to the implications of globalisation for financial supervision. The issue first surfaced in 1974 with the failure of a medium-sized German bank, Bankhaus Herstatt, that had significant foreign currency exposures to other European and American banks. The bank failure triggered fears of a domino-like chain-reaction of solvency problems in each of its major counter-parties, and briefly caused an interruption in the markets for foreign exchange and inter-bank lending markets.

The institutional structure of financial-sector supervision has been closely monitored in many countries around the world (Figure 8.1). Major changes have already taken place, but especially in accession countries, where the history of the financial sector has been a short one, many decisions in this respect are still to come. Beyond the industrialised countries, some countries that have relatively recently set up a supervisory framework, such as the transition countries of Europe and Central Asia, have been examining the case for introducing unified financial supervision authority. Estonia is an example of this.

Events in Asia and Russia have shown us just how interdependent markets have become. Stresses in one part of the world can affect markets, consumer confidence, investor confidence and government everywhere. Due to this, not only the national experience has to be taken into account but also international developments; international organisations and their

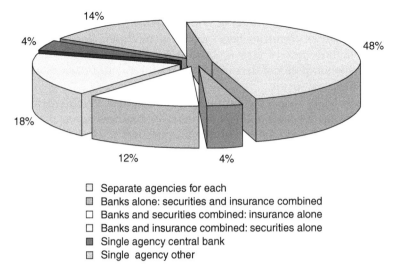

14%

4%

48%

18%

12%   4%

☐ Separate agencies for each
▨ Banks alone: securities and insurance combined
☐ Banks and securities combined: insurance alone
☐ Banks and insurance combined: securities alone
■ Single agency central bank
☐ Single agency other

Figure 8.1 Supervisors of financial market according to the institutional allocation. (Information of 73 agencies.) (Source: *How Countries Supervise their Banks, Insurers and Securities Markets*, 1999.)

decisions also play a crucial role. Increasing emphasis is being given to the general question of whether the efficiency of regulation and supervision in achieving their objectives may be influenced by the particular institutional structure in which they operate.

International financial institutions have set out the main principles for supervision, including good practices for guiding them, but not a single rule is set out for the structure of the regulatory regime.

The most important function of financial supervision is to ensure that financial enterprises are solvent and bring violations of financial legislation to an end. State supervision should ensure the sound management of financial institutions to protect clients' interests. Thus the authority not only requires skilled, able and committed professionals, but also an established organisational structure. The current trend in EU countries is to establish autonomous authorities separate from other governmental bodies, with clearly defined objectives and strategies and a sufficient degree of independence.

Goodhart (1998) has identified several reasons for the emergence of this trend, including the rapid structural change that has taken place in financial markets spurred by the acceleration in financial innovation. This has challenged the assumptions behind the original structuring of regulatory organisations. The increasing complexity of financial business is evidenced by the emergence of financial conglomerates.

A review of international experience indicates a wide variety of institutional structures for financial regulation. Some countries have reduced the number of regulatory agencies and, in some cases (such as the UK, Iceland, Australia, Germany, Finland and Sweden), have created a single 'mega-agency'. Other countries have opted for multiple agencies. Differences reflect a multitude of factors: historical evolution, the structure of the financial system, political structures and traditions, and the size of the country and financial sector.

In his 'Twin Peaks' concept, Taylor (1996) compares a single prudential supervisory agency with a single conduct of business agency. Taylor argues that a regulatory system which presupposes a clear separation between banking, securities and insurance is no longer the best way to regulate a financial system in which these distinctions are increasingly irrelevant. The counter-argument is that, while there has been a degree of convergence between banks and securities firms, there is still a reasonably clear distinction to be made between banks and other financial institutions. Even if banks remain unique and a single institution conducts prudential supervision for everything from banks to insurance companies, it would still need to tailor the rules to meet the characteristics of particular types of business. The new regulator could quickly become a collection of separate 'divisions'.

Another factor justifying an integrated approach to regulation is the need to respond to the formation of financial conglomerates (Taylor and Fleming 1999). An integrated regulatory agency would be an appropriate response to conglomeratisation because it enables regulators to assess risks on a group-wide basis. An integrated regulation should help eliminate the potential for regulatory arbitrage by financial conglomerates. By applying a single set of regulatory requirements across a diversified financial group, a single agency should be able to achieve greater clarity and consistency than specialist agencies, and reduce the scope for one set of regulatory requirements being evaded by transactions being booked elsewhere in the group.

A unified supervision agency should permit the regulatory authority to achieve efficiencies in the deployment of staff with rare intellectual capital. This argument has been especially influential among the Scandinavian and Baltic countries that have needed to maximise their use of scarce human resources if they are to be able to participate fully in international regulatory forums.

There are a variety of other reasons for integration that can be emphasised. The formation of the FSA in the United Kingdom has been justified on similar grounds to those labelled 'small country rational'. Announcing the decision to create the FSA on 20 May 1997, Chancellor Gordon Brown declared that the blurring of boundaries between different categories of financial intermediary necessitated a radical rethink of the structure of regulation.

Behind the creation of a number of single authorities may also have been the desire to improve the quality of supervision of specific industrial sectors. One undoubted benefit of the integrated approach when compared with specialist regulatory agencies is that it is less likely that specific regulatory problems will be lost in the gaps between regulatory jurisdictions. A number of cases had contributed to the perception that too many problems were simply falling between regulatory agencies. In theory, the existence of a single regulatory agency also makes it much easier to extend its powers as new products emerge.

However, there is also a risk in this. A single financial services regulator can suffer from a 'Christmas tree' effect, in which heterogeneous responsibilities are gradually added to its range of functions. This may eventually result in a situation in which it becomes overburdened with a series of functions which are, at best, tangentially connected to the agency's primary objective but of which government departments have been keen to divest themselves.

Llewellyn (2001) has rightly said that all this suggests that there is no obvious 'ideal model' in existence, which could be universally applied. It might, therefore, be necessary to accept the inevitability of an imperfect set of institutional arrangements. While appropriate structures must necessarily reflect the country-specific environment, it is nevertheless instructive to consider whether there are general principles which can inform discussion about the appropriate institutional structure.

It is not self-evident that a single, mega-regulator would, in practice, be more efficient than a series of specialist regulators, based on clearly defined objectives and focused specifically on regulation to meet clearly defined objectives.

How successful has Estonia been in enhancing the efficiency of the financial sector?

Estonia has made strong progress to date in developing a privately owned and market-oriented banking sector, and is achieving fairly rapid expansion of the financial sector in general, including non-bank financial institutions such as leasing, insurance, investment firms and private pension funds. With substantial influence in recent years from strong Nordic strategic investors, productivity and efficiency of the financial sector is rapidly approaching Western European standards (Figure 8.2).

Several assessors in the framework of IMF/World Bank FSAP in 2000 and EU Peer Review in 2001 (followed up in 2003) have appraised Estonia's regulations in the financial sector as harmonised with EU law and international standards. The regulations are supported by institutional mechanisms to implement these laws and, as a result, the country compares very well overall with other accession countries. Estonia's commercial laws are perceived by lawyers in the field as being of the highest standard among the transition countries and can be characterised as reasonably good for supporting investment and other commercial activity.

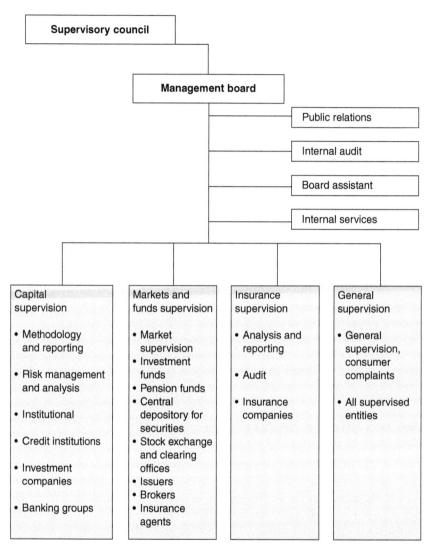

Figure 8.2 The EFSA's organisational structure as of March 2002.

Non-bank financial institutions continue to be much less developed than the credit institutions. The main channels for financing investments continues to be the banking sector, international capital flows and, to a lesser extent, the securities market and leasing. In the structure of debt financing of the real sector, the share of foreign financing is approximately 50 per cent (without intra-company loans, i.e. FDI flows, the share is still 25 per cent). Estonian companies obtain half of their debt financing from banks and one-quarter from other parts of the financial sector.

The share of financing by debt securities has been modest, with outstanding debt securities issued by local companies amounting to less than 3 per cent of GDP. Households' financing is mainly based on bank loans (85 per cent of total household debts), although in total terms household indebtedness only amounts to 10 per cent of GDP. The total credit exposure of Estonian banks and their leasing subsidiaries to real sector enterprises and households has increased to around 40 per cent of GDP by 2002.

The banking sector has been strengthened through the further consolidation behind foreign strategic investors. At the end of 2002, seven banks were operating in the market (down from 42 banks in 1992, and 11 banks in 1997). More than 90 per cent of banking sector capital and 98 per cent of assets are foreign-owned. The Swedish Swedbank owns a 63 per cent stake in Hansabank, the Swedish SEB a 99 per cent stake in Ühispank and the Finnish Sampo group own Sampo Bank. Meanwhile Hansapank broadened its coverage in other Baltic states with the acquisition, in June 2001, of the Lithuanian Savings Bank.

The sector continues to be highly concentrated, with the three largest banks owning 95 per cent of the assets between them. Capital adequacy levels have been remarkably stable since the middle of 2000, fluctuating between 13 per cent–15 per cent, i.e. 3 per cent–5 per cent above the minimum level of 10 per cent. The capital adequacy ratio averaged 14.4 per cent in 2001. The share of non-performing loans at around 1 per cent–1.5 per cent is the lowest among CEB countries. Nevertheless, domestic credit to the private sector was still only around 28 per cent of GDP at the end of 2002, and broad money to GDP stood at 53 per cent of GDP.

The primary legislation governing the Estonian banking sector includes the Law on the Bank of Estonia (BoE), 1993, and the Credit Institutions Act, 1999 (the 'CIA'). Since 1990, the BoE has made considerable progress in strengthening its supervisory framework. Major efforts include introducing principles for consolidated financial statements of credit institutions in 1996, and comprehensive regulations for compiling consolidated statements in 1998. The CIA stipulates prudential ratios for credit institutions such as capital adequacy, large exposures and investments on sole and consolidated bases.

Currently there are seven management companies in Estonia. Under these are managed 36 investment funds, wherefrom 15 are mandatory and four voluntary pension funds. The development of the investment funds industry has been quite rapid in the past few years, and the total assets in investment funds have doubled in the last two years, amounting to 4.1 per cent of GDP. Domestic money market and capital growth funds were the most popular, until the Asian and Russian crises sparked a collapse in share prices and led many funds to shrink in size. Companies in particular became more interested in the money market and interest funds as an alternative short-term investment facility for bank deposits. At the end of the year 2002, the money market and interest funds combined made up approximately 90 per cent of total investment fund assets.

Asset management is regulated by the Investment Funds Act (IFA) dated from 1997. Currently a working party has been established to work out a new IFA in order to promote the investment funds environment in Estonia. The new IFA will be in full compliance with all the relevant EU directives. In addition, the new draft will allow a wider range of collective investment funds (the funds, which do not have the European passport, will be regulated).

In response to the build up of pension liabilities, the Estonian Government moved from the pay-as-you-go pension system to a three-tier partially funded scheme. Going forward, the market should benefit from the evolution of pension reform. In September 2001, Parliament approved legislation to establish the second pillar of the pension system. Payment collections to the second-pillar funds started on 1 July 2002. The fully funded second tier offers additional pension coverage financed by individual contributions. The funded pension is based on preliminary financing – a working person saves for his or her pension, paying 2 per cent of the gross salary to the pension fund. In addition to that, the state adds 4 per cent out of the current social tax that is paid by the employee. Subscription to the funded pension is mandatory for those entering the labour market, i.e. those born in 1983 or later. The funded pension is voluntary for those born before 1983.

Over 200,000 people switched into the second pillar pension system. The introduction of this mandatory, privately managed pillar for pensions helps to deepen the non-banking market and provides alternative sources of financing for local large-scale enterprises, making the country less dependent on high inflows of foreign direct investment.

The supplementary funded pension (the third pillar) is based on each person's voluntary decision to start saving either by contributions to a voluntary pension fund or by entering into a respective insurance contract on the supplementary funded pension with a life insurance company with the respective activity licence. The third pillar was started in 1998. The supplementary funded pension differs from the funded pension or the second pillar due mainly to the fact that contributions are voluntary for everybody and the amount to be contributed is not prescribed by the state.

There are currently 12 insurance companies operating in the Estonian insurance market, of which five are life and seven are non-life insurers. While increasing, the gross premiums of life and non-life insurance companies remain low at only 2.06 per cent of GDP at the end of 2002. Traditionally, the market has been dominated by non-life insurance, the share of which is around 80 per cent, whilst the share of life insurance is 20 per cent. The share of non-life insurance has grown rapidly in recent years following the introduction of compulsory motor TPL-insurance. It is likely that the importance of life insurance will gradually grow. The key problem in the insurance sector has been that companies are small and their operating costs continue to be relatively high.

The Insurance Activities Act was adopted in 2000. This Act strengthened licensing and control requirements, restricted the use of financial derivatives exclusively to manage risk and forbids insurance companies from writing put-options. In addition to these new controls, a Ministry of Finance decree (August 2000) updated the methods for calculating capital adequacy and solvency ratios, and updated the reporting requirements for insurance companies.

The integration of the Helsinki Stock Exchange with the Tallinn Stock Exchange, and improvements in regulation, should enhance the strength of the capital market and its integration into pan-European associations. In May 2001, the owner of the Helsinki Stock Exchange, HEX Group, acquired a majority holding in the Tallinn Stock Exchange, and the integration was completed in February 2002 with the creation of a common trading environment for securities listed on the Helsinki and Tallinn bourses. The take-over by the Helsinki Stock Exchange is likely to benefit the Tallinn Stock Exchange in the future. This move is expected to help both Finnish and Estonian investors to gain access to each other's capital markets and facilitate the integration of the Estonian stock market into the EU markets. The total capitalisation of Tallinn Stock Exchange reached 34.5 per cent of GDP at the end of 2002.

The securities market is regulated by the Securities Market Act, which was passed in October 2001 and came into force in January 2002. This act brought Estonian legislation into line with the requirements of the EU. This Act replaced the existing 1993 provisions and assigned the supervision of the Estonian securities market to the Estonian Financial Supervision Authority (EFSA). It regulates in detail public offers, activities of investment firms (including cross-border services) together with clearing and settlement activities. The Act enforces prudential ratios for investment firms that are non-credit institutions, prohibits markets manipulations and insider trading, regulates the issues of investment firms and regulated market operators. The new Act also includes more extensive regulation of tender-offers, listing particulars, own funds requirements and take-overs.

The Guarantee Fund Act was adopted in February 2002 and came in to force from 1 July 2002. It harmonises European directives on investor-compensation schemes and deposit-guarantee schemes. In addition it oversees a guarantee scheme for the funded pension system.

On 11 June 1997 the Estonian Government included the launching of the Estonian Financial Supervision Authority (EFSA) in its short-term priorities. It was stated in the IMF memorandum, signed on 7 November 1997, that Estonia will work out a plan to reform the financial supervision structure. The same statement was given in the EU Accession Partnership at the end of 1997. These decisions were shortly followed with the crises in the financial sector, of which the most significant was the bankruptcy of the Maapank.

As stated by Taylor and Fleming (1999), in most instances in Eastern Europe and the former Soviet Union, there has been a significant effort to strengthen the supervisory framework for banks, often with substantial technical assistance from international financial institutions or bilateral donors. They point out that the banking crises in a number of emerging countries have intensified the effort to bolster capacity in the banking supervisory functions. Banking supervision has been seen as a priority in transitional, emerging economies which, at least in their early stages, are dominated by banks.

On 28 June 1998, Maapank (Land Bank) was declared bankrupt by the Bank of Estonia after its repeated failure to meet prudential requirements and after its shareholders (the Nordika Insurance Company, Swedfund and EBRD) failed to re-capitalise it. The reasons for the failure of Maapank were mainly due to:

- a high proportion of non-performing loans; and
- a decline in the value of its securities portfolio in the wake of the stock market decline in late 1997 and early 1998.

As stated in the relevant report by Mølgard (1998) the actual size of non-performing loans was far greater than the reported figures. With respect to the securities portfolio, Maapank continued to incorrectly report the higher face value of the securities instead of marking them to market – as required by the Bank of Estonia – thus inflating both its assets and profits.

Mølgard, the establisher of the Danish FSA, was asked by the Government of Estonia and the Bank of Estonia to act as a rapporteur in Maapanks' case. He suggested that it must be the responsibility of the Ministry of Finance to ensure that the supervisory authorities cooperate and coordinate their activities in every respect if needed by new legislation, written instructions or agreements. He recommended changing the law on credit institutions and the supervisory system so that the supervisor takes the final decision if the bank and its auditors disagree with the banking supervisor as to the supervisory issues, particularly as to prudential criteria. Mølgard suggested that the Ministry of Finance should ensure cooperation and exchange of information among the supervisory bodies, if needed by amending the rules on confidentiality in the laws.

Besides the crises in the financial sector, one of the main concerns was the dissatisfaction with the performance of supervisory tasks, mainly relating to the Securities Inspectorate. And it must be stated here that this was not only caused by the insufficient powers given by the old Securities Market Act, from 1993. The staff was young and inexperienced, the management was not following the best principles of supervision. The Securities Inspectorate was not a member of IOSCO. The financing of both the Securities Inspectorate and the Insurance Supervisory Agency was also insufficient, which did not enable the hiring of specialists from the market, the training of the existing employees and the building up of market monitoring systems. Their budgets where incorporated into the state budget, but the market participants financed the Insurance Supervisory Agency whilst funding for Securities Inspectorate came from the state budget. At the same time, the Banking Supervision Department, being a part of BoE, did not have problems with funding, which resulted in higher morale and better qualifications of its inspectors.

Although the IMF and World Bank in the Financial Sector Assessment Programme also stated that the Securities Inspectorate as well as the Insurance Supervision Agency were not independent in their decisions due to the fact that they were Government agencies, I do not agree with this statement completely. It is true that the Minister of Finance made the final decision of granting and withdrawing the licences of the market participants. But in everyday operations there was no possibility for the minister to intervene in the decision-making process. The minister could also have no say when it came to operational matters.

At the beginning of 1999, a working group of specialists, including the author, finished work on a report containing the detailed description of the Estonian financial markets and supervisory institutions, an analysis of the Estonian legal framework and of pros and cons for merging the supervisory institutions (*Finantsjärelevalvete ühendamise töörühma aruanne,* 1999).

Based on a report by a second party formed by the Government, the basic decisions were made in 2000. It was supported by the Government in merging the three supervisory authorities and forming a unified financial supervision authority, as it will enable it to:

- gain an overview of the financial situation of the whole financial group;
- achieve the purposes of supervision with much more flexibility and efficiency;
- better evaluate the possible risks to the whole financial market;
- find loopholes in the legislative acts, etc.

It was agreed that the merging of financial-sector supervision should be carried out taking into account the following conceptual principles.

- The new institution must have sufficient autonomy, authority and responsibility as well as political and financial independence. The balance between independence and responsibilities must be ensured by respective institutional and organisational procedures.
- The merging must not have a negative side-effect or even a temporary

decrease in the quality of supervision. It was required that the efficiency of the separate supervisory institutions must be increased beforehand.

- Taking into account the tasks of the Bank of Estonia and the Government (the Ministry of Finance) in carrying out monetary and economic policies, the necessary relations and institutional connections between the Bank of Estonia, the Ministry of Finance and the joint supervision authority should be ensured.

It was suggested that the independence of a new institution can be achieved by managing system designed in details and sequestered financing system. The tasks and responsibilities of the management (council, board, employees, internal control, etc.) will have to be described in the law (*Asjatundjate komisjoni töö aruanne ja ettepanekud*, 2000).

The Financial Supervision Authority Act, adopted in 2001, established the Estonia Financial Supervision Authority (the EFSA) as an independent institution affiliated with the BoE. The EFSA became operational in January 2002 and assumed the functions of three financial-sector supervision authorities – the Banking Supervision Department of BoE, Securities Inspectorate and Insurance Supervisory Agency (Figure 8.3).

According to the Financial Supervision Authority Act, the Financial Supervision Authority is an agency with autonomous competence and a separate budget. The directing bodies of the Authority are to act and submit reports pursuant to the procedure provided for in this Act.

The independence of the EFSA is supported by its organisational structure. The governing bodies of the EFSA – the Supervisory Council and the Management Board – are not part of the central bank governance hierarchy. EFSA has its own budget formed on the basis of supervision fees required from market participants. When exercising its control functions, designing financial regulations and making decisions regarding market participants, the ESFA is unconditionally independent from any other institution.

The EFSA has formalised cooperation with the Bank of Estonia and the Ministry of Finance in fields of crisis management, development of financial-sector legislation and information sharing in the form of a Memorandum of Understanding. A lesson was learned from the mistakes of the former institutions which, together with the analyses on the changes in the financial sector overall and international developments, was taken into account in establishing the bases for the operation of the EFSA. The legal environment, with the introduction of the EFSA Act and the new Securities Market Act from the beginning of 2002 and the changes in most of the related acts, was taken to a level comparable with the EU member states. The financing of the new institution was remarkably improved, with international assistance in building the organisation, its IT system and training the staff being used. With the Financial Supervision Act, the EFSA was granted operational independence.

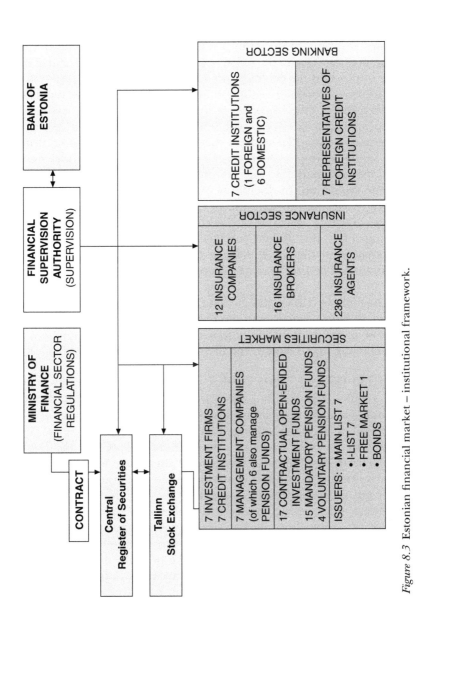

Figure 8.3 Estonian financial market – institutional framework.

The first test for the EFSA was granting licences to the second-pillar mandatory pension funds. This process was to come to an end by 1 April 2002, but in reality it took three more weeks. Still, I am of the opinion that in this process the EFSA showed its strength rather than incapacity. The fund managers, having been used to the low standards of supervision by the former Securities Inspectorate did face the improved approach to the licensing process. The EFSA did not submit to the political and public pressure imposed by the deadline given in the legal acts.

Still, numerous open-ended questions are outstanding. The regulation and supervision of other financial institutions such as leasing, saving and loan association, pawn offices, loan offices, bureaux de change and so on is under review today. The role of the EFSA in supervising these institutions, as well as its responsibility for the supervision of cross-border money transfer, money laundering and consumer protection needs to be specified in the regulation. In discussions it has been mentioned that adding each new obligation to the list of the EFSA's tasks requires more resources, and this again raises the cost of supervision for the market participants. But this should not keep supervision of some financial sectors away from the EFSA. Still, at the same time, two contradictory standpoints must be kept in mind, where balance must be found:

- the warning by Taylor and Fleming (1999) about the 'Christmas-tree' effect, as discussed earlier in this chapter;
- lack of resources must never prevail over the justified argument for maintaining supervision by the EFSA.

Mwenda and Fleming (2001) say that there is some evidence to suggest that the smaller countries, in particular, are seeking to yield the fruits of economies of scale in regulation through improved management of regulatory resources (especially staff) and infrastructure support.

But smaller states, by necessity, cannot afford to have very complex or costly regulatory institutions and systems. A small state with ambitions to be at the forefront of economic development and innovation has the most to lose from individual institutions collapsing or suffering a crisis, and from adverse international business and economic opinion concerning the standards applied in its financial services markets. This tension between the constraints and needs of smaller economies is not merely inevitable but amounts to a challenge to the political and administrative leaders of such societies to be courageous, innovative and clear-minded in their approach to the regulation of the financial services sector.

A year is not sufficient time to conclude that a unified authority has been performing its tasks better or has conducted itself more efficiently. But it has proved that the choices made have been for promoting an efficient financial marketplace in Estonia. The author agrees with McDowell (2001) that small, open economies, especially economies emerging from decades of under-performance, constantly face choices between the need for rapid change and the dictates of high standards of democratic accountability and regulatory integrity. Economic regulation and financial supervision must always be firmly rooted in reality.

What are the implications of future EU membership?

What else is there to do for Estonia in enhancing the financial markets? There has definitely been a success story in building up the financial sector and establishing its regulations. The sector is market-oriented, and developing in a good and reasonable way. Does Estonia now only have to maintain its reputation as a country with an open and competitive economy and just proceed with integrating the new standards set out by the Commission and international organisations?

It is certainly not the main perspective for us. Capital and financial service activity is, in the global economic market, highly mobile. A balance has to be struck between making an economy friendly and supportive to the financial services sector, on the one hand, and the danger of making a state over-indulgent and apparently negligent on the other. In order to attain this, we do have a plan to have our say in working out the international standards and integrating them in Estonian law.

The *acquis communautaire* within the financial services sector is long and has been developed during the last 25-to-30 years. It covers a large number of general principles, detailed technical provisions and provisions on cooperation. Since 1992, EU-based financial institutions operate throughout the EU under a single passport. The basis of the EU single market in the financial field is the system of harmonised prudential rules. The financial markets of accession countries will only face the challenge of operating under a single passport after becoming a member state.

In order to set out the regulatory road map for a fully integrated financial market, in May 1999 the Commission adopted a Financial Services Action Plan. In the framework of this action plan currently the new Investment Services Directive (ISD) is worked out. I would like to use this directive as an example in further analyses on the future implications of EU membership for an accession country.

One of the overarching objectives of the proposal is to establish a regulatory framework to ensure financial transactions are executed in a manner that upholds overall market efficiency and integrity. The proposal addresses, effectively and proportionately, the risks to market efficiency and integrity associated with different types of trade execution functionality. The revised ISD is an opportunity for European legislators and regulators to build on the existing ISD to provide improved conditions in which European capital markets can continue to serve European investors and European business at the cutting edge of innovation and competition.

At the time of writing this chapter in February 2003, the accession countries did not yet have an opportunity to have their say in working out the draft, neither were they included in the range of addressees for receiving draft documentation and consultation papers. By the time of the conference (starting from April 2003), accession countries have the opportunity to take part in the discussions in the system of EC working groups and committees. This new challenge requires high administrative capacity from the regulators, including qualified staff and better allocation of resources.

Speaking more specifically of new ISD, the text under discussion provides a good basis for more detailed discussions on several issues. There is a clear need for revised ISD as, since passing the previous one in 1993, financial markets and the degree of their integration have changed considerably. While providing for the challenges and the changes for the future, a revised ISD must be based on the realities of today.

So as to create a truly integrated financial market in a competitive environment, it must create a level playing-field between all market participants and trading functionalities (MTFs, investment firms, exchanges) throughout the Union, including accession countries. European investors and issuers need efficient and flexible markets to keep the cost of capital low and investment returns high. The quality of price formation on European Securities Markets is one of the greatest assets and has important implications for overall financial markets in Europe. At the same time the regulations must provide an adequate level of protection for the investors that require it to make an informed decision. The key words here are transparency and accessibility of information.

These challenges in working out the new ISD, and also other directives, are familiar to the member states and new for the accession countries. Now the interests of the 'old players' and newcomers have to be brought together.

In the discussion on the draft text of the new ISD, the most significant debate is about pre-transparency rules. Art. 25 (4) says: 'Implementing measures shall ensure the uniform application of pre-trade transparency provisions in a manner which supports the efficient valuation of shares ....' The objective is to create a framework for financial markets in Europe that provides optimum conditions for the price-formation process and optimises the flow of information from trading venues to the market participants. However, an attempt to offer a one-rule-fits-all approach can clearly be detected. I do think that the idea behind regulating pre-trade transparency is to give the market the information necessary for functioning adequately and not just make visible to the market what is not visible. ISD should make visible the information necessary to create a complete picture of the overall markets. As market efficiency can be achieved in several ways, transparency may not always be sufficient in itself to offset the negative effects of fragmentation on market efficiency and investor protection.

So as to accomplish reasonable solutions, intensive work by CESR, members states and now also accession countries must be used to establish appropriate implementation of the desired results.

The regulations must work with the grain of the marketplace. The new marketplace for the accession countries is the single market of the whole of Europe. That is the perspective to keep in mind. It is time to avoid using regulations to protect national markets and make a choice which promotes competition and diversity to the benefit of the future European financial markets.

Conclusions

The objective of this chapter is to exemplify and generalise, through the analysis of actual financial and economic processes, the general principles and legitimacy for the development of efficient financial regulation and, based on that, analysis the developments of a small accession country such as Estonia on the grounds of its changes in regulatory framework.

Financial regulation today is not a domestic matter. The financial markets become more and more integrated both by sectors and nations. The need for common regulatory concepts and approaches is manifested in a range of international associations, committees, working groups and so on. This is done both on a formal and informal level. The legislative work that is constantly proceeding within the EU is very important for accession countries.

In view of critical contributions to economic performance, it is not surprising that the health of the financial sector is a matter of public policy concern and that nearly all national governments have chosen to regulate the financial sector. The author agrees with Menton (1990) when he says that the overall objective of regulation of the financial sector *should be* to ensure that the system functions efficiently in helping to deploy transfer and allocate resources across time and space, as well as under conditions of uncertainty.

In conclusion, it must be stressed that before making any changes in the regulatory environment the key issues have to be considered in national or regional boundaries of the financial markets. It is realised that there are major issues in the financial industry, like structural changes, globalisation, internationalisation, consolidation, increasing demands on conduct of business, advance in technology, as well as the changing regulatory framework that drives the changes. There are many differences that have to be considered for small economies. At the same time, the global aspect represented in the principles and directives by the international organisations like BIS, IOSCO, IAIS, EU and so on, also influence the final decision of the regulatory structure.

A unified financial services supervisory authority would appear to be an attractive option for many countries with small, rapidly evolving financial sectors. It is clear that the decision on whether or not to integrate should be taken after full consideration of the circumstances of each individual country.

A key issue is that the regulatory framework has an impact on the overall effectiveness and efficiency of regulation and supervision, since this is the ultimate criterion, when making judgements between alternative formats.

The responsibility of the regulator is to set up the framework, which then enables the markets to play their disciplining role in an efficient way. If there are differences in national arrangements, this may create uncertainty. And these uncertainties present serious obstacles for a truly functioning single financial market. It is crucial that we do everything to ensure the depositors, investors and other financial market clients' confidence in our financial markets.

References

A New Regulator for the New Millennium, UK Financial Services Authority, London, 2000.

Asjatundjate komisjoni töö aruanne ja ettepanekud: Ühendatud finantsjärelevalve moodustamise aluste ja tegevuskava väljatöötamiseks moodustatud asjatundjate komisjoni töö aruanne ja ettepanekud, Valitsuskomisjoni aruanne, Tallinn, 2000. Online, available at: www.fin.ee.

Australian Financial System Inquiry Discussion Paper, Australian Government Publishing Service, January 1997 [CD ROM Non-Bank Financial Institutions (NBFIs): Development and Regulation Workshop, 2001, Washington, DC, World Bank Background Publications].

Bolkestein, F. (2001) 'New policies for European securities markets', paper presented on the Forum for US–EU Legal Economic Affairs (Mentor Group) Rome, 13 September.

Briault, C.B. (1999) 'The Rationale for a Single national Financial Services Regulator,' Occasional Paper Series No. 2, London: FSA.

Building a New Regulator, Progress Report 1, UK Financial Services Authority, London, 2000, p. 44.

Calomiris, C., Litan, R. and Montrone, P.M. (2001) 'Financial regulation in a global marketplace', [CD ROM Non-Bank Financial Institutions (NBFIs): Development and Regulation Workshop, 2001, Washington, DC, World Bank Background Publications].

Cavalcanti, C. and Oks, D. (1998) 'Estonia: the challenges of financial integration', ECPE Technical Paper, May.

Danthine, J.-P., Giavazzi, F., Vives, X. and Thadden, E.-L. (1999) *The Future of European Banking: Monitoring European Integration*. London: Centre for Economic Policy Research.

Duisenberg, W.F. (2001) 'Finantsturgude Roll Majanduskasvus', *Eesti Panga Bülletään*, 8: 14–18.

EC, DG Internal Market. Online, available at: http://europa.eu.int/comm/internal_market/en/finances/general/index.htm.

Finantsjärelevalvete ühendamise töörühma aruanne, Rahandusministeeriumi ja Eesti Panga töögrupp, Tallinn, 1999. Online, available at: http:www.fin.ee.

Goodhart, C.A.E. (ed.) (1998) The Emerging Framework of Financial Regulation: A Collection of Papers Compiled by the Financial Markets Group of the London School of Economics. London: A Central Bank Publication.

Hadjiemmanuil, C. and Andenas, M. (1999) 'Banking supervision and European monetary union', *The Journal of International Banking Regulation*, June: 84–102.

Herring, R.J. and Santomero, A.M. (1991) 'The role of financial structure in economic performance, in Sweden SNS Forlag, Stockholm' [CD ROM Non-Bank Financial Institutions (NBFIs): Development and Regulation Workshop, 2001, Washington, DC, World Bank Background Publications].

Herring, R.J. and Santomero, A.M. (1999) 'What is optimal financial regulation?' FMA Annual Meeting, October [CD ROM Non-Bank Financial Institutions (NBFIs): Development and Regulation Workshop, 2001, Washington, DC, World Bank Background Publications];

Lannoo, K. (1999) *Financial Supervision in EMU*, Centre for European Policy Studies (CEPS). Online, available at: http://www.ceps.be.

Liive, L. (2001) 'Unified Financial Supervisory Authority to be Launched from 2002', Estonian Securities Market, Fact Book of Tallinn Stock Exchange and Estonian Central Depository for Securities, May.

Llewellyn, D. (1999) 'The economic rationale for financial regulation', FSA Occasional Paper, UK Financial Services Authority, London.

Llewellyn, D.T. (2001) 'The creation of a single financial regulatory agency in Estonia: the global context', *Challenges for the Unified Financial Supervision in the New Millennium*. Tallinn: Ministry of Finance of Estonia, The World Bank Group.

McDowell, M. (2001) 'Challenges for the unified financial supervision: experience of Ireland', *Challenges for the Unified Financial Supervision in the New Millennium*. Tallinn: Ministry of Finance of Estonia, The World Bank Group.

Mäenpää, M. (2001) *The Legislation Related to Securities Markets in the Baltic States.* Nordic Council of Ministers, ANP 2001: 728, Helsinki.

Meigas, H. (1999) 'Facts to be considered when determining institutional framework for integrated financial supervision', *Integrated Financial Sector Regulation and Supervision in the Context of EU Accession*, Prague, June 24–25.

Menton, R.C. (1990) 'The financial system and economic performance', *Journal of Financial Services Research*, 4 (4), December: 263–300.

Mølgard, E. (1998) *A Report on the Eesti Maapanga Case*, 18 December. Online, available at: http://www.ee/epbe/.

Mwenda, K.K. and Fleming, A. (2001) 'International developments in the organisational structure of financial services supervision', *Challenges for the Unified Financial Supervision in the New Millennium*. Tallinn: Ministry of Finance of Estonia, The World Bank Group.

Siibak, K. (2001) 'Finantsregulatsioonid ja finantsjärelevalve, probleemid ja arengud', *Juridica* III.

Srejber, E. (2001) 'Financial markets in a globalised world', speech to the Swedish Mutual Fund Association on 4 September. Online, available at: http://www.centralbanknet.com.

Summers, L. (1999) 'Reflections on managing global integration', *Journal of Economic Perspective*, Spring: 3–18.

Taylor, M. (1996) *Peak Practice: How to Reform the UK's Regulatory System.* London: Centre for Study of Financial Innovation.

Taylor, M. and Fleming, A. (1999) 'Integrated financial supervision: lesson from Northern European experience', Policy Research Working Paper, The World Bank Policy Research Dissemination Centre, Washington, DC.

The FSA's Approach to Regulation of the Market Infrastructure, UK Financial Services Authority, London, 2000, p. 58

The Portal to European Union Law. Online, available at: http://europa.eu.int/eur-lex/en/index.html.

The Structure and Functioning of the Financial Sector in Estonia, Workshop on Financial Sector Issues in Accession Countries, Bank of Estonia, Tallinn 2001, p. 40.

9 The effect of foreign bank entry on domestic banks in Central and Eastern Europe

Peter Zajc[1]

Introduction

In recent decades, especially during the 1990s, financial markets have been liberalised. Banking sectors have been opened for foreign banks,[2] based on the premise that gains from foreign entry to the domestic banking system outweigh losses (Claessens *et al.* 2001). Levine (1996) suggests that foreign banks enhance competition, which leads to a higher quality and greater variety of bank products. Furthermore, they contribute to the development of bank legislation and supervisory systems.

In light of the rapid penetration of foreign banks, several issues of concern emerge. These issues can be grouped into three broad categories: (i) the effect on competition in the host country's banking system; (ii) the effect on the performance and efficiency of banks, especially domestic ones; and (iii) the effect on the stability of the banking system of the host country. There are some papers and case studies dealing with the role of foreign banks, but on the whole empirical evidence of the impact of foreign banks on the domestic banking sector remains sparse.

I examine the impact of foreign bank entry on domestic banks in six advanced transition countries of Central and Eastern Europe (the Czech Republic, Estonia, Hungary, Poland, Slovakia and Slovenia) in the 1995–2000 period. Using micro-data from the BankScope database, I undertake an empirical analysis to determine the effects of foreign bank entry on several indicators of bank performance. The analysis is structured as follows. First, I provide a short literature overview, focusing specifically on two studies by Claessens *et al.* (2001) and Hermes and Lensink (2002). I then present selected accounting ratios of domestic and foreign banks to check whether there are statistically significant differences between these two groups of banks. This is followed by an econometric analysis of the effects of foreign bank entry on domestic banks. Lastly, I conclude with a summary and some comments on results.

Literature review

The issue of rapid foreign bank entry has received substantial attention not only from policymakers and practitioners, but also researchers and academics. There are a number of studies that analyse the effects of foreign bank entry on domestic banks from different perspectives. However, these are mostly descriptive studies, case studies or comparative studies of accounting ratios (for example, Bhattacharya 1994; Crystal *et al.* 2001; Pigott 1986). Crystal *et al.* (2001) note that empirical analysis of the effects of foreign bank entry on domestic banks is relatively limited, which can, in part, be ascribed to the fact that these developments occurred only recently. Accordingly, there is little empirical evidence for Central and Eastern European countries, with a few exceptions (for example Papi and Revoltella, 2000, analyse FDI in the banking sectors of nine Central and Eastern European countries).

Claessens *et al.* (2001; also 1998 as a working paper) performed a comprehensive study of the impact of foreign bank entry on the performance of domestic banks. Several authors have followed this framework: Barajas *et al.* (2000) for Colombia; Clarke *et al.* (2000) for Argentina; Denizer (2000) for Turkey; Hermes and Lensink (2002) for developing countries; and Pastor *et al.* (2000) for Spain.

Claessens *et al.* (2001) use an extensive database of individual bank balance sheets and income statements based on BankScope.[3] They study banks in 80 developed and developing countries in the period 1988–1995. In the first part of the analysis, they extend the work of Hanson and Rocha (1986) and Demirgüç-Kunt and Huizinga (1999), and compare average values of net interest margins, taxes paid, overhead expenses, loan loss provisions and profitability for domestic and foreign banks in individual countries as well as in groups of countries. The results differ between developed and developing countries. In developed countries, foreign banks have lower net interest margins, overhead expenses and profitability than domestic banks. The opposite holds for developing countries.

The second part of their study is an empirical estimation of the consequences of a change in foreign bank presence for the domestic banks. This part extends the work of two of the authors, Demirgüç-Kunt and Huizinga (1999), who used the same database to investigate the relationship between bank variables (including ownership) and net interest margin and profitability. Demirgüç-Kunt and Huizinga (1999) show that, in developing countries, foreign ownership is positively correlated with profitability and net interest margins, and vice versa in developed countries. Claessens *et al.* (2001) take the analysis a step further and concentrate on foreign bank entry, i.e. changes in foreign bank presence, and how it affects domestic banks. Foreign bank presence is measured either as a change in the number of foreign banks as a percentage of all banks present in the banking sector, or as a change in foreign banks' share in total assets. This allows them to test whether the mere presence or the actual market penetration of foreign banks is relevant for changes in the performance of domestic banks (Barajas *et al.* 2000).[4] For domestic banks, they estimate five equations with net interest margin, non-interest revenue, before-tax profit, overhead expenses and loan loss provisions as dependent variables. They regress the dependent variables on foreign bank number (number of foreign banks to the total number of banks),[5] four bank variables (equity, non-interest earning assets, overhead expenses, and customer and short-term funding) and four country-specific variables (real GDP per capita, real GDP growth rate, inflation and real interest rates). Their findings were that an increase in foreign bank presence is statistically significantly related to a reduction in non-interest income, before-tax profit and overhead costs. This may indicate that foreign banks bring modern and efficient technology and business practices which spill over to domestic banks and, in turn, reduce cost and enhance efficiency. Foreign banks also increase competition which forces domestic banks to improve their operations and efficiency, and leads to lower profits.

Hermes and Lensink (2002) have re-done the analysis by Claessens *et al.* (2001) with the same dependent and explanatory variables except for the real interest rate which was dropped because of insufficient data. Using a smaller sample of countries, i.e. 26 developing countries (including four European transition countries) in the 1990–1996 period, Hermes and Lensink (2002) find different results from those of Claessens *et al.* (2001). A rise in foreign bank presence, measured as the number of foreign banks as a percentage of the number of all banks, reduces profits and increases costs of the domestic banks. However, a rise in foreign bank presence, measured as the share of foreign banks in total assets, is associated with an increase in profits, income and costs. Overall, there is a clear positive relationship between change in foreign bank presence and increase in domestic banks' costs. Results for profitability and income are less clear, but Hermes and Lensink (2002) indicate that foreign bank entry generally increases profits, income and costs which is the opposite to the results of Claessens *et al.* (2001). In the last section, Hermes and Lensink (2002) test for non-linearity in the relationship between change in foreign bank presence and performance of domestic banks (inverted U-shaped relationship). They posit that, at low levels of foreign penetration, foreign bank entry has a positive effect on domestic banks, that is, enhancing their profits, income and costs. The spill-over effect dominates the effect of increased competition. A negative effect, such as reducing profits, income and costs, only sets in after a certain minimum threshold of foreign bank penetration has been reached and the competition effect dominates. Higher competition leads to lower profits and income, and to higher efficiency (lower costs). They find that an inverted U-shaped relationship exists for income and costs but not for profits. Thus, income and cost reducing effects of foreign bank entry (increased competition) set in only after the degree of foreign penetration has reached a certain threshold.

Accounting ratios of domestic and foreign banks

Before turning to the effects of foreign bank entry on the performance of domestic banks, I briefly look at five standard accounting ratios to identify differences between domestic and foreign banks.[6] Following Demirgüç-Kunt and Huizinga (1999), I use a simple accounting identity which includes the net interest margin (net interest revenue to total assets), non-interest income, before-tax profit, overhead costs and loan loss provisions, expressed as a percentage of total assets (see also Table 9.2):

$$NIM + NII/TA = PBT/TA + OE/TA + LLP/TA \qquad (9.1)$$

where

NIM = net interest margin
NII = non-interest income
PBT = profit before tax
OE = overhead expenses
LLP = loan loss provisions.

Net interest margin represents income from interest-generating activities, and non-interest margin represents all other (non-lending) sources of income such as fees and commissions. Overhead expenses and loan loss provisioning represent the cost side of bank operations. Table 9.1 presents all variables as 1995–2000 weighted averages with total assets as weights.

Claessens *et al.* (2001) find that, in general, foreign banks in developing countries have higher net interest margins, overhead costs and profitability, while the reverse holds for developed countries. Broken down by geographic region, their findings for transitional economies are in line with those for the six advanced transition economies of Central and Eastern Europe presented in Table 9.1: the net interest margin and both cost variables (overhead costs and loan loss provisions) are lower for foreign banks as compared to domestic banks, while non-interest income and profit before tax are higher.

According to Claessens *et al.* (2001), the higher net interest margin of foreign compared to domestic banks in developing countries reflects market conditions in which foreign banks operate in the host countries. For example, in developing countries, foreign banks may have higher net interest margins than their domestic counterparts because they may be exempt from some restrictive regulations, do not operate on non-commercial criteria as some state-owned banks do, and apply modern

Table 9.1 Net interest margin, profitability and costs for domestic and foreign banks, 1995–2000

Country	Ownership	Net interest margin	Non-interest income	Before-tax profit	Overhead	Loan loss provisions
Czech Republic	D	3.91[1]	1.82[1]	−0.0021	5.19[1]	2.12[1]
	F	2.73[1]	1.49[1]	−0.031	3.67[1]	0.63[1]
Estonia	D	6.03	2.83	1.14	6.28	1.11
	F	5.22	2.89	1.94	5.42	0.82
Hungary	D	5.28[1]	2.43	0.61	6.11[1]	0.48
	F	4.53[1]	2.31	1.23	4.64[1]	0.62
Poland	D	5.83[1]	2.09[1]	2.28	2.64	0.44
	F	4.91[1]	3.66	2.48	2.79	0.51
Slovakia	D	2.75[1]	1.82	−0.14[1]	4.18[1]	0.92
	F	3.61[1]	1.96	2.03[1]	2.91[1]	0.71
Slovenia	D	4.76[1]	1.93[1]	1.4	4.55[1]	1.01
	F	3.39[1]	2.29[1]	1.3	3.74[1]	0.76

Source: author's calculations.

Notes
Weighted averages for the 1995–2000 period. Total assets as weights.
347 observations (305 for loan loss provisions).
Foreign bank: 50 per cent or more of equity owned by foreign entities.
All variables defined as fraction of total assets.
1 statistically significant difference between domestic and foreign banks at 5 per cent level or better.

banking practices that outweigh their information disadvantages. As shown in Table 9.1, this does not seem to apply to the six Central and Eastern European countries (any more). However, if net interest margin is interpreted as a rough indicator of efficiency (Demirgüç-Kunt and Huizinga 1999), foreign banks are more efficient because of their advantages in business practices, product range, organisational structure and experience.[7]

Lower net interest margin and higher non-interest income suggest that the latter is one of the key driving forces behind the high profits of foreign banks in Central and Eastern European countries. Net interest income seems to be less important than non-interest income. This is in line with findings in the literature that foreign banks bring to host markets new sophisticated products which, to a large extent, generate fee and commission (i.e. non-income) revenue. Lower overhead expenses may suggest that foreign banks outsource some of their labour- and technology-intensive operations to their headquarters. Bearing in mind that personnel expenses are the key component of overhead costs, lower overhead costs may also indicate that foreign banks are more flexible in adjusting the number of employees they employ to their operational requirements. Foreign greenfield investments start off with an adequate number of employees, while domestic banks acquired by foreign banks

may adjust the number of employees slower due to restrictive labour legislation, but still faster than other domestic banks which are more likely to
follow other interests in respect to employees. Demirgüç-Kunt and Huizinga
(1999) analyse determinants of net interest margin and find that higher
non-interest income and lower overhead expenses are significantly associated with lower net interest margins which seems to be consistent with the
experience of foreign banks in Central and Eastern Europe (Table 9.1).

Loan loss provisions are a measure of differences in credit quality.
Lower loan loss provisions indicate that foreign banks have a better credit
screening procedure and/or a better-quality client structure (that is, large
companies and high net-worth individuals). The latter is consistent with
the 'cherry-picking' hypothesis, where foreign banks service mostly better
clients and leave customers of lesser quality to domestic banks. However,
loan loss provisions are not comparable across countries because of different provisioning regulation.

Effects of foreign bank entry on the domestic banking system

Hermes and Lensink (2002) suggest that the impact of foreign bank entry
on domestic bank operations is different for developed and developing
countries. Their sample includes only a small number of banks from each
country (that is, one bank each from Hungary, Romania, Bolivia, Peru
and so on), which could imply that the sample is not random and is also
not representative for all developing countries as a group.

In my analysis, I build on and extend the work of Claessens *et al.* (2001)
and Hermes and Lensink (2002). I use their specification of the empirical
model, but specifically concentrate on the effects of foreign bank entry on
domestic banks in six Central and Eastern European countries (the Czech
Republic, Estonia, Hungary, Poland, Slovakia and Slovenia). Subsamples
may result in a selection bias, but I am only interested in making an infer-
ence about the transition economies and not for all countries. Thus, the
sample of the transition economies is sufficient. Within this sample selection,
bias should not be a problem since I include most of the banks. These banks
account for a large share in total assets of the respective banking sectors.

The estimation equation is based on Claessens *et al.* (2001: 905) and is
defined as:

$$\Delta Y_{ijt} = \beta_0 + \beta_1 \Delta FE_{jt} + \beta_2 \Delta XB_{it} + \beta_3 \Delta XC_{jt} + \epsilon_{ijt} \qquad (9.2)$$

where

Y_{ijt} = the dependent variable
FE_{jt} = the foreign entry variable
XB_{it} = bank variables
XC_{jt} = country variables

β = vectors of coefficients to be estimated
ϵ_{ijt} = the error term
i = the bank index
j = the country index
t = the time index.

This equation is estimated for domestic banks only. It is estimated in first differences to possibly correct for endogeneity.[8] It has two specifications with respect to the definition of the foreign entry variable (FE_{jt}): (i) the number of foreign banks in country j and time t as percentage of all banks in country j and time t; and (ii) the share of foreign banks in total assets in country j and time t. Thus, there are two-times-five equations to be estimated. The five dependent variables (Y_{ijt}) are net interest margin, non-interest income, profit before tax, overhead expenses and loan loss provisions, all for bank i in country j and time t. There are four bank-specific explanatory variables (XB_{it}): equity, non-earning assets, customer and short-term funding, and overhead costs. All bank-specific variables are scaled by total assets to control for size. XC_{jt} are country-specific variables (GDP per capita, real growth and inflation). For data unavailability, the real interest rate was not included. A more detailed description of variables and their sources is provided in Table 9.2.

In the empirical estimation, I apply the weighted least squares method on a pooled sample of six countries for the 1995–2000 period. The number of domestic banks is used as a weight to control for the different number of banks in each country under study. All regressions include country dummies to capture some of the remaining differences among countries. Regressions also include time dummies to control for time effects not accounted for by other country-specific variables. Country and time dummies are not reported. The panel is unbalanced because (i) if a bank changes from domestic to foreign, it is excluded from the sample from the next year on; and because of (ii) data availability in some years.

First, I estimate five equations with the number of foreign banks as the explanatory variable (Table 9.3). The p-value of the F-statistic for the model shows the overall significance of the models (equations). Explanatory variables are jointly significant. I also report p-values for joint tests for country and time dummies, and White heteroskedasticity corrected standard errors. The number of observations is 347, except for loan loss provisions where the data availability is more limited (305 observations).

Coefficients in the estimated equations show that foreign bank number (i.e. an increase in the share of foreign banks in the total number of banks) is significantly associated with a reduction of non-interest income (significant at 1 per cent) and before-tax profit (1 per cent), and an increase in the overhead costs (5 per cent). Foreign bank number is not statistically significantly associated with the net interest margin (p-value of 0.12, not reported) and loan loss provisions (0.23, not reported). A negative relationship with

Table 9.2 Description of variables

Variable	Source	Description
Foreign bank number	Central banks, EBRD	Number of foreign banks as percentage of all banks in a given country and year
Foreign bank share	Central banks, BankScope	Share of foreign banks of total assets of banking sector in a given country and year
Net interest margin	BankScope	Net interest revenue (interest income minus interest expense) over total assets
Non-interest income	BankScope	Total operating income minus net interest revenue over total assets
Before-tax profit	BankScope	Profit before tax over total assets
Overhead expenses	BankScope	Total operating expense (all but interest expenses) over total assets
Loan loss provisions	BankScope	Loan loss provisions over total assets
Equity	BankScope	Equity over total assets
Non-earning assets	BankScope	Cash, non-interest-bearing interbank deposits, intangible and other non-earning assets to total
Customer and short term funding	BankScope	Short- and long-term deposits, and other non-deposit short-term funding over total assets
GDP per capita	IFS and CIA	GDP per capita in euros
Real growth	EBRD	Real GDP annual growth rate
Inflation	IFS	Annual CPI change

Sources: Central banks: various publications and home pages; CIA Factbook 2001; http://www.cia.gov/cia/publications/factbook; EBRD Transition Reports, various years; Fitch IBCA's BankScope database; IMF's International Financial Statistics (IFS) CD ROM 2001.

Note: all variables are expressed as percentages except GDP per capita (in euros, 2000 prices).

the profitability measure (before-tax profits) indicates that foreign bank entry enhances the level of competition in the banking sector and thus reduces non-interest income and profits of domestic banks. A rise in overhead costs suggests that foreign bank entry induces domestic banks to enhance and upgrade their operations and infrastructure, which means higher investment costs that can be spread out over some years. In sum, foreign bank entry seems to reduce profits and income, and increase costs (consistent with the finding of Hermes and Lensink 2002).

Turning to control variables, it is interesting to note that an increase in overhead expenses (explanatory variable) is significantly and strongly associated with an increase in non-interest income. Banks in Central and Eastern Europe are refocusing their businesses and are concentrating more on non-interest income. This requires setting up systems to provide

Table 9.3 Foreign bank number and its impact on the performance of domestic banks

Explanatory variables	Dependent variables				
	Net interest margin	Non-interest income	Before-tax profit	Overhead	LLP
Foreign bank number	−0.0360	−0.1725***	−0.1031***	0.1306**	0.0514
	(0.0229)	(0.0327)	(0.0339)	(0.0606)	(0.0431)
Equity	0.1045**	0.0941	0.1305*	−0.4554**	−0.1128***
	(0.4938)	(0.0745)	(0.0726)	(0.2238)	(0.0417)
Non-earning assets	−0.5781*	0.0930	0.0521	−0.0789	0.0486*
	(0.3247)	(0.0702)	(0.0706)	(0.1108)	(0.0285)
Customer and ST funding	−0.0153	0.0154	0.0309	−0.0006	0.0104
	(0.0153)	(0.0273)	(0.0283)	(0.0403)	(0.0173)
Overhead	0.0189	0.4659***	−0.6200***		0.5017***
	(0.0479)	(0.0677)	(0.0856)		(0.1411)
GDP per capita	−0.0029	−0.0074**	−0.0124***	0.0092*	0.0012
	(0.0021)	(0.0030)	(0.0033)	(0.0049)	(0.0032)
Real growth	−0.0379	0.1816	0.1763	−0.2947	−0.0768
	(0.0690)	(0.1312)	(0.1425)	(0.2053)	(0.1288)
Inflation	0.0298	0.1206	−0.0183	−0.1931	−0.1362*
	(0.0664)	(0.0850)	(0.0972)	(0.1547)	(0.0703)
F model[1]	0.0000	0.0000	0.0000	0.0040	0.0000
F time dummies[1]	0.1752	0.0035	0.0117	0.0104	0.8464
F country dummies[1]	0.0999	0.0139	0.0514	0.7570	0.6498
Number of observations	347	347	347	347	305

Source: author's calculations.

Notes
Heteroskedasticity corrected standard errors in parentheses.
* Significant at 10 per cent level; ** significant at 5 per cent level; *** significant at 1 per cent level.
1 P-values for the F-test.
All variables are in first differences.
Unbalanced panel.
LLP are loan-loss provisions. ST is short-term.

for fee- and commission-generating services which bring about additional costs but also revenues from the new services offered (non-interest revenues). Overhead expenses are also significantly correlated with lower profits and, somewhat surprisingly, with higher loan loss provisions. Results for overhead expenses (as an explanatory variable) accord with the results of Hermes and Lensink (2002) and Claessens *et al.* (2001).

Coefficients on the country-specific variables are insignificant with few exceptions. Higher GDP per capita is significantly associated with lower profits, which is contrary to the findings in the literature.

The same five equations were also estimated in the alternative or second specification, that is, with the share of foreign banks in total assets as the dependent variable. Estimated coefficients (Table 9.4) are similar

Table 9.4 Foreign bank share and its impact on the performance of domestic banks

Explanatory variables	Dependent variables				
	Net interest margin	Non-interest income	Before-tax profit	Overhead	LLP
Foreign bank share	−0.0161*	−0.0702***	−0.0516***	0.0486*	−0.0148
	(0.0088)	(0.0141)	(0.0135)	(0.0253)	(0.0163)
Equity	0.1072**	0.1052	0.1391*	−0.4648**	−0.1128***
	(0.4905)	(0.0782)	(0.0738)	(0.2258)	(0.0402)
Non-earning assets	−0.0598*	0.0855	0.0451	−0.0748	0.0436
	(0.0326)	(0.0733)	(0.0712)	(0.1102)	(0.0296)
Customer and ST funding	−0.0112	0.0352	0.0422	−0.0159	0.0057
	(0.0157)	(0.0258)	(0.0271)	(0.0453)	(0.0200)
Overhead	0.0186	0.4623***	−0.6192***		0.5249***
	(0.0474)	(0.0686)	(0.0832)		(0.1443)
GDP per capita	−0.0020	−0.0028	−0.0092***	0.0060	0.0016
	(0.0022)	(0.0029)	(0.0035)	(0.0058)	(0.0032)
Real growth	−0.0944	−0.0728	0.0027	−0.1132	−0.0813
	(0.0828)	(0.1215)	(0.1250)	(0.2199)	(0.1335)
Inflation	0.0113	0.0299	−0.0697	−0.1236	−0.0980
	(0.0660)	(0.0839)	(0.0913)	(0.1462)	(0.0696)
F model[1]	0.0000	0.0000	0.0000	0.0000	0.0000
F time dummies[1]	0.2303	0.0123	0.0168	0.0158	0.5953
F country dummies[1]	0.0772	0.4071	0.3125	0.9478	0.6496
Number of observations	347	347	347	347	305

Source: author's calculations.

Notes
Heteroskedasticity corrected standard errors in parentheses.
*Significant at 10 per cent level; ** significant at 5 per cent level; *** significant at 1 per cent level.
1 P-values for the F-test.
All variables are in first differences.
Unbalanced panel.
LLP are loan-loss provisions. ST is short-term.

to those under the first specification. An increase of foreign banks' share in total assets is statistically significantly associated with a decline in profitability, non-interest income and net interest margin, and positively associated with overhead expenses. Thus, foreign bank entry reduces income and profits, and increases costs. For income and profits this is the reverse of the Hermes and Lensink (2002) results, while the overhead expenses are in line with their results. Claessens *et al.* (2001) do not find any coefficients statistically significant under the second specification of the model.

A summary of results is presented in Table 9.5. Overall, the results seem to be robust and consistent across both specifications; that is, the number of foreign banks and their share in total assets have the same effects on domestic banks in terms of income, profitability and costs. This is different to the results of Hermes and Lensink (2002), who report converse results for both specifications, and to those of Claessens *et al.* (2001), who only find significant coefficients in the first specification (number of foreign banks) but not in the second. Hence, foreign bank entry in the six Central and Eastern European countries is significantly associated with a decline in income and profits (in line with Claessens *et al.* 2001), and a rise of overhead costs of domestic banks (in line with Hermes and Lensink 2002). This may suggest that the argument of Hermes and Lensink (2002) holds, that is, that foreign bank entry has different impacts on domestic banks in developed and developing economies.[9] However, my results disagree in part with those of Hermes and Lensink (2002), which might imply that Central and Eastern European countries behave differently from countries they included in their sample.

Table 9.5 Summary of results and a comparison with other studies

	Model specification	Net interest margin	Non-interest income	Before-tax profit	Overhead expenses	Loan-loss provisions
Results	FBN	ns	−	−	+	ns
	FBS	−	−	−	+	ns
Claessens *et al.* (2001)	FBN	ns	−	−	−	ns
	FBS	ns	ns	ns	ns	ns
Hermes and Lensink (2002)	FBN	ns	−	−	+	+
	FBS	ns	+	+	+	ns

Source: author: Claessens *et al.* (2001) and Hermes and Lensink (2002).

Notes
FBN – foreign bank number, FBS – foreign bank share.
ns indicates a relationship that is not significant statistically.
+ indicates a significant positive correlation.
− indicates a significant negative correlation.

Testing for non-linearity in foreign bank entry effects on domestic banks

The impact of foreign bank entry on domestic banks works through increased competition and enhanced efficiency (Claessens *et al.* 2001). Increased competition puts downward pressure on income and profits. Foreign banks put pressure on domestic banks to enhance their efficiency by adopting more efficient management techniques and taking advantage of new technology introduced by foreign banks (spill-over effect). This eventually leads to lower costs, but initially the costs of domestic banks might rise to reflect efforts to reorganise and invest in new technology. In the short term, if domestic banks still have some market power, they may increase interest margins and non-interest income to cover higher costs (Hermes and Lensink 2002). Costs of domestic banks may also rise because increased competition can weaken their loan portfolios and require higher loan loss provisioning.

The inverted U-shape impact of the foreign bank entry scenario posits that foreign bank entry may first bring positive and eventually negative effects for domestic banks. Initially, the efficiency effect is stronger than the effect of increased competition, and income, profits and costs rise upon foreign bank entry. Later on, after a certain threshold of foreign bank presence has been reached, negative effects (such as a decrease in costs, income and profit) may take place (competition effect dominates). To check for a non-linear relationship (inverted U-shaped relationship) between the entry variable and domestic bank performance variables, I follow Hermes and Lensink (2002) and estimate Equation (9.3):

$$\Delta Y_{ijt} = \beta_0 + \beta_1 \Delta FE_{jt} + \beta_2 \Delta FE_{jt}^2 + \beta_3 \Delta XB_{it} + \beta_4 \Delta XC_{jt} + \epsilon_{ijt} \qquad (9.3)$$

where

Y_{ijt} = the dependent variable
FE_{jt} = the foreign entry variable
XB_{it} = bank variables
XC_{jt} = country variables
β = vectors of coefficients to be estimated
ϵ_{ijt} = the error term
i = the bank index
j = the country index
t = the time index.

Equation (9.3) includes a quadratic term for the foreign bank entry variable. A significant positive coefficient on the foreign entry variable and a significant negative coefficient on the quadratic foreign entry variable would indicate an inverted U-shaped effect of foreign bank entry on domestic banks. Estimation results are presented in Table 9.6 and Table 9.7.

Table 9.6 Foreign bank number and its impact on domestic bank performance, allowing for non-linear relationship

Explanatory variables	Dependent variables				
	Net interest margin	Non-interest income/TA	Before-tax profit/TA	Overhead/ TA	LLP/TA
Foreign bank number	−0.0417	−0.2608***	−0.0766	0.2491	−0.2141*
	(0.0655)	(0.0969)	(0.1135)	(0.1977)	(0.1199)
(Foreign bank number)^2	0.0079	0.1221	−0.0366	−0.1641	0.3654*
	(0.0823)	(0.1396)	(0.1630)	(0.2851)	(0.2095)
Equity/TA	0.1044**	0.0925	0.1310*	−0.4523**	−0.1324***
	(0.0496)	(0.0766)	(0.0728)	(0.2224)	(0.0455)
Non-earning assets	−0.0578*	0.0924	0.0523	−0.0780	0.0428
	(0.0325)	(0.0718)	(0.0708)	(0.1095)	(0.0279)
Customer and ST funding	−0.0154	0.0135	0.0315	0.0020	−0.0015
	(0.0155)	(0.0271)	(0.0293)	(0.0428)	(0.0230)
Overhead/TA	0.0190	0.4674***	−0.6205***		0.4959***
	(0.0476)	(0.0678)	(0.0853)		(0.1369)
GDP per capita	−0.0028	0.0048	−0.0131**	0.0057	0.0091
	(0.0032)	(0.0045)	(0.0055)	(0.0080)	(0.0055)
Real growth	−0.0423	0.1146	0.1963	−0.2040	−0.2907
	(0.0955)	(0.1701)	(0.1903)	(0.2782)	(0.2191)
Inflation	0.0291	0.1093	−0.0149	−0.1776	−0.1754
	(0.0675)	(0.0842)	(0.0959)	(0.1567)	(0.0769)
F model[1]	0.0000	0.0000	0.0000	0.0051	0.0000
F time dummies[1]	0.1776	0.0053	0.0177	0.0063	0.4260
F country dummies[1]	0.1022	0.0132	0.0944	0.7862	0.5874
Number of observations	347	347	347	347	305

Source: author's calculations.

Notes
Heteroskedasticity corrected standard errors in parentheses.
* Significant at 10 per cent level;
** significant at 5 per cent level;
*** significant at 1 per cent level.
1 P-values for the F-test.
All variables are in first differences.
Unbalanced panel.
LLP are loan-loss provisions. ST is short-term.

Table 9.7 Foreign bank share and its impact on domestic bank performance, allowing for non-linear relationship

Explanatory variables	Dependent variables				
	Net interest margin	Non-interest income/TA	Before-tax profit/TA	Overhead/ TA	LLP/TA
Foreign bank share	−0.0400	0.1019	0.0596	0.0440	−0.1576
	(0.0529)	(0.0735)	(0.0818)	(0.1520)	(0.1176)
(Foreign bank share)^2	0.0269	0.1939**	−0.1253	0.0051	0.1608
	(0.0591)	(0.0825)	(0.0894)	(0.1644)	(0.1232)
Equity/TA	0.1074**	0.1032	0.1378*	−0.4648**	−0.1114***
	(0.0489)	(0.0773)	(0.0733)	(0.2267)	(0.0399)
Non-earning assets	−0.0598*	0.0859	0.0453	−0.0748	0.0430
	(0.0326)	(0.0728)	(0.0711)	(0.1104)	(0.0296)
Customer and ST funding	−0.0107	0.0314	0.0398	−0.0158	0.0071
	(0.0155)	(0.0244)	(0.0264)	(0.0441)	(0.0192)
Overhead/TA	0.0186	0.4624**	−0.6191***		0.5217***
	(0.0474)	(0.0681)	(0.0830)		(0.1426)
GDP per capita	−0.0018	−0.0041	−0.0100***	0.0060	0.0027
	(0.0023)	(0.0031)	(0.0037)	(0.0060)	(0.0035)
Real growth	−0.1028	−0.0118	0.0420	−0.1148	−0.1325
	(0.0858)	(0.1303)	(0.1373)	(0.2260)	(0.1586)
Inflation	−0.0038	0.1391	0.0009	−0.1264	−0.1907**
	(0.0728)	(0.0900)	(0.0895)	(0.1460)	(0.0900)
F model[1]	0.0000	0.0000	0.0000	0.0000	0.0000
F time dummies[1]	0.2584	0.0179	0.0141	0.0192	0.5238
F country dummies[1]	0.0974	0.0642	0.2699	0.9875	0.6384
Number of observations	347	347	347	347	305

Source: author's calculations.

Notes
Heteroskedasticity corrected standard errors in parentheses.
* Significant at 10 per cent level;
** significant at 5 per cent level;
*** significant at 1 per cent level.
1 P-values for the F-test.
All variables are in first differences. Unbalanced panel.
LLP are loan-loss provisions. ST is short-term.

Estimated coefficients indicate that an inverted U-shaped relationship is not confirmed by the data; that is, there seems to be no non-linear (i.e. quadratic) relationship among the foreign bank entry variables and the five dependent variables. Thus, it cannot be inferred that foreign bank entry initially, when foreign bank presence is still relatively low, has a different effect on the performance of domestic banks than later when foreign bank presence has reached a certain threshold. The result is not in line with Hermes and Lensink (2002), who found that cost and income decrease only after the foreign bank presence has reached a certain minimum level.

The result has to be interpreted within the time span of the sample (1995–2000) and a relatively short time period. Although an inverted U-shaped relationship between foreign bank entry and costs of domestic banks has been rejected by the analysis, domestic banks in Central and Eastern Europe may still be on the rising side of the inverted U-shaped curve. Thus, there may be a time lag and eventually their costs may start decreasing.

For profits, the argument is less clear; that is, different scenarios could be possible. As mentioned before, the efficiency effect may initially outweigh the competition effect resulting in rising profits, which only start falling after the competition effect has reached a certain threshold (inverted U-shaped relationship). However, this was rejected by the analysis. Another scenario could be a U-shaped relationship between foreign bank entry and domestic bank profitability. Initially profits of domestic banks fall, but eventually (some) domestic banks resolve their bad-debt problem and enhance their efficiency to such levels that the efficiency effect outweighs the competition effect, and profits start to rise. Also, after reaching a substantial market share, foreign banks might reduce their efforts to increase their market share further (perhaps it would be too costly to lure over loyal clients of other banks). The level of competition could decline (stabilise) and profits may rise. In such a scenario, there would be a U-shaped relationship between foreign bank entry and domestic bank profitability. But for empirical verification of these hypotheses one needs to extend the sample to include some of the future years.

Comment and conclusion

This chapter empirically analysed the effect of foreign bank entry on the performance of domestic banks in six Central and Eastern European countries (the Czech Republic, Estonia, Hungary, Poland, Slovakia and Slovenia) in the 1995–2000 period. Results show that foreign bank entry, measured both as the number of foreign banks and as the foreign banks' share in total assets, reduces net interest margin, income and profits, and increases the costs of domestic banks. A reduction of the net interest margin and of profits suggests that foreign bank entry enhances competition in the banking sector. A rise in costs may indicate that domestic banks react to new competitors and invest in refocusing their businesses and in introducing new products.

The results partly diverge from those of Claessens *et al.* (2001), who use a sample including both developed and developing countries. Foreign bank entry seems to have a different effect on domestic banks in developed and developing countries. However, the results are also different from those of Hermes and Lensink (2002), who analyse developing countries only, but their sample might suffer from selection bias. Thus, Central and Eastern European countries seem to warrant a separate analysis. The experience with foreign bank entry in other countries or geographic regions such as South America or Asia might be informative, but policymakers should keep in mind the specificities of Central and Eastern Europe. Foreign banks have undoubtedly been playing an important role in Central and Eastern European countries, but their role should not be overemphasised, i.e. they should not be treated as a panacea for all the problems of the banking sectors.

Notes

1 The author would like to thank Claudia Buch, Stijn Claessens and Robert Lensink for valuable comments.
2 I define a foreign bank (domestic bank) as a bank in which 50 per cent or more of equity is held by non-residents (residents).
3 BankScope is a database of individual bank accounting information compiled by Fitch-IBCA. It is standardised and thus enables international comparisons. For more details on BankScope see, for example, Mathieson and Roldos (2001).
4 See Green *et al.* (2002) for a critique of the number of foreign banks as a measure of foreign bank entry.
5 All five regressions were also estimated using foreign bank share in total assets. Coefficients on this variable were statistically insignificant.
6 Demirgüç-Kunt and Huizinga (1999: 382) note that 'although it may be misleading to compare accounting ratios without controlling for differences in macroeconomic environment in which banks operate and the differences in their business, product mix, and leverage, it is still useful as an initial indicator of differences across countries.'
7 Net interest margin can be interpreted as a proxy for efficiency. However, this concept of efficiency is not directly related to the concept of frontier efficiency (x-efficiency).
8 Following Claessens *et al.*(1998: 16) I implicitly assume that the foreign entry variable (FE_{jt}) is exogenous. One way for this assumption to hold would be if the foreign bank presence at time t were determined by other variables (entry incentives) at time $t-1$. See also Amel and Liang (1997).
9 Papi and Revoltella (2000: 441) also note that the impact of foreign banks is different in developed and developing countries, which may 'present a further stimulus to investigate Central and Eastern European countries as a special case'.

References

Amel, D.F. and Liang, J.N. (1997) 'Determinants of entry and profits in local banking markets', *Review of Industrial Organisation*, 12: 59–78.
Barajas, A., Steiner, R. and Salazar, N. (2000) 'Foreign investments in Colombia's

financial sector', in C. Claessens and M. Jansen (eds), *The Internationalization of Financial Services*. The Hague: Kluwer Law International.

Bhattacharya, J. (1994) 'The role of foreign banks in developing countries: a survey of the evidence', mimeo, Iowa State University.

Claessens, S., Demirgüç-Kunt, A. and Huizinga, H. (1998) 'How does foreign entry affect the domestic banking market?', Policy Research Working Paper No. 1918. World Bank.

Claessens, S., Demirgüç-Kunt, A. and Huizinga, H. (2001) 'How does foreign entry affect domestic banking markets?', *Journal of Banking and Finance*, 25: 891–911.

Clarke, G., Cull, R., D'Amato, L. and Molinari, A. (2000) 'On the kindness of strangers? The impact of foreign entry on domestic banks in Argentina', in C. Claessens and M. Jansen (eds), *The Internationalization of Financial Services*. The Hague: Kluwer Law International.

Crystal, J.S., Dages, B.G. and Goldberg, L.S. (2001) 'Does foreign ownership contribute to sounder banks? The Latin American experience', in R.E. Litan, P. Masson and M. Pomerleano (eds), *Open Doors – Foreign Participation in Financial Systems in Developing Countries*. Washington, DC: Brookings Institution Press.

Demirgüç-Kunt, A. and Huizinga, H. (1999) 'Determinants of commercial bank interest margins and profitability: some international evidence', *The World Bank Economic Review*, 13: 379–408.

Denizer, C. (2000) 'Foreign entry in Turkey's banking sector, 1980–97', in C. Claessens and M. Jansen (eds), *The Internationalization of Financial Services*. The Hague: Kluwer Law International.

Green, C.J., Murinde, V. and Nikolov, I. (2002) 'Foreign bank penetration in domestic banking markets: evidence on Central and Eastern Europe', in T. Kowalski, R. Lensink and V. Vensel (eds), *Foreign Bank and Economic Transition – Papers in Progress*. Poznan: Poznan University.

Hanson, J.A. and Rocha, R.d.R. (1986) *High Interest Rates, Spreads, and the Cost of Intermediation*. Industry and Finance Series Volume 18, World Bank.

Hermes, N. and Lensink, R. (2002) 'The impact of foreign bank entry on domestic banks in less developed countries: an econometric analysis', in T. Kowalski, R. Lensink and V. Vensel (eds) *Foreign Bank and Economic Transition – Papers in Progress*. Poznan: Poznan University.

Levine, R. (1996) 'Foreign banks, financial development, and economic growth', in C.E. Barfield (ed.), *International Financial Markets – Harmonization versus Competition*. Washington, DC: AEI Press.

Mathieson, D.J. and Roldos, J. (2001) 'Foreign banks in emerging markets', in R.E. Litan, P. Masson and M. Pomerleano (eds), *Open Doors – Foreign Participation in Financial Systems in Developing Countries*. Washington, DC: Brookings Institution Press.

Papi, L. and Revoltella, D. (2000) 'Foreign direct investment in the banking sector: a transitional economy perspective', in C. Claessens and M. Jansen (eds), *The Internationalization of Financial Services*. The Hague: Kluwer Law International.

Pastor, J.M., Perez, F. and Quesada, J. (2000) 'The opening of the Spanish banking system: 1985–98', in C. Claessens and M. Jansen (eds), *The Internationalization of Financial Services*. The Hague: Kluwer Law International.

Pigott, C.A. (1986) 'Financial reform and the role of foreign banks in Pacific Basin nations', in H.S. Cheng (ed.), *Financial Policy and Reform in Pacific Basin Countries*. Lexington, KY: Lexington Books.

10 Are foreign banks in Central and Eastern Europe more efficient than domestic banks?[1]

Christopher J. Green, Victor Murinde and Ivaylo Nikolov

Introduction

One of the central issues in the move to a market economy by the transition economies of Central and Eastern Europe is the development of an efficient financial system. In most transition economies, a key policy element has been the opening up of the banking system to foreign competition at a relatively early stage in the transition process. The motivation for this policy is that foreign banks can immediately import financial management, organisational skills and general banking experience which are likely to be in short supply among domestic entrepreneurs. Foreign banks may therefore provide a clear competitive yardstick against which domestic banks can be evaluated by customers and regulators, and thus themselves develop efficient banking practises more rapidly. Irrespective of their precise motives, or methods of penetration, banks have rapidly become among the most important foreign investors in the European transition economies (Mathieson and Roldos 2001).[2]

The purpose of this chapter is to examine more rigorously the prevailing belief that the banking sector in Central and Eastern Europe benefits substantially, in terms of efficiency, from the entry of foreign banks. Hence, the main questions addressed by this chapter are twofold. First is the question of whether foreign ownership is an important factor in reducing a bank's total costs. Second is the issue of whether foreign banks operate more efficiently, in terms of economies of scale and scope, than domestic banks in Central and Eastern Europe.

Several recent papers have addressed the issue of foreign bank ownership in Central and Eastern Europe. However, most of these papers have concentrated either on the determinants of entry or on a country-specific study of X-inefficiency. The main contribution of this chapter is that it is, to our knowledge, the first cross-country study which carries out a systematic estimation of economies of scale and scope in banks located in the transition economies. We implement an innovative research methodology by estimating and testing a system of equations, consisting of an augmented translog cost function and the associated cost share equations, on a panel of 273 foreign and domestic banks which operated in Bulgaria, Croatia, the Czech Republic, Estonia, Hungary, Latvia, Lithuania, Poland and Romania during 1995–1999.

We find evidence that, in general, banks in Central and Eastern Europe operate at a reasonable level of efficiency in terms of economies of scale and scope. Moreover, we generally reject the hypothesis that foreign banks are more efficient than domestic banks in the sample European transition economies: the evidence suggests that, in terms of efficiency, foreign banks are, on average, not substantially different from domestic banks. Indeed, in some cases, domestic banks are more efficient. In addition, we do not find any empirical grounds to sustain the argument that bank ownership (foreign versus domestic) is an important factor in reducing banks' total operating and interest costs.

The remainder of this chapter is structured into four sections. The next section presents a short review of the relevant literature. This is followed by a discussion of econometric methodology. An empirical model is specified as a system of equations, comprising a multiproduct translog total cost function and two share equations, followed by a discussion of measurement and data. The section that follows this reports the empirical results, concentrating on the evidence on economies of scale and scope, and the tests of differences between domestic and foreign-owned banks. The final section contains some concluding remarks.

Background literature

The main questions addressed in this chapter derive from a synthesis of two strands of the literature: that on bank efficiency and that on the impact of foreign bank entry on the domestic banking sector.

The literature on bank efficiency is based on two different approaches to efficiency measurement: the first measures efficiency in terms of economies of scale and scope; the second uses the efficient frontier concept, or *X*-inefficiency, which may be disaggregated into technical and allocative inefficiency. Until recently, measurement of scale and scope economies dominated the theoretical and empirical literatures. In this approach, banks are assumed to be operating on a cost function, and inefficiencies may arise either from the use of inefficient technology (associated with higher costs along all or part of the cost function), or from an inefficient scale or scope (product mix). In principle, inefficient scale or scope may be attributable to either the management of the individual bank or to the structure of the market and the number of competing banks. The more recent, frontier efficiency, literature measures inefficiency with reference to a production (or cost, or profit) frontier, estimated using parametric or non-parametric techniques from the technologies used by sample banks. Deviations inside the frontier are ascribed primarily to inefficiencies in management.

In comparing the two approaches, Molyneux *et al.* concluded that 'differences in managerial ability to control costs or maximise revenues seem to be larger than the cost effects of the choice of scale and scope of production (1996: 252)'. This would suggest the use of frontier efficiency to study banks in Central and Eastern Europe. However, the disadvantage of the frontier approach is that the method does not readily offer possible remedies for inefficient firms since, by construction, inefficiency is attributable primarily to unobservable management actions. In contrast, as Berger and Humphrey (1991, 1997) and others have argued, measures of economies of scale and scope provide a natural framework for informing bank management on possible bank branching and cost reduction strategies, and informing regulators about the efficient number of banks in the market.

There are few existing studies on the efficiency of banks in the transition economies of Europe, and these do not explicitly distinguish between foreign-owned and locally-owned banks; see, for example, Yildirim and Philippatos (2002), Mertens and Urga (2001) and Kraft and Tirtiroglu (1998). More recently, there have been some country-specific studies of bank efficiency using the cost frontier approach. Weill (2003) and Havrylchyk (2003) studied small samples of banks in the Czech Republic and Poland, and both authors found some evidence that foreign banks were more efficient than domestic banks. These studies are, however, limited by the small samples and short time period studied.

The second strand of the literature concerns the impact of the entry of foreign firms into emerging markets. Litan *et al.* (2001) point to a steadily rising presence of foreign firms in the financial sector during the past decade. They argue that foreign firms bring important benefits to the markets they enter: improved technologies, increased investment and more experienced management. In the banking sector in particular, foreign entrants bring more sophisticated risk management techniques and greater financial stability because they tend to be more diversified than their domestic counterparts. It is also argued that, for the most part, foreign banks have helped increase the competitiveness and efficiency of the domestic banks in the host markets. Mathieson and Roldos (2001) show results whereby efficiency gains are reflected in lower operating costs and smaller margins between interest rates on loans and deposits among the foreign banks as well as the domestic banks.

In addition, foreign banks seem to enjoy higher profits than their local counterparts. Using 7,900 bank observations from 80 countries for 1988–1995, Claessens *et al.* (2001) examine the extent and effect of foreign presence in domestic banking markets by investigating how net interest margins, overheads, taxes paid and profitability differ between foreign and domestic banks. It is found that foreign banks have higher profits than domestic banks in developing countries, while the opposite holds true in industrial countries. An increased presence of foreign banks is also associated with a reduction in profitability and margins for domestic banks. These results are consistent with the evidence obtained by Demirgüç-Kunt and Huizinga (1999).

There is also evidence to suggest that the efficiency benefits of foreign bank entry are amplified by financial liberalisation. Bhattacharyya *et al.* (1997) examine the productive efficiency of 70 Indian commercial banks during the early stages of liberalisation (1986–1991), using a combination of data envelopment analysis and stochastic frontier analysis. It is found that publicly-owned Indian banks have been the most efficient, followed by foreign-owned banks and privately-owned Indian banks. In addition, there was a temporal improvement in the performance of foreign-owned banks, virtually no trend in the performance of privately-owned Indian banks, and a temporal decline in the performance of publicly-owned Indian banks, following a period of liberalisation.

Further, it may be argued that, given the strategies by host governments in the European transition economies, we would particularly expect foreign banks to have important effects on efficiency and the cost structure of the banking system in these countries. In these economies, foreign bank entry has responded to two main approaches used by governments to transform the banking sector (Claessens 1997). First, existing banks and especially the debt-burdened big state banks have been rehabilitated (the 'rehabilitation' approach). Second, new entrants have been allowed into the system or a completely new and parallel banking system has been allowed to emerge (the 'new entry' approach). In responding to these, foreign banks have maintained a clear focus on their motives for entry (Konopielko 1999). The most common reason for foreign bank entry is the need to support the client base, especially in Poland and the Czech Republic. Other reasons include: a response to international competitive pressures; and the search for new business opportunities, reflecting the belief in the growth potential of the transition economies (Konopielko 1999: 468).

However, the existing evidence does not point to there being unalloyed benefits from foreign bank entry. The experience of Latin America in the 1990s suggests that, in some countries, whereas local banks acquired by foreign owners became stronger in comparison with their domestic counterparts, their profitability was only comparable to or weaker than that of domestic banks. Moreover, efficiency gains may be eroded if foreign-owned banks adversely affect the stability of domestic bank credit by providing additional channels for capital flight. On these issues see Dages *et al.* (2000) and Claessens *et al.* (2001). Indeed, it may be argued that, if other dangers of foreign bank entry prevail, as in the case when foreign-owned banks withdraw rapidly from the domestic market in the face of a financial crisis, as witnessed during the recent experience in South East Asia, or when foreign banks may aggravate the risk profile of domestic banks by using their financial power to pick the most lucrative aspects of the domestic market ('cherry picking') thereby marginalising the domestic banks and pushing them to more risky business, domestic bank competitiveness and efficiency is achieved *before* rather than *after* the entry of foreign banks; that is, efficiency is a pre-condition rather than a result of foreign bank entry.

A seminal effort to weave together these two strands of the literature is offered by Berger *et al.* (2003), who discuss the issue of domestic versus foreign bank efficiency and provide a review of the key issues in the literature. However, they view foreign bank entry as part of a broader paradigm of the globalisation of financial institutions and the cross-border consolidation of banks. No attention is paid to Central and East European markets or to the entry of foreign banks there; instead, the paper focuses on evidence from the major industrialised nations.

The contributions of this chapter are twofold: first, we provide further general evidence on the efficiency of foreign banks in emerging markets; second, we empirically contest the intuitive argument that the banking sector in Central and Eastern Europe necessarily benefits greatly, in terms of efficiency, from the entry of foreign banks. We therefore contribute to one of the major directions for future research proposed by Berger *et al.* (2003), namely to investigate whether banks in emerging markets have 'home field advantages' or, alternatively, whether banking markets in these economies support a limited form of the 'global advantage hypothesis': i.e. that foreign banks from certain foreign countries are more efficient after all.

Econometric methodology

The empirical model

We specify a multi-product, three-input, three-output model to capture the cost and output behaviour of banks in European transition economies. The model is estimated using a translog cost function and two share equations.[3] However, the cost function is augmented with a foreign–domestic ownership dummy, as follows:

$$LnTC = \alpha_0 + \sum_{j=1}^{3} \alpha_j LnY_j + \sum_{i=1}^{3} \beta_i LnP_i + 0.5 \sum_{j=1}^{3} \sum_{k=1}^{3} \sigma_{jk} LnY_j LnY_k +$$

$$0.5 \sum_{i=1}^{3} \sum_{h=1}^{3} \gamma_{ih} LnP_i LnP_h + 0.5 \sum_{j=1}^{3} \sum_{i=1}^{3} \delta_{ji} LnY_j LnP_i + \eta F + \epsilon \qquad (10.1)$$

Here, *TC* is the total cost; $\sigma_{ik} = \sigma_{ki}$, $\gamma_{jh} = \gamma_{hj}$ (the symmetry restrictions); Y_j are the output variables; P_i the input prices; and F is a dummy variable for foreign banks. The coefficients to be estimated are: α, β, σ, γ, δ, and η; the coefficient of special interest to this study is the foreign dummy coefficient (η); subscripts j and k denote each of the three outputs, and subscripts i and h denote each of the three input prices.

The regularity conditions are:

$$\sum_{i=1}^{3} \beta_i = 1, \sum_{i=1}^{3} \gamma_{ih} = 0 \text{ and } \sum_{i=1}^{3} \delta_{ji} = 0.$$

These conditions provide the unique correspondence between the cost function and the underlying production function; for details see, for example, Gropper (1991: 719–720). Accordingly, the cost function must be homogeneous of degree one and concave in factor prices, as well as non-decreasing in both factor prices and output quantities. The cost share equations (derived using Shephard's lemma) are expressed as:

$$SH_i = \partial \ln TC / \partial \ln P_i = \beta_i + \sum_{h=1}^{3} \gamma_{ih} \ln P_h + \sum_{j=1}^{3} \delta_{ji} \ln Y_j \tag{10.2}$$

with $i = 1,2$ denoting the two cost share equations to be estimated.

Our general approach was to estimate the cost function (equation 10.1) and the two share equations (equation 10.2) simultaneously for each country using the seemingly unrelated regression (SUR) method to impose the necessary cross-equation restrictions. As explained later in this section, we estimated a different model for each country and then compared the results.

On the basis of the system of equations (10.1) and (10.2), we estimate multi-product economies of scale (MSE) according to the following specification:

$$MSE = TC(Y,P) / \sum_{j=1}^{3} Y_j MC_j = 1 / \sum_{j=1}^{3} \omega_{cyj} \tag{10.3}$$

where $j = 1,2,3$ denotes each of the three types of outputs, MC_j is the marginal cost with respect to the j-th output, and $\omega_{cyj} = \partial \ln TC / \partial \ln Y_j$ is the cost elasticity of the j-th output. A bank is operating with economies or diseconomies of scale according as $MSE > / < 1$ (respectively). The formula for the elasticities (following Drake 1992: 213), derived from the differentiated translog, is:

$$\omega_{cyj} = \alpha_j + \sum_{j=1}^{3} \sigma_{jk} \ln_k + \sum_{i=1}^{3} P_i \tag{10.4}$$

We then proceed to estimate economies of scope (SC) based on the following:

$$SC = \frac{TC(Y_1 - 2\epsilon_1, \epsilon_2, \epsilon_3) + TC(\epsilon_1, Y_2 - 2\epsilon_2, \epsilon_3) + TC(\epsilon_1, \epsilon_2, Y_3 - 2\epsilon_3)}{TC(Y_1, Y_2, Y_3)} \tag{10.5}$$

where $\epsilon_j = 1$ per cent of Y_j for each available bank/year output observation. This is a common empirical approach to get around the difficulty that the logarithm of a zero output is not defined: we reduce each of the three outputs in turn by 2 per cent, while we hold the remaining two outputs at 1 per cent of their values. A bank is operating with economies or diseconomies of scope according as SC $>/<1$ (respectively).

In this framework, the impact of foreign bank participation is modelled in three ways. First, the foreign dummy coefficient, η, models any absolute differences in cost efficiency. If, as is usually hypothesised, $\eta < 0$ and significant in Equation (10.1), this implies that foreign banks have an absolute cost advantage over domestic banks.[4] This sheds light on the question of whether foreign ownership is an important factor in reducing banks' total costs. The second measure of foreign bank participation emerges from the estimates for economies of scale and scope. We estimate economies of scale and scope for all banks, and separately for domestic and for foreign banks. These measures give information about the position on the cost curve that domestic and foreign banks choose, and therefore shed light on whether foreign banks are more scale- or scope-efficient than domestic banks. Of course, one reason why banks may have an inefficient scale may be the size of the market, which is outside the control of individual banks. However, the economies of scope measure is less ambiguous, and the impact on scope economies of differences in product mix may help shed light on the argument that foreign banks tend to cherry pick business rather than to improve competitive efficiency in the whole banking market. Third, we estimate different cost functions for different economies in Central and Eastern Europe, on the grounds that the different national banking markets are sufficiently different as to warrant a separate treatment (for instance, in methods of privatisation, regulation, and patterns of saving, lending and money transmission). This allows us to compare the impact of foreign banks across different countries. Overall, therefore, we would argue that our framework provides a multi-dimensional assessment of the impact of foreign banks on banking efficiency in Central and Eastern Europe.

Measurement

The empirical variables in the translog cost function and the related cost share equations fall into three groups: total cost, outputs and input prices. Total costs consist of operating costs and interest costs. We specify inputs and outputs using the intermediation approach, viewing banks as financial intermediaries employing inputs, consisting of labour, capital and deposits, to produce outputs consisting of loans, other earning assets and non-interest income. This approach is preferred in many studies, because it captures the varied nature of modern banking firms; see Berger and Humphrey (1991).

The variables and their empirical counterparts are shown in Table 10.1. The three types of outputs that enter the analysis are loans, other earning assets and non-interest income (Y_1, Y_2, Y_3). The first two are preferred in more recent efficiency studies and generally cover the bulk of the banking business, especially within the traditional view of banks as deposit collectors and loan makers. Non-interest income is included as the third output in line with the recent banking literature, which points out that banks are turning to alternative, fee-based, activities and markets (for example, Hunter *et al.* 1990: 513; Drake 1997: 12). Off-balance-sheet activities by banks arguably constitute a natural response to increased competition in markets where entry barriers and inter-industry segmentations have been significantly eroded during the last decade. An intriguing feature of the banking systems of Central and Eastern Europe, which partly explains the rapid developments there, is that they are very much exposed to pressures and tendencies typical of the mature neighbouring markets. There is, therefore, little doubt that the off-balance-sheet component of the banks' business should be included in a well-specified model of banks in European transition economies.[5]

The variables for inputs and their prices are measured in accordance with the concept of the multi-product, multi-input banking firm. In an attempt to better encompass various aspects of the production process in

Table 10.1 Variables used in the estimation of the cost function

Variable	Empirical/observable variables
Total costs (TC)	interest expenses + operating expenses (operating expenses = commissions + fees + trading expenses + personnel + other admin. costs + other operating costs)
Outputs	
Loans (Y_1)	total customer loans
Other earning assets (Y_2)	total other earning assets
Non-interest income (Y_3)	commissions + fees + trading income + other operating income + non-operating income
Inputs	
Labour (IN_1)	number of employees
Capital (IN_2)	fixed assets
Deposits (IN_3)	deposits + money-market funding + other funding
Input prices	
Labour (P_1)	total personnel expenses/number of employees
Capital (P_2)	(other admin. expenses + other operating expenses)/total fixed assets
Deposits (P_3)	interest expense/(deposits + money-market funding + other funding)
Foreign/domestic (F)	1–0 Dummy

banking in transition economies, the input prices reflect the three types of inputs that are considered relevant: labour, capital and deposits.

The data

We started by collecting bank-specific data using the universe of all banks in all European transition countries, as reported in the BankScope database as at 25–28 June 2001. There were many missing observations, both across time and banking units. The short commercial banking history of Central and Eastern Europe has been marked by bank mergers,[6] bankruptcies or privatisation deals, and this may partly explain why observations were often missing in BankScope. However, the main reason for the gaps in the data was the irregular reporting practices of banks in the region.

We retrieved from BankScope data relevant to the translog functional form used in this chapter. For each bank, data availability was checked for the period 1995–1999. If there were no observations for one year, it was assumed that the bank did not exist at the time (not an unrealistic assumption in view of the short and unstable banking history of the region); thus, data were left missing for the respective bank/year. If there was at least one entry for a certain year, this was taken as evidence that the bank existed at the time (which does not necessarily mean the bank was fully functioning). The missing observations were then attributed to reporting failure or that the bank was not fully operational in that year.[7]

The main problem with the data concerned personnel expenses and the number of employees, which were missing in many cases. If a bank existed and functioned in some way, it would surely have had employees and expenses. Unfortunately, for the countries of Central and Eastern Europe, employee-related data are among the least reported statistics. (Data for some countries are totally missing, as in the case of Bulgaria.) Therefore, the following country-by-country procedures were followed. Where the data were missing, the number of employees was estimated using the authoritative International Labour Organisation (ILO 2001) database. The country figures from that database were taken, subject to certain limitations. The 'total employment by economic activity' criterion was applied. As the ILO convention for most countries has been changed since 1996, the current one (ISIC Rev.3 'J' which covers financial intermediation in total, not only banks) was chosen. The relevant figures were averaged over the years 1996–1999 (which coincides approximately with our sample period) and the industry figure was obtained (assuming dominance of banking over other financial activities) as 90 per cent of the average annual ILO figure for each country. To get the missing number of employees, each bank was assigned a 'bank/year weight' (as a ratio of total fixed assets for that bank/year to total fixed assets for all banks and all years; in all cases taking only the sample banks). As a rule, the total fixed assets data were available everywhere. In the very few cases where that was not the case, the number of employees and personnel expenses were left blank (assuming the existence of that bank was a legal rather than a practical fact). However, due to the few missing observations on personnel expenses, the final dataset was necessarily unbalanced. Hence, we ended up with an unbalanced panel data set for nine countries: Bulgaria, Croatia, the Czech Republic, Estonia, Hungary, Latvia, Lithuania, Poland and Romania, within the period 1995–1999.[8] Even so, this amounted to a large sample for this kind of research, with a total of 273 banks.

Our analysis was, in some respects, shaped by the limitations of the data set. Unavailability of banking data has always obstructed research into Central and Eastern Europe. In this context, this study is perhaps pioneering, and almost certainly the most comprehensive study in the area. However, some theoretical and practical considerations are worth noting. The units of the panel data set are 'banks', as filtered from the original database. According to the definitions used by BankScope, banks fall into a number of categories, but for analytical convenience and to reflect the reality of the banking sector in European transition economies, we selected only three categories: commercial banks, savings banks and cooperative banks. Banks were classified as foreign or not according to the BankScope convention. Specifically, a bank is classified as foreign if it has shareholders settled in foreign countries holding altogether a minimum of 51 per cent of the ordinary share capital; added to that number are banks which have at least one foreign shareholder when the percentage of ownership was not available; also, a foreign bank may include local shareholders if they hold altogether less than 50 per cent of the bank's share capital. Technically, this classification may differ from national legal or regulatory specifications (such as local branches of foreign banks versus non-branch domestic entities whose shareholders are predominantly foreign). Another important consideration is that BankScope classifies banks as being foreign or not at the time the database is last updated. This means that no historical observations were available for the foreign dummy. This is a significant drawback, within the context of the analysis, as Central and Eastern Europe has experienced many different forms of foreign banks' penetration, including the privatisation of existing banks. A bank may have been domestic in the early years of observation, but foreign today. Thus, each bank was assigned an ownership dummy of 1 (foreign) or 0 (domestic) across units, according to these criteria, but the dummy did not vary over time. Clearly this is an important limitation of the research. However, the relatively short maximum time period of each bank's data (five years) would suggest that it may not be too severe.[9]

In some instances, the same bank appeared more than once in BankScope, due to the application of different consolidation codes or accounting standards. In such cases, we used only the unconsolidated statements, as this is the most widely used format in the database as a whole. This procedure is consistent with the assumption that, because the financial markets in the sample countries were under-developed, banking accounted for the bulk of the financial sector. Likewise, we used only variables reported under the international accounting standard (IAS). When the same bank appeared in BankScope more than once due to different consolidation and accounting formats, priority was given to the unconsolidated reporting criterion.

The number of banks included in the dataset for each country is reported in Table 10.2.[10] In each of the nine markets it can be seen that foreign banks increased in number during the five-year period. However, those numbers are not perfectly correlated with either the size of the markets or the number of domestic banks. Turning to the length of the dataset, annual data for five consecutive years (1995–1999) were extracted. BankScope contained data for 1993–2001, but in the case of Central and Eastern Europe, relatively little data was available outside the 1995–1999 period.

Empirical results

The system of the total cost function and the two share equations with all symmetry and regularity conditions was estimated for each country using SUR. The estimates satisfy the usual diagnostic tests and provide a sensible econometric model of bank costs. Given the rapid pace of change in Central and Eastern Europe, this is a satisfactory finding. The details of the parameter estimates and diagnostics are omitted from the chapter to save space,[11] as the main interest in the results concerns the estimates of scale and scope economies and the role of foreign banks. We therefore turn next to our findings on these issues.

Absolute differences in cost-efficiency (η)

Estimates of the foreign–domestic dummy (η) are given in Table 10.3 and, *prima facie*, would appear to challenge the ideas that ownership matters, and that foreign banks are generally more cost-efficient than domestic banks. The estimated values of η are generally small and insignificant. In only half of the countries (Croatia, the Czech Republic, Lithuania and Romania) does foreign ownership seem to be associated with an absolute reduction in costs ($\eta < 0$) and only in one case (Lithuania) is that cost reduction significant (at the 0.05 level). The definite conclusion, therefore, is that foreign ownership was not an immediate factor in reducing costs in banks in Central and Eastern Europe.

Table 10.2 Number of banks analysed

Country	Domestic (Foreign)						Total					
	1995	1996	1997	1998	1999	Total	1995	1996	1997	1998	1999	Total
Bulgaria (BG)	10 (5)	10 (7)	12 (7)	13 (8)	12 (9)	17 (9)	15	17	19	21	21	26
Croatia (CR)	27 (5)	32 (5)	37 (8)	32 (7)	32 (7)	37 (8)	32	37	45	39	32	45
Czech Republic (CZ)	21 (7)	22 (8)	22 (8)	17 (8)	11 (7)	24 (8)	28	30	30	25	18	32
Estonia (EE)	10 (0)	11 (0)	11 (0)	4 (0)	4 (0)	12 (0)	10	11	11	4	4	12
Hungary (HU)	18 (12)	19 (13)	18 (13)	14 (12)	12 (12)	20 (14)	30	32	31	26	24	34
Latvia (LV)	14 (4)	14 (5)	17 (7)	17 (6)	4 (6)	21 (7)	18	19	24	23	10	28
Lithuania (LT)	8 (1)	9 (2)	9 (2)	8 (2)	7 (2)	11 (2)	9	11	11	10	9	13
Poland (PL)	27 (13)	31 (17)	29 (17)	24 (17)	21 (17)	35 (18)	40	48	46	41	38	53
Romania (RO)	5 (3)	8 (3)	8 (6)	15 (13)	13 (12)	16 (14)	8	11	14	28	25	30
Total	140 (50)	156 (60)	163 (68)	144 (73)	109 (72)	193 (80)	190	216	231	217	181	273

Table 10.3 Effects of ownership: absolute differences in cost efficiency

	BG	CR	CZ	EE	HU	LV	LT	PL	RO
η	0.1072	-0.0013	-0.0325	0	0.0676	0.0588	-0.2201**	0.1074	-0.1494
	(0.2183)	(0.1209)	(0.045)	(0)	(0.038)	(0.0888)	(0.109)	(0.057)	(0.0947)

Note
**denotes significantly different from zero at the 5 per cent level.

Economies of scale

Economies of scale were estimated separately for each observation (that is, separately for each bank-year) and over all outputs and input prices following Equation (10.3). In presenting summary statistics we, of course, distinguish between domestic and foreign-owned banks and we report our results in a format that facilitates comparisons with other European studies following similar methodology (see Mendes and Rebelo 1999). This adds to the significance of the current study, considering the shortage of European bank efficiency literature, and the non-existence of a study on the European transition economies. Table 10.4 summarises the results on economies of scale.

These results suggest that, on average, banks in Central and Eastern Europe have exhibited small or negligible economies of scale and are effectively operating at or close to scale-efficient levels. With the exception of the Czech Republic, all the mean and median economies of scale measures are close to unity for both domestic and foreign banks, and in no case are the means significantly different from unity. In the case of the Czech Republic, there is a relatively wide variation in the economies of scale measures so that, although the means are high, they are, nevertheless, not significantly different from unity.[12] In terms of the traditional analytical pattern of the U-shaped cost curve for scale efficiency, all but one of the median and mean measures exceed unity, suggesting that all the Central and Eastern European banking markets are on the downward-sloping part of their average cost curves, close to the scale-efficient level of output.

Turning to a comparison between domestic and foreign banks, the mean economies of scale measure for foreign banks is generally somewhat greater than that for domestic banks (dom-for <0). However, this difference is significant only for Croatia and Romania and, in the case of Latvia, domestic banks exhibit a significantly greater economies-of-scale measure. Moreover, it could be argued that the main impact of foreign banks is unlikely to be on every existing bank in the host country. The least efficient domestic banks are less likely to improve than are those which are already operating closer to international standards. To check this point we recalculated the *t* tests for Croatia, Romania and Latvia excluding one quartile of the sample: the lowest for Croatia and Romania, the highest for Latvia (determined by the sign of the difference between the means: dom-for). The right-most column of Table 10.4 shows that this eliminates the significant difference between domestic and foreign banks for Croatia and Latvia (but not Romania). This is not to claim that there 'really' is no difference between domestic and foreign banks in these two economies, but that the source of the difference appears to lie mainly in a group of domestic banks operating at a significantly different scale from other domestic and foreign banks in the economy. The overall conclu-

Table 10.4 Economies of scale for domestic and foreign banks in Central and Eastern Europe

	No. of bank-years			Range			Median				Mean and T-test				
	Total	Domestic	Foreign	Total	Domestic	Foreign	Total	Domestic	Foreign	Dom-for	Total	Domestic	Foreign	Dom-for	Dom(Q)-for
BG	78	44	34	0.1386	0.1386	0.1277	1.0742	1.0746	1.0742	0.0004	1.0697	1.0668	1.0733	−0.0065	
t											0.74	0.74	0.74	−0.30	
CR	163	133	30	0.2435	0.2141	0.4690	1.2797	1.2797	1.2823	−0.0026	1.3241	1.3062	1.4034	−0.0972	−0.0267
t											1.30	1.59	0.97	−1.94**	−0.52
CZ	100	64	36	0.9766	1.1238	0.4573	1.2025	1.2348	1.1869	0.0480	4.5928	6.7483	0.7608	5.9875	
t											0.10	0.13	−0.05	0.81	
EE	38	38	0	0.2180	0.2180	na	1.1241	1.1241	na	na	1.1670	1.1670	na	na	
t											0.72	0.72			
HU	72	43	29	0.3770	0.3451	0.3555	1.0874	1.0978	0.9384	0.1594	1.2786	1.4103	1.0833	0.3270	
t											0.19	0.22	0.29	0.95	
LV	85	62	23	0.0908	0.0926	0.0495	1.1047	1.1302	1.0659	0.0643	1.1148	1.1266	1.0831	0.0434	0.0148
t											1.69	1.75	2.03**	2.72**	1.35
LT	45	38	7	0.4237	0.3416	0.8101	1.2127	1.1958	1.4515	−0.2557	1.4338	1.4214	1.5007	−0.0793	
t											0.46	0.42	1.02	−0.20	
PL	160	102	58	0.1727	0.1856	0.1291	1.0337	1.0244	1.0368	−0.0124	1.0311	1.0284	1.0360	−0.0076	
t											0.25	0.21	0.35	−0.38	
RO	56	31	25	0.3041	0.2250	0.2369	1.0473	0.9645	1.1197	−0.1553	1.0655	1.0061	1.1391	−0.1330	−0.0956
t											0.39	0.04	0.86	−3.16**	−2.19**

Notes

The economies of scale measures are calculated from equation (10.3).

No. of bank-years gives the total number of observations in each category.

Range is the interquartile range of the sample.

Median and mean are calculated in the usual way for each sample.

Dom-for is the difference between the medians or means of domestic and foreign banks.

Dom(Q)-for is the difference between the means of domestic and foreign banks when the sample excludes domestic banks in the lowest (dom-for < 0) or highest (dom-for > 0) quartile by economies of scale.

T-test (t) is a test against the null that the economies of scale measure is unity in the sample (total, domestic and foreign); or that the difference between the domestic and foreign means is zero (dom-for, dom(Q)-for). ** denotes significant at the 5 per cent level.

na: not applicable

sion, therefore, is that foreign banks are not systematically more scale efficient than the average domestic bank in our sample European transition
economies.

Economies of scope

Economies of scope were estimated separately for each observation (that
is, separately for each bank-year) and over all outputs and input prices
following Equation (10.5). The presentation of results in Table 10.5
follows that for economies of scale. There is substantially more evidence
of economies of scope than economies of scale, with all the measures
exceeding unity and, apart from the Czech Republic, all significantly
greater than unity. This result may be consistent with the argument that
banking markets in the transition economies are still developing. It may
be that, during the early stages of development of the banking market,
banks have to produce a more varied output mix in order to remain in the
market. Certainly, the data suggest that multi-product banking firms do
have a cost advantage over more specialised banks.

However, when we turn to a comparison between domestic and foreign
banks, we again find few significant differences: only in Croatia, Bulgaria
and Latvia. Following our procedure for economies of scale, we re-
performed the t tests on these countries omitting the relevant outlying
quartile of domestic banks, and again we see in the right-most column of
Table 10.5 that this eliminates the significant difference between domestic
and foreign banks for Croatia and Latvia (but not Bulgaria). These results
again suggest that there is no evidence of a systematic difference in efficiency (in this case in economies of scope) as between domestic and
foreign banks. These results also cast some doubt on the cherry-picking
hypothesis. If indeed, foreign banks cherry pick the best business, we
would expect to see some more differences in the economies of scope
measures as between domestic and foreign banks. Of course, our input
and output measures are relatively aggregated and cherry picking may
occur at a more disaggregated level. However, at our level of aggregation,
it is difficult to see much support for the hypothesis.

Conclusions

This chapter has attempted to fill a serious gap in the literature by pioneering the modelling of bank efficiency in Central and Eastern Europe,
and by using the largest feasible sample of banks in order to explore the
scale and scope dimensions of bank efficiency. A central finding of our
chapter is that it contests the widespread belief that foreign banks are
more efficient than their domestic counterparts. The empirical results
suggest that banks in Central and Eastern Europe are scale efficient for
the sample period (1995 to 1999) and that they enjoy significant

Table 10.5 Economies of scope for domestic and foreign banks in Central and Eastern Europe

	No. of bank-years			Range			Median				Mean and T-test				
	Total	Domestic	Foreign	Total	Domestic	Foreign	Total	Domestic	Foreign	Dom-for	Total	Domestic	Foreign	Dom-for	Dom(Q)-for
BG	78	44	34	0.1728	0.1252	0.1069	1.9493	1.8869	2.0241	-0.1372	1.9354	1.8909	1.9930	-0.1022	-0.0550
t											7.38	7.36**	8.95**	-3.83**	-2.31**
CR	162	132	30	0.0678	0.0626	0.0740	2.2404	2.2350	2.2714	-0.0364	2.2410	2.2353	2.2663	-0.0310	-0.0105
t											21.65**	24.10**	16.97**	-2.73**	-1.03
CZ	100	64	36	4.8831	7.7287	4.0995	7.6908	7.2567	7.8223	-0.5656	6.9285	6.6522	7.4196	-0.7675	
t											0.32	0.25	1.16	-0.20	
EE	38	38	na	0.1146	0.1146	na	1.8823	1.8823	na	na	1.8732	1.8732	na	na	
t											12.84**	12.84**	na		
HU	72	43	29	0.2887	0.3198	0.1087	3.0581	3.0808	3.0539	0.0269	3.1878	3.2194	3.1410	0.0783	
t											5.32**	4.38**	10.74**	0.79	
LV	85	62	23	0.0613	0.0686	0.0586	2.0295	2.0229	2.0429	-0.0200	2.0187	2.0106	2.0404	-0.0297	-0.0018
t											16.65**	16.68**	17.72**	-2.03**	-0.17
LT	45	38	7	0.1785	0.1604	0.2528	2.4270	2.4324	2.2778	0.1546	2.4686	2.4943	2.3294	0.1649	
t											6.56**	6.73**	6.97**	1.84	
PL	160	102	58	0.0441	0.0473	0.0343	2.1736	2.1693	2.1750	-0.0058	2.1708	2.1686	2.1745	-0.0059	
t											38.06**	35.73**	43.71**	-1.17	
RO	56	31	25	0.0879	0.0940	0.0570	1.9299	1.9546	1.9252	0.0293	1.9402	1.9527	1.9247	0.0279	
t											15.88**	14.74**	19.02**	1.79	

Notes

The economies of scope measures are calculated from equation (10.5).

No. of bank-years gives the total number of observations in each category.

Range is the interquartile range of the sample.

Median and mean are calculated in the usual way for each sample.

Dom-for is the difference between the medians or means of domestic and foreign banks.

Dom(Q)-for is the difference between the means of domestic and foreign banks when the sample excludes domestic banks in the lowest (dom-for < 0) or highest (dom-for > 0) quartile by economies of scope.

T-test (*t*) is a test against the null that the economies of scope measure is unity in the sample (total, domestic and foreign); or that the difference between the domestic and foreign means is zero (dom-for, dom(Q)-for). ** denotes significant at the 5 per cent level.

na: not applicable.

economies of scope. There is virtually no evidence in our data that foreign banks are more efficient than the average domestic bank in any of the nine European transition economies: in terms of an absolute cost advantage, or in terms of economies of scale or scope.

A shortlist of future research priorities includes the estimation of product-specific scale economies, scope economies for subsets of products and, most important of all, X-efficiency, as more data become available.

Notes

1 This chapter was presented at the 24th SUERF Colloquium on *Stability and Efficiency of Financial Markets in Central and Eastern Europe*, held on 12–14 June 2003 in Tallinn. We thank participants in this conference for their useful comments on the chapter. We also thank Robert Lensink and participants at the ACE Workshops on *Foreign Banks and Economic Transition* held at Poznan University of Economics, Poland, 14–16 September 2001, and in Tallinn, Estonia, on 10–12 May 2002, for their comments on the chapter. We gratefully acknowledge financial support from the European Commission's PHARE/ACE Programme 2001–2002 under Contract No. P98-1082-R. However, the interpretations and conclusions expressed in this chapter are entirely those of the authors and should not be attributed in any manner to the European Commission or any other organisation.

2 By the end of the 1990s, the share of banking assets under foreign control in Central Europe had reached more than 50 per cent (Mathieson and Roldos, 2001: 17).

3 A formal derivation of the translog cost function from a translog production function using duality theory can be found in several places, for example: Diewert (1974), Cornes (1992) and Coelli *et al.* (1999).

4 Note that we do not consider different slope coefficients for domestic and foreign banks. Different slope coefficients would suggest that domestic and foreign banks use completely different cost technologies whose relative advantage is practically difficult to compare, since it will depend on the precise point on the different cost functions on which each bank is operating. The usual argument about foreign banks is based primarily on the hypothesis of a direct cost advantage. The clearest way to test this hypothesis is with the simple shift dummy (F) which we employ.

5 Banks in Central and East European markets exhibit patterns which are similar to those of more developed markets in that non-interest income is increasingly becoming an important business and revenue source. However, we did not undertake sensitivity analysis to find out what happens if non-interest income is not included as an output.

6 We were not able to adjust the BankScope data in order to tease out periods of mergers and acquisitions (M&A) in Central and East European banks. Given that M&A activity is only one method of foreign bank entry, our data incorporates the information in an aggregate manner. Further research is necessary to shed light on how M&A activities feature in foreign bank entry.

7 Fee and trading expenses are not reported by banks in most countries of the sample, apart from Estonia, Latvia and Lithuania. Such expenses are either not captured by local accounting conventions, or are not incurred. Where such expenses were missing, we assumed they were zero.

8 We did not carry out a sensitivity test to find out what happens if the ILO conventions were not just used in case the employee data were missing but,

instead, for all observations. In any event, the panel was not completely balanced even after all the adjustments and the inclusion of ILO data.

9 It is also possible that domestic banks that were taken over by foreign banks within the sample were, before the time of takeover, already qualitatively different from those that remained domestically owned throughout.

10 Given that there are no foreign banks in the sample for Estonia, we could have easily removed the country from the analysis. However, we bear in mind that this chapter not only looks for the comparisons between foreign and domestic banks, but also analyses bank efficiency in Central and Eastern Europe in general.

11 The parameter estimates and diagnostics are available from the authors on request.

12 Some of the economies of scale measures for the Czech Republic are implausibly high or low, suggesting that, for this country, there may be some particular problems with the data. However, similarly anomalous findings are not unusual even in the limited European bank efficiency research (see Altunbas and Molyneux 1996: 371).

References

Altunbas, Y. and Molyneux, P. (1996) 'Economies of scale and scope in European banking', *Applied Financial Economics*, 6: 367–375.

Berger, A.N. and Humphrey, D.B. (1991) 'The dominance of inefficiencies over scale and product mix economies in banking', *Journal of Monetary Economics*, 28(1): 117–148.

Berger, A.N. and Humphrey, D.B. (1997) 'Efficiency of financial institutions: international survey and directions for future research', Working Paper. The Wharton School, University of Pennsylvania: Financial Institutions Centre.

Berger, A.N., Dai, Q., Ongena, S. and Smith, D.C. (2003) 'To what extent will the banking industry be globalized? A study of bank nationality and reach in 20 European nations', *Journal of Banking and Finance*, 27(3): 383–415.

Bhattacharyya, A., Lovell, C.A.K. and Sahay, P. (1997) 'The impact of liberalization on the productive efficiency of Indian commercial banks', *European Journal of Operational Research*, 98(2): 332–345.

Claessens, S. (1997) 'Banking reform in transition countries.' Policy Research Working Paper, No. 1642. Washington, DC: The World Bank.

Claessens, S., Demirgüç-Kunt, A. and Huizinga, H. (2001) 'How does foreign entry affect domestic banking markets?', *Journal of Banking & Finance*, 25(5): 891–911.

Coelli, T., Rao, D.S.P. and Battese, G. (1999) *An Introduction to Efficiency and Productivity Analysis*. Boston, MA: Kluwer Academic Publishers.

Cornes, R. (1992). *Duality and Modern Economics*. Cambridge: Cambridge University Press.

Dages, B.G., Goldberg, L. and Kinney, D. (2000) 'Foreign and domestic bank participation in emerging markets: lessons from Mexico and Argentina', *Federal Reserve Bank of New York Economic Policy Review*, 6(3), September: 17–36.

Demirgüç-Kunt, A. and Huizinga, H. (1999) 'Determinants of commercial bank interest margins and profitability: some international evidence', *The World Bank Economic Review*, 13(2): 379–395.

Diewert, W. (1974) 'Applications of duality theory', in M.D. Intriligator and D.A. Kendrick (eds), *Frontiers of Quantitative Economics*, Vol. II. Amsterdam: North-Holland.

Drake, L. (1992) 'Economies of scale and scope in UK building societies: an application of the translog multiproduct cost function', *Applied Financial Economics*, 2: 211–219.

Drake, L. (1997) 'Measuring efficiency in UK banking', Department of Economics Research Paper No. 97/18. Loughborough: Loughborough University.

Gropper, D.M. (1991) 'An empirical investigation of changes in scale economies for the commercial banking firm, 1979–1986', *Journal of Money, Credit and Banking*, 23: 718–727.

Havrylchyk, O. (2003) 'Efficiency of the Polish banking industry: foreign vs. national banks', Paper presented at the 24th SUERF Colloquium on *Stability and Efficiency of Financial Markets in Central and Eastern Europe*, June 12–14, Tallinn.

Hunter, W.C., Timme, S.G. and Yang, W.K. (1990) 'An examination of cost subadditivity and multiproduct production in large U.S. banks', *Journal of Money, Credit and Banking*, 22, 4, November: 504–525.

International Labour Organisation (2001) *The Labour Statistics Database*. Online, available at: http://laborsta.ilo.org.

Konopielko, L. (1999). 'Foreign banks' entry into Central and Eastern European markets: motives and activities', *Post-communist Economies*, 11(4): 463–486.

Kraft, E. and Tirtiroglu, D. (1998) 'Bank efficiency in Croatia: a stochastic-frontier analysis', *Journal of Comparative Economics*, 26(2): 282–300.

Litan, E.R., Masson, P. and Pomerleano, M. (2001) 'Introduction', in E.R. Litan, P. Masson and M. Pomerleano (eds), *Open Doors: Foreign Participation in Financial Systems in Developing Countries*. Washington, DC: Brookings Institution Press, pp. 1–14.

Mathieson, D.J. and Roldos, J. (2001) 'Foreign banks in emerging markets', in E.R. Litan, P. Masson and M. Pomerleano (eds), *Open Doors: Foreign Participation in Financial Systems in Developing Countries*. Washington, DC: Brookings Institution Press, pp. 15–58.

Mendes, V. and Rebelo, J. (1999) 'Productive efficiency, technological change and productivity in Portuguese banking', *Applied Financial Economics*, 9(5): 513–522.

Mertens, A. and Urga, G. (2001) 'Efficiency, scale and scope economies in the Ukrainian banking sector in 1998', *Emerging Markets Review*, 2(3): 292–308.

Molyneux, P., Altunbas, Y. and Gardener, E.P.M. (1996) *Efficiency in European Banking*. Chichester: John Wiley & Sons.

Weill, L. (2003) 'Banking efficiency in transition economies: the role of foreign ownership', Paper presented at the 24th SUERF Colloquium on *Stability and Efficiency of Financial Markets in Central and Eastern Europe*, June 12–14, Tallinn.

Yildirim, H.S. and Philippatos, G.C. (2002) 'Efficiency of banks: recent evidence from the transition economies of Europe: 1993–2000', Research Paper, Department of Economics, Knoxville, TN: University of Tennessee.

11 The efficiency of banking systems in CEE

Inequality and convergence to the EU

Mariana Tomova, Nikolay Nenovsky and Totka Naneva

Introduction

Financial-sector development and efficiency have always been considered as key factors to the successful implementation of economic reforms. Recently their importance took on new dimensions in the context of European integration. Both market and regulatory actions may drive financial institutions to consolidate into a single European market (Berger 2003). Central and Eastern European (CEE) countries' banking sectors are naturally aspiring to these processes and their successful convergence can both be influenced by and influence the enhancement of European integration in the financial services industry.

The aim of this chapter is to investigate to what extent CEE economies' banking systems have been successful in the transformation and convergence to the EU as measured by their relative operational efficiency. The study looks at Bulgaria, the Czech Republic, Croatia, Estonia, Hungary, Latvia, Poland, Romania, Slovenia, the Slovak Republic and selected EU countries based on the IBCA BankScope database for the period 1993–2001.

Banking sector development and efficiency have implications for the enhancement of the European integration process from various perspectives. First, the development of more sophisticated and efficient financial systems is needed to support faster economic growth in transition economies that would enable them to catch up with the euro-area. Although the causal link between finance and growth is controversial, it is generally agreed that financial and economic development is a two-way street, and the pursuit of real convergence towards the current euro-area member countries implies that the financial sector should be larger and better able to foster investments and savings possibilities at the end of the convergence process.

Second, developing the financial sector is also important for nominal convergence, as it fortifies the interest-rate-based monetary policy transmission mechanism and helps to provide a stable macroeconomic environment. At present, the exchange rate channel is still the main tool for the transmission of monetary impulses to accession countries. This reflects three specific aspects: the high degree of openness in all countries, the relatively low level of intermediation through the domestic financial system and the relatively developed foreign exchange markets, which also benefited from early capital account liberalisation and large capital inflows.

The purpose of this chapter is to provide a synoptic view of the efficiency of banking sectors in the CEE countries under common regional and European frontiers, answering the following questions:

1   are there significant disparities in banking operating efficiency across countries in Central and Eastern Europe, due to perceived differences in technological capabilities, banking innovations and regulatory systems?
2   do countries with more efficient banking systems converge faster to the EU?
3   are banks in CEE economies more successful in achieving the corporate goal of profit maximization than in complying with the central banks objectives perceived as facilitating economic growth and development?
4   do banks in countries with currency board arrangements exhibit higher efficiency in achieving the central bank regulatory objectives?

Special attention is paid to the empirical investigation of financial sectors in countries with currency board systems in order to attempt to trace the consequences of the functioning of this arrangement on banking operational efficiency and performance.

The reminder of the chapter is organized as follows: the first part discusses the economic environment in the CEE economies' banking systems in the 1990s, tracing their common features and specific characteristics. The next part evaluates the technical efficiency in ten transition economies and selected EU member states' banking systems between 1993–2001, employing data envelopment analysis. In order to differentiate the various functions performed by banks, two models are analyzed using different sets of inputs and outputs. First, the performance of banks in achieving the corporate goal of profit maximization is studied. Second, the technical efficiency of commercial banks is analyzed with respect to their ability to comply with the central bank regulatory objective to facilitate economic growth while, at the same time, preserving the safety and soundness of the banking system. The third part investigates the link between banking efficiency and financial convergence in both the regional and European dimensions. The final part concludes.

Our principal findings are:

1   No matter what measures of performance are used, the technical efficiency of banks in CEE countries in obtaining both sets of objectives was converging to that in the evaluated EU member states in the period 1993–2001 in terms of decreasing variability.
2   The greatest decrease in the heterogeneity of banking efficiency in transition countries and between CEE and EU member states could be observed in the year 2000, following the launch of the European Monetary Union. For that period the null hypothesis that, with respect to revenue generation, banks in two groups of countries are drawn from the same population cannot be rejected.
3   Despite the trend of decreasing dispersion of performance measures, differences in efficiency levels are still great and only banks in the Czech Republic and the Slovak Republic are, on average, indistinguishable from that in the EU in terms of their ability to obtain commercial banks' objectives.

The development of banking systems in CEE – common trajectories and specific characteristics

Current and past changes in the competitive process have significantly reshaped the world banking industry. Even if some regional and euro-area integration has been achieved as trade and investment flows progressively and significantly increased, the CEE countries still retain some of the characteristics of transition economies, reflecting also the idiosyncrasy of each country's transformation path. The adjustments that need to be achieved in order for the banking sectors in accession countries to reach euro-area standards still remain significant (Solans 2002).

With the enlargement of the EU, banks in CEE will have to compete in a market in which there are no barriers to the movement of capital. Within such a remodeled financial environment, CEE economies have initiated a profound metamorphosis of their banking industry. First, authorities implemented a rapid deregulation and liberalization phase, giving priority to the competitive aspect of bank restructuring. Subsequently, CEE economies have been (and in some cases still are) confronted with a consolidation and privatization trend.

Disparities between banking systems

Despite the influence of market forces and regulatory action leading to integration, differences are persistant both between CEE banking systems and between transition economies and the EU member states.

Banking sectors in CEE differ in terms of diversification of portfolios, market penetration, technological progress and financial services infrastructure. For instance, in Poland and Croatia, retail lending represents 31 percent and 42 percent respectively of total lending activities while this ratio is 13 percent in Slovakia and 20 percent in Bulgaria (Nicastro *et al.* 2002).

Differences between banks in CEE and EU countries are more pronounced and have greater influence over the cross-country comparisons. Transition economies differ from European countries both in terms of microeconomic measures of efficiency and macroeconomic indicators for financial structure and development. Table 11.1b describes selected operating income ratios for CEE and some EU countries. The main "stylized facts" characterizing the specific features of banking structure and efficiency in CEE can be summarized as follows.

Microeconomic efficiency measures

HIGHER NET INTEREST MARGINS

Numerous studies, although in most of the international comparative research, transition economies are not included, have confirmed that banks in under-developed financial systems usually tend to have higher profits and margins (Demirgüç and Huizinga 2000). Greater banking development brings about tougher competition and lower profits. High interest margins are treated as a sign of lower efficiency with respect to the intermediation function of banks and are highly correlated with the degree of equity capitalization, inflation and real GNP per capita (Demirgüç and Huizinga 2000). It could not be reasonable to expect the level of interest rates in transition economies to be the same as that in the EU, as the risks for depositors are greater and, on the other hand, the return to capital may also be higher in these countries due to the opportunities offered by the restructuring of the economic activity (Brada and Kutan 2001). Table 11.1b describes the trends in net margins (calculated as the ratio between net interest and total earning assets). The differences between net margins

Table 11.1a Number of banks, by country and year, 1993–2001

	1993	1994	1995	1996	1997	1998	1999	2000	2001
Bulgaria	3	3	7	11	14	20	30	34	33
Czech Republic	10	23	27	25	26	23	29	25	26
Estonia	4	8	10	11	11	4	4	4	5
Croatia	8	24	26	29	42	36	34	37	37
Hungary	6	18	25	26	27	27	32	40	31
Latvia	1	11	13	15	19	19	21	19	19
Poland	16	35	38	46	48	45	42	43	31
Romania	1	2	2	2	7	21	25	25	23
Slovenia	2	10	16	16	20	19	20	20	17
Slovak Republic	0	9	10	11	10	9	10	12	13
CEE	51	143	174	199	224	223	247	259	235

Table 11.1b Selected ratios, 1993–2001

	1993	*1994*	*1995*	*1996*	*1997*	*1998*	*1999*	*2000*	*2001*
Cost-to-income ratio (operating expenses over gross income)									
Bulgaria		52.00	74.60	40.08	34.57	−21.47	74.57	69.49	84.75
Czech Republic	24.10	46.10	48.70	20.66	45.07	95.41	85.81	96.26	63.95
Estonia	64.30	69.80	56.60	63.30	54.90	1,155	66.80	57.30	49.70
Croatia	22.90	72.00	89.00	62.60	65.50	82.10	60.30	67.50	64.90
Latvia	66.70	59.70	0.625	60.10	60.70	1,778	72.80	69.00	64.30
Hungary		111.21	112.98	73.55	76.75	115.77	87.00	84.00	77.70
Poland	42.87	49.83	46.85	49.35	53.74	61.30	62.50	64.22	66.21
Romania	22.20	19.10	22.60	38.40	50.40	39.60	55.20	68.80	99.30
Slovenia	46.20	67.20	65.07	35.00	59.60	60.60	34.70	56.70	64.00
Portugal	56.19	61.77	64.94	64.28	60.06	55.42	58.51	58.80	57.10
France	64.30	78.70	4.10	75.80	74.90	74.20	70.80	67.90	69.90
Spain	59.53	59.11	64.07	63.81	63.30	61.23	64.38	60.70	57.70
Net interest revenue/gross income									
Bulgaria		4.10	27.10	25.40	24.70	49.90	55.00	63.50	62.30
Czech Republic	79.71	116.71	67.25	67.88	68.23	63.57	62.23	47.80	53.50
Estonia	63.80	61.20	61.20	52.00	49.60	73.70	45.00	49.20	63.20
Croatia	45.20	45.40	52.20	55.90	60.20	63.00	64.50	65.70	64.40
Latvia	33.30	65.20	60.90	61.50	44.40	113.3	51.80	49.80	49.60
Hungary		169.19	166.62	97.10	86.08	129.47	88.84	52.80	56.70
Poland	67.95	73.50	75.37	75.77	71.49	68.79	61.02	58.80	45.30
Romania	50.00	46.20	47.40	51.30	58.70	76.60	67.60	67.00	64.80
Slovenia	56.00	60.50	62.70	65.00	68.80	65.80	65.30	68.50	64.90
Portugal	75.99	77.92	76.04	68.88	68.18	65.17	69.37	62.10	65.00
France	63.80	58.80	59.80	56.50	54.80	47.70	39.80	33.00	32.80
Spain	68.43	74.83	71.65	67.52	64.82	63.40	63.74	66.50	67.10
Other operating income/gross income									
Bulgaria		9.59	72.90	74.60	75.30	50.10	45.00	36.50	37.70
Czech Republic	20.29	−16.71	32.75	32.12	31.77	36.43	37.77	52.20	46.50
Estonia	36.20	38.80	38.80	48.00	50.40	26.30	55.00	50.80	36.80
Croatia	54.80	54.60	47.80	44.10	39.80	37.00	35.50	34.30	35.60
Latvia	66.70	34.80	39.10	38.50	55.60	−13.30	48.20	50.20	50.40
Hungary		−69.19	−66.62	2.90	13.92	−29.47	11.16	47.20	43.30
Poland	32.05	26.50	24.63	24.23	28.51	31.21	38.98	41.20	54.70
Romania	50.00	53.80	52.60	48.70	41.30	23.40	32.40	33.00	35.20
Slovenia	44.00	39.50	37.30	35.00	31.20	34.20	34.70	31.50	35.00
Portugal	24.01	22.08	23.96	31.12	31.82	34.83	30.63	37.90	35.00
France	36.20	41.20	40.20	43.50	45.20	52.30	60.20	67.00	67.20
Spain	31.57	25.17	28.35	32.43	35.18	36.56	36.26	33.50	32.90
Net interest margin (net interest revenue/total earning assets)									
Bulgaria	10.00	0.20	1.80	6.40	4.10	5.30	5.40	5.30	5.10
Czech Republic	4.00	4.50	3.40	2.90	3.20	3.40	3.00	2.70	3.50
Estonia	1.10	7.20	7.50	5.70	4.30	4.00	3.90	3.40	4.80
Croatia	16.80	1.90	2.90	3.00	4.00	4.20	4.20	4.00	3.80
Latvia	6.30	12.20	10.6	8.50	4.70	6.60	4.90	3.70	3.40
Hungary	4.00	6.40	6.40	5.10	4.90	5.00	4.70	4.50	4.60
Poland	7.60	7.30	7.96	7.47	6.95	6.59	5.33	4.82	3.34
Romania	6.10	8.40	6.90	6.50	8.70	15.90	15.2	12.00	8.80
Slovenia	9.20	4.50	3.90	4.80	4.50	4.50	4.10	4.40	3.70
Portugal	4.00	3.40	2.90	2.50	2.60	2.50	2.30	2.10	2.20
France	1.10	1.70	1.60	1.60	1.40	1.70	1.00	1.00	0.90
Spain	2.96	3.00	3.00	2.80	2.80	5.30	2.70	2.50	3.00
CEE			9.80	4.60	4.50	4.70	4.40	4.20	3.50
SE			9.40	4.60	4.40	4.70	4.40	4.20	3.50
EU			3.80	1.80	1.60	1.90	1.30	1.30	1.40

Sources: OECD, *Bank Profitability*, 2000; BankScope Database.

for CEE and SE countries tends to be minimal, while there are great disparities between bank net margins in transition economies and the EU; the former being higher. Interest spreads are constantly wider in Bulgaria, Croatia, Latvia and Romania, but in all countries they are decreasing and tending to approach the levels in the EU.

HIGHER COST-TO-INCOME RATIOS

Banks in transition economies usually exhibit higher cost-to-income ratios, which is currently one of the most focused-on performance indicators. Its levels are highest in Romania, Latvia and the Czech Republic. The ratio (calculated as overheads over the income before provisions, with income measured as the sum of net interest revenues and other operating income) indicates the cost of running the bank and is a measure of operating efficiency. Given the range of margins in transition economies, the high levels of cost-to-income ratios in these countries may be an indicator of overstaffing and excessive branch networks. The ratio is improving in almost all CEE and SE countries, which could be a sign of high net income or successful transformations and removal of excess staffing, as salaries are normally the major element of this coefficient.

SMALLER RANGE OF BUSINESS AND PRODUCT MIX

Banks in transition economies offer less-sophisticated portfolios of services and products to their customers than their counterparts from the European countries.

EXCESS CAPACITY

The insufficient amount of productive investment opportunities and over-restrictive prudential regulation, especially in the countries with currency boards, are likely to have created greater liquidity and excess capacity in some CEE banking systems.

Macroeconomic financial development and structure measures

LOWER BANK INTERMEDIATION LEVEL

Despite the long-lasting transformation and restructuring processes, CEE countries still have lower levels of financial development indicators.

HIGHER INFLATION

The economic environment in which most banks in CEE countries operate is characterized by higher inflation that tends to distort the ROE and ROA coefficients and has to be taken into account while interpreting operating income and profit ratios.

The level of investment in information technologies and financial infra-structure strongly influences, as well as being influenced by, transactions and payment systems in CEE countries.

HIGHER CONCENTRATION RATIOS

In most of transition economies, the financial sector is highly concen-trated and still characterized by lower levels of competition.

Banking efficiency analysis

Methodology for analyzing efficiency in banking

In order to monitor and enhance the banking system's operational effi-ciency, policymakers in CEE countries need to be able to measure its improvements.

One of the approaches to this end is to use accounting data and compare the operating assets, income and equity ratios either before and after the reform or in terms of cross-country studies. The most closely and extensively studied ratio is the net interest margin. This approach has several deficiencies. The main criticisms are that neither coefficient can capture the whole range of services banks provide. Bank operating ratios can also be severely distorted by differences in capital structure, account-ing practices for reporting reserves and provisions, the level of inflation, the range of business and product mix (Vittas 1991).

The alternative empirical methodology is to use parametric (such as the stochastic frontier approach, SFA, or the distribution-free approach, DFA) or non-parametric (such as data envelopment analysis, DEA) fron-tier techniques to estimate an index of bank operational efficiency. The SFA has the advantage that it performs well in small and "noisy samples". For that reason it is often chosen for analysis of transition economies' banking systems. The main disadvantage of this approach is that a specific functional form for the production frontier has to be assumed. The distri-bution-free approach requires a constant level of efficiency over time that, in the case of transition economies, is difficult to assume.

The non-parametric DEA approach has the advantage that the produc-tion frontier is derived based on the sample under investigation and there is no need to make preliminary assumptions about it. This gives the tech-nique a great potential for identifying the best-practices benchmark and evaluating the performance of banks in comparison to it. The main disadvantage of this approach is that the derived efficiency scores are very sensitive to outliers and shocks because they are treated as a sign of inefficiency.

Both approaches suffer from the usual difficulty of having to construct an index for bank output capturing the whole range of functions that these institutions perform. Additional problems arise if the samples that are combined under a common frontier exhibit too-great a heterogeneity, which can lead to higher inefficiency scores (Mester 1997).

Studies on banking efficiency in transition

An increasing number of studies of efficiency in banking in transition economies that apply parametric or non-parametric methodology are filling the gap that existed until recently in the academic literature in this area. The prevailing part of these studies is analyzing the efficiency of banking systems in individual countries. Hasan and Marton (2003) trailed the dynamics of profit and cost efficiency for Hungarian banks and the factors that correlate to their performance. Using SFA, they estimated the overall profit and cost inefficiency to be 28.76 and 34.50 respectively. Taci (2000) analyzed the cost efficiency of the Czech financial sector in conjunction with the size, ownership structure and performance status of banks using the distribution-free approach (DFA) in a cross-sectional estimation and fixed effects approach in panel data estimation. Kraft and Tirtiroglu (1998) studied X-efficiency and scale efficiencies of both new and old, state and private banks in Croatia. Using the SFA and data for the period 1994–1995, they found that the new banks are more X-inefficient and more scale-inefficient than either old privatized banks or old state banks. However, according to this study, new, private banks are highly profitable. Consequently, a negative, but only weakly statistically significant, relationship between profitability and X-efficiency was found to emerge in Croatia.

A growing number of international comparative studies use banking system efficiency scores for various countries, including transition economies, to derive policy recommendations and analyze different aspects of financial structure architecture or performance. Yildirim and Philippatos (2002) analyze the cost and profit efficiency of 12 transition economies, excluding Bulgaria and Yugoslavia, for the period 1993–2000. Using both the SFA and DFA, they found that the average cost efficiency level for the 12 countries was 72 percent and 76 percent respectively. The profit efficiency levels were estimated to be significantly lower: almost one-third of banks' profits are lost to inefficiency according to the SFA and almost one-half by DFA. Drakos (2002) analyzed the effect of reforms on banking efficiency using a dealership model for micro datasets of six CEE countries' banks during the period 1993–1999. In a recent study, Grigorian and Manole (2002) investigated the determinants of banking efficiency in 16 transition countries, employing DEA and a variation of the value-added approach to the definition of bank output for the period 1995–1998. They defined two types of indexes – revenue-based and service-based, differentiated according to different banking functions.

Specification of input and output variables

The exact definition of input and output variables in banking is still a controversial issue. According to Berger and Humphrey (1992), inputs and outputs in banking can be specified using either the assets (or intermediation) approach, the user-cost approach or the value-added (or production) approach. In recent empirical studies, more attention has been given to the intermediation approach, treating deposits as inputs and defining loans and investments as outputs. According to this approach, interest on deposits is considered as part of total costs.

In this study, following Leightner and Lovell (1998), we adopt a different stance, defining two specifications of the type of services that banks provide, depending on whether they follow their own objectives or the regulatory objectives of the central bank. In the first model, we treat commercial banks as profit-maximizing corporate firms and specify their output as total operating income (sum of net interest revenue and other net operating income). In the second model we examine the behavior of commercial banks while they follow the objectives of central banks, which can be summarized as the attempt to make the financial system support faster economic development and investments while, at the same time, preserving its stability. In this case, we use as an output vector investments (other earning assets) and the net amount of total loans (after deducting problem loans and loan-loss provisions). The substraction of problem loans is aimed at reflecting risk-taking behavior in lending. In both models, inputs are total customers and short-term funding (total deposits), equity and total operating costs.

Convergence of efficiency in banking analysis

Methodology for analyzing convergence in banking

Financial convergence has been modeled using time-series, cross-section and panel data techniques with respect to various aggregate and firm-level variables. Although there is no universally agreed definition of the term "convergence", there are two predominant concepts in the growth literature (Quah 1993) which also inspire the studies of banking system evolution. One concept, referred to as "beta convergence", is related with regression to the mean and implies, in the banking context, that financial systems with lower bank output, expressed relative to a given steady state

level (usually the start of the reforms period in 1993 in the case of transition economies), tends to grow faster over time (Murinde *et al.* 2000).
The other concept, known as "rho convergence", concerns cross-sectional
dispersion and applies if the variability, measured as a change in the standard deviation of a given variable (such as Government Bond Yield) or
performance measure (such as the ratio of non-interest income to gross
income), declines over time (Calcagnini *et al.* 2000). De Guevara and
Maudos (2002) and Altunbas and Chakravarty (1998) analyze the importance of productive specialization and the country effect in the explanation of the differences in efficiency of the banking sectors in the
European Union using Theil indexes decomposition.

Numerous papers have investigated the existence and implications of
financial convergence in Europe especially in relation with and after the
introduction of the euro. Convergence in banking is normally analyzed by
testing the time trends of numbers of aggregate and micro-level indicators.
Calcagnini *et al.* (2000) use a statistical cost-accounting approach to investigate whether there is convergence of marginal rates of return on costs
and liabilities in Europe. Another approach is to estimate and test a model
of growth of output in banking using different measures of bank outputs
such as loans to government sectors, loans to public enterprises or bank
loans to the private sectors (Murinde *et al.* 2000). Almost all authors in the
extensive literature on scale and scope economies in banking have looked
at the convergence of efficiency scores, although there are no studies concentrated on explicitly testing a hypothesis for the type of banking evolution based on parametric or non-parametric efficiency measures.

Convergence of banking efficiency in transition economies

In this chapter, convergence is investigated by employing a sigma test for a
decrease in the dispersion of average banking systems' efficiency scores
and ANOVA F-test for measuring the appropriateness of the construction
of a common European frontier and panel data analysis.

The first test exploits the hypothesis that convergence in banking can
be sought primarily in the decrease of differences in the variability of efficiency across countries although the heterogeneity in efficiency levels is
preserved.

The second test builds upon the hypothesis that, although there are differences in the average level of banking efficiency across countries and
regions, the two samples of banks for the CEE and EU member states are
drawn from the same population and, consequently, the construction of a
common frontier is justified.

Further, the micro-level differences in banking performance across
countries are explored using panel data analysis with time effects, fixed
effects and country specific variables.

The study gives insight into the relationship between banking efficiency and economic convergence by suggesting new indicators for the state of development of banking systems based on measures of relative microeconomic efficiency. This approach, although unexplored in the existing convergence literature, can give insights into the importance and speed of banking system integration, the inequalities of financial-sector development across Europe, highlighting the CEE countries' relative performance in this respect.

Data description

The information used is annual firm-level data from bank balance sheets and income statements for a sample of 12 European countries between 1993 and 2001, obtained from BankScope, OECD financial accounts and other sources such as central banks' statistics.

The available micro-data has significant drawbacks both in terms of coverage per country and of definitions of variables. The coverage per country is likely to create a sample bias that does not run in favor of the countries with more developed banking systems, as they may be reporting a larger share of their banks, including both good and bad banks. Cross-country comparisons based on micro-level data are also difficult because of the differences in accounting practices, which are especially wide in the case of CEE countries. However, these data appear to be a natural starting point for a comparative analysis since they provide better insight into financial-system structure and the market behavior of individual commercial banks. Hence, they allow a more detailed evaluation of a financial system than a description of banking-sector-aggregated indicators concentrated on size. The aggregate measures primarily reflect the financial intermediation function of banks and are not that flexible in qualifying the behavior of banks as profit-maximizing firms.

The CEE countries included are: Bulgaria, the Czech Republic, Croatia, Estonia, Hungary, Latvia, Poland, Romania and Slovenia. For the panel data estimation, Spain and the Slovak Republic are also included. From the initial sample we excluded bank holding companies and banks with missing observations on a model variable or with negative values due to efficiency estimation specifications. Despite the strong influence of outliers on the DEA efficiency score, in order to avoid sample selection bias no banks were excluded based on these considerations. To preserve the number of observations, efficiency estimations were made separately on cross-sectional data for each year. Table 11.1a lists the number of banks in the sample by country and year, while Table 11.2 reports the descriptive statistics for model variables for 1999. All data are reported in thousands of US dollars as a reference currency and are corrected for inflation using the IMF's International Financial Statistics GDP deflators.

There are substantial differences in average bank size and performance across countries. The average bank in Poland has generated more loans

Table 11.2a Descriptive statistics of banks in the sample by country for 1999

Country	N	Total loans – net	Net interest revenue	Other operating income	Total operating income	Customer and short-term funding	Equity	Total operating expenditures	Total fixed assets
Bulgaria	30	1,207,897	199,345	172,290	366,433	3,262,259	780,713	224,017	254,652
Czech Republic	29	22,546,766	1,459,009	1,237,846	2,693,222	45,855,224	4,566,255	490,134	2,138,662
Estonia	4	1,480,069	91,112	111,005	1,237,846	1,921,091	433,513	134,928	92,077
Croatia	34	5,483,717	481,570	258,016	201,914	8,087,689	1,848,874	444,976	620,096
Latvia	21	1,235,249	123,886	114,523	238,358	2,419,511	288,891	174,114	147,054
Hungary	32	13,623,576	1,362,964	4,097,638	2,048,819	29,152,900	2,851,504	1,957,567	1,243,724
Poland	42	41,835,129	3,328,022	2,163,074	5,491,097	71,152,112	7,623,801	3,464,855	2,789,795
Romania	25	2,165,905	1,023,354	359,756	1,383,111	5,659,065	1,252,202	623,373	922,823
Slovenia	20	6,709,419	476,090	252,784	728,874	8,244,807	1,329,162	252,784	512,702
Slovak Republic	8	4,110,964	395,713	548,775	944,490	12,551,617	654,235	476,708	543,791
Spain	76	214,370,558	9,988,396	5,584,148	15,572,548	333,361,093	26,444,427	9,651,621	8,376,407
France	146	751,767,168	19,169,144	29,349,245	48,518,399	890,623,873	78,629,846	34,505,464	27,026,261
Portugal	42	156,966,024	7,429,082	5,273,755	12,702,838	238,568,860	20,161,815	10,586,124	6,619,441

Notes

N – number of banks included in the sample.

All quantity variables are in thousands of US dollars, corrected for inflation.

Total number of banks, N = 195 for CEE sample and N = 383 for the pooled EU and CEE sample.

Table 11.2b Descriptive statistics of banks in the sample by country for 1999

Country	N	Total loans – net		Total operating income		Total operating expenditures		Equity	
		Mean	St. Dev.	Mean	St. Dev.	Mean	St. Dev.	Mean	St. Dev.
Bulgaria	30	40.163	53.977	12.214	18.823	7.467	9.065	26.024	54.581
Czech Republic	29	777.475	1.344.951	92.870	166.207	16.901	50.961	157.457	269.726
Estonia	4	370.017	380.067	50.478	57.120	33.732	33.628	108.378	131.237
Croatia	34	161.286	297.789	21.495	38.078	13.088	22.947	54.379	100.518
Latvia	21	58.821	82.767	11.351	13.743	8.291	8.477	13.757	16.239
Hungary	32	425.737	522.370	64.026	111.739	61.174	96.818	89.109	102.972
Poland	31	996.075	1.381.425	130.740	187.522	82.497	133.459	181.519	213.084
Romania	25	86.636	206.006	55.324	109.314	24.935	43.050	50.088	43.050
Slovenia	20	335.471	512.268	36.444	58.195	12.639	18.872	66.458	87.503
Total	226								
France	146	5.114.062	23.272.422	330.057	1.383.977	234.731	984.521	534.897	2.378.117
Portugal	42	4.111.818	5.991.359	257.562	395.580	254.331	489.248	447.786	669.757
Total	414								

Notes
N – number of banks included in the sample.
All quantity variables are in thousands of US dollars, corrected for inflation.
Total number of banks, $N = 195$ for CEE sample and $N = 383$ for the pooled EU and CEE sample.

than the average bank in the other CEE countries, followed by Czech and Hungarian banks. Banks in Bulgaria have given the smallest amount of credits, which can be explained with the restrictive policy imposed by the currency board arrangement in the country. Polish banks also lead with respect to the operating income and level of equity. However, the average Polish bank also has the highest amount of expenditure in its income statements, followed by Hungarian and Estonian banks. Czech banks are operating at relatively lower cost-to-income ratios in comparison to Polish and Hungarian banks. Banks in EU member states are not exactly comparable with CEE banks in terms of loans. The average French bank has in its balance sheet more than six times more credits than even the average bank in the Czech Republic. On the other hand, the average bank in the EU member states in the sample has considerably lower total operating income than the average bank in the CEE countries, which can be explained with the persistently higher net interest margins in transition economies.

Empirical results

DEA technical efficiency analysis – CEE countries

We analyzed the technical efficiency of banks in CEE and the EU according to two different scenarios: the first is based on the profit-maximizing behavior of banks, while the second is based on the economic-growth-generating objectives of the regulatory authorities. Table 11.3 reports results based on data envelopment analysis of annual cross-sectional data for CEE based on the regulatory authorities' objectives in Panel 1 and on commercial banks' objectives in Panel 2 for the period 1993–2001.

We performed DEA separately for a sample of banks in CEE for the period 1993–2001 and for a pooled sample of banks in CEE and selected EU member states (France, Portugal and Spain). Because of the differences in the selected input and output variables, and the differentiation of two types of bank outputs, the scores obtained cannot be directly compared with those from other studies. The efficiency scores are relatively low, far from reaching the world average of 0.86 (Berger and Humphrey 1997) or the average efficiency level reported by the European Commission (1997) equal to 0.79. Still, they are in the range of other recent studies using DEA. For instance, Sathye (2001) found the mean technical efficiency level to be 0.67 for Australian banks; Dietsch and Weil (1998) estimated the average efficiency level in the EU to be 0.64 in 1996. As in most of these studies, a single set of bank outputs is used; the lower efficiency scores obtained while estimating two separate sets of outputs reflecting the different bank objectives are just confirming the complexity of functions performed by these institutions. Obviously banks cannot be treated only as ordinary firms seeking to maximize profits, or just as

Table 11.3 Mean DEA technical efficiency scores, VRS, CEE countries

	1993	1994	1995	1996	1997	1998	1999	2000	2001	Mean
Panel 1: regulatory authorities' objectives										
Bulgaria	0.7963	0.8961	0.6260	0.8561	0.6308	0.6801	0.6138	0.6398	0.4498	0.4684
Czech Republic	0.6853	0.8456	0.7398	0.9371	0.8695	0.9301	0.8569	0.8854	0.5929	0.6245
Croatia	0.6054	0.9265	0.6530	0.8170	0.6452	0.7753	0.4894	0.5640	0.4318	0.4724
Estonia	0.8654	0.7059	0.5727	0.8598	0.7098	0.9585	0.5718	0.7380	0.5650	0.5773
Hungary	0.7171	0.7482	0.6982	0.8850	0.6686	0.8284	0.6308	0.6789	0.5241	0.5360
Latvia	0.9783	0.7368	0.7246	0.8537	0.5526	0.8375	0.5806	0.6812	0.4014	0.4196
Poland	0.5683	0.6866	0.6467	0.8431	0.6630	0.8057	0.6401	0.6959	0.5811	0.5539
Romania	0.6417	0.6725	0.5040	0.8290	0.3990	0.7102	0.6072	0.5237	0.3957	0.3695
Slovenia	0.7113	0.7847	0.4990	0.8481	0.6584	0.8125	0.5902	0.6070	0.4501	0.5457
St. dev.	0.1306	0.0921	0.0886	0.0351	0.1249	0.0904	0.0992	0.1057	0.0782	
Panel 2: commercial banks' objectives										
Bulgaria	0.2263	0.9330	0.5697	0.7454	0.8757	0.5061	0.4767	0.6455	0.4542	0.6036
Czech Republic	0.2955	0.5121	0.3367	0.5972	0.7044	0.7349	0.6239	0.5058	0.4238	0.5260
Croatia	0.6106	0.5358	0.3171	0.3969	0.3151	0.4699	0.2818	0.5216	0.3316	0.4201
Estonia	0.8205	0.6608	0.5383	0.5680	0.4144	0.3618	0.3375	0.6254	0.5014	0.5364
Hungary	0.4998	0.7318	0.4423	0.5131	0.4377	0.4464	0.2845	0.5668	0.4492	0.4857
Latvia	0.7260	0.7977	0.6773	0.7199	0.3652	0.6168	0.3591	0.5949	0.3582	0.5794
Poland	0.6526	0.7336	0.3829	0.4815	0.4955	0.5130	0.3313	0.6716	0.4553	0.5241
Romania	0.3280	1.0000	0.4695	0.6860	0.5729	0.7858	0.5131	0.7518	0.4397	0.6163
Slovenia	0.3875	0.5216	0.2417	0.4219	0.3705	0.4090	0.3294	0.5633	0.3241	0.3965
St. dev.	0.2086	0.1767	0.1378	0.1277	0.1831	0.1452	0.1178	0.0776	0.0622	

intermediaries and service-providing institutions. Taking this into account, the results are in line with those found in efficiency studies based on differentiated bank functions (Grigorian and Manole 2002).

Although cross-country efficiency estimates need to be interpreted with caution because of the differences in regulatory framework, economic environment (Berger and Humphrey 1997), as well as the selection of input and output variables and accounting practices, low mean efficiency scores imply that:

1   banks in CEE countries have to further improve efficiency so as to achieve world and European best practices. Governments and regulatory authorities should help financial institutions in this respect by creating an economic environment that is more favorable to efficiency enhancement. As both efficiency with respect to commercial and central banks' objectives were found to be relatively low, these measures should concern bank credit operations and the possibilities for further financial services liberalization.

2   as is confirmed in numerous studies, efficiency levels are negatively correlated with the degree of concentration of the banking sector (Berger and Hannan 1989; Sathye 2001; Yildirim and Philippatos 2002). More than half of the banks in the sample exhibit decreasing returns to scale.

Technical efficiency reflects the productivity of inputs. In order to increase efficiency, banks in CEE have to enhance the productivity of the three inputs used – total operating costs, loanable funds and equity. With the progress of privatization and the increasing competition from both local and foreign-owned firms, banks in transition countries have been persistently improving their cost-to-income ratios by decreasing excess staff and closing branches. The switch to Internet banking, considered a cost effective way of delivering banking services, is still not well developed in CEE countries due to insufficient investments in information technologies and infrastructure.

The changes in the average DEA efficiency scores reported in Table 11.3 can be classified in three periods. In the first period, the start of the transition process is characterized with high levels of efficiency with respect to regulatory authorities' objectives and lower scores with respect to efficiency in terms of profit maximization. The second period is encompassing the continuous transformation processes involving privatization, liberalization and consolidation. It is interesting to observe the change in efficiency scores for Romania and Bulgaria during the bank crisis period of 1996–1997. In both countries efficiency in obtaining central banks' objectives is relatively low while scores for efficiency in achieving commercial banks' goals are quite high. This is due mainly to the high non-interest revenue of banks in this period. It can partially be explained by the fact that most of the banks that have been closed after the banking crisis in Bulgaria are not included in the sample because of the lack of data. The last period following the main reforms is characterized by slightly increasing levels of efficiency.

The composition of the efficiency frontier, presented in Table 11.4 permits an analysis of the relative position of each country. The efficiency frontier comprises banks that are efficient and thus represent a benchmark constituting the reference technology for the sample. An improvement in the position can be observed for almost all countries except Estonia, Slovenia and Latvia. The influence of banks in each country changes slightly in response to environmental and country-specific factors. The importance of Czech banks is decreasing in favor of Polish banks. The continuous presence of Bulgarian banks on the efficient frontier is due primarily to the influence of foreign-owned banks. The changes in the composition of the efficiency frontier give insight into the range of heterogeneity in the banking systems and country-specific processes characterizing their evolution.

DEA technical efficiency – CEE and EU countries

To analyze the efficiency of banks under a common European frontier, we pooled the data for CEE countries and France and Portugal, and estimated technical efficiency using DEA for the period 1993–2001. The estimation of banking efficiency for the pooled sample resulted in lower technical efficiency scores for the CEE countries as almost half of the frontier was built by French banks. The results are presented in Table 11.5 and Table 11.6. Even though banks from the EU were predominantly selected as the benchmark for efficiency for the joint sample, the overall average efficiency levels for France and Portugal were not always much greater than those of CEE banking systems. This can be explained with the diversity of specialization and efficiency levels of banks in those countries. The same differences in efficiency with respect to time periods can be observed.

Convergence of banking efficiency?

First, we were interested to see whether there is a regional convergence in banking efficiency in CEE countries or if the disparities between countries in that respect are predominant and increasing. Second, we analyzed whether there is convergence in bank efficiency and a decrease of heterogeneity as European integration proceeds for the CEE and selected EU member states sample.

We made regressions on time of cross-sectional standard deviations of average technical efficiency scores per each country for the period 1993-2001. Table 11.7 presents the results of the regressions. All coefficients for the time trends have negative signs and those for the efficiency of achieving

Table 11.4 Composition of the efficient frontier, VRS, CEE countries

Number of efficient banks	1993	1994	1995	1996	1997	1998	1999	2000	2001
Panel 1: regulatory authorities' objectives									
Bulgaria	1	3	2	2	2	1	5 (4)	4 (4)	6 (3)
Czech Republic	4	5 (1)	4 (1)	8 (4)	7 (2)	8 (3)	7 (2)	3 (2)	4 (2)
Croatia	2	3 (1)	2 (1)	3 (1)	2 (1)	6 (4)	0	0	2 (1)
Estonia	1	0	0	1	1	1	0	0	0
Hungary	5 (5)	0	1 (1)	0	0	2 (2)	1 (1)	4 (3)	5 (4)
Latvia	2 (1)	1	2 (1)	2 (1)	0	4 (2)	0	0	1
Poland	2	2	1 (1)	2 (1)	2	2	3	5	4 (1)
Romania	0	0	0	1 (1)	0	2	1	1 (1)	0
Slovenia	3 (1)	3 (1)	0	0	0	0	1	1	0
Total	20 (7)	17 (3)	12 (5)	19 (8)	14 (3)	26 (11)	18 (7)	17 (10)	21 (11)
Panel 2: commercial banks' objectives									
Bulgaria	0	2 (1)	1	3 (2)	7 (4)	2	5 (4)	6 (5)	5 (2)
Czech Republic	0	4 (1)	4 (1)	7 (2)	9 (3)	9 (3)	8 (2)	1	1
Croatia	1	3 (1)	2 (1)	1 (1)	1 (1)	3 (1)	0	1 (1)	0
Estonia	1	0	1	0	0	1	0	0	0
Hungary	1 (1)	5 (1)	3	3	2	1	1	4 (2)	2 (1)
Latvia	0	4 (1)	2 (1)	3 (2)	1 (1)	3 (1)	0	0	0
Poland	4 (1)	7 (5)	4 (2)	2	4 (1)	3 (1)	1	3	2 (1)
Romania	0	2	0	0	0	6 (1)	4	7 (2)	3 (1)
Slovenia	0	0	0	0	0	0	0	0	0
Total	7 (2)	27 (12)	17 (5)	19 (7)	24 (10)	27 (7)	19 (6)	21 (10)	13 (5)

Note
Numbers in brackets = the number of foreign-owned banks on the efficient frontier.

Table 11.5 Mean DEA technical efficiency scores, VRS, CEE countries and selected EU member states

	1993	1994	1995	1996	1997	1998	1999	2000	2001	Mean
Panel 1: regulatory authorities' objectives										
Bulgaria	0.5683	0.7353	0.4115	0.5241	0.4520	0.4490	0.4927	0.4813	0.4414	0.5062
Czech Republic	0.4558	0.5350	0.3887	0.5182	0.4707	0.5755	0.6267	0.3670	0.3664	0.4782
Croatia	0.5513	0.7463	0.3717	0.3394	0.2907	0.4888	0.3503	0.3151	0.3506	0.4227
Estonia	0.8116	0.5698	0.3956	0.4711	0.3565	0.4928	0.3788	0.3736	0.4200	0.4744
Hungary	0.4468	0.4549	0.3432	0.3687	0.2868	0.4028	0.3668	0.3281	0.3446	0.3714
Latvia	0.8913	0.5902	0.4959	0.6039	0.2366	0.6620	0.4393	0.3678	0.3547	0.5157
Poland	0.3787	0.4336	0.3253	0.3246	0.3111	0.4037	0.3664	0.3026	0.3180	0.3515
Romania	0.4873	0.3940	0.2970	0.4960	0.2167	0.5348	0.4163	0.3344	0.3767	0.3948
Slovenia	0.4963	0.4287	0.2661	0.3204	0.2922	0.3963	0.3974	0.2379	0.3049	0.3489
Slovak Republic	–	0.4914	0.2942	0.3862	0.3600	0.4457	0.4849	0.2616	0.2963	0.3775
Selected EU m.s.	0.5542	0.7016	0.4769	0.5101	0.5102	0.5662	0.5398	0.4883	0.4900	0.5375
St. dev.	0.1630	0.1329	0.0733	0.1007	0.1017	0.0880	0.0897	0.0770	0.0575	
Panel 2: commercial banks' objectives										
Bulgaria	0.2263	0.9330	0.5651	0.7445	0.8626	0.4808	0.4740	0.5935	0.4419	0.5763
Czech Republic	0.2729	0.4912	0.3269	0.5972	0.7007	0.7196	0.6238	0.4157	0.3840	0.5473
Croatia	0.6106	0.4912	0.3119	0.3969	0.2945	0.4516	0.2769	0.4531	0.3012	0.4232
Estonia	0.8205	0.6391	0.5361	0.5680	0.3770	0.3510	0.3215	0.4990	0.4364	0.4725
Hungary	0.4345	0.7066	0.4055	0.5125	0.4090	0.4196	0.2733	0.4568	0.3838	0.5250
Latvia	0.7260	0.7973	0.6735	0.7199	0.3441	0.5946	0.3567	0.5031	0.3333	0.5065
Poland	0.6138	0.7973	0.3642	0.4810	0.4513	0.4880	0.3165	0.5355	0.3933	0.5654
Romania	0.3110	0.9920	0.4640	0.6860	0.4814	0.7374	0.5064	0.6465	0.4317	0.6347
Slovenia	0.3665	0.5186	0.2321	0.4219	0.3490	0.3912	0.3213	0.4396	0.2591	0.4372
Slovak Republic	–	0.5977	0.2910	0.3375	0.4070	0.5936	0.3636	0.4574	0.2943	0.4178
Selected EU m.s.	0.5013	0.5310	0.3132	0.3842	0.3917	0.4283	0.3135	0.5031	0.4035	
St. dev.	0.2005	0.1856	0.1379	0.1338	0.1787	0.1340	0.1165	0.0716	0.0609	

Table 11.6 Composition of the efficient frontier, VRS, CEE countries and selected EU member states

Number of efficient banks	1993	1994	1995	1996	1997	1998	1999	2000	2001
Panel 1: regulatory authorities' objectives									
Bulgaria	0	2	0	2	2 (1)	1	5 (4)	4 (4)	4 (3)
Czech Republic	0	0	2 (1)	2	2 (1)	3	4 (1)	0	1
Croatia	2	3 (1)	2	1 (1)	0	2 (1)	0	0	1
Estonia	3	0	0	0	0	0	0	0	0
Hungary	0	0	0	1 (1)	0	0	0	2 (1)	1 (1)
Latvia	1 (1)	2 (1)	1	2	1	3	0	1	0
Poland	0	1	1 (1)	1	1	0	1	1 (1)	0
Romania	0	0	0	0	0	3	1	1 (1)	2 (1)
Slovenia	0	0	0	0	0	0	0	0	0
Selected EU m.s.	5	28	21	19	27	22	21	31	24
Total	11	36	27	28	32	36	31	39	33
Panel 2: commercial banks' objectives									
Bulgaria	0	2 (1)	1	2	8 (2)	2	6 (4)	5 (4)	5 (2)
Czech Republic	0	2 (1)	2 (1)	7 (2)	9 (3)	7 (3)	8 (3)	1	1
Croatia	3	2	2 (1)	1 (1)	0	3 (1)	0	1 (1)	0
Estonia	1	0	1	0	0	0	0	0	0
Hungary	0	3 (1)	2	4 (1)	1	1	0	3 (2)	1
Latvia	0	5 (1)	5 (1)	2	0	2 (1)	0	1	0
Poland	3 (1)	5 (4)	2 (1)	2	3	2 (1)	1	2	1
Romania	0	1	0	0	0	3 (1)	4	4 (2)	1 (1)
Slovenia	0	0	0	0	0	0	0	0	0
Selected EU m.s.	4	16	11	10	11	11	8	21	17
Total	11	36	26	28	32	31	27	38	26

Note
Numbers in brackets = the number of foreign-owned banks on the efficient frontier.

Table 11.7 Regressions of technical efficiency scores standard deviations on time

	Constant	Trend	R-squared	St. error	F-statistic	Probability
Regulatory objectives						
CEE countries	0.102	−0.002	0.022	0.029	0.16	0.002
	(0.021)	(0.004)				
CEE countries and selected EU member states	0.146	−0.009	0.649	0.020	12.96	0.000
	(0.015)	(0.003)				
Commercial banks' objectives						
CEE countries	0.213	−0.016	0.739	0.026	19.86	0.000
	(0.019)	(0.003)				
CEE countries and selected EU member states	0.214	−0.016	0.796	0.023	27.29	0.000
	(0.017)	(0.003)				

commercial banks' objectives are higher in magnitude. The results imply that there is convergence in efficiency both in regional and European dimension and the decrease of divergences is faster when the EU member states are included in the sample. This can be explained both with the heterogeneity between CEE countries' banking systems and by the fact that, in the joint sample, the efficiency comparison is made against a frontier composed predominantly of banks from EU member states.

Then, in order to perform the ANOVA test, DEA was applied separately on the samples of CEE countries and the pooled sample of CEE countries and EU member states for the years 2000 and 2001. The results of testing the null hypothesis that the two samples are drawn from the same population are presented on Table 11.8. Evaluating efficiency separately for both samples avoids the problem of inherent dependency of the relative efficiency scores and complies with the sample independence assumption of the ANOVA test. The tests were done for efficiency in both obtaining central banks' and commercial banks' objectives. The results from the equality of variances test imply that, in terms of commercial banks' efficiency in pursuing their own objectives, for year 2000 and to a lesser extent for year 2001, the null hypothesis of having no significant differences between the two groups of banks cannot be rejected. The tests for equality of means suggest that there are strong disparities between the average levels of banking efficiency in the two regions.

To gain a better insight on banking systems' performance at disaggregate level, we made a panel data regression of the estimated technical efficiency score of every bank on control variables as well as on country-specific and time-specific dummy variables. The country-specific variables are controlling for the type of monetary policy regime and the presence of currency board arrangement and the level of inflation. Banks in countries with currency boards are expected to have higher liquidity and thus lower efficiency both in terms of generating revenues and

Table 11.8 ANOVA tests of differences between banking systems' efficiency levels in CEE and selected EU member states

			Equality of variance			*Equality of means*		
				Value	*Prob.*		*Value*	*Prob.*
Regulatory objectives	2001	F-test		1.549 (191; 208)	0.0020	*t*-test	7.181 (399)	0.000
						ANOVA F-test	51.57 (1; 399)	0.000
	2000	F-test		1.496 (243; 223)	0.0023	*t*-test	5.796 (466)	0.000
						ANOVA F-test	33.60 (1; 466)	0.000
Commercial banks' objectives	2001	F-test		1.279 (199; 220)	0.0740	*t*-test	6.47 (419)	0.000
						ANOVA F-test	41.86 (1; 419)	0.000
	2000	F-test		1.127 (248; 223)	0.3590	*t*-test	3.13 (471)	0.0019
						ANOVA F-test	9.79 (1; 0471)	0.0019

providing services. Inflation is a proxy for shocks and is expected to have a positive sign because of the increase of both input and output variables.

The country-specific dummy variables test whether there are systematic differences between bank efficiency among countries. For identification purposes, the dummy variables for EU member states are excluded, so that the estimated coefficients measure the relative technical efficiency of banks in transition economies relative to the EU countries.

The time-specific dummy variables test whether there are systematic differences in efficiency levels over time. Again, for identification purposes, the dummy variable for 1993 is excluded so that the time dummies measure the time effect relative to 1993.

Table 11.9 presents the regression results with efficiency scores as dependent variables for the two models of banking efficiency in obtaining the commercial banks' and central banks' objectives. The *t*-statistics are calculated using the White (1980) heteroscedasticity-consistent standard errors. Currency boards have a significantly negative influence on both types of efficiency scores while inflation, as expected, has a positive impact on banking performance.

Regarding the country-effect dummies, all but Estonia and Latvia (both countries with currency boards) have significantly negative coefficients, indicating lower performance on average than in the EU member states with respect to central banks' objectives and positive coefficients with respect to commercial banks' objectives. The performance of banks in the Czech Republic and the Slovak Republic is indistinguishable from that of

Table 11.9 Panel data analysis of technical efficiency (*t*-statistics and probabilities in parentheses)

	Regulatory objectives	*Commercial banks' objectives*
Currency board	−1.043	−0.521
	(0.065), (0.000)	(−2.028), (0.000)
Inflation	0.001	0.001
	(1.580), (0.000)	(2.327), (0.000)
Bulgaria	−0.10	0.192
	(−6.322), (0.000)	(3.255), (0.000)
Czech Republic	−0.047	−0.013
	(0.006), (0.000)	(−1.818), (0.069)
Croatia	−0.086	−0.034
	(0.003), (0.000)	(−8.706), (0.000)
Estonia	0.998	0.599
	(1.560), (0.000)	(2.223), (0.000)
Hungary	−0.124	0.042
	(−4.166), (0.000)	(7.459), (0.000)
Latvia	0.976	0.597
	(1.526), (0.000)	(2.390), (0.000)
Poland	−0.094	0.104
	(−1.916), (0.000)	(1.236), (0.000)
Romania	−0.169	0.096
	(−1.710), (0.000)	(8.103), (0.000)
Slovenia	−0.119	−0.016
	(−3.726), (0.000)	(−3.411), (0.000)
Slovak Republic	−0.094	−0.012
	(−3.287), (0.000)	(−1.411), (0.158)
1994	0.620	0.0526
	(1.370), (0.000)	(9.912), (0.000)
1995	0.400	0.202
	(9.779), (0.000)	(4.333), (0.000)
1996	0.434	0.376
	(1.227), (0.000)	(8.144), (0.000)
1997	0.421	0.342
	(1.280), (0.000)	(8.001), (0.000)
1998	0.521	0.474
	(1.640), (0.000)	(1.153), (0.000)
1999	0.511	0.279
	(1.610), (0.000)	(7.014), (0.000)
2000	0.424	0.437
	(1.254), (0.000)	(1.158), (0.000)
2001	0.439	0.285
	(1.650), (0.000)	(7.277), (0.000)
Adjusted R^2	0.745	0.643
Number of observations	3,825	3,879

Note
White heteroscedasticity-consistent standard errors.

banks in EU with respect to commercial banks' objectives, as indicated by their coefficients that are not significant enough to reject the null hypothesis of equality of efficiency levels in the two sets of countries.

All of the time-effect dummies have significantly positive coefficients indicating that, in the period 1993–2001, on average efficiency levels were increasing with respect to both types of banking objectives. While efficiency in obtaining the regulatory objectives is relatively constant and more gradually improving, efficiency in following commercial banks' own objectives is more volatile, exhibiting particular increases in 1998 and 2000.

Summary

This chapter reports results from analyzing the comparative efficiency of banks in two groups of countries under a common frontier in obtaining the objectives of revenue generation and services provision. On average, banks in transition economies tend to have higher efficiency scores on the first set of objectives and lower performance on the second ones. Differences in efficiency levels are significant and null hypothesis of equality of performance between banks in CEE countries and EU member states with respect to efficiency in revenue generation is rejected for all countries except the Czech Republic and Slovak Republic. The efficiency of banks in those two countries in obtaining the commercial banks' own objectives is virtually statistically indistinguishable from those of banks in the EU.

The observed significant trend of decrease in the dispersion of average performance measures across countries confirms the ongoing financial integration and convergence in banking efficiency not only for the EU countries but also for transition economies. Moreover, the equality of variance tests suggests that, after the start of the European Monetary Union, for years 2000 and 2001, the variability of the efficiency scores obtained in performing DEA analysis separately on the two groups of CEE and EU member states does not permit a rejection of the null hypothesis that the two samples of countries are the same with respect to revenue generation.

References

Altunbas, Y., Gardener, E.P.M., Molyneux, P. and Moore, B. (2000) "Efficiency in European banking", *European Economic Review*, 45(10), December: 1931–1955.

Altunbas, Y. and Chakravarty, S.P. (1998), "Efficiency measures and the banking structure in Europe", *Economics Letters*, 60.

Berger, A. (2003) "The efficiency effects of a single market for financial services in Europe", *European Journal of Operational Research*, 150 (3), November: 466–481.

Berger, A.N. and Hannan, T.H. (1989) "The price-concentration relationship in banking", *The Review of Economics and Statistics*, 71: 291–299.

Berger, A.N. and Humphrey, D.B. (1997) "Efficiency of financial institutions:

international survey and directions for future research", *European Journal of Operational Research*, special issue.

Berger, A.N. and Humphrey, D.B. (1992) "Measurement and efficiency issues in commercial banking", in *Output Measurement in the Service Sectors*. National Bureau of Economic Research Studies in Income and Wealth. Vol. 56. Chicago: The University of Chicago Press.

Brada, J. and Kutan, A. (2001) "The convergence of monetary policy between candidate countries and the European Union", *Economic Systems*, 25.

Calcagnini, G., Farabullini, F. and Hester, D. (2000) "Financial convergence in the European monetary union?".

Casu, B. and Molyneux, P. "A comparative study of efficiency in European banking", School of Accounting, Banking and Economics, University of Wales, Bangor.

Davis, E.P. and Salo, S. (1998) "Excess capacity in EU and US banking sectors: conceptual, measurement and policy issues", LSE Financial Markets Group special papers series, 105.

Demirgüç, A. and Huizinga, H. (2002) "Financial structure and bank profitability", World Bank.

De Guevera, J. and Maudos, J. (2002) "Inequalities in the efficiency of the banking sectors in the European Union", *Applied Economics Letters*, 9.

Dietsch, M. and Weil, L. (1998) "Banking efficiency and European integration: productivity, cost and profit approaches", Paper presented at the 21st Colloquium of SUERF, Frankfurt, 15–17 October.

Drakos, K. (2002) "The efficiency of banking sector in Central and Eastern Europe", *Russian and East European Finance and Trade*, 38(2) March–April.

European Commission (1997) "Credit institutions and banking", Vol. 4, Subseries II, *Impact on Services*, The Single Market Review. London: Kogan Page.

European Commission (1997) *The European Union: Key Figures* Brussels: EUROSTAT.

Grigorian, D. and Manole, V. (2002) "Determinants of commercial banks' performance in transition: an application of data envelopment analysis", IMF Working Paper 146.

Goddard, J., Molyneux, P. and Wilson, J. "Dynamics of growth and profitability in banking".

Gomel, G. (2002) "Banking and financial sector in transition countries and convergence towards European integration".

Hasan, I. and Marton, K. (2003) "Development and efficiency of the banking sector in a transitional economy: Hungarian experience", *Journal of Banking and Finance*, 27 (12), December: 2249–2271.

Kraft, E. and Tirtiroglu, D. (1998) "Bank efficiency in Croatia: a stochastic frontier analysis", *Journal of Comparative Economics*, June.

Leightner, J.E. and Lovell, C.A.K. (1998) "The impact of financial liberalization on the performance of Thai banks – theory, methodology and applications", *Journal of Economics and Business*, March.

Mester, L. (1997), "Measuring efficiency at U.S. banks: accounting for heterogeneity is important", *European Journal of Operational Research*, 98.

Murinde, V., Agung, J. and Mulineux, A. (2000) "Banking system convergence in Europe", in D. Dickinson and A. Mullineux (eds), *Financial and Monetary Integration in the New Europe: Convergence Between the EU and Central and Eastern Europe*. Elgar.

Nicastro, R., Steinbichler, A. and Revoltella, D. (2002) "Banking sectors in transition–comparisons, experiences and results", National Bank of Slovakia.

OECD (2000) *Bank Profitability: Financial Statements of Banks 2000.*

Sathye, M. (2001) "X-efficiency in Australian banking: an empirical investigation", *Journal of Banking and Finance*, 25: 613–630.

Solans, E. (2002) "The relevance of financial sector developments for accession countries", Speech delivered at *The Economist* conferences – 3rd Cyprus Summit on "Countdown to European Accession", Nicosia.

Taci, A. (2000) "Efficiency in the Czech banking sector", CERGE-EI, Doctoral dissertation.

Vittas, D. (1991) "Measuring commercial banks' efficiency: use and misuse of bank operating ratios", World Bank.

White, H. (1980) "A heteroscedasticity-consistent covarience matrix estimator and a direct test for heteroscedasticity", *Econometrica*, 48.

Yildirim, H.S. and Philippatos (2002) "Efficiency of banks: recent evidence from the transition economies of Europe – 1993–2000", University of Tennessee.

12 The internationalization of Estonian banks

Inward versus outward penetration

Mart Sõrg, Janek Uiboupin, Urmas Varblane and Vello Vensel

Introduction

The banking sector in Estonia has been among the frontrunners in understanding the opportunities and risks of the internationalization process. The internationalization of banks in Estonia has been twofold. On one side, foreign banks have intensively entered into the Estonian banking market, and currently more than 86 per cent of the aggregated share capital of Estonian banks is owned by foreign residents. At the same time, some Estonian banks have tried to enlarge their activities in neighbouring foreign markets. The aim of this chapter is to analyse the foreign-entry strategies of Estonian banks and foreign banks entering into the Estonian banking market. We also discuss main entry motives and possible effects of foreign bank entry in Estonia and other CEE (Central and Eastern European) transition countries.

The chapter is structured as follows. In first section we discuss the main theoretical and empirical literature explaining the internationalization of banks. Then we give an overview of the main potential effects of foreign bank entry on transition countries. In the second section we empirically analyse strategies used by Estonian banks going abroad. Then, regression analysis is used to point out differences between foreign banks compared with domestic banks in Estonia and ten other CEE countries. After this, we analyse motives and the impact of foreign entry into the Estonian banking market, some comparisons are made with other CEE countries.

Literature overview

Major theories explaining the internationalization process of banks

There are many theories which are trying to explain why firms start to internationalize. Although there is a growing literature on FDI, we are still lacking a comprehensive approach, which would explain all different types of FDI. In line with the objectives of our analysis, we found that the most relevant theories are the ones which explain why firms at certain development stages start investing abroad, how this will be executed and the development implications of such activities.

The most general theoretical framework is Dunning's eclectic paradigm, or OLI theory (Dunning 1973, 1981, 1993). It explains why firms decide to start investing abroad, the preconditions (firm specific advantages), where they invest (where the location advantages complementing their ownership-specific advantages are available), and why they select FDI out of many forms of foreign market entry (maximization of their rents). The important aspect of OLI theory is that the location and ownership advantages are necessary, but not sufficient, conditions for FDI. They should be complemented by internationalization, which helps in taking the advantage of such conditions.

Yannopoulus (1983) applied the eclectic paradigm to the banking sector. He argued that there are locational advantages, which may include follow-the-client, country-specific regulations and entry restrictions. Ownership advantages can be, for example, easy access to vehicle currency. Internationalization advantages can be informational advantages and access to local deposit bases.

Another theory with approach to eclectic paradigm is IDP (investment development path paradigm), the dynamic paradigm proposed by Ozawa (1992) based on Japan experiences. Inward and outward FDI are regarded as development catalysts. Ozawa claims that firms that start losing comparative advantages, because of the growth of wages for instance, start to invest abroad in order to keep their competitiveness by taking advantage of low wages abroad. The dynamic paradigm is very similar to IDP model. This theory has been used in working out relocation models explaining the behaviour of multinationals.

The Nordic or sequential internationalization model (Luostarinen 1970; Johanson and Vahlne 1977; Johanson and Wiedersheim-Paul 1975) is mainly a descriptive theory. Originally it looked only at which firms start to invest abroad and in which forms they enter foreign market. It also partly answered the question of why internationalization in certain activities takes place earlier than in others and where such internationalization happens. The basic idea is that internationalization follows stages, that firms start the process through less-demanding, simple activities (export) and their sales functions and only later, through accumulating experiences, do they enter into more sophisticated forms of activities, in more-distant countries. First, they internationalize mostly in neighbouring countries, countries with similar cultures and in simple products and activities. Only later are more sophisticated products and forms of internationalization started. The first activity to be internationalized is the marketing function and the last is the production function. Later, in the 1990s, this model also began to include an inward dimension (Luostarinen 1994).

Resource-based and evolutionary-based theories (Cantwell 1989, 1994; Kogut and Zander 1993) are based on the capabilities of firms. These theories, along with sequential internationalization models (Luostarinen 1970; Johanson and Vahlne 1977; Johanson and Wiedersheim-Paul 1975) have their earlier roots in the theory of the firm. They explain some OFDI, although it may be said that the eclectic or OLI paradigm already incorporated a capabilities perspective, as Dunning (1993) acknowledges. A basic postulation of resource-based theories is that the accumulation of a firm's specific advantages is a cumulative process, and it is important to differentiate between the public and tacit components of technology.

Recently, more attention has been given to the network approach to internationalization since it was established that many firms' international activities are strongly interconnected. Swedish researchers have developed this approach (Mattsson 1985; Johansson and Mattson 1986). Yet it is impossible to talk about one stream of this theory; there are several approaches. Not least among them is a more sociological approach, which concentrates on the types of relationships within the network and not only on why such networks are established.

The theory of multinational banking was first developed by Grubel (1977) and later researchers tried to answer some of the questions posed in his paper (Aliber 1984). This theory of international banking was based on the theory of FDI in manufacturing. According to this theory, multinational banks have some comparative advantages. Banks go abroad to better serve their domestic clients, who have also gone abroad; this is called the 'gravitational pull' effect. Banking internationalization grows in parallel with FDI as banks try to meet the demand for banking services of multinational firms abroad. This bank behaviour of moving abroad is seen as a defensive strategy necessary to assure the continued business with the domestic parents of foreign subsidiaries so that the existing flow of information resulting from the bank–client relationship will not be pre-empted by a competitor bank. Second, multinational service banks also do some business with local and wealthy individuals by offering them specialized services and information required for trade and capital market dealings within their native countries (Paula 2002).

The internationalization of banks has been significantly affected by structural changes in world trade, the growth of direct investments into foreign countries, development of military aid programmes and so on. The 1973 oil crisis was one example of these macroeconomic factors. Because of the crisis, monetary resources began to accumulate in the oil-exporting countries where they remained idle, but the oil-importing countries suffered money scarcity due to the deficit in their balance of payments. The disproportion between the location and demand of money resources gave a powerful boost to the internationalization of banks – with the banks setting up subsidiaries in the oil states. Thus, an opportunity was given to pump money from the oil-producing countries back to the oil-importing countries.

In the last decade, the end of the Cold War and the breakdown of the communist regime in Eastern Europe have become especially important factors for the internationalization of banks. The Western banks rush to conquer the emerging markets, especially the largest, Russian market. The recent wave of bank internationalization is characterized not only by following their existing clients. According to Focarelli and Pozzolo (2002) the 'follow the clients' determinant for bank internationalization is only relevant for small banks, while the behaviour of larger banks is determined by more complex diversification policies.

There are some recent works that try to establish a pattern of expansion for the recent wave of banking internationalization. One of the most common explanations is related to the effects of the increase in banking competition caused by financial deregulation (Pauli 1994; Berger *et al.* 2000). As margins and fees are tightened in domestic financial markets, banks seek to expand cross-borders to generate higher returns. Thus, with banks' net interest margins under downward pressure due to the increase of banking competition, and as the big financial institutions, in general, have a low potential for growth, some banks seek to diversify geographically in markets with potential of growth and/or with greater net interest margins. The benefits from earnings diversification may increase bank value in several ways, since diversification may lower bank risk and reduce the possibility of failure (Berger *et al.* 2000).

There is already a limited amount of literature dealing with the question of whether there exists a difference in foreign market entry for production firms and service providers. Findings differ. Both Terpstra and Yu (1988) and Agarwal and Ramaswami (1992) concluded that no basic differences could be outlined between production and service firms in this respect. But a shortcoming of their research was the limitation of analyses with leasing and advertising firms. With these services, the physical location of the firm in relation to the customer is not important. Dunning (1993) has concluded that the basic factors are similar, but the very realization of internationalization differs between production and service firms.

Important input into the analyses about the specific aspects of service-sector internationalization was given by Erramilli (1990) and Erramilli and Rao (1993). He classified internationally traded services into two groups: soft services and hard services, which serve as a useful tool in analysing the pattern of internationalization of services. Hard services could be exported in a similar manner to manufactured goods. Soft services require close contact and physical proximity between producers and consumers (trade, financial services). Firms producing soft services are typically not able to enter foreign markets by exporting initially. Therefore they have to use more sophisticated methods (franchise, investments) from the beginning of the internationalization process. Consequently, they do not gain prior experience and knowledge and have to face the risks of foreign markets at the beginning of their internationalization process (Pietikäi-nen 1994). It means that, in the case of soft services, the pattern of inter-nationalization can hardly fit the Scandinavian sequential model.

Management theories are also to be taken into account when designing policies of internationalization. What seems particularly important is the development of a global mindset, a state of mind able to understand a business, an industry sector or a particular market on a global basis. Firms from evaluated transition economies seem to be more ambitious than simply aiming to become a regional multinational. Some among them have already taken a more global approach, are expanding outside the region, into wider Europe, and other continents. What is still lacking, however, is the strategic management approach according to which all the firms' activities are to be intertwined in one system, in one decision-making process, regardless of the location of the activity.

Besides the macroeconomic factors that rule the internationalization of banks, the ambitions of bank managers also play an important role. From the bankers' viewpoint, the motives of internationalization can be divided into five groups (Rugman and Kamath 1987):

1   to use the potential ability of a bank more completely. For example, domestic management and sales skills may enable banks to offer ser-vices abroad at lower costs. It also enables the local companies' sub-sidiaries abroad to use competent information about the possibilities and conditions in the mother country.

2   to use the reputation of a parent bank. Subsidiaries set up abroad may get competitive advantages; as a rule, an international bank is con-sidered more reliable than local banks. Opinion poll research con-ducted with Estonian companies in the period 1994–2000 showed that, when choosing a bank, the trustworthiness of the bank was the first order criterion for 29.9 per cent, second order criterion for 16.1 per cent and third order criterion for 16.7 per cent of the companies (Aarma and Vensel 2002).

3   to reduce banking regulations. In many cases, the main purpose of setting up subsidiaries and branches abroad is to overcome the restric-tions on moving capital abroad.

4   to reduce risks. As the economic situation, legislation, political situ-ation and other circumstances may change, being present will enable the banks to recognize the risks in time and take necessary counter-measures.

5   because of special bank–customer relationships. If a bank follows its major customers abroad (the 'follow-the-customer' hypothesis (Grubel 1977)), then it already knows whom it is going to serve, and that provides considerable advantages (Taeho 1993: 42).

The impact of foreign bank entry

Banking sectors in the European Union (EU) countries have been subjected to deregulatory and liberalization changes with the aim to liberalize capital movements among the member states. It is argued that liberalization will significantly affect the degree of cross-border competition in the integrated banking sector of the EU and banking industry performance and efficiency (see Claessens *et al.* 1998, 2001; Gual 1999; De Brandt and Davis 2000; Hasan *et al.* 2000; Berger *et al.* 2000; Hickson and Turner 2000). Recent studies have stressed the importance of differences in the banking structure across the EU, country-specific environmental conditions and banking technology differences (Allen and Rai 1996; Pastor *et al.* 1997; Altunbas and Chakravarty 1998; Bikker 1999; Dietsch and Weill 2000; Dietsch and Lozano-Vivas 2000; Repullo, 2000; Garcia Blandon 2000).

There are a growing number of empirical studies to suggest that the overall economic development of a country is a positive function of the development of its financial sector, especially the banking system. Recent studies have shown that countries with well-developed financial institutions tend to experience more rapid rates of real GDP per capita growth (Levine 1997; Levine and Zervos 1998; Rajan and Zingales 1998). More importantly, empirical studies have shown that there is a positive correlation between foreign ownership of banks and the stability of the banking system (Caprio and Honohan 2000; Goldberg *et al.* 2000).

In addition, there is also the experience of the impact of foreign banks' participation in different countries. For example, Dages *et al.* (2000) examined the lending patterns of domestic and foreign banks and found that foreign banks typically have stronger and less volatile lending growth than their domestic counterparts. They also found that diversity of ownership contributes to the greater credit stability in times of financial system turmoil and weakness. Weller (2000) showed that an increase in multinational banks' entry into Poland resulted in a lower credit supply by Polish national banks during the early transition phase. Comparisons of domestic-owned and foreign-owned banks' performance in the US market are reported by Chang *et al.* (1998) and Peek *et al.* (1999). Benefits of increased foreign participation in the banking sector are discussed by Martinez *et al.* (1999), Gruben *et al.* (1999), Buch (2000) and Lardy (2001). Demirgüç-Kunt and Detragiache (1998) noticed that, over the period 1988–1995, and for a large sample of countries, foreign banks' entry was generally associated with a lower incidence of local banking crises.

The question of whether foreign bank entry and foreign direct investment (FDI) in the financial sector of the host country promote efficiency growth is a complicated issue. Graham (2001) emphasized the question of what exactly is meant by 'efficiency' in the financial sector:

Does it mean, for example, that financial institutions themselves are efficient in the sense that, for any output, they minimise input of resources, i.e. that these institutions are cost-efficient? (This concept of efficiency is often termed 'x-efficiency'.) Or, alternatively, does it mean that, given the volume of national savings that an economy generates, these institutions intermediate these savings into the best possible end-uses, taking into account the risk characteristics of alternative end-use possibilities? The first concept is about efficiency of individual financial institutions, whereas the second is about efficiency of the entire financial system as it affects the performance of the economy. (Graham 2001: 8).

Unfortunately, these two concepts of efficiency do not coincide fully with each other.

Theoretical considerations suggest that foreign banks may be more *X*-efficient than domestic banks, but not necessarily so. Fortunately, a large number of empirical studies have shown that many banks, operating outside their own country, are typically more *X*-efficient than domestic locally-owned banks (see Berger *et al.* 2000 for a review of the recent relevant literature). Berger *et al.* (2000) studied the relative efficiencies of foreign versus domestically-owned banks in five developed industrial countries (the USA, the UK, France, Germany and Spain) and their main finding was that foreign-owned banks from particular countries of origin (especially the US banks) tended to be more efficient than either domestically-owned banks or foreign-owned banks from other countries (the authors called this phenomenon 'limited global advantage'). In developing countries, foreign-owned banks are generally more efficient than domestically-owned ones; that is, 'global advantages' dominate over 'home field advantages' (see Claessens *et al.* 2001).

An equally important issue for emerging market economies is whether foreign banks' entry will contribute to the banking system stability and be a stable source of credit, especially during periods of crisis. Mathieson and Roldos (2001) pointed out two related issues: whether the presence of foreign banks makes systemic banking crises more or less likely to occur, and whether there is a tendency for foreign banks to 'cut and run' during the crises periods (2001: 23). In general, it has been suggested that foreign banks can provide a more stable source of credit because branches and subsidiaries of large international banks can draw on their parent (which typically hold more diversified portfolios) for additional funding. Large international banks are likely to have better access to global financial markets and the entry of foreign banks can improve the overall stability of the host country's banking system (stronger prudential supervision; better disclosure, accounting and reporting practice and so on).

There are also some concerns that foreign banks' entry may worsen the stability of the banking system in the host country. For example, if domestic banks are relatively inefficient, they may respond to increased competition by undertaking higher-risk activities to earn returns, or they may be forced into bankruptcy. Foreign banks may tend to take over the most creditworthy domestic customers, leaving domestic banks to serve other, more risky customers and thereby worsen the profit, risks and capital position of domestic banks. There have also been concerns about the behaviour of foreign banks during the crisis periods, although recent empirical studies have shown that greater foreign bank participation was a stabilizing factor during the crises periods (see Demirgüç-Kunt and Detragiache 1998; Palmer 2000; Goldberg *et al.* 2000).

The main expected benefits and drawbacks from the entry of foreign banks are clearly defined by Bonin *et al.* (1998) (see also Dages *et al.* 2000; Murinde and Ryan 2000; Doukas *et al.* 1998). The main expected benefits include:

- the introduction of new banking technology and financial innovations (for foreign banks, it is relatively easy to introduce new products and services to the local market).
- possible economies of scale and scope (foreign banks can help to encourage the consolidation of the banking system; they have knowledge and experience of other financial activities such as insurance, brokerage and portfolio management services).
- an improvement of the competition environment (foreign banks represent potent competitors to local banks).
- the development of financial markets (foreign banks' entry may help deepen the inter-bank market and attract business from customers that would otherwise have gone to foreign banks in other countries).
- an improvement of the financial system infrastructure (transfer of good banking practice and know-how, accounting, transparency, financial regulation, supervision and supervisory skills).
- attracting foreign direct investments (foreign banks' presence may increase the amount of funding available to domestic projects by facilitating capital inflows, diversifying the capital and funding basis).

Pomerleano and Vojta identified some new factors which are stimulating participation of foreign banks in emerging-market banking systems and which derive from current trends in banking development (2001: 3–4).

- The banking sector is consolidating on a global basis and the global economy is increasingly interconnected in real and financial terms. A small number of very large global banking institutions are emerging and smaller domestic banks in emerging markets do not have the necessary resources and/or do not desire to build competitive global networks. Domestic banks have to create alliances with these global banks to provide global financial services to their customers.

- The development of local capital markets, often fuelled by pension reforms. Development of local capital markets requires the import of foreign expertise in the form of foreign branches, joint ventures and such.
- The global financial system is in the process of supporting a movement to achieve universal acceptance of global standards and best practices. Compliance with these standards requires linkages with foreign expertise by domestic banks.
- The increased foreign direct participation in domestic banks, which is related to privatization and the restructuring of the domestic banking system as a result of transition to a market economy in CEECs.

The main arguments against foreign banks' entry are (Anderson and Chantal 1998: 65):

- fear of foreign control (control over the allocation of credit implies substantial economic power in any economy);
- banking as an infant and special industry (this argument is a version of the general infant industry argument and banks are subject to various special protections due to their central role in the economy);
- foreign banks may have different objectives (foreign banks may be only interested in promoting exports from the home country, or in supporting projects undertaken by home-country firms);
- regulatory differences (supervisors of the host country lose regulatory control and, if the home country has weak bank supervision, this may lead to unsound banking in the host country).

Hellmann (1996) distinguishes between three internationalization strategies: 'customer-following' strategy, 'market-seeking' strategy and 'following-the-leader' strategy. All three features may contribute to internationalization at the same time. The question is which strategy is more important at the present time. None of the strategies alone is sufficient to guarantee profitable international operations. It has been observed that 'following-the-customer' may be a motive in the early stages of internationalization, but its importance may decrease over time (Li and Guisinger 1992).

Internationalization of banks in Estonia: empirical evidence

Expansion of Estonian banks to foreign markets

At the beginning of the 1990s, Estonia began to build up its market economy and also to integrate into the global economy. This forced Estonian banks to pass through, in a short period of time, the stages of internationalization that the banking institutions in developed countries had gone through in decades. The first steps of the Estonian commercial banks in the process of internationalization were most probably made in order to offer clients better transaction services. The very first step was the opening of correspondent accounts in foreign banks. In 1991, four banks among the 27 registered commercial banks had a foreign currency licence (Eesti Sotsiaalpank, Tartu Kommertspank, Eesti Tööstuse ja Ehituse Kommertspank ja Balti Ühispank). By the end of 1993 most of the banks had licences for foreign currency and correspondent accounts opened at least in the banks of the Nordic countries.

The Bank of Estonia was interested in issuing the licences because, according to the regulations effective in 1992–1994, a bank, before converting foreign cash into kroons, had to transfer the money to an account in a foreign bank. Only after that was it allowed to transfer the money to the correspondent Bank of Estonia account abroad. Table 12.1 shows that, by the end of 1993, Estonian banks had correspondent accounts in America, Asia and Australia, as well as those in Europe, and it was possible to make transfers in 17 different currencies.

Table 12.1 also clearly demonstrates the orientation towards Europe: 90 per cent of the correspondent accounts were located in Europe, and all 17 currencies were represented. Further, all Estonian banks had correspondent relations in Europe but only few of them had connections in other continents. Four banks (Hansapank, Põhja-Eesti Pank, Eesti Ühispank and Eesti Tööstuse ja Ehituse Kommertspank) had correspondent accounts abroad for all 17 currencies. The Estonian currency – the kroon – was fixed to the German Deutschmark (8:1). The Bank of Estonia also quoted 18 foreign currencies (17 currencies of the developed countries and the ECU). In addition to DEM and USD, correspondent relations were closest with Estonia's main trade partners – Finnish and Swedish currencies. Accounts were opened in USD and DEM and many other hard currencies in Finnish and Swedish banks.

The strategy of better payment service made the establishment of correspondent accounts in foreign banks quite burdensome for the commercial banks. For example, at the end of 1993 the liabilities of commercial

Table 12.1 The correspondent accounts of the Estonian commercial banks in foreign banks by the end of 1993

Continent	Number of banks owning correspondent accounts	Number of correspondent accounts	Number of different currencies used
Europe	18	246	17
America	12	24	2
Asia	4	6	2
Australia	2	2	1
Total	18	278	17

Source: Sõrg 2002.

banks to foreign banks were 1,151 million Estonian kroons, or 18.1 per cent of their total liabilities. By the end of 1994, the foreign currency resources in foreign banks had grown to 2,242 million kroons and already formed 21.8 per cent of the total liabilities. But this significantly lessened the possibilities of granting credits and complicated internal liquidity management.

Another motive of internationalization for Estonian banks was the possibility to invest their loan resources in foreign countries more favourably and with lower risk, or buy the resources for a cheaper price. The process was started by the Tartu Kommertspank, which granted credit outside Estonia under conditions of the former Soviet Union with higher interest rates than would have been possible in the domestic market. The notorious story of the ten million dollars of the Põhja-Eesti Pank lost in Switzerland also shows that deposits in foreign countries were offered high interests. At the end of 1994, the non-resident liabilities already formed 28.8 per cent and assets 8.4 per cent of the total assets of commercial banks.

Estonian commercial banks also had high ambitions in non-financial business outside Estonia. In such business deals, a bank preferred not to lend resources but did the business directly, trying to make use of the large disparities in prices in transition countries. Thus the main reasons for liquidity difficulties, and later crashes, of Otepää Ühispank and Revalia Pank were unsuccessful international commercial deals (respectively, the trade of MAZ trucks and the purchase of large quantities of low-quality nickel). Estonian newspapers have written about other similar cases of fraud by Estonian banks.

After the first banking crises, the remaining banks recovered and learned a lot. Foreign banks trusted them once more, granting them credit. In the middle of 1997, the commercial banks could proudly announce that the four major banks had gained subordinated loans of 2.4 billion kroons from foreign markets for re-lending. Mr Aare Järvan, the head of the central bank policy department of the Bank of Estonia, expressed the opinion that banks had become too careless again and a tiny crisis would suit them well (Ideon 1997). This carelessness began to cause headaches when the stock market crashed in October 1997 and became a serious problem for Estonian commercial banks after the Russian financial crisis in autumn 1998. Table 12.2 shows that, until 1997, the assets and profits of the banks had increased rapidly but then this expansive growth, which was achieved mostly by entering foreign markets, began to generate losses in similar amounts.

In general the internationalization of the Estonian banking sector could be divided into two stages. The first period started at the beginning of the 1990s and concluded by the end of 1998, when a majority of shares of the leading Estonian banks were bought by foreign banks. The first stage of internationalization therefore mainly represents the strategic

Table 12.2 Profitability indicators of Estonian commercial banks

	1994	1995	1996	1997	1998	1999	2000	2001
Total assets at the end of a year (billion EEK)	10.1	14.9	21.9	38.8	41.0	47.1	57.8	68.4
Annual profit (million EEK)	68.7	288.5	517.4	963.1	498.5	637.0	625.1	1,685.4
Equity multiplier (%)	11.7	12.6	10.4	10.7	8.4	6.3	7.1	7.8
Return on equity, (ROE)(%)	5.7	30.5	30.6	34.9	−10.1	9.2	8.4	20.9
Return on assets (ROA) (%)	0.5	2.4	2.9	3.3	−1.2	1.5	1.2	2.7
Profit margin (%)	0.0	0.2	0.2	0.2	−0.1	0.1	0.1	0.2
Assets utilization (%)	15.9	15.6	18.2	20.1	11.5	12.0	11.1	11.4
Earnings per share (%)	8.6	40.4	47.9	74.3	−29.8	31.6	29.5	n.a.

Source: Bank of Estonia 2003.

plans of Estonian banks to go abroad. It resulted in a significant outflow of investments into Latvia and Lithuania and peaked in 1999 (see Figure 12.1). The second stage started in 1999 and continues up to the present. It reflects the strategic interests of not only Estonian managers, but also foreign banks. Therefore it could not be analysed in isolation of the strategic goals of foreign investors. This stage has produced an initial decline

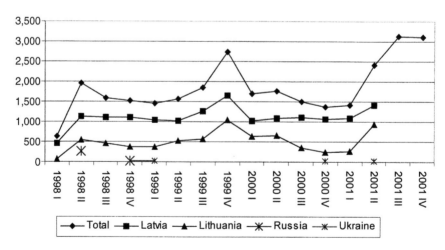

Figure 12.1 The distribution of the stock of Estonian outward investments of banking sector by target countries 1998–2001 (in millions of EEK). (Source: Sõrg and Varblane 2002.)

in the stock of outward investments but, starting from the beginning of 2001, new and rapid growth began.

There are several reasons why Estonian banks started to move into neighbouring countries (see Table 12.3). From the list of different theories explaining foreign market entry processes (see pages 251–255), the most relevant to the Estonian banking sector are the eclectic model, network theory and the management-oriented model. The classical Scandinavian-stage model of entering foreign markets holds only partly with regard to the internationalization of the Estonian banking sector. It is suitable to explain the selection of foreign markets, but does not hold with respect to movements from simple to more complicated methods of market entry.

As a list of motives of internationalization, Table 12.3 includes both proactive and reactive factors. It seems that proactive motives were still dominating in decision-making about Estonian banks going abroad. The Estonian banking crisis in 1992 resulted in a strong consolidation of the banking sector. In the process of consolidation a complete restructuring of banks also occurred. It covered all aspects of the banking industry starting with improvements in the quality of loan portfolios and ending with boosted innovation. This increased competitiveness of Estonian banks when compared with neighbouring Baltic countries, Russia and the Ukraine.

The main reason for the internationalization of Estonian banks was explained with the 'market-seeking' argument – the domestic market was very limited in size and competition was intensive. Therefore, Estonian banks started to use their created strategic assets in entering Latvian and

Table 12.3 Motives of internationalization in the Estonian banking sector

	Internal triggers	*External triggers*
Proactive	Search for market power, increase market share	Strategic presence vis-à-vis competitors
	Distinctive service and brand. Increase brand identity	Increasing concentration (through acquisitions and mergers)
	Extend product range and life cycle	Improvements in information technology
	Visionary leadership	Improvements in physical infrastructure (communication networks)
	Diversification	
Reactive	Improve levels of business performance	Decline, saturation of local/national market
	Have excess capacity (human capital, technology)	Intensity of competition
	Suitable situation to obtain foreign bank (default)	Avoid entry by cross-border rivals
		Service existing customers who have 'gone international'

Source: compiled by authors based on results of the survey among Estonian outward investors (Sõrg and Varblane 2002).

Lithuanian markets. This process also included a strong element of competition between Estonian banks themselves in order to obtain the strategic advantage of first entry. Foreign banks were still not interested in entering Latvian and Lithuanian markets, Estonian banks were therefore able to take advantage of the situation. An important additional aspect in entering Latvian and Lithuanian markets was the need to serve domestic firms, which moved into these markets intensively after early 1995. Latvia and Lithuania together by that time formed around 15 per cent of Estonian total exports. This is a traditional reason of the internationalization in services, mentioned earlier in literature (Terpstra and Yu 1988). As the stability of the local banking sector in Latvia and Lithuania was very weak, Estonian firms were looked to for stable financial services, and it was provided by subsidiaries of Estonian banks there.

The Estonian banks have used three strategies in their internationalization:

1   setting up subsidiaries and branches (green-field);
2   buying up local banks (complete take-over);
3   acquiring a significant stake in a local bank.

The first bank to succeed was Hansapank who, in 1996, used suitable opportunity to acquire a Latvian bank (Deutsche Lettische Bank), which had defaulted. The former name of the bank was changed into Hansapank-Latvija, the shares of the former shareholders were exchanged for the shares of Hansapank, and the management of the subsidiary was changed. Because the credibility of Latvian banks had weakened, Hansapank, with its reputation insured, ensured that, by the second half-year of 1997, Hansapank-Latvija was already earning profit. Later the name was changed to Hansapanka and the bank has grown rapidly.

After the success of Hansapank became known, the other competing Estonian commercial banks began to make plans for buying up banks in the Latvian, Lithuanian, Russian and Ukrainian markets. Eesti Hoiupank acquired FABA bank in Moscow for 7.2 million kroons in September 1997. As, in the course of the take-over, it became evident that the assets of the bank were weaker than expected, Eesti Hoiupank abandoned the Russian bank, because holding the bank did not conform to the bank's Russian strategy. In 1998, they bought 72.4 per cent of Zemes Banka in Latvia and, later, Hansapank obtained this share due to a merger with the Estonian Savings Bank. The activity of the Tallinn Bank in acquiring Saules Bankas in Lithuania was successful, too. In 1996 the bank started with the share of 20 per cent and, in March 1998, just before Tallinna Pank joined Eesti Ühispank, it already held a controlling block of 79.5 per cent of the shares. But the activities of Forekspank in Pioneer Bank in Moscow lasted only two months. The possible share of 51 per cent was abandoned in June 1998 because the bank was declared to be without prospects.

As acquisition usually means taking over a poorly-functioning bank, which needs restructuring or re-capitalization; obtaining a strategic share can create reluctance from other banks and the central bank. Thus, the tactic of starting from scratch is often chosen. Hansapank has reiterated its intentions to establish a subsidiary in Lithuania, although the first two attempts failed. On 7 July 1999, Hansabankas Lithuania opened its doors to clients in Vilnius as a typical green-field investment. It only had 200 clients, but the subsidiary expected to seize 5 per cent of the Lithuanian banking sector in the following three years. In reality, much more rapid expansion in the Lithuanian market occurred. In addition to strong organic growth, the Hansabank Group also completed the acquisition of the largest retail bank in Lithuania, Lietuvos Taupomasis Bankas (LTB) after a long privatization process. In April 2001, Hansabank paid €43 million for its holding of 99.3 per cent of the share capital of LTB. This acquisition significantly strengthened Hansabank's position in Lithuania, as well as in the whole Baltic market. In Lithuania, the market share rose to 30 per cent and the Hansabank controls over one-third of the banking market in the Baltics. With this transaction, Hansabank doubled its customer base and workforce – at the end of June, the group had over 2.7 million customers.

Eesti Ühispank (Union Bank of Estonia) had especially high-flying plans. In autumn 1997, the bank announced its plans to establish a subsidiary bank with total assets of 1.5 billion Estonian kroons (EEK) in St Petersburg (the total assets of Eesti Ühispank this time were c.9.5 billion EEK). Even at the beginning of 1998 the value of Eesti Ühispank had not changed essentially as the bank was planning to spend a billion kroons on opening a branch in Helsinki and a bank office in Stockholm. Tallinna Pank had even more ambitious plans. In January 1998 the Chairman of the Board announced the bank's goal of gaining a market share of 35 per cent in the Baltic market. The future internationalization of Ühispank was cancelled in 1999, after Swedish SEB took over a majority of shares. Since 1999 up to 2002, the SEB started to create a Baltic network of SEB subsidiaries and Ühispank lost its subsidiaries in Latvia and Lithuania.

The first stage in the internationalization of Estonian banks has provided both positive and negative experiences. We can reach general conclusions that the internationalization was directed towards the East, where Estonian banks had created a specific advantage (knowledge, technology, organizational culture, and so on). But a move in that direction raised the risk level for Estonian domestic banking and its sensitivity to crises, due to the higher risks and unbalanced character of internationalization. The second conclusion is that the realization of internationalization plans is being dragged out, thus it will not be as successful as expected. It indicates that either the banks were not able to foresee the risks of

internationalization or they used the announcement of their internationalization plans to the public at this stage as a means of advertising
and improving their image.

The researchers of bank globalization have concluded that excessive
eagerness in entering foreign markets without sufficient preliminary
knowledge about local economic conditions may increase the vulnerability
of such banks (Balino and Ubide 2000). The Estonian banks' experiences
of the East expansion have proved this conclusion once more.

Foreign banks' entry into Estonia: motives and impact

The opposite process – the entry of foreign banks into Estonia – has
accompanied the internationalization of Estonian banks who had been
entering into neighbouring countries since the mid-1990s. Foreign banks
just waited for a suitable moment to 'run to help' the local banks who
have been too reckless in their business.

The Bank of Estonia did not allow any foreign share in Estonian commercial banks before the currency reform in 1992. Therefore Balti Ühispank had to except their Latvian shareholders from the register in 1991
before it got a licence. But the new regulations for the issuance of banking
licences after currency reform did not impose such restrictions. Therefore, on 26 August 1992, Ameerika-Balti Ühispank (Baltic American
Union Bank), whose sole proprietor was a US businessman, received a
licence. The INKO Balti Pank (INKO Baltic Bank), the subsidiary bank of
the Ukrainian INKO Bank, received its licence on 29 September 1994. But
the Board of the Bank of Estonia did not approve all applications. For
example, the representatives of the Austrian Doonau Bank had to return
empty-handed. In September 1994, Merita Bank established a branch in
Tallinn. The first two banks, created on the basis of foreign capital, did
not find their place in Estonia and had lost their licences. Merita-Nord-
banken (now Nordea), after a long period of quiet growth, has begun to
apply an expansion strategy and wishes to increase its market share in
Estonia significantly.

The major foreign banks have always been waiting for a suitable
moment to come to Estonia. Schleswig-Holstein Landesbank, based in the
German capital, started a bit too early and, in autumn 1997, met the resistance from the management of Eesti Investeerimispank (Estonian Investment Bank) when it expressed an interest in acquiring 60 per cent of the
shares of the Estonian bank. The resistance was justified because of a
desire to continue its activities as an investment bank and not to turn to a
retail bank. However, this did not occur.

Foreign banks got the opportunity to acquire shares in Estonian banks
because the local banks turned to quote companies. Hansapank was the
first to reach the foreign stock exchanges in 1994. The banks also faced a
need to raise foreign capital in connection with the schedule of the

growth of share capital and equity capital prescribed by the central bank. By the end of 1995, foreigners held 35 per cent of the share capital of Estonian banks (foreign banks' ownership formed 29.2 per cent while 5.7 per cent were clients of foreign banks).

The major Swedish banks (Swedbank and SEB) managed to bide their time. They bought the cheapened shares of the Estonian major banks from the stock exchange. Then, in 1998, they were able to acquire, without resistance, an essential portion of the share capital of Hansapank and Eesti Ühispank, when both were facing financial difficulties. The question of why the Scandinavian banks were and still are active in the Baltics has its own logic. The Baltic region is geographically ideal for Scandinavian banks in their expansion spree. Decisive action can be observed in Estonia, which is the most advanced Baltic State as far as the banking sector is concerned (Tiusanen and Jumpponen 2000: 53).

By the end of 1998, the share capital of Eesti Ühispank and Hansapank were mainly in the hands of Swedish credit institutions (68.4 per cent and 64.9 per cent respectively) and the foreign portion in the share capital of Estonian banks had increased to 57.8 per cent. By the end of 2002, 86.6 per cent of the shares of Estonian commercial banks were in the ownership of non-residents (see Figure 12.2).

In June 2000, Optiva Pank, established by the merger of Eesti Investeerimispank and Sampo Finance Ltd, acquired Forekspank in favourable conditions. This is a joint company owned by the Finnish banking and insurance company Sampo-Leonia and the Estonian Kaleva Mutual Insurance Company. The new owners turned Optiva Pank into Sampo Pank, offering both insurance and banking services.

Vice-Governor of the Bank of Estonia, Mrs Helo Meigas, concluded that, with the entry of Swedish banks, the maturity structure in Estonian banking improved, creating sufficient buffers. The share capital of Estonian commercial banks increased and the capital adequacy of banks improved from 12.4 per cent to 17 per cent (Meigas 1999).

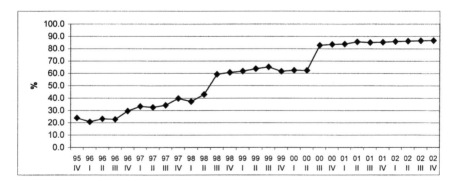

Figure 12.2 Share capital owned by foreign residents in Estonian banks 1995–2002. (Source: Bank of Estonia 2003, authors' calculations.)

But the penetration of foreign banks into Estonia is still continuing. In Tallinn, German Landesbank Schleswig-Holstein Girozentrale, Swedish Svenska Handelsbanken and Osuuspankkien Keskuspankki OY (OKOBANK) have opened representative offices. Of course, the EBRD has shares in Estonian banks and other financial institutions, and several other banks have also been interested in the Estonian banking market.

Foreign banks have their own objectives in coming to Estonia. This is the special problem in dealing with OFDI in Estonia and other transition countries – the link between inward and outward FDI. There is no single theory on foreign direct investment that would evaluate its inward and outward dimensions. The role of foreign investors in designing the internationalization strategy of the Estonian banking sector has significantly increased during the last two-to-three years. We could distinguish two different types of approaches. First is the approach followed by Swedfund, the majority owner of Hansabank Group. They have basically used a very decentralized approach, by which managers in Estonia are still developing and executing their plans for foreign market expansion. An opposite approach is presented by the case of Skandinaviska Enskilda Banken (SEB), the majority owner of Ühispank. They took over the role of strategic expansion planner and are working hard in creating a Baltic banking net, which will include the banks in all the three Baltic States, controlled by SE Banken. Vast differences exist, of course. While it is true for Hungary and less for the Czech Republic and Estonia, it is not for Slovenia where domestic companies are major investors abroad. The issue here is whether foreign firms, which could be called indirect investors, have a better competitive position as compared to local Estonian firms. Do they have a more global perspective? Do they have more experienced management structures? Do they have more flexibility in using and reallocating funds? If the answer is positive, the inward flow of foreign investments improves the competitiveness of the Estonian banking sector in other markets and also gives positive feedback to the home-country banks.

It is interesting to study what characterizes foreign banks in CEE markets; are foreign banks somehow different from domestic banks in transition countries? To test this, we used binomial logit estimation, and regression results are shown in Table 12.4. Notations of variables are given in Appendix 12.1.

We used time–series from 1992–2001, from 11 CEE countries, mostly from EU accession countries: Estonia, Latvia, Lithuania, Poland, the Czech Republic, Hungary, Romania, Bulgaria, Slovenia, Slovakia and Croatia. Balance-sheet data and income-statement data from the BankScope database, provided by the Bank of Estonia, was used. EVIEWS 4 was used to calculate regression coefficients.

The results indicate that foreign banks' assets tend to be more profitable, but foreign banks also have higher costs with respect to total assets. Foreign banks pay comparatively less tax, but this coefficient is not statisti-

Table 12.4 Regression output for logit estimation

Dependent variable: FD variable	Coefficient	Std. error	z-Statistic	Prob.
C	0.699753	0.121450	5.761643	0.0000
PNI/TA	0.010327	0.004511	2.289442	0.0221
TOE/TA	0.014108	0.003298	4.278356	0.0000
TAX/TA	−0.024341	0.013005	−1.871603	0.0613
LLR/GL	−0.020303	0.006147	−3.302723	0.0010
NIM	−0.022678	0.012728	−1.781812	0.0748
Mean dep. var.	0.632584	S.D. dep. var.		0.482372
Obs. with Dep. = 0	327	Total obs.		890
Obs. with Dep. = 1	563			

Sources: authors' calculations.

cally very significant. The same holds for the net interest margin of foreign banks. It can be concluded that foreign banks have better risk-management techniques. The regression shows that foreign banks have smaller loan loss reserves; this indicates lower credit risk. We haven't included macroeconomic variables into this equation, but in further research we plan to analyse the effect of foreign banks on domestic markets in CEE countries.

In Table 12.5 we report the result of pooled regression, where the dependent variable was total operating expense over total assets. Regression results indicate that TOE/TA and FD are positively correlated. But

Table 12.5 Regression results of operating costs

Variable	Coefficient	Std. error	t-statistic	Prob.
C	3.132711	1.391216	2.251779	0.0245
FD	2.727790	1.796013	1.518803	0.1291
TNA/TA	0.228693	0.019719	11.59761	0.0000
TLN/TA	0.040295	0.004550	8.856620	0.0000
AR(1)	0.384967	0.019216	20.03375	0.0000
R-squared	0.602206	Mean dep. var.		11.23244
Adjusted R-squared	0.600730	S.D. dep. var.		28.28416
S.E. of regression	17.87215	Sum squared resid.		344328.0
F-statistic	407.9861	Durbin-Watson stat.		1.838329
Prob (F-statistic)	0.000000			

Sources: authors' calculations.

Notes
Dependent variable: TOE/TA
Method: Pooled Least Squares
Sample (adjusted): 1993–2000
Total panel (unbalanced) observations: 1,083

the regression coefficient for FD is not statistically very significant, $p = 0.12$. At the same time, logit estimation results in Table 12.4 indicate that foreign banks tend to have higher operating costs. Therefore we can conclude that there is some evidence that foreign banks tend to have higher operating costs, but further testing is needed.

All arguments for and against internationalization and foreign-bank entry need additional empirical testing. An interview study questionnaire was elaborated with this aim in mind, using the experience and lessons of other analogous studies (see Konopielko 1999; Kraft and Galac 2000; Pomerleano and Vojta 2001). The survey of foreign and domestic banks, using this questionnaire, was carried out during 2001–2002 in Estonia, Lithuania, Poland and Romania, some comparative data were also available from the Croatian (CR) analogous study (Kraft and Galac 2000).

All four foreign banks, six representative offices of foreign banks and three domestically-owned banks in Estonia were questioned about the motives for foreign banks' entry and the preliminary effects of it. The response rate of domestic banks was 100 per cent, response rates of foreign banks and representative offices were 50 per cent and 67 per cent respectively. In Poland, 40 banks (out of over 60 banks) were asked to answer the questionnaires. The response rate of domestically-controlled banks was higher than that of foreign-controlled ones. Altogether, a general response rate reached the level of 65 per cent.

All foreign and domestic banks in the Romanian banking system were asked about the effects of foreign-bank entry. The proposed questionnaire was similar to those for foreign and domestic banks with some obvious differences. The response rate was 60 per cent for domestic banks and 50 per cent for foreign banks. This rate proves the lack of time and availability of officials of these banks, as well as their privacy policy in evaluating the competitors within the market. A survey on the role of foreign banks was conducted in Lithuania between June–December 2001. All foreign and domestically-owned banks were asked about motivations and preliminary effects of foreign banks' entry. The response rate for domestic banks was around 80 per cent; the response rate for foreign banks and representative offices was about 70 per cent. Banks in all countries were asked to evaluate different questions on a five-point scale.

The main reasons for entry to the host countries markets are presented in Table 12.6. The same questions regarding motives were put to both domestically- and foreign-controlled banks. In the case of the first group, we intended to get information on the domestic banks' perception of the foreign-controlled banks' motives and strategies. It appears that the most important motive for foreign banks' entry is new business opportunities in all observed countries (the average grades given by domestic banks and foreign banks respectively were 4.68 and 4.58). The expansion strategies of foreign banks were evaluated as the second most important reason for entry to the host-country market. Following existing clients was a very

Table 12.6 Main reasons for entry to the host-country market

Reason	Domestic banks					Foreign banks				
	ES	LI	PO	RO	Mean	ES	LI	PO	RO	Mean
Following the existing clients	4.0	3.8	3.0	3.9	3.68	4.0	3.2	3.0	3.1	3.33
Looking for new business opportunities	4.7	4.8	4.5	4.7	4.68	4.4	4.8	4.2	4.9	4.58
International trade financing	3.7	3.0	2.6	3.0	3.08	3.6	3.5	2.7	3.4	3.30
Meeting competition of other banks	3.7	2.3	3.3	2.0	2.83	2.8	3.3	3.4	3.2	3.18
Following expansion strategy	4.3	4.5	2.9	4.5	4.05	2.8	4.3	4.2	4.2	3.88
Supporting the local client base	2.7	3.5	3.6	3.2	3.25	4.0	3.7	3.4	3.6	3.68
Foreign exchange trading	1.0	2.0	2.3	2.0	1.83	2.2	2.5	2.4	2.0	2.28
Portfolio management	2.3	3.5	2.3	3.2	2.83	2.4	2.5	2.2	2.0	2.28

Sources: Dubauskas (2002); Florescu (2002); Kowalski *et al.* (2002).

Note
ES, Estonia; LI, Lithuania; PO, Poland; RO, Romania.

important reason for foreign banks' entry into Estonia, but not in other countries. Supporting and developing the local client base was also mentioned by respondents as a quite important motive (average grade 3.25 and 3.68). Hellmann (1996) has pointed out three potential internationalization strategies of banks: 'customer-following' strategy, 'follow-the-leader' strategy and 'market-seeking' strategy. Our results suggest that banks have probably followed all three strategies. Foreign exchange trading, portfolio management and/or meeting competition of other banks were not highly evaluated in all observed countries.

It can be said that the classical important host country determinants of FDI are also important in the banking sector. Again, it is not possible to distinguish the most important factor underlying the foreign-entry decision, because they are equally important and are quite different in different countries, (see Table 12.7). Nevertheless, respondents (both domestic and foreign banks) in all countries evaluated macroeconomic and political stability in the country highly, as well as liberal economic policy, a good potential for future EU membership, and existing clients and potential new client base (average grades given by domestic banks, respectively, 4.28, 3.63, 4.08 and 3.90 points; grades given by foreign banks, 4.10, 3.43, 3.73 and 3.80 points). Surprisingly, good tourism and/or industry development opportunities were evaluated in all countries as not as important as the host-country's market specifics. We can say that, in transition countries, both see the 'customer-following' strategy and 'market-seeking' strategy as important. Our results are similar to Aliber (1984), Li and Guisinger (1992), Hellmann (1996) and many others.

Table 12.7 Importance of different host-country market specifics

Specific feature	Domestic banks					Foreign banks				
	ES	LI	PO	RO	Mean	ES	LI	PO	RO	Mean
Macroeconomic and political stability	4.0	4.5	3.8	4.8	4.28	4.6	3.8	4.0	4.0	4.10
Liberal economic environment	4.7	3.3	3.3	3.2	3.63	3.8	3.2	3.6	3.1	3.43
Potential for future EU membership	4.3	3.8	4.5	3.7	4.08	4.0	3.3	4.4	3.2	3.73
Relatively high interest spreads	4.0	3.5	3.3	3.4	3.55	3.0	2.5	3.5	2.3	2.83
Good expansion opportunities	3.7	4.0	3.8	3.8	3.83	3.8	3.7	4.0	3.5	3.75
Geographical, cultural, proximity	4.3	2.3	2.0	3.0	2.90	3.4	3.0	1.6	3.0	2.75
Existing clients and potential new clients	3.7	4.3	3.6	4.0	3.90	3.8	3.8	3.6	4.0	3.80
Presence of competitor banks	2.7	3.0	3.3	2.5	2.88	2.8	2.3	3.3	2.0	2.60
Tourism development opportunities	3.0	1.5	1.8	1.0	1.83	2.0	1.7	1.5	2.0	1.55
Industry development opportunities	3.0	3.3	2.2	3.2	2.93	2.0	2.5	2.3	2.3	2.28

Sources: Dubauskas (2002); Florescu (2002); Kowalski *et al.* (2002).

Note
ES, Estonia; LI, Lithuania; PO, Poland; RO, Romania.

It is commonly agreed that foreign banks have several advantages over domestic banks in transition economies (see Bonin *et al.* 1998; Kraft and Galac 2000; Konopielko 1999). The respondents' evaluations of the advantages and disadvantages of foreign banks in Estonian, Lithuanian, Polish and Romanian banking markets are presented in Table 12.8. The results of our comparative study suggest that foreign banks have quite different advantages over domestic banks in different countries. For example, Estonian foreign banks have significant advantages over Estonian domestic banks in terms of: (1) less expensive in funding sources; (2) better loan interest rates; and (3) competition threat to domestic banks (see Table 12.8). Lithuanian, Polish and Romanian respondents evaluated the following foreign banks' advantages more highly: (1) reputation of foreign banks; (2) better range and quality of banking innovations; (3) better risk management. In general, the reputation of foreign banks was evaluated as their most important advantage, followed by the range and quality of banking innovations (Estonia is an exception). The main advantage of domestic banks is a better knowledge of customers and closer bank–customer relations.

Table 12.8 Advantages and disadvantages of foreign banks

Advantage/disadvantage	Domestic banks					Foreign banks				
	ES	LI	PO	RO	Mean	ES	LI	PO	RO	Mean
Expensiveness of funding sources	3.3	3.8	3.3	4.0	3.60	4.2	3.5	2.7	3.5	3.48
Loan interest rates	4.3	3.8	3.3	4.0	3.85	3.8	3.5	3.5	3.5	3.58
Employee quality and competence	4.0	2.8	3.7	3.0	3.38	3.0	3.3	3.9	3.5	3.43
Range and quality of banking innovations	3.0	2.8	4.3	3.0	3.28	2.4	3.8	4.4	4.0	3.90
Knowledge of the local client	2.3	2.5	1.6	2.0	2.10	2.4	3.0	2.0	3.0	2.60
More diversified portfolio	3.3	2.3	3.5	2.0	2.78	3.0	2.7	2.9	3.0	2.90
Superior mix of financial services	3.3	2.8	3.8	3.0	3.23	3.0	3.5	4.1	3.0	3.40
Better risk management	4.0	2.5	4.2	2.5	3.30	3.2	3.5	4.1	3.0	3.45
Reputation of foreign banks	4.0	3.5	–	3.7	3.73	3.4	4.2	4.5	4.0	4.03
Success of advertizing campaigns	2.3	3.0	4.1	3.0	3.10	2.6	3.0	3.0	3.0	2.90
Legal impediments	3.0	3.0	2.5	1.0	2.38	2.4	2.3	2.7	2.0	2.35
Internal communication	3.0	2.8	3.0	1.0	2.45	3.0	2.5	2.5	2.0	2.50
Competition threat to domestic banks	3.3	2.5	3.6	2.0	2.90	3.8	3.2	3.8	3.5	3.58

Sources: Dubauskas (2002); Florescu (2002); Kowalski *et al.* (2002).

Note
ES, Estonia; LI, Lithuania; PO, Poland; RO, Romania.

Our results also indicate that foreign and domestic banks in different countries have somewhat different target customer groups (see Table 12.9). The most important client groups for domestic banks in Estonia are small and medium-sized domestic companies (SMEs) and high-income individuals (the average grade for both client groups, 4.3 points). The main target client groups for foreign-owned banks are as follows: large domestic companies (average 4.0 points), home-country companies (3.8 points) and large exporters (also 3.8 points). This result indicates that foreign banks have followed their home-country customers into the Estonian market.

The main target groups of domestic and foreign banks in Poland and Romania are different from in Estonia. Among the most important target groups of Polish domestic banks were households and high-income individuals (both 4.0 points) and sole proprietors (3.9 points). Foreign banks' main target groups in the Polish market are domestic SMEs and high-income individuals (average grade 4.5 points) followed by large domestic

Table 12.9 Main target groups of foreign and domestic banks

Target clients group	Domestic banks				Foreign banks				
	ES	*PO*	*RO*	*Mean*	*ES*	*CR*	*PO*	*RO*	*Mean*
Large domestic companies	2.0	–	4.0	3.00	4.0	3.4	4.1	4.0	3.88
Small and medium-size domestic companies	4.3	–	4.5	4.40	2.8	4.4	4.5	3.8	3.88
Home-country companies	2.7	–	4.0	3.35	3.8	3.2	3.3	4.5	3.70
International corporations	1.7	1.3	3.5	2.17	3.4	3.0	3.4	4.5	3.83
Foreigners and foreign investors	3.7	1.9	3.5	3.03	3.4	2.7	3.3	4.0	3.35
Large exporters	2.0	2.6	4.5	3.03	3.8	4.0	3.4	4.5	3.93
Households	3.7	4.0	4.0	3.90	3.0	4.5	3.8	2.0	3.33
High-income individuals	4.3	4.0	4.0	4.10	3.6	4.8	4.5	3.0	3.98
Sole proprietors	2.3	3.9	3.0	3.07	2.8	4.1	3.8	3.0	3.43

Sources: Kraft and Galac (2000); Florescu (2002); Kowalski *et al.* (2002).

Note
ES, Estonia; PO, Poland, RO, Romania; CR, Czech Republic.

companies (4.1 points). This phenomenon is quite understandable if we remember the different size and structure of Estonian and other observed countries' economies. The most important target groups of Romanian domestic banks are large exporters and domestic SMEs (average grades, 4.5 points); for foreign banks, home-country companies, international corporations and large exporters (average grade also 4.5 points). High-income individuals, households and domestic EMEs are the main target groups for Croatian foreign banks; that is, these are surprisingly more oriented to retail banking activities in the host country's banking market

Our study results indicate that there are no very significant differences between foreign and domestic banks in the main fields of activities. Differences are higher in different countries' markets and banking activities depend more on country-specific factors. The specific banking activities are not very essential in Estonia because all active banks there are universal banks (see Table 12.10). However, corporate financing is the most important field of activity for both domestic and foreign banks (the average grade, 4.3). Foreign-exchange trading, cash and assets management and capital market transactions were mentioned by Estonian domestic banks as being among the more important other fields of activities.

Corporate financing and, differing from the Estonian case, retail banking activities were evaluated by Polish and Romanian domestic and foreign banks more highly (average grade, 4.0 points). Project financing was also evaluated highly by both domestic and foreign Romanian banks. It is quite interesting to mention that non-financial activities are quite highly evaluated by both Estonian domestic and foreign banks (grade, 3.0

Table 12.10 Main fields of activity of foreign and domestic banks in Estonia

	Domestic banks				Foreign banks				
	ES	PO	RO	Mean	ES	CR	PO	RO	Mean
Corporate financing	4.3	3.7	4.5	4.17	4.2	4.6	4.2	4.0	4.25
Foreign exchange trading	4.0	2.3	4.0	3.42	2.4	3.5	3.4	3.8	3.28
International trade financing	2.3	1.9	3.5	2.57	3.0	4.5	3.3	3.5	3.58
Project financing	2.7	2.5	4.0	3.07	3.4	–	3.0	4.0	3.47
Dealing in securities market	3.0	2.5	3.0	2.83	2.6	3.2	3.3	2.0	2.78
Retail banking activities	3.3	3.9	4.0	3.73	3.2	4.8	4.0	4.0	4.00
Leasing	3.0	2.1	4.0	3.03	3.6	3.2	3.2	2.0	3.00
Cash and assets management	4.0	3.2	3.0	3.40	3.6	1.6	2.6	3.5	2.83
Capital market	4.0	2.3	3.0	3.07	3.2	2.4	2.6	2.0	2.55
Insurance activities	2.3	1.9	2.0	2.07	2.5	3.1	2.5	2.0	2.53
Non-financial activities	3.0	1.8	2.0	2.26	3.3	–	1.0	2.0	2.10

Sources: Kraft and Galac (2000); Florescu (2002); Kowalski *et al.* (2002).

Note
ES, Estonia; PO, Poland; RO, Romania; CR, Czech Republic.

and 3.3 points), but not by Polish and Romanian domestic and/or foreign banks.

It seems that Estonian banks are more universal in their activities – they are also more active in participating in leasing, capital market and insurance activities in comparison with Polish and Romanian domestic and foreign banks. Retail banking activities, corporate financing and international trade financing were evaluated by Croatian respondents as the main fields of foreign banks in Croatia.

Respondents reported the following entry modes and year of entry into the Estonian banking market:

1   take-over of existing Estonian domestic bank (in 1998);
2   setting up a representative office (in 1992), and setting up a branch (in 1994);
3   setting up a representative office (in 1994);
4   setting up a representative office (in 1995).

All respondent foreign banks' strategies foresee long-term stays in the Estonian and Romanian banking markets (see Table 12.11). Among the most important motives for staying (both in Estonian and Romanian markets) included good future prospects for the development of the local client base (average grade, 4.00 points), as well as good future prospects for doing business with home-country clients (3.85 points).

Table 12.11 Foreign banks' motives for long-term stay in Estonian and Romanian markets

Reason	ES	RO	Mean
Good future prospects of doing business with home-country clients	3.6	4.1	3.85
Good future prospects of development for the local client base	4.0	4.0	4.00
Prospects for financing international trade	3.6	3.0	3.30
Regional expansion strategy of the bank for entry to other regional markets	3.2	3.5	3.35
Potential for development of capital markets	2.6	3.0	2.80
Continued pressure of competitor banks	3.0	1.0	2.00
Good future prospects for foreign-exchange trading	1.6	3.0	2.00
Inter-bank money market participation opportunities	1.8	3.0	2.40

Sources: Florescu (2002); Uiboupin and Vensel (2002).

Note
ES, Estonia; Ro, Romania

We received quite limited information from respondents about the general sectoral structure of both domestic and foreign banks' direct investments and participation on the boards of targeted firms. For example, only a limited number of Estonian respondents mentioned investments into leasing and insurance (financial sector); one respondent mentioned investment into manufacturing industries; trade and other services (non-financial sector). Some banks also mentioned that they have representatives in both financial- and non-financial-sector firms' boards. Only one domestic bank reported that they have 100 per cent control over the targeted leasing firm. The average proportion of foreign clients' deposits in total deposits was reported to be about 20 per cent, and the average share of foreign clients' credits in total credits was reported to be about 5 per cent.

All banks in Estonia and Romania use a German-type, two-tier board model for bank governance. The total number of the Managing Board members vary in foreign-owned banks from three to ten, in domestic banks from three to five. The Managing Boards consist mainly of executive directors; one domestic bank reported also having private shareholders and a non-executive director in their Managing Board. The total number of Supervisory Board members in Estonia varies in foreign banks from six to ten; in domestic banks, the average is five-to-six members. One majority foreign-owned Estonian bank reported the exact structure of the Supervisory Board: five institutional shareholders, four consumer representatives and one private shareholder (total number of the Board members, ten). There are mostly institutional and private shareholders sitting on the Supervisory Boards of domestic banks.

Table 12.12 The main decision-makers in foreign banks (% of respondents)

The main decision-maker	General strategic policies		Capital policy		Dividend policy	
	ES	RO	ES	RO	ES	RO
The 'mother' bank	37	60	50	40	75	80
Shareholders' assembly	9	–	–	–	–	–
Supervisory board (SB)	9	–	10	30	–	20
Managing board (MB)	18	20	20	15	25	–
SB and MB	9	20	10	–	–	–
MB and 'mother's' MB	18	–	10	15	–	–

Sources: Florescu (2002); Uiboupin and Vensel (2002).

Note
ES, Estonia; RO, Romania.

Some Estonian and Romanian foreign-owned banks (or representative offices of foreign banks) and domestic banks reported who are making key strategic decisions in the bank (see Tables 12.12 and 12.13). In general, the mother bank is the main strategic decision-maker. Additionally the Managing Board of the foreign-owned bank, either alone or with the Managing Board of the mother bank, make some important strategic decisions (especially in working out general strategic policies and/or capital policy). The shareholders' assembly and the Managing Board play key roles in strategic decision-making in domestic banks. It is quite interesting that Estonian and Romanian respondents responded quite differently to this question.

Table 12.13 The main decision-makers in domestic banks (% of respondents)

The main decision-maker	General strategic policies		Capital policy		Dividend policy	
	ES	RO	ES	RO	ES	RO
Shareholders' assembly	34	60	25	40	25	60
Supervisory board (SB)	34	15	–	15	–	31
Managing board (MB)	16	15	75	15	25	10
SB and MB	16	10	–	30	50	–

Source: Florescu (2002); Uiboupin and Vensel (2002).

Note
ES, Estonia; RO, Romania.

Table 12.14 Evaluations of the adoption of mother bank's policies and systems

Adjustments	ES	RO	Mean
Information systems	3.3	2.0	2.65
Credit policy	4.5	3.0	3.75
Personnel policy	3.5	2.0	2.75
Price policy	2.8	2.0	2.40
Product/service mix policy	3.0	2.0	2.50
Risk management	4.7	4.0	4.35
Cost management	3.8	4.0	3.90
Choice of activities	3.5	4.0	3.75
Choice of target groups	3.3	3.0	3.15

Sources: Florescu (2002); Uiboupin and Vensel (2002).

Note
ES, Estonia; RO, Romania.

The share of foreign high-level managers in foreign-owned Estonian banks was reported by two banks to be about 10 per cent–12 per cent (two banks reported this share only 1 per cent) and very few of them have experience in transition countries. Quite surprisingly, one domestic bank also reported the share of foreign managers at about 20 per cent; about 20 per cent of them having experience in transition countries.

Evaluations of the adoption of the mother bank's various policies, systems and management techniques from Estonian and Romanian foreign-owned bank respondents are presented in Table 12.14. Risk-management techniques, cost-management and credit-policy methods are evaluated by respondents to be the most relevant innovations. In general, all listed adjustments are evaluated quite highly and we may conclude that the mother bank's impact on the foreign-owned bank operation is relatively high.

The transfer of various kinds of know-how from foreign banks has been important, especially for foreign-owned banks' management (see Table 12.15).

The transferred know-how of interest-rate, solvency and credit-risk management techniques was evaluated by respondents more highly (over 4.0 points by Estonian foreign banks' respondents). Liquidity risk-management techniques, information systems, credit policy and personnel policy transfer from foreign banks is also evaluated by Estonian domestic banks quite highly. Average grades from Polish domestic banks are somewhat different: the transfer of information systems and banking services/products mix policy were evaluated as the most important know-how transfers from foreign banks (4.3 and 4.2 grades respectively).

The assistance in borrowing from international markets and the financial assistance in times of crises or other financial troubles are evaluated by Estonian respondents as the most important forms of assistance by the

Table 12.15 The relevance of the transfer of know-how from foreign banks

Transferred know-how	Estonian banks			Polish Domestic Banks
	Foreign	Domestic	Total	
Liquidity-risk management	4.0	4.0	4.0	3.8
Interest-rate risk management	4.7	3.7	4.2	3.9
Solvency-risk management	4.7	3.3	4.0	3.4
Credit-risk management	4.3	3.3	3.8	3.9
Overhead-costs management	4.0	3.0	3.5	3.9
Information systems	–	3.7	3.7	4.3
Credit policy	–	3.7	3.7	2.8
Personnel policy	–	3.7	3.7	3.1
Price policy	–	2.7	2.7	3.3
Product/service mix policy	–	3.3	3.3	4.2

Source: Uiboupin and Vensel (2002).

mother bank (4.3 and 4.0 grades respectively, see Table 12.16). All other listed assistance forms are also evaluated quite highly, so that the mother bank, in general, strongly supports Estonian foreign-owned bank operations and activities in the market. This conclusion is very important taking into account the openness of the Estonian economy, sensitiveness to external shocks and the small scale of the Estonian market.

The impact of foreign banks' entry into the observed CEECs banking markets (as evaluated by respondent domestic banks) is presented in Table 12.17. We may argue that foreign banks' entry increased the overall competition in the banking market significantly (average grade, 4.0 points in Estonia and in Romania, 4.5 in Poland) and reduced the profitability and operating efficiency of domestic banks. All other impacts were

Table 12.16 The mother bank's assistance and participation in decision-making

Assistance/participation in decision-making	Grade (1–5)
Financial assistance in times of crisis/trouble	4.0
Participation in largest credits approval	3.8
Assistance in strategic planning and decision-making	3.8
Assistance in operational planning and decision-making	3.3
Assistance in borrowing from international markets	4.3
Assistance in introducing banking innovations, new systems	3.3
Assistance in correspondent banking	3.8

Source: Uiboupin and Vensel (2002).

Table 12.17 The impact of foreign banks' entry into the host-country's market

Impact	ES	CR	PO	RO	Mean
Increased the overall competition in the market	4.0	4.6	4.5	4.0	4.28
Reduced the profitability and efficiency of domestic banks	3.3	4.2	3.1	3.0	3.40
Forced to re-organize the bank's organization to increase efficiency	2.0	4.2	4.1	3.0	3.33
Forced to change financial regulations by the central bank	2.0	3.6	2.4	2.5	2.63
Improved corporate governance of private firms	1.7	–	2.9	2.5	2.37
Forced to introduce new bank products/ services	2.7	4.2	3.9	3.0	2.45
Forced to improve the quality of existing bank products/services	2.7	4.2	3.9	3.0	2.45

Sources: Florescu (2002); Kraft and Galac (2000); Uiboupin and Vensel (2002).

Note
ES, Estonia; CR, Czech Republic; PO, Poland; RO, Romania.

evaluated by Estonian respondents as not important, even corporate governance in private firms (average grade only 1.7 points). Polish respondents were of the opinion that foreign banks' entry forced banks to significantly re-organize their internal organization to raise efficiency (4.1 points), it also forced the introduction of new banking services/products and the improvement of the quality of existing banking products and services (both 3.9 points). It is quite interesting that Croatian respondents evaluated the impact of foreign banks' entry into the Croatian banking market higher than respondents of other countries.

Respondent domestic banks' evaluations of the degree of competitive pressure that resulted from foreign banks' entry are given in Table 12.18. Quite clearly, long-term loans to first-class business clients (average grade, 4.4 points) dominated among the other market segments of competitive pressure from foreign banks. Mortgage loans to households (average grade 4.0 points) were mentioned as the most important market segments in Estonian banking market, which were influenced by pressure from foreign banks. Lithuanian, Polish and Romanian respondents' evaluations are somewhat different: short-term loans to first-class business clients were mentioned as the most important competitive market segment (average grades, respectively, 4.0, 4.2 and 4.0 points). Romanian respondents also cited long-term loans to other business clients and demand deposits of business clients as important market segments for competitive pressure from foreign banks (both 4.0 points).

Respondents from Estonian and Lithuanian domestic banks are very optimistic about the prospects for future independent survival. Even in

Table 12.18 The degree of competitive pressure from foreign banks

Market segment	ES	LI	PO	RO	Mean
Short-term loans to first-class business clients	3.0	4.0	4.2	4.0	3.80
Short-term loans to other business clients	2.7	3.5	3.3	3.0	3.13
Long-term loans to first-class business clients	4.3	4.5	4.0	4.8	4.40
Long-term loans to other business clients	3.7	3.5	3.2	4.0	3.60
Consumer credits to households	2.7	2.5	2.4	3.0	2.65
Mortgage loans to households	4.0	3.3	3.3	3.0	3.40
Demand deposits of business clients	2.0	3.5	3.3	4.0	3.20
Demand deposits of households	2.0	2.3	2.8	3.0	2.53
Short-term time deposits	2.7	2.8	3.2	3.0	2.68
Long-term time deposits	2.7	3.0	3.3	3.5	3.13
Saving accounts	2.7	2.5	2.6	3.0	2.70
Payment services to business clients	2.7	3.5	2.5	3.0	2.93
Payment services to households	2.0	2.8	3.8	3.5	3.03

Sources: Dubauskas (2002); Florescu (2002); Uiboupin and Vensel (2002).

Note
ES, Estonia; LI, Lithuania; PO, Poland; RO, Romania.

the long-term perspective (see Table 12.19), Estonian banks evaluated prospects of merging with a foreign bank and/or selling a majority of ownership to a foreign partner to be much higher in comparison with merging with a domestic and/or selling the majority ownership to a domestic partner, especially in the long-term (average estimates, respectively, 4.5 and 4.5 points, and 3.0 and 2.0 points). Respondent domestic

Table 12.19 Evaluations of the prospects for independent survival

	Mid-term					Long-term				
	ES	LI	PO	RO	Mean	ES	LI	PO	RO	Mean
Independent survival	5.0	4.0	2.7	3.0	3.68	4.5	3.0	2.1	4.0	3.40
Merging with a DB	2.5	2.1	3.8	3.0	2.85	3.0	3.0	3.6	3.0	3.15
Selling ownership to DB	2.0	1.0	2.0	1.0	1.50	2.0	1.0	1.7	2.0	1.68
Merging with a FB	3.5	2.0	1.4	2.0	2.23	4.5	2.0	1.4	2.0	2.48
Selling ownership to FB	4.0	4.0	2.2	1.0	2.80	4.5	4.0	2.5	2.0	3.23
Hostile minority stake-bid by a FB	1.0	2.0	1.3	1.0	1.33	2.0	2.0	1.6	2.0	1.90
Hostile majority stake-bid by a FB	1.0	2.0	1.3	1.0	1.33	1.0	2.0	1.4	2.0	1.60

Sources: Dubauskas (2002); Florescu (2002); Uiboupin and Vensel (2002).

Note
ES, Estonia; LI, Lithuania; PO, Poland; RO, Romania.

banks in all countries do not see any prospects of a hostile minority or majority stake-bid by a foreign bank.

Respondents from Polish and Romanian domestic banks are less optimistic. Merging with another domestic bank was evaluated by respondents as the most likely mid- or long-term prospect (3.8 and 3.6 points, respectively, given by Polish respondents and 3.0 by Romanian respondents). All other prospects are evaluated as not very likely outcomes. But, surprisingly, Romanian domestic banks also evaluated independent survival prospects in the long-term quite highly (4.0 points).

Conclusions

It is argued, and empirical studies have also shown, that there is a positive correlation between foreign ownership of banks and stability of the banking sector. The main expected benefits and drawbacks resulting from the entry of foreign banks are well known, but these arguments need additional empirical testing. The main special feature of the internationalization of the Estonian banking sector was that they had to reconstruct themselves and join the globalization process at the same time. The internationalization of Estonian banks has given both positive and negative experiences. We can make some general conclusions.

- The internationalization is directed towards neighbouring transition countries, particularly towards Latvia and Lithuania. The eastern direction of internationalization has raised the risk level for Estonian domestic banking and its sensitivity to crises, due to the higher risks and unbalanced character of internationalization.
- The main reason for the internationalization of Estonian banks can be found in the 'market-seeking' argument – the domestic market was very limited in size, and competition was intense. Therefore, Estonian banks started to use their created strategic assets in entering Latvian and Lithuanian markets.
- An additional important aspect in entering Latvian and Lithuanian markets was the need to serve domestic firms, which had moved intensively into these markets from early 1995. As the stability of the local banking sector was very weak, Estonian firms looked for stable financial services which were provided by subsidiaries of Estonian banks there.
- The Estonian banks have used three strategies in their internationalization: setting up subsidiaries and branches; buying up local banks; and acquiring a significant stake in a local bank.
- The realization of internationalization plans is often drawn out, thus it will not be as successful as may be expected. It indicates either that the banks are not able to foresee the risks of internationalization or they use the announcement of their internationalization plans as the means of advertising and improving their image.

- A positive example of internationalization is the case of Hansabank, which has developed from a very small bank in Estonia into a leading commercial bank in the Baltics, now placed 15th in the ranking of the top Central European banks. Hansabank has created an extensive network of subsidiaries in all Baltic countries covering different financial services.

The results of regression analysis based on bank-level data indicate that foreign banks' assets tend to be more profitable, but foreign banks also have higher costs with respect to total assets in CEECs. Further testing is needed to analyse the activities of foreign banks in Estonia and other CEECs.

A special questionnaire was elaborated with the aim of studying foreign banks' entry motives and impact, using the experience and lessons of other analogous studies. Some important conclusions can be drawn on the basis of this empirical study, carried out in Estonia and some other CEECs.

- The most important motive for foreign banks' entry is the potential of new business opportunities in all observed countries (the average grades given by domestic banks and foreign banks, respectively, 4.68 and 4.58). The second more important reason for entry to the host country market was following the expansion strategy of the foreign bank. Both the results of regression analysis and the questionnaire confirm that the 'customer-following' strategy was important for foreign banks' entry into Estonia, but not in other countries. Supporting and developing the local client base was also mentioned by respondents as quite an important motive.
- Respondents (from both domestic and foreign banks) in all countries evaluated macroeconomic and political stability in the host country highly, as well as a liberal economic policy, a strong potential for future EU membership, and existing clients and potential new client-base as important host-country market specifics. Surprisingly, good tourism and/or industry development opportunities were evaluated in all countries as not important to the host-country market specifics.
- The results of our comparative study suggest that foreign banks have quite different advantages over domestic banks in different countries. In general, the reputation of foreign banks was evaluated as the most important advantage of foreign banks, followed by the range and quality of banking innovations (Estonia is an exception). The main advantage of domestic banks was a better knowledge of customers and closer bank–customer relations. The results fit with the main theory of internationalization of banks.
- Foreign-owned and domestic banks have somewhat different target client groups of activities in the host countries' banking markets, and

these depend on the host-country's specific features. Our study's results indicate that there are no very significant differences between foreign and domestic banks in the main fields of activities, and corporate financing is the most important field of activity for both domestic and foreign banks in all observed countries.

- All respondent foreign banks' strategies foresee a long-term stay in the Estonian and Romanian banking markets. Among the most important motives mentioned for the stay (in both Estonian and Romanian markets) were good future prospects of the development of the local client base, as well as good future prospects of doing business with home-country clients. The mother bank is the main strategic decision-maker in foreign-owned banks, also the Managing Board of the foreign-owned bank alone or with the Managing Board of the mother bank are making some important strategic decisions (especially in working out general strategic policies and/or capital policy). The shareholders' assembly and the Managing Board play the key role in strategic decision-making in domestic banks.

- Although there are differences between observed countries, the transfer of various kinds of know-how from foreign banks has been important, especially for foreign-owned banks' risk management. The transfer of information systems and banking services/products mix was also evaluated by respondents as important know-how transfer from foreign banks. Assistance in borrowing from international markets and financial assistance in times of crises or other financial troubles are evaluated by Estonian respondents as most important forms of assistance from the mother bank. All other listed assistance forms are also evaluated quite highly, so that the mother bank, in general, supports foreign-owned bank operations and activities in the host-country market.

- Foreign banks' entry significantly increased overall competition in the banking market and reduced the profitability and efficiency of operating domestic banks in the host country. Polish respondents were of the opinion that foreign banks' entry forced banks to significantly re-organizse their internal organization to raise efficiency, as well as forcing them to introduce new banking services/products and to improve the quality of existing banking products and services.

- Long-term loans to first-class business clients dominated among the other market segments of competitive pressure from foreign banks. Mortgage loans to households were mentioned as the most important market segments in the Estonian banking market, which were influenced by pressure from foreign banks. Lithuanian, Polish and Romanian respondents' evaluations were somewhat different: short-term loans to first-class business clients were mentioned as the most important competitive market segment. Romanian respondents also evaluated long-term loans to other business clients and demand deposits of business clients as highly important market segments for competitive pressure from foreign banks.

- Respondents from Estonian and Lithuanian domestic banks were very optimistic about the prospects for future independent survival, even in the long-term. Evaluated prospects of merging with a foreign bank and/or selling a majority of ownership to a foreign partner are much higher in comparison with merging with a domestic and and/or selling the majority ownership to a domestic partner, especially in the long-term. Respondent domestic banks in all countries do not see any prospects of a hostile minority or majority stake-bid by a foreign bank.
- Foreign banks' entry has improved service quality and innovation in the host country's banking sector. For example, the biggest Estonian banks, with a large share of foreign capital, have excelled in their highly-developed Internet banking services. Improved bank risk management can also be considered as a positive effect of foreign banks' activities. Foreign capital has made banks more reliable and borrowing from international markets has become less expensive for banks and their customers.

Appendix

A12.1 definition of variables

FD	dummy variable with value 1 if bank is foreign-owned and 0 if otherwise. Bank is taken as foreign if at least 51 per cent of its share capital is foreign-owned.
PNI/TA	published net income over total assets.
TOE/TA	total operating expense over total assets.
TAX/TA	taxes paid over total assets.
LLR/GL	loan loss reserve over gross loans.
NIM	net interest margin.
ROAA	return on average assets.
CIN	costs-to-income ratio.
TLN/TA	total loans net over total assets.
TNA/TA	total non-earning assets over total assets.
AR(1)	first order autocorrelation operator.

Bibliography

Aarma, A. and Vensel, V. (2002) 'Bank–customer relationships development in majority foreign owned banking system', TTUWPE No. 02/65.

Agarwal, S. and Ramaswami, S.N. (1992) 'Choice of foreign markets entry mode: impact of ownership. Location and internalization factors', *Journal of International Business Studies*, 23(1): 1–28.

Aliber, R. (1984) 'International banking: a survey', *Journal of Money, Credit and Banking*, XVI(2): 661–678.

Allen, L. and Rai, A. (1996) 'Operational efficiency in banking: an international comparison', *Journal of Banking and Finance*, 20: 655–672.

Altunbas, Y. and Chakravarty, S. P. (1998) 'Efficiency measures and the banking structure in Europe', *Economic Letters*, 60: 205–208.

Anderson, R.W. and Chantal, K. (1998) *Transition Banking: Financial Development of Central and Eastern Europe*. Oxford: Clarendon Press.

Balino, T.J.T. and Ubide, A. (2000) 'The new world of banking', *Finance & Development*, June: 41–43.

Bank of Estonia (2003) Official Homepage. Online, available at: http://www.eestipank.info (accessed 4 July 2003).

Berger, A.N., DeYoung, R., Genay, H. and Udell, G.F. (2000) *Globalization of Financial Institutions: Evidence from Cross-border Banking Performance*. Brookings-Rochester Economic Series, Vol. 3.

Bikker, J.A. (1999) *Efficiency in the European Banking Industry*. Amsterdam: De Nederlandische Bank.

Bonin, J., Miszei, K., Szekely, I. and Wachtel, P. (1998) *Banking in Transition Economies: Developing Market Oriented Banking Sectors in Eastern Europe*. Vermont: Edward Elgar Brookfield.

Buch, C.M. (2000) 'Why do banks go abroad? Evidence from German data', *Financial Markets, Institutions and Instruments*, 9(1) February: 33–67.

Cantwell, J. (1989) *Technological Innovation and Multinational Corporations*. Oxford: Basil Blackwell Ltd.

Cantwell, J. (1994) *Transnational Corporations and Innovatory Activities*, United Nations Library on Transnational Corporations, Vol. 17, UNCTAD Program on Transnational Corporations. London and New York: Routledge.

Caprio, G. and Honohan, P. (2000) *Finance for Growth: Policy Choices in a Volatile World*. Washington, DC: The World Bank.

Chang, C.E., Hasan, I. and Hunter W.C. (1998) 'Efficiency of multinational banks: an empirical investigation', *Applied Financial Economics*, 8, 6: 1–8.

Claessens, S., Demirgüç-Kunt, A. and Huizinga, H. (1998) 'How does foreign entry affect the domestic banking market?' World Bank Policy Research Working Paper No. 1918.

Claessens, S., Demirgüç-Kunt, A. and Huizinga, H. (2001) 'How does foreign entry affect domestic banking markets?' *Journal of Banking and Finance*, 25(5): 891–911.

Dages, B.G., Goldberg, L. and Kinney, D. (2000) 'Foreign and domestic bank participation in emerging markets: lessons from Mexico and Argentina', *Federal Reserve Bank of New York Economic Policy Review*, 6(3) September: 17–35.

De Brandt, O. and Davis, P. (2000) 'Competition, contestability, and market structure in European banking sectors on the eve of EMU', *Journal of Banking and Finance*, 24, 6/7.

Demirgüç-Kunt, A. and Detragiache, E. (1998) 'The determinants of banking crises in developing and developed countries', *International Monetary Fund Staff Papers*, 45, March: 81–109.

Dietsch, M. and Lozano-Vivas, A. (2000) 'How the environment determines banking efficiency: a comparison between French and Spanish industry', *Journal of Banking and Finance*, 24(6/7): 985–1004.

Dietsch, M. and Weill, L. (2000) *The Evolution of Cost and Profit Efficiency in the European Banking Industry.* Research in Banking and Finance, JAI Press.

Doukas, J., Murinde, V. and Wihlborg, C. (1998) 'Main issues in financial sector reform and privatization in transition economies', in: J. Doukas, V. Murinde and C. Wihlborg (eds), *Financial Sector Reform and Privatization in Transition Economies.* Amsterdam: Elsevier Science B.V., pp. 1–18.

Dubauskas, G. (2002) 'Motivation of foreign banks' entry into the emerging economies: the case of Lithuania', in: T. Kowalski, R. Lensink and V. Vensel (eds), *Papers of the 5th Conference on Financial Sector Reform in Central and Eastern Europe: The Impact of Foreign Banks' Entry*, 26–27 April, Tallinn. TTUWPE(BFE) No. 02/69. Tallinn: TTU, Department of Economics and Business Administration, pp. 63–72.

Dunning, J.H. (1973) 'The determinants of international production', Oxford Economic Papers, 25.

Dunning, J.H. (1981) *International Production and the Multinational Enterprise.* London: Allen and Unwin.

Dunning, J.H. (1993) *Multinational Enterprises and the Global Economy.* Wokingham: Addison-Wesley Publishers.

Erramilli, M.K. (1990) 'Entry mode choice in service industries', *International Marketing Review*, 7(5): 50–62.

Erramilli M.K. and Rao, C.P. (1993) 'Service firm's international entry-mode choice. A modified transaction costs analysis approach', *Journal of International Marketing*, 57(3) July: 19–39.

Florescu, G. (2002) 'Foreign banks entry into Romania', in: T. Kowalski, R. Lensink and V. Vensel (eds), *Papers of the 5th Conference on Financial Sector Reform in Central and Eastern Europe: The Impact of Foreign Banks' Entry*, 26–27 April, Tallinn. TTUWPE(BFE) No. 02/71. Tallinn: TTU, Department of Economics and Business Administration, pp. 83–94.

Focarelli, D. and Pozzolo, A.F. (2000) 'The determinants of cross-border bank shareholdings: an analysis with bank-level data from OECD countries', unpublished manuscript.

Garcia Blandon, J. (2000) 'Cross-border banking in Europe: an empirical investigation', Universitat Pompeu Fabra Working Paper No. 509, October.

Goldberg, L.B., Dages, G. and Kinney, D. (2000) 'Foreign and domestic bank participation: lessons from Argentina and Mexico', Federal Reserve Bank of New York Working Paper.

Graham, E.M. (2001) 'Opening up the banking sector to competition from foreign-owned banks: issues and strategies', Paper presented at the World Bank, IMF, and Brookings Institution 3rd Annual Financial Markets and Development Conference, 19–21 April, New York.

Grubel, H. (1977) 'A theory of multinational banking', *Banka Nazionale del Lavozo*, Quarterly Review, 123, 1997: 349–363.

Gruben, W., Koo, J. and Moore, R. (1999) 'When does financial liberalization make banks risky? An empirical examination of Argentina, Canada and Mexico', Federal Reserve Bank of Dallas, Center for Latin American Economics Working Paper No. 0399.

Gual, J. (1999) 'Deregulation, integration and market structure in European banking', *Journal of the Japanese and International Economy*, 13: 372–396.

Hasan, I., Lozano-Vivas, A. and Pastor, J.T. (2000) 'Cross-border performance in

European banking', Bank of Finland Discussion Papers, 24/2000. Bank of Finland, Helsinki.

Hellman, P. (1996) *Internationalization of the Finnish Financial Service Sector.* Turun Kauppakorgeakoulun Kirjasto.

Hickson, C. and Turner, J. (2000) 'Banking stability under limited liability: an historical perspective', *Taiwan Journal of Political Economy*, 3(1): 43–67.

Ideon, A. (1997) Pangauksest hakkab voolama rahajõgi, *Postimees*, June 5.

Johanson, J. and Mattsson, L.-G. (1986). 'International marketing and internationalization processes – a network approach', in S. Paliwoda and P.N. Turnbull (eds), *Research in International Marketing*. London: Croom Helm.

Johanson, J. and Vahlne, J.E. (1977) 'The internationalization of the firm', *Journal of International Business Studies*, 8, spring/summer: 23–32

Johanson, J. and Wiedersheim-Paul, F. (1975) 'The internationalization of the firm – four Swedish cases', *Journal of Management Studies*, 12(3): 305–322.

Kogut, B. and Zander, U. (1993) 'Knowledge of the firm and the evolutionary theory of the multinational corporation', *Journal of International Business Studies*, 4th Quarter: 625–646.

Konopielko, L. (1999) 'Foreign banks' entry into Central and East European Markets: motives and activities', *Post-Communist Economies*, 11(4): 463–485.

Kowalski, T., Uiboupin, J. and Vensel, V. 'Motives of foreign banks entry into the transitional economies' in T. Kowalski, R. Lensink and V. Vensel (eds) *Papers of the 5th Conference on Financial Sector Reform in Central and Eastern Europe: The Impact of Foreign Banks Entry*, TTUWPE (BFE) No. 02/78, Tallinn, TTU: 688–726.

Kraft, E. and Galac, T. (2000) 'The impact of foreign banks on the Croatian banking market', Paper presented at the 6th European Association of Comparative Economic Systems, Barcelona, 7–9 September.

Lardy, N.R. (2001) 'Foreign financial firms in Asia', Paper presented at the World Bank, IMF and Brookings Institution 3rd Annual Financial Markets and Development Conference, 19–21 April, New York.

Levine, R. (1997) 'Financial development and economic growth: views and agenda', *Journal of Economic Literature*, 33: 688–726.

Levine, R. and Zervos, S. (1998) 'Stock markets, banks, and economic growth', *American Economic Review*, 88: 537–558.

Li, J. and Guisinger, S. (1992) 'The globalization of service multinationals in the "Triad" regions: Japan, Western Europe and North America', *Journal of International Business Studies*, 23(4): 675–696.

Linnamo, J. and Vanamo, I. (1980) 'Kansainvälisesta pankkikilpailusta ja pankkirikistä', *Kansantaloudellinen Aikauskirja*, 1: 14–31.

Luostarinen, R. (1970) *Foreign Operations of the Firm*, 1st Edn, Helsinki.

Luostarinen, R. (1994) 'Internationalization of family enterprises', Helsinki: CIBR Working Papers Series Z–1, Helsinki School of Economics.

Martinez, P., Soledad, M. and Schmukler, S.L. (1999) 'Do depositors punish banks for "bad behavior"? Market discipline in Argentina, Chile, and Mexico', World Bank Policy Research Paper No. 2058.

Mathieson, D.J. and Roldos, J. (2001) 'The role of foreign banks in emerging markets', Paper presented at the World Bank, IMF and Brookings Institution 3rd Annual Financial Markets and Development Conference, 19–21 April, New York.

Mattsson, L.-G. (1985) 'An application of a network approach to marketing:

defending and changing market positions', in N. Dholakia and J. Arndt (eds), *Alternative Paradigms for Widening Marketing Theory*. Greenwich, CT: JAI press.

Meigas, H. (1999) 'Estonian banking: an outline of its dynamics', *The Baltic Review*, 17: 33–34.

Murinde, V. and Ryan, C. (2000) 'The implications of World Trade Organization and the General Agreement on Trade in services for the banking sector in sub-Saharan Africa', in V. Murinde (ed.), *The Free Trade Area for the Common Market for Eastern and Central Africa*. Aldershot: Ashgate Publishing.

Ozawa, T. (1992) 'Foreign direct investment and economic development', *Transnational Corporations*, 1(1), February: 27–54.

Pastor, J. M., Perez, F. and Quesada, J. (1997) 'Efficiency analysis in banking firms: an international comparison', *European Journal of Operational Research*, 98(2): 395–407.

Paula, L.F. (2002) *Banking Internationalization and the Expansion Strategies of European Banks to Brazil during 1990s*. SUERF Studies No. 18, Vienna.

Pauli, R. (1994) Pankkitoiminnan rakennemuutos Suomessa, Suomen Pankkki, Helsinki.

Peek, J., Rosengren, E.S. and Kasirye, F. (1999) 'The poor performance of foreign bank subsidiaries: were the problems acquired or created?', *Journal of Banking and Finance*, 22(6): 799–819.

Pietikäinen, M. (1994) Obstacles to and Strategies of the Internationalization of Finnish Service Companies. Helsinkin Kauppakorkeakoulu julkaisuja: D–199, Helsinki.

Pomerleano, M. and Vojta, G.J. (2001) 'What do foreign banks do in emerging markets? An institutional study', Paper presented at the World Bank, IMF and Brookings Institution 3rd Annual Financial Markets and Development Conference, 19–21 April, New York.

Rajan, R.G. and Zingales, L. (1998) 'Financial dependence and growth', *American Economic Review*, 88: 559–586.

Repullo, R. (2000) 'A model of takeovers of foreign banks', CEPR Discussion Paper No. 2639.

Rugman, A.M. and Kamath, S.J. (1987) 'International diversification and multinational banking in recent developments', in S. J. Khoyry and A. Ghosh (eds) *International Banking and Finance*. London: McGraw-Hill.

Sõrg, M. (2002) 'Estonian banks' internationalization and entry to the foreign market. Foreign banks and economic transition', Tadeusz Kowalski, Robert Lensink and Vello Vensel (eds) Poland: The Poznan University of Economics, pp. 157–178.

Sõrg, M. and Varblane, U. (2002) 'Expansion of Estonian banks to foreign markets', in T. Kowalski, R. Lensink and V. Vensel (eds), *Papers of the 5th Conference on Financial Sector Reform in Central and Eastern Europe: The Impact of Foreign Banks' Entry*, 26–27 April, Tallinn. TTUWPE(BFE) No. 02/81. Tallinn: TTU, Department of Economics and Business Administration, pp. 217–238.

Taeho, K. (1993) *International Money and Banking*. Routledge.

Terpstra, V. and Yu, C.-M. (1988) 'Determinants of foreign direct investments of US advertising agencies', *Journal of International Business Studies*, 19, spring: pp. 33–46.

Tiusanen, T. and Jumpponen, J. (2000) 'The Baltic States in the 21st century. Western investors in Estonia, Latvia and Lithuania', *Studies in Industrial Engineering and Management*, Lappenranta University of Technology, No. 11.

Uiboupin, J. and Vensel V. (2002) 'The impact of foreign banks' entry into the Estonian banking market', in T. Kowalski, R. Lensink and V. Vensel (eds), *Papers of the 5th Conference on Financial Sector Reform in Central and Eastern Europe: The Impact of Foreign Banks' Entry*, 26–27 April, Tallinn. TTUWPE(BFE) No. 02/82. Tallinn: TTU, Department of Economics and Business Administration, pp. 239–249.

Weller, C.E. (2000) 'Financial liberalization, multinational banks and credit supply: the case of Poland', *International Review of Applied Economics*, 14(2): 193–211.

Yannopoulus, G. (1983) 'The growth of transnational banking', in Mark Casson (ed.), *The Growth of International Business*. London: George Allen and Irwin.

13 An early-warning model for currency crises in Central and Eastern Europe[1]

Franz Schardax

Introduction

The many financial crises that erupted in the course of the 1990s have ignited great interest in the development of early-warning models for financial crises. At the same time, advances in economic theory suggest that the development of reliable early warning systems for financial crises is likely to meet with considerable difficulties. While empirical studies for broad samples of emerging markets are relatively abundant, rather few investigations have been made for geographically constrained samples. This is particularly true for the Central and Eastern European transition countries, where the scarcity of available data imposes additional limitations on empirical research. On the other hand, the ongoing processes of liberalization of capital flows and convergence toward the present EU member states is likely to pose considerable challenges for the macroeconomic stability of these countries. As a result, tools for the detection of vulnerabilities in these countries could make an important contribution to stable macroeconomic development in the region and the smooth integration of candidate countries into the European Union and – finally – into the euro area.

The focus of this study lies on one particular type of disturbance to macroeconomic stability, namely currency crises. In the course of this chapter, the terms 'currency crisis' and 'balance of payments crisis' will be used synonymously. As will be outlined in more detail later in the chapter, the definition of crises used herein focuses on discrete events rather than on continuous measures of downward pressure on a currency. The first section of this chapter contains a brief overview of the relevant theoretical literature on this subject along with a categorization and discussion of existing empirical studies. Next, the so-called 'signal approach', which is strongly associated with the work of Kaminsky, Lizondo and Reinhart (1998), will be applied to a sample of quarterly data from 12 Central and Eastern European transition economies. In this section, the aim is to identify the empirical relevance of individual economic indicators for the prediction of currency crises. The selection of these indicators is based mainly on the results of Berg and Pattillo (1998). In a further step, the appropriateness of the functional form implicitly embedded in the signal approach will be investigated. On the basis of this analysis, the aim of the subsequent part of this chapter is to develop a multivariate probit model incorporating all relevant economic variables simultaneously, with a dummy crisis variable as the regressand. Finally, the predictive power of such a model will be evaluated by a number of statistical tests which provide the basis for the conclusions presented in the chapter's conclusion.

Literature review

Theory

Although this chapter has an empirical focus, I should like to very briefly review some key insights from the theory of currency crises, as this theory makes some important predictions regarding the ability of empirical models to correctly forecast currency crises. The so-called first-generation crisis models, pioneered by Krugman (1979), strongly emphasize economic fundamentals in their explanation of balance of payments/ currency crises. According to Krugman (1979), currency crises are the consequence of inconsistencies in economic fundamentals with governmental attempts to maintain a fixed exchange-rate peg. In Krugman's model, the root of currency turbulence lies in an excessive expansion of domestic credit used to finance fiscal deficits or to support a weak banking system. A critical assumption is the government's inability to fulfill its financing needs by tapping capital markets, which results in a monetization of deficits. The expansion of money supply leads to downward pressure on domestic interest rates, capital outflows and losses of official reserves. As a result, the vulnerability of the currency to a speculative attack increases. There are a number of extensions of Krugman's (1979) initial model (for instance, Flood and Garber 1984; Connolly and Taylor 1984), but a common feature of these models is the explanation of currency crises by the inconsistency of a fixed peg with domestic policies. Therefore, according to these models, currency crises are predictable.

The difficulties of first-generation models in explaining contagion effects, and the occurrence of balance-of-payments crises in countries with relatively sound fundamentals, led to the development of second-generation models. In this approach, features of speculative attacks are explicitly incorporated. Second-generation models regard currency crises as shifts between different monetary policy equilibriums in response to self-fulfilling speculative attacks. According to Kaminsky, Lizondo and Reinhart (1998), a crucial assumption of these models is that economic policies are not predetermined, but respond instead to changes in the economy and that economic agents take this relationship into account in forming their expectations. At the same time, the expectations and actions of economic agents affect some variables to which economic agents respond. This circularity creates the possibility for multiple equilibria; the economy may move from one equilibrium to another without a change in fundamentals. Thus, the economy may initially be in an equilibrium consistent with a fixed exchange rate, but a sudden worsening of expectations may lead to changes in policies that result in a collapse of the exchange rate regime, thereby validating agents' expectations. For instance, Obstfeld (1994, 1996) presents models in which a loss in confidence increases the costs of maintaining a fixed peg for the government. In the former model, expectations of a currency crash drive up wages, which negatively affects output. In the latter model, higher interest rates increase the government's debt-servicing costs. In both models, the government decides to abandon the peg as the cost of maintaining the peg exceeds the cost of abandoning it. Because of the much more important role of unpredictable changes in market sentiment in this approach, these models suggest that currency crises are very difficult to predict. Nevertheless, economic fundamentals do still play a role.

However, more recent theoretical work – often referred to as 'generation two-and-a-half models' – places more weight on the importance of economic fundamentals. In a contribution from Morris and Shin (1998), uncertainty among market participants with respect to economic fundamentals and other market participants' beliefs about the state of the economy inhibits highly coordinated behavior of speculators. As a result, easy shifts between different equilibria are no longer possible and a single equilibrium emerges. Morris and Shin's (1998) model is able to identify states of fundamentals below which a speculative attack always occurs, and states above which an attack on the currency never occurs. Thus, according to this model, the occurrence of currency crises and weak fundamentals are expected to be strongly related.

Empirical studies

The large number of financial crises that occurred in emerging markets in the course of the 1990s has ignited great interest in early-warning models for financial crises. As a result, literature on this subject has become abundant. Vlaar (2000), who provides an excellent methodological comparison of currency crises models, distinguishes three main types of such models. The first type comprises case studies concentrating on specific episodes of financial turmoil. These models are less geared toward predicting the exact timing of financial crises; rather, they aim at explaining the severity of financial crises. Papers by Blanco and Garber (1986), Sachs, Tornell and Velasco (1996) or Bussiére and Mulder (1999) are notable examples for this kind of model class.

A second category of studies, which may be summarized under the label 'signal approach', is strongly associated with the work of Kaminsky,

Lizondo and Reinhart (1998), Kaminsky (1998) Kaminsky and Reinhart (1999), as well as Goldstein, Kaminsky and Reinhart (2000). In their papers, the levels of individual variables, such as the real exchange rate or the export growth rate during a specified period before the outbreak of a crisis, are compared with tranquil periods. A variable is deemed to issue a signal if it exceeds a certain threshold. The threshold is set such that the noise-to-signal ratio (defined as the share of wrong signals that are preceded by tranquil periods divided by the share of correct signals that are followed by crises) is minimized.

The third type of model consists of limited dependent (probit or logit) regression models. In these models, the currency crisis indicator is modeled as a zero–one variable, as in the signal approach. However, unlike in the signal approach, the explanatory variables do not take the functional form of a dummy variable, but enter the model mostly in a linear fashion. Moreover, the significance of all variables is analyzed simultaneously, while the signal approach investigates the relationship between dependent and explanatory variables in a bivariate way. Frankel and Rose (1996), Berg and Pattillo (1998) and Kumar, Moorthy and Perraudin (2002) may be cited as examples of this genre. Vlaar (2000) presents a model which combines elements of the severity of crises and the limited dependent regression approach.

There are a number of advantages and disadvantages associated with each methodological approach. While the case-study type of papers are able to avoid the need to define crises as discrete events, they focus on times of crisis only. As a consequence, they neither incorporate information from tranquil times, nor are they well suited for predicting the timing of a crisis.

The signal approach uses information from crisis and non-crisis times and takes the timing of crises explicitly into account. A major advantage of this method is the evaluation of each indicator's predictive power on an individual basis, which facilitates the establishment of indicator rankings. Moreover, this method is useful for designing policy responses, as the economic variables which issue warning signals can be immediately identified. However, owing to the bivariate character of this approach, the interaction among indicators is not taken into account. A related drawback is the fact that these models do not directly produce a composite early-warning indicator that incorporates all available information from individual indicators. Kaminsky (1998) offers a solution to this problem by proposing a single composite early warning indicator that is calculated as a weighted sum of the individual indicators. In Kaminsky's paper, each indicator is weighted according to the inverse of its noise-to-signal ratio.

Another potentially problematic aspect of this approach is the implicit assumption of a very specific functional relationship between explanatory and dependent variables. The probability of crisis is modeled as a step function of the value of the indicator, taking on a value of zero when the indicator variable is below the threshold and a value of one if the opposite is true. Thus, for instance, these models do not distinguish whether the indicator variable just exceeds the threshold or whether it does so by a wide margin. Finally, the signal approach does not easily allow the application of some standard statistical evaluation methods, such as the testing of hypotheses.

Most of the disadvantages associated with the signal approach are resolved in limited dependent regression models: results are easily interpreted as probabilities for the outbreak of a crisis and standard statistical tests are immediately available. Moreover, these models capture the effect of all explanatory variables simultaneously, and they are flexible enough to deal with different functional forms for the relationship between dependent and explanatory variables, inclusive of dummy variables. A problem is posed to these models by the fact that the number of crises in the underlying sample is usually very small in comparison with the number of tranquil periods. As a result, the statistical properties of limited dependent regressions are often rather poor.

Most empirical studies dealing with currency crises use a broadly based sample of emerging markets. In some cases industrial countries are also included, while the number of studies that focus exclusively on a particular region are relatively scarce. A recent example for a regionally focussed study is provided by Wu, Yen and Chen (2000) who estimate a logit model for South-East Asian countries. Studies which are based on samples with a large number of countries have the advantage of being able to produce very strong results, as they are neither subject to the criticism of using too small or biased samples. However, such studies could produce less reliable warning signals for a specific region that is characterized by common structural features. According to Weller and Morzuch's (2000), results, it seems plausible to assume that the Central and Eastern European transition economies (CEECs) bear some common structural features that affect their proneness to financial crises and differentiate them from other emerging economies. Therefore, an early-warning model based entirely on a sample of Central and Eastern European countries could be capable of producing superior results in terms of predictive power compared to a horizontally strongly diversified sample. Empirical studies dealing with early-warning models for currency crises in Central and Eastern Europe are scarce, mainly for the obvious reason of the shortness of time series. Notable examples include Brüggemann and Linne (1999, 2001) and Krkoska (2001). Brüggemann and Linne (1999, 2001) basically apply the Kaminsky-Lizondo-Reinhart (1998) framework with a few extensions to 13 CEECs and three Mediterranean countries (Cyprus, Malta and Turkey). Krkoska (2001) estimates a VAR-model for four countries (the Czech Republic, Hungary, Poland, and the Slovak Republic) with an index of speculative pressure (comprising changes in exchange rates, international reserves and interest rates) as a dependent variable measuring downward pressure on the exchange rate (in a linear fashion).

An early-warning model for currency crises in Central and Eastern Europe

The approach employed in this chapter draws greatly from the work of Berg and Pattillo (1998). For a 23-country sample with monthly data covering the time period from 1970 to April 1995, they identify: (1) the deviation of the real exchange rate from a trend; (2) the current account; (3) the growth of reserves; (4) the growth of exports; (5) the ratio of M2/reserves; and (6) the growth of M2/reserves as statistically significant variables for explaining currency crises. In addition to these variables, the budget balance/GDP is used in this chapter. In a first step, the predictive power of these variables is analyzed according to the signal approach. Next, I run probit regressions on the dummy crisis variable for each explanatory variable separately, but with different functional specifications for the explanatory variable in order to check whether the dummy variable specification employed in the signal approach or alternative specifications seem more appropriate. Finally, I will present a probit model using the variables mentioned above.

Data and definitions

This study uses all available quarterly data from 12 transition countries from the beginning of 1989 up to the third quarter of 2002. Data sources include the Vienna Institute for Comparative Studies' database, the IMF's international financial statistics, the BIS database and national central banks' statistics. However, data for all variables and countries generally do not exist for the full 1989–2002 period. Mostly, time series start in the first quarter of 1992 and end in the third quarter of 2002. The country dimension of the sample consists of: Bulgaria, Croatia, the Czech Republic, Estonia, Hungary, Latvia, Lithuania, Poland, Romania, Russia, Slovak Republic and Slovenia. All explanatory variables are measured in percentiles of the country-specific distribution of this variable. In my definition of currency crises, I focus on the following events which were identified by Brüggemann and Linne (1999) as the beginning of currency crises.

Bulgaria

January 1997: hyperinflation and massive depreciation of the lev. Later, currency stability is re-established by means of a currency board.

The Czech Republic

May 1997: after ten days of heavy pressure on the koruna, the fixed exchange rate regime is abandoned and the koruna is left to float.

Hungary

December 1994: the government acknowledges the necessity for the government launch of an austerity package (including a 9 percent one-off devaluation of the forint and the introduction of a crawling peg regime) after the current account deficit has exceeded 9 percent. Actual measures took effect in March 1995.

Romania

January 1997: the lei devalues 20 percent in the space of one week.

Russia

August 1998: forced devaluation of the rouble, switch to a flexible exchange rate regime, moratorium on debt payments.

In addition to these events, the following episodes were defined as currency crises.[2]

Poland[3]

February 1992: having a crawling peg exchange rate regime in place, Poland has to undertake an extra-devaluation of the zloty of 10.7 percent.

Russia

First quarter of 1994: following an episode of hyperinflation, the rouble begins to fall sharply versus the US dollar. In the course of the first quarter of 1994, the rouble's depreciation amounts to more than 40 percent relative to the end of the preceding quarter.

Slovak Republic

October 1998: abandonment of the fixed exchange rate regime after prolonged downward pressure on the koruna.

There are a few other episodes of sharp falls in Central and Eastern European currencies. However, these events occurred in the early 1990s for which data are not available and, thus, these events are not represented in the sample. Given the crisis definitions listed above, in the following sections the dependent variable always equals one if there is a crisis and zero otherwise. In the regression equations reported later in this chapter, not only were the periods marking the beginning of a crisis set equal to zero, but also the eight periods preceding the crisis. This procedure, which was successfully applied by Berg and Pattillo (1998), has some important advantages: provided the signals of a crisis are indeed visible two years before the actual event, this method identifies the optimal model which is able to issue warnings two years in advance. Taking account of the time lag until data are published, the signaling horizon is long enough to take action in response to the predictions of the model. Obviously this also avoids the need to work with lagged variables. From the statistical point of view, this procedure strongly increases the number of 'ones' in the sample, which is beneficial for the statistical properties of the model.

Using the signal approach

In the signal approach, an indicator is understood to issue a signal if the level of the indicator exceeds a certain threshold. The threshold, in turn, is defined relative to the percentiles of the country-specific distribution of the indicator. For instance, if the threshold for the current account is set at the eightieth percentile, all values of the current account that exceed the eightieth percentile in country A would constitute a signal. Obviously, the time horizon between the signal's time of issuance and the outbreak of the crisis needs to be set appropriately: signals that are sent too early to credibly stand in any relationship with subsequent crises should be avoided, as should signals that are sent too late to prompt action. In this study, I opted for a signaling horizon of eight quarters for the evaluation of indicators. An indicator is considered to send a 'good signal' if the indicator variable exceeds the threshold and a crisis occurs within the limits of the signaling horizon. Correspondingly, a signal is deemed 'bad' if the indicator emits a signal, but no crisis follows during the signaling horizon.

The performance of each indicator can be evaluated according to the following matrix, as proposed by Kaminsky, Lizondo and Reinhart (1998):

	Crisis (within 8 quarters)	No crisis (within 8 quarters)
Signal was issued	A	B
No signal was issued	C	D

In this matrix, A means the number of months in which a good signal was sent, B is the number of bad signals, C is the number of months in which the indicator failed to issue a signal (which would have been a good signal) and D is the number of months in which the indicator rightly refrained from emitting a signal, as it was not followed by a crisis in the signaling horizon. Using the input from the matrix, the noise-to-signal (NtS) ratio for an indicator can be computed according to the following formula:

$$NtS = [B/(B+D)]/[A/(A+C)] \qquad (13.1)$$

Table 13.1 Performance of indicators according to the signal approach

	Number of observations used in calculation	Good signals, % of possible good signals $A/(A + C)$	Bad signals, % of possible bad signals $B/(B + D)$	Noise-to-signal ratio (NtS)
% change in M2/gross official reserves, yoy	461	4	18	0.24
M2/gross official reserves	520	43	79	0.54
% change in exports in USD, yoy	455	10	16	0.62
Real effective exchange rate, deviation from HP trend	590	14	21	0.64
Budget balance, % of GDP	364	74	88	0.84
Gross official reserves	539	70	73	0.96
% change in gross official reserves, yoy	477	100	100	1.00
Current account, % of GDP	443	100	100	1.00

The signaling threshold is to be set such that the NtS reaches a minimum. Ideally, one would want a NtS that comes as close as possible to zero. In the literature,[4] a distinction is often made between indicators providing useful information that is reflected in a noise-to-signal ratio below one and indicators that have a noise-to-signal ratio above one. Results for each indicator are reported in Table 13.1.

Most of the variables identified as relevant indicators by Berg and Pattillo (1998) exhibit noise-to-signal ratios below one in our sample. However, NtS ratios are generally lower than in Brüggemann and Linne (1999). A possible explanation could be the relatively small number of observations per country, which results in rather crude country-specific distributions. Among the various external and fiscal indicators, the budget balances, as a percentage of GDP, seem to be relatively less important than in Brüggemann and Linne (1999), where these indicators were among the most important.

Is there a case for an alternative functional specification?

Having confirmed the empirical relevance of a number of variables as early-warning indicators according to the signal approach methodology, I will deal next with the question of whether the implicitly embedded functional relationship between the (0,1) crisis variable and individual indicators is justified. According to Vlaar (2000), the transformation of the indicator variable into a dummy variable, based on the criterion of whether its value is above or below the threshold, can be expected to yield the best results if there is a clear distinction between crisis periods and periods of tranquillity. Presumably this condition is best fulfilled if only the most severe crises are above the threshold or if the crisis definition is related to a currency peg.

Although the crisis definition employed in this study is probably largely in line with this condition, the results reported in Table 13.1 raise the possibility that functional specifications other than the step function relationship between the crisis variable and the indicators could be more appropriate for some variables. In particular, this seems to be the case for the current account, which is assigned a prominent role by *ex ante* knowledge, but does not do well according to the NtS ratio. In order to investigate this question in more detail, I run probit regressions on the crisis variable for the pooled panel with different functional specifications for one particular explanantory variable, as suggested by Berg and Pattillo (1998). For each indicator, I estimate equations which assume the following format:

$$\text{Prob } (c8 = 1) = f(\alpha_0 + \alpha_1 p(x) + \alpha_2 I + \alpha_3 I(p(x) - T)) \qquad (13.2)$$

Where $c8 = 1$ if a crisis occurs during the next eight quarters, $p(x)$ is the percentile of the variable x and $I = 1$ if the percentile is above some threshold, T, and zero otherwise. For the threshold, T, the results from the signal approach calculations are used. Thus, if the threshold concept provides an appropriate functional specification, only the coefficient α_2 should be significantly different statistically from zero. Significant coefficients α_1 and α_3 would point to a linear functional relationship between crisis variable and indicator and a different (higher) slope coefficient when the indicator is above the threshold, respectively. Table 13.2 summarizes the results of these regressions.

For a number of indicators the closeness of thresholds to one end of the distribution resulted in meaningless estimation results, which is indicated by the empty cells. In these cases the equation was estimated again without the variable causing the problems. Although the jump coefficients (α_2) are statistically significant in a number of cases, the results reported in Table 13.2 provide empirical support for more general specifications, too. This hypothesis gains further support from Berg and Pattillo's (1998) observation that the procedure applied above produces a bias in favor of finding significant jump coefficients. As the data themselves were used to identify the biggest jumps (through the signals method), the subsequent tests will tend to find that the jumps identified in the preceding section are unusually large. Thus, the *t*-tests performed on these regressions overestimate the statistical significance of the dummy variable coefficient α_2.

Generally, the variables specified as changes seem to be better captured by linear specifications. Considering the nature of the variables, this is a very plausible result, as it seems difficult to imagine, for instance, that

Table 13.2 Bivariate probit regressions for individual indicators

Variable	Coefficients for alternative specifications, z-statistics in brackets			Number of observations used
	Percentile (α_1)	*Dummy (α_2)*	*Dummy* (percentile threshold) (α_3)	
% change in M2/gross official reserves, yoy	0.776649 (2.791867)	n.a.	n.a.	461
M2/gross official reserves	1.619717 (1.960928)	0.714314 (2.490426)	n.a.	509
% change in exports in USD, yoy	−0.717464 (−2.156131)	0.592093 (2.099215)	n.a.	476
Real effective exchange rate, deviation from HP trend	−0.126836 (−0.407691)	0.375466 (1.585253)	n.a.	578
Budget balance, % of GDP	−1.330619 (−2.571187)	1.045350 (2.830427)	n.a.	360
Gross official reserves	−2.620193 (−5.981929)	1.209670 (4.903024)	n.a.	526
% change in gross official reserves, yoy	−0.137938 (−2.787291)	n.a.	n.a.	477
Current account, % of GDP	−1.283212 (−4.217102)	n.a.	n.a.	445

there is a threshold for the growth rate of exports that is associated with a jump in a country's propensity for a financial crisis. On the contrary, it seems extremely possible that the probability of a currency crisis decreases with every unit of an increase in the growth rate of exports. However, even for some level variables, such as the balances of the budget and the current account, the linear specifications seem to make more sense than the dummy variable specification.

A multivariate probit-based extension

As the results already established in this chapter are favorable for using specifications other than the dummy variable specification implicitly embedded in the signal approach, a multivariate probit model seems to be the natural extension of the analysis presented in the previous section. In particular, it is the most natural way to incorporate the information provided in different indicators at the same time. Table 13.3 shows the results of the multivariate probit model which simultaneously includes all variables. The functional form of variables was specified according to the

Table 13.3 Multivariate probit regression including all variables (included observations: 331)

Variable	Coefficient	Std. error	z-statistic	Prob.
C	−0.466919	0.689395	−0.677288	0.4982
BUD	−0.103423	0.369640	−0.279795	0.7796
C_A	−1.732702	0.517407	−3.348821	0.0008
CH_EXP	−0.698780	0.476502	−1.466477	0.1425
D_M2_RES	0.639023	0.227558	2.808179	0.0050
CH_M2_RES	−0.307973	0.376546	−0.817888	0.4134
CH_RES	−0.319054	0.407101	−0.783723	0.4332
REER_DEV	1.012057	0.504933	2.004337	0.0450
RES	−0.852282	0.516421	−1.650363	0.0989
Mean dep. var.	0.075529	S.D. dep. var		0.264643
S.E. of regression	0.237875	Akaike info. criterion		0.470253
Sum squared resid.	18.22025	Schwarz criterion		0.573634
Log likelihood	−68.82686	Hannan–Quinn criter.		0.511486
Restr. log likelihood	−88.61225	Avg. log likelihood		−0.207936
LR statistic (8 d.f.)	39.57077	McFadden R-squared		0.223281
Probability (LR stat.)	3.85E-06			

results of Table 13.2. In general, the variables were specified according to the specification with the highest t-ratio (with the right sign). Interestingly, some variables that were significant in the bivariate regressions are no longer statistically significant in the multivariate setting. Conversely, the real exchange rate variable becomes significant, thus confirming the relevance of considering the interaction of variables.

Based on the results reported in Table 13.3, insignificant variables were gradually eliminated, until the most parsimonious representation of the data was achieved. The final result of this procedure is shown in Table 13.4.

Table 13.4 Multivariate probit regression – 1-most parsimonious representation of data (included observations: 442)

Variable	Coefficient	Std. error	z-Statistic	Prob.
C	−0.423979	0.331248	−1.279943	0.2006
C_A	−1.720424	0.325591	−5.283995	0.0000
D_M2_RES	0.785602	0.200218	3.923730	0.0001
RES	−0.958195	0.400313	−2.393616	0.0167
Mean dep. var.	0.115385	S.D. dep. var.		0.319848
S.E. of regression	0.293606	Akaike info. criterion		0.597901
Sum squared resid.	37.75755	Schwarz criterion		0.634927
Log likelihood	−128.1362	Hannan–Quinn criter.		0.612505
Restr. log likelihood	−158.0712	Avg. log likelihood		−0.289901
LR statistic (3 d.f.)	59.87002	McFadden R-squared		0.189377

In the most parsimonious specification reported in Table 13.4, the real exchange rate variable is no longer statistically significant. Due to the lack of budget data for the early parts of the sample, the elimination of this variable strongly increases the number of observations in Table 13.4 in comparison to the specification which includes all variables. Possibly, the real exchange rate variable is no longer significant because of the introduction of the early years of transition. As most countries undertook sharp nominal and real devaluations of their currencies in the early transition period, deviations from the trend in the real effective exchange rate were probably less important than in more recent times.

The alternative specification, shown in Table 13.5, introduces country dummies. This step was motivated by the fact that the measurement of variables as percentiles of country-specific distributions does not take enough account of differences in riskiness across countries. In particular, this problem is most evident in countries which are characterized by a high level of macroeconomic stability throughout the whole sample period. Thus, in this case, the model reacts very sensitively with respect to a slight worsening of macroeconomic conditions from a very sound level to a still satisfactory level in absolute terms.

The introduction of country dummy variables – which have a similar effect as fixed effects in a panel estimate – removes this drawback. However, due to the limited number of observations per country, it was not possible to keep all country dummies simultaneously in the estimation equation. Thus, several specifications with different combinations of country dummies were investigated. It turned out that the statistical

Table 13.5 Multivariate probit regression – 2-most parsimonious representation of data (included observations: 442)

Variable	Coefficient	Std. error	z-statistic	Prob.
C	−1.731861	0.547115	−3.165440	0.0015
C_A	−2.033841	0.397123	−5.121433	0.0000
D_M2_RES	0.804060	0.272097	2.955053	0.0031
RES	−1.140742	0.552542	−2.064536	0.0390
BU	2.206178	0.449009	4.913439	0.0000
CZ	1.970408	0.437243	4.506434	0.0000
RO	2.489734	0.473733	5.255564	0.0000
SK	1.873702	0.442295	4.236321	0.0000
RU	2.018091	0.441452	4.571487	0.0000
HU	1.540617	0.446826	3.447910	0.0006
Mean dep. var	0.115385	S.D. dep. var.		0.319848
S.E. of regression	0.257466	Akaike info. criterion		0.471335
Sum squared resid.	28.63680	Schwarz criterion		0.563898
Log likelihood	−94.16500	Hannan-Quinn criter.		0.507844
Restr. log likelihood	−158.0712	Avg. log likelihood		−0.213043
LR statistic (9 d.f.)	127.8124	McFadden R-squared		0.404287

significance of certain country dummy variables was quite robust with respect to different combinations of country dummies in the specification. The same holds true for the economic variables in the model. Table 13.5 reports the specification inclusive of the statistically significant country dummies. Judged by AIC and Schwarz criterions, the specification including country dummies represents an improvement relative to the specification without country dummies.

Results

Expectation/prediction tables

For a probit model serving as an early-warning device, clearly the most important criterion to evaluate its performance is its predictive power. The standard evaluation method of a probit model is a comparison of its estimated crisis probabilities against realized results. For this purpose, a cut-off level for crisis probabilities has to be defined. In case the probab-

Table 13.6a Expectation/prediction table for specification 1 (included observations: 442; prediction evaluation (success cut-off, $C = 0.25$))

	Estimated equation			Constant probability		
	Dep = 0	Dep = 1	Total	Dep = 0	Dep = 1	Total
$P(\text{Dep} = 1) < = C$	354	27	381	391	51	442
$P(\text{Dep} = 1) > C$	37	24	61	0	0	0
Total	391	51	442	391	51	442
Correct	354	24	378	391	0	391
% correct	90.54	47.06	85.52	100.00	0.00	88.46
% incorrect	9.46	52.94	14.48	0.00	100.00	11.54
Total gain[1]	−9.46	47.06	−2.94			
Percent gain[2]	NA	47.06	−25.49			

	Estimated equation			Constant probability		
	Dep = 0	Dep = 1	Total	Dep = 0	Dep = 1	Total
$E(\# \text{ of Dep} = 0)$	353.06	38.01	391.07	345.88	45.12	391.00
$E(\# \text{ of Dep} = 1)$	37.94	12.99	50.93	45.12	5.88	51.00
Total	391.00	51.00	442.00	391.00	51.00	442.00
Correct	353.06	12.99	366.05	345.88	5.88	351.77
% correct	90.30	25.47	82.82	88.46	11.54	79.59
% incorrect	9.70	74.53	17.18	11.54	88.46	20.41
Total gain[1]	1.84	13.93	3.23			
Percent Gain[2]	15.91	15.75	15.83			

Notes
1 Change in '% correct' from default (constant probability) specification.
2 Percentage of incorrect (default) predictions corrected by equation.

Table 13.6b Expectation/prediction table for specification 2 (included observations: 442; prediction evaluation (success cut-off, $C = 0.25$))

	Estimated equation			Constant probability		
	Dep = 0	Dep = 1	Total	Dep = 0	Dep = 1	Total
$P(\text{Dep} = 1) <= C$	354	10	364	391	51	442
$P(\text{Dep} = 1) > C$	37	41	78	0	0	0
Total	391	51	442	391	51	442
Correct	354	41	395	391	0	391
% correct	90.54	80.39	89.37	100.00	0.00	88.46
% incorrect	9.46	19.61	10.63	0.00	100.00	11.54
Total gain[1]	−9.46	80.39	0.90			
Percent gain[2]	NA	80.39	7.84			

	Estimated equation			Constant probability		
	Dep = 0	Dep = 1	Total	Dep = 0	Dep = 1	Total
$E\ (\text{\# of Dep} = 0)$	361.90	29.41	391.31	345.88	45.12	391.00
$E(\text{\# of Dep} = 1)$	29.10	21.59	50.69	45.12	5.88	51.00
Total	391.00	51.00	442.00	391.00	51.00	442.00
Correct	361.90	21.59	383.49	345.88	5.88	351.77
% correct	92.56	42.33	86.76	88.46	11.54	79.59
% incorrect	7.44	57.67	13.24	11.54	88.46	20.41
Total gain[1]	4.10	30.79	7.18			
Percent gain[2]	35.49	34.81	35.15			

Notes
1 Change in '% correct' from default (constant probability) specification.
2 Percentage of incorrect (default) predictions corrected by equation.

ility of crisis exceeds the cut-off level, the model is considered to send a signal and vice versa. Using a cut-off level for the probability of crisis of 50 percent, the model issues hardly any wrong signals, but it misses all the crises in the sample. As shown in Table 13.6, lowering the cut-off level to 25 percent leads to a strong improvement in the model's ability to recognize crises in advance, while the number of wrong signals rises only moderately.

Similar to the statistical properties, the predictive power of specification 2 is somewhat better than specification 1.

Quadratic probability scores and the Pesaran–Timmermann test

While the results presented in Table 13.5 and Table 13.6 clearly look highly promising, the strong predictive power of both models is confirmed by the Pesaran–Timmermann test (P–T test) (1992) and the Quadratic Probability Score (QPS)[5] test. The QPS test measures the discrepancy between a realization, R_t, and the estimated probability, P_t (as predicted by the probit model) for the realization. In this case, R_t is either one (if there is a crisis period) or zero (in tranquil periods). The QPS can be computed according to the following formula:

$$QPS = \frac{1}{N} \sum_{t=1}^{N} 2(P_t - R_t)^2 \qquad (13.3)$$

As the formula shows, the values of the QPS are between zero and two, where zero is the best result. The QPS test statistics for both specifications are provided in Table 13.7. With values of 0.17 and 0.13, both speci-fications achieve markedly better scores than in comparable studies. For instance, Berg and Pattillo (1998) report quadratic probability scores in the order of 0.23 for their probit-based extensions of Kaminsky, Lizondo and Reinhart's (1998) model. Brüggemann and Linne's (2001) signal-approach-based early-warning composite indicator achieves a QPS of 0.297.

As the QPS test does not allow conclusions regarding the statistical significance of the results, I computed the P–T test in addition. The P–T test evaluates the predictions of a model (in this case, for a binary depend-ent variable) against the null hypothesis that the forecasts are no better than random guesses. As the squared P–T test statistics follow the Chi-Square distribution with one degree of freedom, it can be evaluated as a common Chi-Square test. As shown in Table 13.7, for both probit speci-fications the null hypothesis can be rejected with a very low error probab-ility for a cut-off level of 0.25. Only for a cut-off level of 0.5 does specification 1 not outperform random guesses. Thus, these results provide empirical support for 'first-generation crisis' models and 'genera-tion two-and-a-half' models.

Table 13.7 Quadratic probability score and Pesaran–Timmermann test

	Probit specification 1		Probit specification 2	
	Cut-off level		*Cut-off level*	
	25%	*50%*	*25%*	*50%*
QPS	0.170849	0.170849	0.129578	0.129578
Squared Pesaran–Timmermann test statistics	53.6	0.53	156.18	94.83
P-value of P-T-statistics	8.01E–011	0.47	7.49E–011	6.19E–011
Critical value for squared P-T-statistics, 5% significance level, 1 degree of freedom		3.841		

Individual country results

Having statistically confirmed the predictive power of the probit model specifications, the charts in Figure 13.1 show the development of predicted crisis probabilities of specification 2 against empirical observations for a cut-off level of 25 percent.

As expected from the statistical tests, the graphical inspection on an individual country basis confirms the good fit of the model's predictions with actual observations. In particular, the Hungarian, Romanian and Slovak crisis episodes can be very well explained. Nearly all currency crises are associated with repeated signals. The model's most recent predictions also appear to be rather plausible, predicting in general rather low probabilities for most countries, but with a pronounced rise in Hungary.

A possible drawback of the use of country dummy variables becomes evident for countries which did not experience crises: in these cases, the predicted crises probabilities appear unrealistically low – particularly in comparison to their peer group.

Finally, it would of course be very interesting to evaluate the out-of-sample forecasting abilities of the two model specifications proposed above. However, owing to the limited number of observations available per country, this type of analysis faces very tight limits. For instance, as no crisis occurred in the most recent time periods, it is impossible to check whether the model would have correctly predicted these events.

Conclusions

In this study, an early-warning model for currency crises was developed for a sample of quarterly data from 12 Central and Eastern European transition countries. After reviewing the relevant literature, it was shown that a number of indicators contain useful information for early-warning purposes when evaluated according to the signal approach. However, in addition to some known drawbacks inherent to the signal approach, the noise-to-signal ratios for some indicators reached a maximum at the extreme ends of the indicator-specific distributions. Thus, in a next step, the appropriateness of the signal appoach's underlying functional specification was investigated by means of bivariate regressions on one economic variable in different functional specifications.

On the basis of this analysis, two multivariate probit regressions with all statistically significant economic variables on a (0,1)-distributed crisis variable were estimated. For in-sample forecasts, the predictions of both model specifications proved to perform significantly better than random guesses as well as some comparable early-warning models. Overall, the model appears to track developments in individual countries rather well, although the importance of some variables seems to change over time. With respect to economic interpretations, the results of this study lend

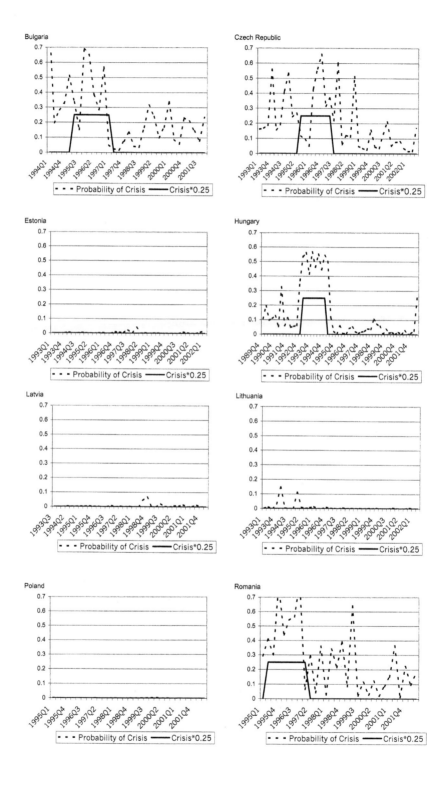

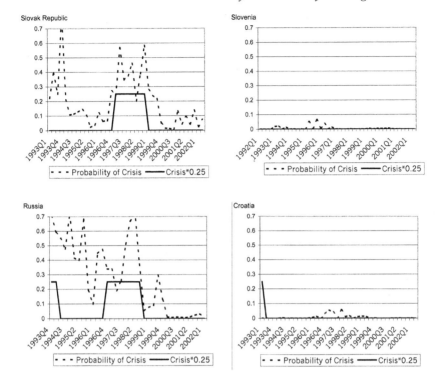

Figure 13.1 In-sample forecasts of specification 2 versus realizations.

support to 'first generation' and 'generation two-and-a-half crisis' models which heavily emphasise economic fundamentals in explaining currency crises.

Notes

1 An earlier version of this chapter was written during the author's stay at the Oesterreichische Nationalbank. The views expressed herein are those of the author and do not represent the position of Capital Invest Kapitalanlagege-sellschaft or of the Oesterreichische Nationalbank. I am particularly indebted to Alois Geyer and Jesus Crespo-Cuaresma for valuable methodological sugges-tions. This version also benefits from remarks from Axel F.A. Adam-Müller, Axel Jochem and from participants of the Oesterreichische Nationalbank's HVW-Diskussionsrunde and from participants of the Hungarian Nationalbank's Macroeconomic Workshop on Macroeconomic Policy Research in October 2002. I would also like to thank Andreas Nader for excellent statistical support and Susanne Steinacher for excellent language advice.

2 A few other episodes of sharp currency depreciation occurred during the sample period, but there are no data for the economic variables available.

3 This crisis episode was used in some, but not all, investigations as most, but not all, data are available for these time periods.

4 For instance, Berg and Pattillo (1998).
5 See Diebold and Rudebusch (1989).

References

Berg, Andrew and Pattillo, Catherine (1998) 'Are currency crises predictable? A test', IMF Working Paper WP/98/154. Washington, DC: International Monetary Fund.

Blanco, Herminio and Garber, Peter M. (1986) 'Recurrent devaluation and speculative attacks on the Mexican peso', *Journal of Political Economy*, 94: 148–166.

Brüggemann, Axel and Linne, Thomas (1999) 'How good are leading indicators for currency and banking crises in Central and Eastern Europe? An empirical test', Diskussionspapiere des Instituts für Wirtschaftsforschung Halle, Nr. 95 (April).

Brüggemann, Axel and Linne, Thomas (2001) 'Weiterentwicklung und Anwendung eines Frühwarnindikatorensystems zur Betrachtung und Bewertung von Finanzkrisen in EU–Beitrittskandidatenländern und ausgewählten Staaten Mittel- und Osteuropas', Sonderheft 4/2001, Institut für Wirtschaftsforschung Halle.

Bussiére, Matthieu and Mulder, Christian (1999) 'External vulnerability in emerging market economies: how high liquidity can offset weak fundamentals and the effects of contagion', IMF Working Paper 99/88. Washington, DC: International Monetary Fund.

Connolly, Michael B. and Taylor, Dean (1984) 'The exact timing of the collapse of an exchange rate regime and its impact on the relative price of traded goods', *Journal of Money, Credit and Banking*, 16: 194–207.

Diebold, Francis X. and Rudebusch, Glenn (1989) 'Scoring the leading indicators', *Journal of Business*, 62: 369–392.

Flood, Robert and Garber, Peter (1984) 'Collapsing exchange-rate regimes: some linear examples', *Journal of International Economics*, 17: 1–13.

Frankel, Jeffrey A. and Rose, Andrew K. (1996) 'Currency crashes in emerging markets: an empirical treatment', *Journal of International Economics*, 41: 351–366.

Goldstein, Morris, Kaminsky, Graciela L. and Reinhart, Carmen M. (2000) 'Assessing financial vulnerability, an early warning system for emerging markets', Institute for International Economics, June.

Kaminsky, Graciela L. (1998) 'Currency and banking crises: the key warnings of distress', Board of Governors of the Federal Reserve System, International Finance Discussion Papers, No. 629, October.

Kaminsky, Graciela L. and Reinhart, Carmen M. (1999) 'The twin crises: the causes of banking and balance-of-payments problems', *American Economic Review*, 89(3): 473–500.

Kaminsky, Graciela, Lizondo, Saul and Reinhart, Carmen M. (1998) 'Leading indicators of currency crises', *International Monetary Fund Staff Papers*, 45(1): 1–48, Washington, DC: International Monetary Fund.

Krkoska, Libor (2001) 'Assessing macroeconomic vulnerability in Central Europe', *Post-Communist Economies*, 13(1): 41–55.

Krugman, Paul (1979) 'A model of balance-of-payments crises', *Journal of Money, Credit, and Banking*, (11): 311–325.

Kumar, Manmohan S., Uma, Moorthy and Perraudin, William (2002) 'Predicting emerging market currency crashes', IMF Working Paper WP/02/7. Washington, DC: International Monetary Fund.

Morris, Stephen and Shin, Hyun Song (1998) 'Unique equilibrium in a model of self-fulfilling attacks', *American Economic Review*, 88(3): 587–597.

Obstfeld, Maurice (1994) 'The logic of currency crises', NBER Working Paper No. 4640.

Obstfeld, Maurice (1996) 'Models of currency crises with self-fulfilling features', *European Economic Review*, 40, April: 1037–1047.

Pesaran, M.H. and Timmermann, A. (1992) 'A simple nonparametric test of predictive performance', *Journal of Business and Economic Statistics*, 10: 461–465.

Sachs, J.D., Tornell, A. and Velasco, A. (1996) 'Financial crises in emerging markets: the lessons from 1995', *Brookings Papers on Economic Activity*, pp. 147–198.

Vlaar, Peter J.G. (2000) 'Currency crisis models for emerging markets', DNB Staff Reports 2000, No. 45. Amsterdam: De Nederlandsche Bank.

Weller, Christian E. and Morzuch, Bernard (2000) 'International financial contagion – why are Eastern Europe's banks not failing, when everybody else's are?', *Economics of Transition*, 8(3): 639–663.

Wu, Yih-Jiuan, Yen, Tzung-Ta and Chen, Pei-Wen (2000) 'Early warning system for currency crises: an empirical study of SEACEN countries', The South East Asian Central Banks (SEACEN) Research and Training Centre, Kuala Lumpur.

14 Institutional vulnerability indicators for currency crises in Central and Eastern European countries[1]

Dirk Effenberger

Introduction

In the 1990s, emerging markets around the globe experienced several full-scale currency crises with often devastating economic, social and political effects. A number of Central and Eastern European countries (CEECs) were among those affected. There was not only the much-reported crisis in Russia in 1998, but also the turmoils in Bulgaria (1997), Romania (1997), the Czech Republic (1997) and Hungary (1994–1995).

Early warning indicators play an important role in assessing a country's vulnerability to currency crises and in detecting financial market weaknesses. It has been standard practice to use a large number of macroeconomic variables in early-warning systems. Indicators providing information on the nature and quality of a country's institutional setting have rarely been included. It is only recently that attempts have been made, as in Ghosh and Ghosh (2002) and Mulder *et al.* (2002), to incorporate institutions more systematically into early-warning systems. But this has just started and a systematic way in which to model the crisis-relevant institutional setting has not yet been found.

Early-warning models focussing solely on CEECs have completely neglected institutional factors. Generally, empirical studies on CEECs are scarce, despite the special importance of detecting vulnerabilities not only in the run-up to the CEECs' membership of the EU, but especially later on during ERM II participation. This chapter takes a first step to fill the gaps by extending the macro- and micro-based discussion of currency crises to the institutional level, and by applying empirical analysis to the CEECs. The chapter is structured as follows. First, a look is taken at the theoretical approaches adopted to explain currency crises. This part particularly seeks to show the channels through which institutions can influence a country's vulnerability to currency crises. In the second section, an econometric logit model is used to examine the extent to which institutional factors can serve as early-warning indicators for currency crises in Eastern Europe. The final section outlines the conclusions that can be drawn and gives suggestions for further research.

Theoretical background

Existing models for explaining currency crises

The literature now covers three generations of currency crisis models. The first generation (Krugman 1979) attributes the outbreak of a currency crisis to fundamental economic weaknesses in an economy. Most of the early warning indicators found in empirical studies (such as current account deficit, level of reserves, budget deficit and so on) are based on the thinking of the first generation. A second generation of crisis models emerged in response to the crisis of the European Monetary System in 1992–1993. It stresses the existence of multiple equilibria (Obstfeld 1996), in which self-fulfilling expectations of market participants cause a currency crisis to erupt. For the development of early-warning indicators, the finding of the second generation is frustrating. For, if a crisis is triggered less by economic factors than by a sudden swing in expectations, which themselves are caused by stochastic sunspot events, then crises are almost unpredictable. In this case, indicators of the sentiment among market participants would be the only pointers that might provide warning of an impending crisis. A third generation of crisis models was developed in the wake of the Asian crisis. These models stress the importance of microeconomic weaknesses and seek to explain the coexistence of bank and currency crises (twin crises). Here, for the first time, institutions are explicitly considered as major determinants of a currency's vulnerability to crises. However, most of these models only look separately at individual institutions, such as the quality of banking supervision or the existence of a government safety net. As Chai and Johnston (2000) correctly noted, a country's institutional framework and its incentive structure as a whole have not yet been taken into account for assessing crisis potentials in any systematic way.

While the currency crises experienced so far in the CEECs are often regarded as typical first-generation crises (Dabrowski 2001; Schardax 2002), it must be said that microeconomic factors also played a part in some cases. Arvai and Vincze (2000) rightly point out that this applies particularly to the crises in Romania, Bulgaria and Russia. The last two can, in fact, be seen as twin crises as described by the third-generation models, owing to the parallel emergence of both a banking and a currency crisis. A word of warning, though, against categorising the crises in the CEECs too strictly: this would suggest that elements of other types of crisis are absent, and that is not usually the case in reality. Consequently, the institutional influences set out in this chapter are regarded as complementary – not alternative – explanations for currency crises.

How institutions can affect a country's vulnerability to currency crises

The ways in which institutions affect economic outcomes are highly complex. A detailed theoretical analysis would go far beyond the scope of this chapter, especially if the investigation is not restricted to individual institutions but covers the entire institutional setting that is assumed to be crisis-relevant. Nonetheless, an outline of channels through which institutions have a major influence on a country's vulnerability to crises is given below. These channels could then serve as the starting point for the development of a more comprehensive model to explain the ways in which institutions can affect countries' vulnerability to crises.

Channel 1: institutions determine the credibility of policymakers' decisions

In second-generation crisis models, a lack of credibility and the problem of time inconsistency are important factors for explaining currency crises. Certain institutional arrangements can increase credibility and, in this way, convince the markets that policy makers will keep exchange rates stable.[2] The probability that economic and political shocks will lead to a currency crisis is then lower. A currency board is generally considered to have such an effect (for example, Irwin 2001; Ghosh *et al.* 2000). Castren and Takalo (2000) and Pitt (2001) show that further institutional aspects, such as the implementation and application of rules on corporate governance, and the quality of banking supervision, can increase currency credibility.

Channel 2: institutions reduce information asymmetries

Information asymmetries and the related problems of moral hazard and adverse selection are known to be a systemic problem in financial markets (especially in emerging markets and transition economies such as the CEECs). It is also known that the existence of such agency problems implies that lenders will lend less than they otherwise would. Pursuing this idea further, Mishkin (2001) sees a financial crisis as 'a disruption to financial markets in which adverse selection and moral hazard problems become much worse'. If, then, a financial crisis represents an escalation of the agency problem (Mishkin finds the escalation itself to be primarily due to economic disruptions), it is necessary to ask which institutions are helpful in reducing the extent of the underlying information asymmetries and in better absorbing exogenous disruptions. Such institutions are already known from neo-institutional financial theory, but have so far seldom been analysed as explanatory factors for currency and financial crises. Relevant institutions include: first, extensive transparency and disclosure requirements for companies; second, prudential banking and financial supervision; and third, broad corporate governance rules. The latter aim not only to secure the rights of shareholders and creditors, but also to establish clear and binding property rights.

Channel 3: institutions produce information asymmetries

Moral hazard is also a problem when it results in excessive risk-taking by borrowers (overborrowing).[3] Large losses on loans in the future may then bring a boom (previously partly fuelled by the effects of moral hazard) to an abrupt end. McKinnon and Pill (1996, 1999) show that government guarantees, ineffective banking supervision and different types of exchange rate regime can, in this way, lead to overborrowing and, hence, increase the risk of a crisis. This tendency is amplified if the economy is being liberalised at the time, which is quite obviously now the case in the CEECs.

The three institutional channels are therefore particularly relevant for the CEECs. It should be noted, though, that the channels do not affect a country's vulnerability separately, but in interaction with one another. For example, while an exchange rate regime anchored in law, such as a currency board, can raise the credibility of a fixed currency peg, it may also inspire overly strong confidence in the stability of the exchange rate and hence contribute to overborrowing. In such cases, from a theoretical point of view, the net effect on the country's vulnerability to crisis is not clear.

Even though the above arguments focus on institutions, economic and political developments are still considered to have a significant influence on countries' vulnerability to crisis. The interplay of economic and institutional factors is of elementary importance as institutions can either help a country to better absorb the effects of economic or political shocks (channels 1 and 2), or they can themselves influence the economic development by encouraging overborrowing (channel 3). This means that, in the following empirical analysis, both economic and institutional variables have to be incorporated into an early-warning system.

An empirical early-warning system with institutional indicators

Below, this chapter sets out to examine whether various institutional factors can serve as indicators of Eastern European countries' vulnerability to currency crises.

Methodology

The empirical study uses monthly data from 11 transition countries from January 1993 to July 2002. The sample includes the ten CEE accession countries (Bulgaria, the Czech Republic, Estonia, Hungary, Latvia, Lithuania, Poland, Romania, the Slovak Republic and Slovenia) as well as Russia.

The study estimates a multivariate logit model with a binomial crisis variable and pooled data. Specifically, the model asks whether a crisis will occur during alternative periods of time (18-month and 24-month crisis windows are checked).

The crisis variable is specified as follows:[4] first, as in Goldstein *et al.* (2000), an indicator is constructed that measures the pressure in the forex market (FMPI).

$$\text{FMPI}_t = \frac{\Delta e_t}{e_{t-1}} - \frac{\sigma_e}{\sigma_R} * \frac{\Delta R_t}{R_{t-1}}$$

where e = local currency/euro

R = domestic reserves

σ_e = standard deviation of Δ_e/e

σ_R = standard deviation of Δ_R/R.

Contrary to the usual procedure, the exchange rate to the euro is taken, not the rate against the dollar. The euro seems more appropriate, not only in light of the close trade ties with the euro-area countries, but especially because the CEECs are likely to participate in the ERM II quite soon. In this study, a crisis is said to exist when the FMPI exceeds the country-specific mean by more than two standard deviations. Hence:[5]

$$c_{it} = \begin{cases} 1 & \text{if FMPI*}_{it} > \overline{\text{FMPI}}_i \\ 0 & \text{otherwise,} \end{cases} \quad \text{where } \overline{\text{FMPI}}_i = 2{,}0 * \sigma_{\text{FMPI}_i} + \mu_{\text{FMPI}_i}$$

In order to define the dependent variable of the logit model, it is also necessary to model the forecast horizon of, initially, 18 months. For this, each observation y_{it} is allotted to one of the two following periods:[6]

- *Pre-crisis period.* This is the period immediately before a crisis. The duration of the pre-crisis period is determined by the choice of forecast horizon: in the present case, it is 18 months.
- *Tranquil period.* This is the period not followed by a currency crisis within the 18-month forecast horizon.

Since the early-warning indicators are meant to recognise a crisis within the forecast horizon, the crisis variable $C_{i,t}$, which refers to a point in time, is transformed into a forward looking variable, $Y_{i,t}$. In the empirical analysis this is done by giving the dependent variable the value 1 during a pre-crisis period and the value 0 during a tranquil period. Hence:

$$Y_{i,t} = \begin{cases} 1 & \text{if } \exists k = 1....18 \text{ s.t. } C_{i,t+k} = 1. \\ 0 & \text{otherwise} \end{cases}$$

In a logit model the coefficient of the explanatory variables – the early-warning indicators – is calculated by maximising the log-likelihood function LL, which in a panel model looks as follows:

$$LL = \sum_{t=1}^{T} \sum_{i=1}^{N} [\ln Y_{it}\{F(\beta' X_{it})\} + (1 - Y_{it})\ln(1 - F(\beta' X_{it}))],$$

where F is the cumulative distribution function of the indicators and β the vector of its unknown coefficients. Both institutional and (several) macro-economic control variables serve as indicators. Since other crisis models (for example, Bussiére and Fratscher 2002; Schnatz 1998) and our own tests give no clear advice on whether to include country-specific fixed effects or random effects, here it was refrained from using them. Furthermore, Demirgüç-Kunt and Detragiache (1998) show that in a fixed effects logit estimation, countries in which there was no crisis during the sample period are automatically excluded from the panel. This would ultimately lead to important information being disregarded.[6]

In order to be able to assess the forecast quality of an early-warning system with institutional indicators, first a model is estimated that consists solely of economic indicators. This model then serves as a benchmark model in the further analysis. In a second step, various institutional factors are introduced into the model.

The macroeconomic benchmark model

Studies that focus on Eastern Europe should provide a particularly good guide in selecting the economic variables (Schardax 2002; Brüggemann and Linne 2002, Krkoska 2000). In order to obtain an appropriate benchmark model, however, it is necessary that the indicators also prove to be significant in this particular case and that they provide good prediction results. Consequently, the selection and specification of individual variables has been modified slightly compared with the original literature. The economic indicators included in the empirical tests are described below; for detailed information about data sources see Appendix A14.1. Table 14.1 gives the results of the benchmark model with a forecast horizon of 18 months (results of alternative regressions are available upon request).

Real exchange rate overvaluation [RERV]

Both in theory and in empirical studies, an overvaluation of the real exchange rate is regarded as one of the main determinants of a currency crisis. The degree of real overvaluation is calculated here as the percentage deviation of the real exchange rate from its long-term trend.[8] Thus a negative deviation represents a real overvaluation. In this study a real

Table 14.1 Results of the macroeconomic benchmark model

Variable	Coefficient	Std. error	z-statistic	Prob.
C	−2.8619	0.2114	−13.5404	0.0000
RERV_DEV	−0.0401	0.0089	−4.5106	0.0000
EXDEBT	1.0209	0.1798	5.6784	0.0000
MONEY_CHANGE	0.0173	0.0035	4.8743	0.0000
CREDIT	0.2070	0.0321	6.4400	0.0000
CA_AVE	−0.1114	0.0179	−6.2228	0.0000
Akaike info. criterion	0.9771			
McFadden R^2	0.1829			
Obs. with Dep = 0	734	Total obs.		1,016
Obs. with Dep = 1	282			

overvaluation proves to be highly significant according to the *z*-statistic and thus confirms the results of other studies.

Current account deficit [CA_AVE]

First-generation models consider a large current account deficit to be one of the main causes of the outbreak of a currency crisis. In the present study, too, a current account deficit (expressed as a percentage of GDP) proved to be significant, thus confirming the results obtained by Schardax (2002), among others.[9] Other current account indicators, such as various specifications of a country's export growth, prove, on the other hand, to be non-significant, and in some cases even show a non-expected sign. It is therefore not possible to confirm the results of Brüggemann and Linne (2001), who rate export growth as a very important factor in the early recognition of crises in Eastern Europe.

Liquidity ratio [MONEY]

Tests here also confirm the high informative value of the ratio of M2 to forex reserves (using the 12-month percentage change) in assessments of the vulnerability of the CEECs.

External debt [EXDEBT]

If a country has high external debt and if, in addition, a large proportion of the debt is in the form of short-term credit, then the country, according to the third-generation models, is at greater risk of a combined banking and currency crisis. This risk potential is proxied here by the ratio of short-term external debt to domestic forex reserves.[10] This indicator is also included as significant in the regression equation.

Lending and deposit rates [SPREAD]

According to Brüggemann and Linne (2001), banks in the CEECs often respond to an increase in non-performing loans by widening their profit margins. One indicator to measure the profit margin is the difference between (or alternatively the quotient of) the lending and deposit rates. A widening of this spread should therefore point to growing problems in the banking sector and, according to the third-generation models, to greater vulnerability to currency crises. In the present case, however, the spread proved to be non-significant (results are not shown here).

Domestic credit [CREDIT]

Prior to crises, excessive expansion of domestic credit volume can frequently be observed. As mentioned on page 315, this may be a result of liberalisation and/or the provision of additional government guarantees. In any case, when credit expands excessively, the number of non-performing loans rises. This tends to increase the vulnerability of the banking system and, hence, according to the twin-crises theory, the vulnerability to currency crises. In this test, too, the ratio of credit volume to GDP proves to be a useful indicator for predicting crises in Eastern Europe.

In order to evaluate the overall goodness of fit and thus the real forecast quality of the model, use was made of so-called prediction or classification tables (Table 14.2). These summarise the estimated probabilities ($P(Dep)$) and the actual observations (Dep). Since the logit model provides probability values between 0 and 1, it is necessary to define a cut-off level, above which an estimated probability is interpreted as a crisis. Strictly speaking, it is necessary to weigh up economic costs and benefits before

Table 14.2 Prediction table 'Benchmark Model 18 Month' (cut-off level $C=0.25$)

	Estimated equation		
	Dep = 0	*Dep = 1*	*Total*
$P(Dep = 1) < = C$	471	83	554
$P(Dep = 1) > C$	263	199	462
Total	734	282	1,016
% correct	64.17	70.57	65.94
% incorrect	35.83	29.43	34.06

setting this threshold. For, the lower the threshold, the more crisis signals the model will report and the better the model will predict actual crises. However, it will also signal a crisis more often if no crisis occurs during the forecast period (type II error). A high threshold has the opposite effect: type II errors are then less frequent, but the number of crises that the model fails to signal is high (type I error). It is therefore necessary to compare the costs caused by type I errors (costs of a crisis not prevented by precautionary measures) with those caused by type II errors (costs of unnecessary economic policy measures).[11]

In this case, a cut-off level of 25 per cent was found to be appropriate as it correctly predicts a relatively high portion of the actual crises (70.57 per cent) and does not give too many false alarms. Using a forecast horizon of 18 months, the cut-off level of 25 per cent was also found to be optimal in Bussiere and Fratscher (2002).

The results indicate that past crises in Eastern Europe can be largely explained by the macroeconomic factors used in the benchmark model. This is consistent with the findings of Dabrowski (2001), Brüggemann and Linne (2001) and Schardax (2002), though the economic indicators found to be significant may differ somewhat. The forecast quality of the institutions-based model developed further on in this chapter must be measured against these results.

An institutions-based early-warning model

A descriptive view

How has the institutional environment of the CEECs changed since the transition process began? Going by various institutional indicators of the European Bank for Reconstruction and Development (EBRD), for example, the quality of the institutional setting in the 11 CEECs considered here has improved continuously since 1993 (Figure 14.1). This would suggest that the improved institutional setting is one reason why there have recently been fewer currency crises in the CEECs. The empirical relevance of this supposition is tested below using logit analysis.

Results of category-specific tests

Some of the institutions considered to be crisis-relevant are now tested for their ability to function as early-warning indicators for currency crises in the CEECs (details of the indicators are given in Appendix A14.3). It must be remembered that linear functional relationships between two or more explanatory variables (multicollinearity) can occur more frequently here than in the case of economic variables. This is particularly true of indicators with similar content. In order to avoid multicollinearity causing large standard errors of the estimated coefficients, institutional indicators are

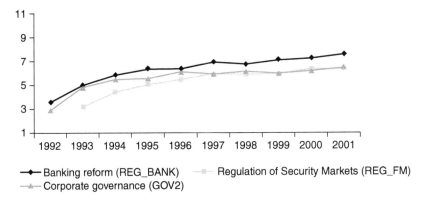

Figure 14.1 Quality of the institutional setting in CEECS. (Source: EBRD (Transition Report), own calculation).

Note
The scale used by the EBRD [1 to 4+] has been transformed to a scale ranging from 1 to 11, where 11 is the best value. The chart shows the index value as an average of the countries considered. The indicators are explained in Appendix 14.1. The parenthesis refers to the indicator's name as used in the regression.

allocated to certain categories. Owing to the possibility of high multi-collinearity within a category, indicators of the same category are tested separately in different regressions. As the exchange-rate regime indicators are not constructed as ordered ranking indices, but as binary dummy variables, this does not apply to them. In the following, the results are described with regard to each institutional category.

EXCHANGE RATE REGIMES

Most theoretical crisis models assume – at least implicitly – that a fixed rate regime is in place. The IMF has found, however, that almost 50 per cent of all currency crises between 1975 and 1996 happened in flexible rate systems (IMF 1997: 91). Currency crises also occurred in CEECs within such systems. The outstanding example is Bulgaria, where the crisis in 1997 paradoxically marked not the end, but the beginning of a fixed rate regime. Although the IMF finding was partly due to the fact that officially promulgated exchange rate policies often differ from those pursued in practice, it nonetheless suggests that the type of regime plays a more varied role in the eruption of currency crises than is usually assumed. In light of this, it is difficult to understand why most empirical early-warning systems do not take the type of exchange rate regime into account. In this study the currency systems of the CEECs are assigned to the following four categories: currency board (CB), conventional fixed (FIXED), crawling peg (CP) and flexible rates (FLEXIBLE).[12] As far as possible, a regime change is reflected in the month in which it occurred (see Appendix A14.2 for the assignment of the CEECs' exchange rate system to the categories). For each category, a 0/1 dummy variable was constructed. It is important to note that all dummies cannot be included simultaneously in the logit model as the dummy variable of one sub-category is always a perfect linear function of the other dummy variables. If they were all included, the regression equation could not be estimated owing to perfect multicollinearity. The Regime 1 and 2 regressions therefore test different dummy variations (Table 14.3).

Table 14.3 shows that either only CB and FLEXIBLE or only CP and FIXED are significant in the regression equation. The two variations are therefore tested separately in the Regime 3 and 4 regressions. The results are clear: if all other indicators remain constant, the vulnerability of the CEECs to currency crises is reduced significantly with a currency board or a flexible regime (despite the Bulgarian crisis). The existence of a conventional fixed rate regime or a crawling peg raises the vulnerability. The results also indicate that the vulnerability of fixed rate regimes depend on their institutional setting. A conventional fixed rate regime (whether a formal or a *de facto* regime) raises vulnerability, whereas a fixed rate regime with a strict institutional anchor – such as a currency board – reduces it significantly.[13] Both the dummy variations CB/FLEXIBLE and CP/FIXED can therefore be used as early-warning indicators. In the remainder of this study the dummies CP and FIXED are included in the early warning system.[14]

It is important to warn against applying these results directly to a situation in which the Eastern European currencies are more strongly linked with the euro in ERM II. Formally, this would be tantamount to a conventional fixed exchange rate as defined in the IMF classification. But ERM II would have much greater credibility than the type of fixed rate system described here as vulnerable, owing to the bilateral intervention obligations.

To understand the results of the indicators shown in Table 14.4 it is important to know that, for all indicators, higher index values correspond to a better institutional setting, except for ECON_FREE where the interpretation is somewhat different (see page 325). Detailed information for each indicator is given in Appendix A14.3.

REGULATORY AND SUPERVISORY SYSTEM

Earlier in the chapter (page 314), the quality of banking supervision and financial market regulation was also said to affect the crisis vulnerability of currencies. Two indicators published by the EBRD are available for empir-

Table 14.3 Logit model with exchange rate regimes

	REGIME							
	1		2		3		4	
	dF/dx	|z|	dF/dx	|z|	dF/dx	|z|	dF/dx	|z|
RERV_DEV	−0.037	4.014***	−0.037	4.014***	−0.037	3.967***	−0.038	4.010***
EXDEBT	1.065	5.570***	1.065	5.570***	1.030	5.401***	1.077	5.631***
MONEY	0.022	5.755***	0.022	5.755***	0.021	5.646***	0.021	5.728***
CREDIT	0.182	4.848***	0.182	4.848***	0.177	4.741***	0.169	4.963***
CA_AVE	−0.106	5.323***	−0.106	5.323***	−0.112	5.690***	−0.111	5.883***
CB	−0.973	3.830***			−0.833	3.554***		
FIXED	−0.349	1.389	0.973	3.830***			1.104	5.336***
CP	−1.195	5.142***	0.624	2.231**			0.778	3.553***
FLEXIBLE			−0.221	0.879	−1.019	5.207***		
Pseudo R² (McFadden)	0.211		0.211		0.209		0.210	
Obs.					1,016			
Crises					282			
Non-crises					734			

Notes
*, **, ***denote significance at the 10, 5 and 1 per cent level, respectively. All economic variables are significant at the 1 per cent level in each regression.

Table 14.4 Logit model with institutional indicators

	INST							
	1		2		3		4	
	dF/dx	|z|	dF/dx	|z|	dF/dx	|z|	dF/dx	|z|
RERV_DEV	−0.033	3.121***	−0.033	3.308**	−0.045	4.351***	−0.009	4.349**
EXDEBT	1.077	4.518***	0.572	1.922**	0.801	3.271***	0.223	3.289**
MONEY	0.027	6.727***	0.024	5.428***	0.023	4.656***	0.004	5.836***
CREDIT	0.101	1.954**	0.257	6.003***	0.151	3.585***	0.039	4.592***
CA_AVE	−0.075	3.892***	−0.075	3.972**	−0.077	3.628***	−0.020	5.151**
CP	1.166	4.089***	1.882	5.239***	1.080	3.653***	0.269	4.941**
FIXED	0.703	3.165***	0.414	1.665	0.971	3.631***	0.232	3.324**
REG_BANK					−0.348	3.061***	−0.114	2.300*
REG_FM	−0.659	6.270***	−0.656	5.588**				
GOV1	0.646	5.573***			−0.079	0.717		
GOV2			−0.065	0.687			0.158	0.733
LAW_ORDER	0.273	1.666*						
LAW_WB			−0.711	1.292				
COR_WB							0.342	0.791
COR_IT					0.011	0.067		
ECON_FREE			−2.340	6.357**	−1.714	4.795***	−0.340	4.699**
Pseudo R^2 (McFadden)	0.246		0.263		0.232		0.233	
Obs.	954		906		798		1,016	
Crises	282		256		238		282	
Non-crises	672		650		560		734	

Notes
*, **, *** denote significance at the 10, 5 and 1 per cent level, respectively.

ical analyses in this field (REG_BANK; REG_FM). In the regressions shown in Table 14.4, both indicators REG_BANK, which measures the quality of banking supervision and regulation (for example, convergence with BIS standards), and REG_FM, which indicates the quality of financial market regulation (for example, convergence with IOSCO standards) prove to be significant at least at the 5 per cent level. Hence a more efficient regulatory and supervisory system seems to reduce the probability of currency crises in the CEECs and can be considered as an important factor for financial market stability in these countries.

CORPORATE GOVERNANCE

Here, too, there is a choice of two indicators published by the EBRD: GOV1 and GOV2 depict the degree of implementation of corporate governance rules and their effectiveness. Both indicators prove to be non-significant in most of the regression. GOV2 is significant in one regression, but has a non-expected sign. Furthermore, GOV2 turns out to react very sensitively to even little changes in model specification, which suggest that the indicator is not reliable in signal crisis vulnerability. The weak performance of governance indicators might be partly explained by the fact that capital market financing still plays only a small role in many CEECs. Bank intermediation tends to be the main channel for financing – which is also the reason why currency crises affected banking rather than the corporate sector whenever they were preceded by microeconomic disruptions (for example, Romania, Bulgaria and Russia). In the near future, though, capital market financing will become much more important in most CEECs, so effective corporate governance can be expected to take on greater significance in determining the crisis vulnerability of the CEECs in the coming years.

RULE OF LAW

In assessing the quality of the legal setting in a country, use is made of indicators that measure the quality of the legal system (LAW_ORDER and LAW_WB) as well as indicators of the degree of corruption (COR_WB and COR_IT). However, none of these indicators proves to be significant in any of the regressions. Furthermore the corruption as well as the LAW_ORDER indicator shows a non-expected sign. One explanation for these counterintuitive results might be the difficulty of an indicator to give a correct picture of such a hidden phenomenon as corruption.

INDEX OF THE INSTITUTIONAL SETTING VERSUS DEGREE OF LIBERALISATION

In addition to the variables for individual institutions, an indicator of the entire institutional setting in each country is also tested. One that is frequently used is the index of economic freedom (ECON_FREE) published by the Heritage Foundation. Here, this index proves significant in the assessment of the CEECs' vulnerability, but the sign is initially unexpected. Since declining index values indicate an improving situation, the negative significance found in this case suggests that the better the institutional environment, the greater the vulnerability to crisis. This conclusion, however, probably springs from a misinterpretation of the index that is sometimes found in the relevant literature. The index depicts the institutional setting in an economy mainly by measuring the degree of liberalisation and privatisation. In the case of a currency crisis, the results therefore indicate that the probability of a currency crisis in the CEECs increases, the more liberalised they are. This, too, may be surprising at first sight, as domestic liberalisation and privatisation are right at the top of the CEECs' economic policy agenda. But the result becomes understandable if the 'degree of liberalisation' is applied to international capital flows, for instance. Economies that are closed in this respect are obviously less vulnerable to an outflow of international capital and hence to currency crises. This result is also consistent with the empirical work of Demirgüç-Kunt and Detragiache (1998), who conclude that, in a weak institutional environment, banking crises are also more likely to occur in liberalised economies. But these results definitely do not permit the conclusion that liberalisation is inherently detrimental to prosperity. They point instead to certain risks, which have to be considered carefully when opening up an economy.

The results of the category-specific analysis are divided. Some of the institutional variables prove to be useful as indicators of vulnerability in the CEECs. Others turn out to be non-significant. Apart from the fact that the latter are indeed irrelevant, this result may be partly due to a general snag with institutional indicators: they seek to measure qualitative factors in quantitative terms. Institutional indicators in general have several weaknesses.

- Most of the selected indicators do not portray exactly those factors that are considered crisis-relevant. Many contain an assessment of other institutional arrangements as well. GOV1, for example, does not focus solely on corporate governance, but also provides information on privatisation and subsidy policy.
- Certainly, the nature and quality of institutional arrangements change only slightly over time. Nonetheless, indicators whose values are determined just once or twice during the observation period of almost ten years give an inadequate picture of the institutional setting in an economy. This seems to be especially true for the CEECs, as the institutional setting is subject to more frequent changes than is the case in other countries. It is striking, for example, that the World Bank indicators (COR_WB, GOV_WB and LAW_WB), which were determined only twice during the period, prove to be non-significant.

• Indicators based on annual data give a much more accurate picture of the institutional environment. But even they can only reflect changes *ex post* (for example, the introduction of new corporate governance regulations), when they are next published. And the (linear) transformation into monthly figures still does not fully overcome this deficiency.

Quality of the institutions-based early-warning model

In order to be able to compare an early-warning system comprising both institutional and economic variables with the purely economic benchmark model, four institutional early-warning indicators that have proved to be significant (CP, FIXED, ECON_FREE and REG_FM) are added to the benchmark model. The results of this hybrid model are then compared with those of the benchmark. Table 14.5 shows the full results of the hybrid model. All indicators are significant at the 1 per cent level and show the expected sign. In order to obtain information on the quality of the model, a prediction table is calculated (Table 14.6). A comparison of the results there with those in Table 14.2 shows that the hybrid model is able (a) to predict for more crises correctly (82.6 per cent), and (b) to recognise tranquil periods (68.4 per cent) as such more often. The

Table 14.5 Prediction table 'Hybrid Model 18 month' (cut-off level, $C = 0.25$)

	Estimated equation		Total
	Dep = 0	*Dep = 1*	
$P(Y_{it} = 1) < = C$	502	49	551
$P(Y_{it} = 1) > C$	232	233	465
Total	734	282	1,016
% correct	68.39	82.62	72.34
% incorrect	31.61	17.38	27.66

Table 14.6 Prediction table 'Hybrid Model 24 Month' (cut-off level $C = 0.35$)

	Estimated equation		Total
	Dep = 0	*Dep = 1*	
$P(\text{Dep} = 1) < = C$	493	61	554
$P(\text{Dep} = 1) > C$	161	301	462
Total	654	362	1,016
% correct	75.38	83.15	78.15
% incorrect	24.62	16.85	21.85

forecast quality of the hybrid model is thus definitely better than that of the purely economic model.

A test is now run to see whether the forecast horizon can be lengthened without impairing the forecast quality of the hybrid model. Table 14.7 shows the results of the hybrid model for a forecast period of 24 months.[15] The quality is obviously better than that of the benchmark model for 18 months (Table 14.2). The hybrid model also outperforms a purely economic model with a forecast horizon of 24 months (Table 14.7). It can therefore be said that with an institutions-based model it is possible to lengthen the forecast period and at the same time improve the forecast quality compared with a purely economic model. Even if compared to the 18-month hybrid model, the 24-month hybrid model performs better. In Appendix A14.4, the result of the 24-month hybrid model is illustrated graphically for each country.

How does the 24-month hybrid model perform in comparison with models of other studies? Tables 14.8–14.11 show the prediction results obtained by Schardax (2002), Bussiere and Fratscher (BF) (2002), Kaminsky *et al.* (KLR) (1998) and Goldman Sachs (GS).[16] It can be seen that the model developed here (Table 14.7) outperforms the KLR and GS models, as it correctly signals more crises and correctly recognised tranquil periods

Table 14.7 Prediction table 'Benchmark Model 24 Month' (cut-off level, $C = 0.35$)

| | *Estimated equation* | | *Total* |
	Dep = 0	*Dep = 1*	
$P(\text{Dep} = 1) < = C$	463	112	575
$P(\text{Dep} = 1) > C$	191	250	441
Total	654	362	1,016
% correct	70.8	69.06	70.18
% incorrect	29.2	30.94	29.82

Table 14.8 Prediction table 'Schardax'

| | *Estimated equation* | | *Total* |
	Dep = 0	*Dep = 1*	
$P(Y_{it} = 1) < = C$	270	16	268
$P(Y_{it} = 1) > C$	36	32	68
Total	306	48	354
% correct	88.24	66.67	85.31
% incorrect	11.76	33.33	14.69

Sources: Schardax (2002).

Table 14.9 Prediction table 'BF-Model'

	Estimated equation		Total
	Dep = 0	Dep = 1	
$P(Y_{it} = 1) < = C$	1,536	129	1,665
$P(Y_{it} = 1) > C$	238	177	415
Total	1,774	306	2,080
% correct	86.58	57.84	82.36
% incorrect	13.42	42.16	17.64

Source: Bussiere and Fratzscher (2002:17).

Table 14.10 Prediction table 'KLR-Model'

	Estimated equation		Total
	Dep = 0	Dep = 1	
$P(Y_{it} = 1) < = C$	1,834	200	2,034
$P(Y_{it} = 1) > C$	704	298	1,002
Total	2,538	498	3,036
% correct	72.26	59.84	70.22
% incorrect	27.74	40.16	29.78

Source: Bussiere and Fratzscher (2002:17).

Table 14.11 Prediction table 'GS-Model'

	Estimated equation		Total
	Dep = 0	Dep = 1	
$P(Y_{it} = 1) < = C$	543	50	593
$P(Y_{it} = 1) > C$	279	98	377
Total	822	148	970
% correct	66.06	66.22	66.08
% incorrect	33.94	33.78	33.92

Source: Bussiere and Fratzscher (2002:17).

more often. With regard to the 'Schardax' and 'BF' models, the results are not as clear-cut. Our model recognises more crises correctly than the others, but fewer of the tranquil periods. This means that the costs due to error type I are lower, whereas type II costs are higher in the hybrid model. Ultimately, a decision in favour of one or other system will depend on an assessment of the respective economic costs and benefits.

Conclusions and suggestions for further research

The type and the quality of institutions influence the vulnerability of currencies to crises. The study aimed to shed light on this connection, using three channels through which institutions particularly influence a country's vulnerability to crises. This connection was used to derive institutional early-warning indicators. Various institutional indicators were tested for significance using a multivariate logit model with panel data. It was found that, above all, the type of exchange rate regime, the quality of the regulatory and supervisory setting, and the degree of liberalisation of an economy significantly influence the probability of a currency crisis. In addition, an early-warning system that included these factors provided much better forecast quality than a purely economic benchmark model. The inclusion of institutional indicators in the early warning system also made it possible to extend the forecast horizon without impairing the forecast quality. In fact, the quality was still higher than that of purely economic models for the same or a shorter forecast period and of the hybrid model with an 18-month prediction horizon. However, it should be emphasised that institutional indicators are not a substitute for macroeconomic variables used in traditional early-warning models; rather, they play an important complementary role in assessing crisis vulnerability.

These findings have far-reaching economic policy implications for the CEECs. First, they underscore the importance of having appropriate institutions in the CEECs, especially during an ERM II membership. Second, a longer forecast horizon enables policymakers to take pre-emptive measures at an earlier stage. This should be more successful in preventing crises or at least in limiting their negative outcomes once they occur.

Despite the relatively good results, the study raises a number of questions that could be interesting for further research.

1   A basic problem of qualitative indicators is that they do not depict the relevant conditions precisely. It therefore seems sensible to continue the search for suitable institutional indicators in order to obtain a more exact picture of the environment that is relevant to the outbreak of a currency crisis.

2   The good in-sample performance of the hybrid model needs to be confirmed in corresponding out-of-sample tests. Schardax (2002) points out that this could be problematic in the case of the CEECs as reliable data are available for only a limited period and there have been no crises in these countries since the end of the observation period. However, out-of-sample tests could be based on other Eastern European countries where crises have occurred (such as Ukraine or Moldova), or on countries outside Eastern Europe that have comparable structures (such as Turkey).

3   The quantitative methodology needs to be refined in order to better

capture the complex effects of institutions as well as their interaction with each other and with economic variables. By using so-called binary recursive trees, Ghosh and Ghosh (2002) have put forward very promising proposals.

4   Although this study focuses on currency crises in particular, it can be presumed that the results are also applicable to more broadly defined financial crises, meaning that institutional indicators might also be helpful in detecting weaknesses in financial markets and/or the banking sector in CEECs.

This study is therefore a first step towards greater use of institutional early-warning indicators for currency crises in the countries of Eastern Europe.

Appendix

A14.1 Sources of data

Variable	Source[1]
Nominal exchange rate	IFS line 00RF
Exports	IFS line 70_D
Current account deficit[2]	WMM
Money M2	IFS line 34 + line 35
Reserves	IFS line IL_D
Deposit rate	IFS line 60L
Lending rate	IFS line 60P
Consumer price index	IFS line 64; IFS line 64H (for Euroland)
Short-term external debt[2]	BIS 'statistics on external debt' – series G
Nominal GDP[2]	IFS line 99b (EBRD for Russia)

Notes
1 IFS = IMF International Financial Statistics; WMM = World Market Monitor (DRI–WEFA).
2 Annual or quarterly available data are linearly interpolated into monthly data.

A14.2 *Classification of exchange rate regimes*

	1993	1994	1995	1996	1997	1998	1999	2000	2001	2002
Bulgaria	4	4	4	4	1	1	1	1	1	1
Czech Republic	2	2	2	2	4	4	4	4	4	4
Estonia	1	1	1	1	1	1	1	1	1	1
Hungary	2	2	3	3	3	3	3	3	4	4
Latvia	4	4	2	2	2	2	2	2	2	2
Lithuania	4	1	1	1	1	1	1	1	1	1
Poland	3	3	3	3	3	3	3	4	4	4
Romania	4	4	4	4	4	4	4	4	4	4
Russia	2	4	2	3	3	4	4	4	4	4
Slovakia	2	2	2	2	2	4	4	4	4	4
Slovenia	4	4	4	4	4	4	4	4	4	4

Notes
Based on the new IMF classification the meaning of the codes is: 1 (CB) = currency board; 2 (FIXED) = conventional fixed peg, exchange rate within horizontal bands; 3 (CP) = crawling peg, exchange rate within crawling bands; 4 (FLEXIBLE) = managed floating, independent floating. For CEEC regimes prior to 1999, the classification has been facilitated by the work of Zhou (2002). Although the table shows annual data, the indicator was adjusted in a month in which a regime change occurred.

A14.3 Source and description of institutional data

Indicator[1]	Description[2]	Scale[3]	Source
Exchange rate regime	See Appendix 14.1	0/1 Dummy	IMF (Annual Report on Exchange Arrangements and Exchange Restriction)
Corporate governance			
GOV1[4]	Provision for corporate governance; protection for shareholder rights. The indicator covers extensiveness and effectiveness of law settings.	[1–11]	EBRD (Law in Transition): 'Company law'
GOV2	Corporate governance, e.g. corporate control mechanism; enterprise restructuring (e.g. enforcement of bankruptcy legislation).	[1–11]	EBRD (Transition Report): 'Governance and enterprise reform'
Regulatory and supervisory system			
REG_BANK	Effectiveness of prudential supervision; convergence with BIS standards; functioning of banking competition; degree of interest rate liberalisation.	[1–11]	EBRD (Transition Report): 'Banking sector reform'
REG_FM	Quality of securities laws; effectiveness of regulation in security markets; convergence with IOSC standards; quality of settlement procedure; protection of minority shareholders.	[1–11]	EBRD (Transition Report): 'Security markets and non-bank financial institutions'
Rule of law			
LAW_ORDER	Strength and impartiality of the legal system.	[0–6]	ICRG (International Country Risk Guide)
LAW_WB[4]	Rule of law	[0–5]	World Bank[5]
COR_WB[4]	Index of corruption	[0–5]	World Bank[5]
COR_IT	Index of corruption	[0–10]	Transparency International
Index of economic freedom			
ECON_FREE	Degree of liberalisation and privatisation; efficiency of regulation	[1–5]	Heritage Foundation

Notes

1 All institutional indicators – with the exception of the regime indicators – are annual data and were linearly interpolated into monthly data.

2 See data source for more detailed description.

3 Higher index values correspond to a better institutional setting, except for ECON_FREE. The EBRD scale [1–4+] has been rescaled to [1–11]; the World Bank scale [−2.5–2.5] has been rescaled to [0–5].

4 These indicators were not available for the entire sample period or were not updated frequently. Therefore values have also been used as proxies for periods they are not explicitly meant for.

5 http://www.worldbank.org/wbi/governance/govdata2001.htm.

A14.4 *Country-specific results of the hybrid model*

The figures show the crises probabilities ρ (where $0 \leqslant \rho \leqslant 1$) for each country estimated by the hybrid model with a 24-month forecast horizon from January 1994 to June 2002. The pre-crises periods are demarcated. The horizontal line represents the cut-off level $c = 0.35$, above which an estimated probability is interpreted as a crisis.

Bulgaria

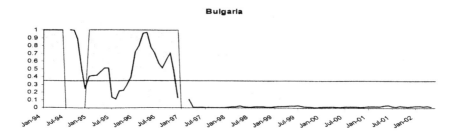

Czech Republic

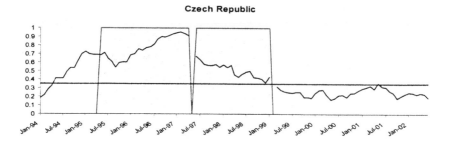

Estonia

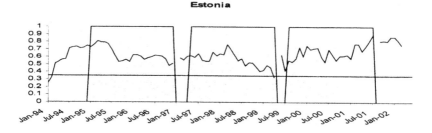

Hungary

Latvia

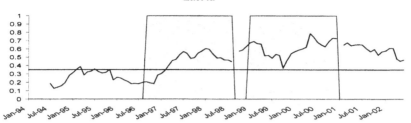

Lithuania

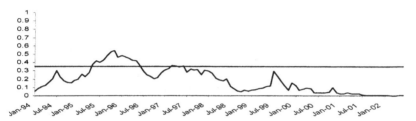

Poland

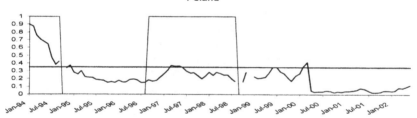

Rumania

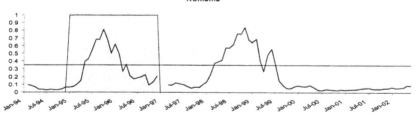

Slovakia

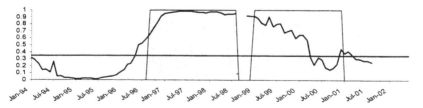

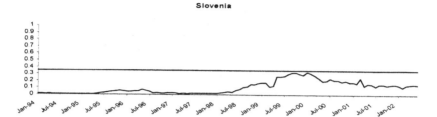

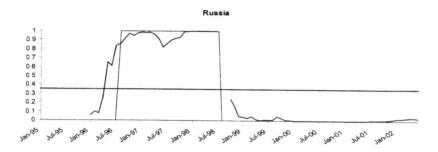

Notes

1 This chapter was originally presented at the 24th SUERF Colloquium in Tallinn, Estonia, 12–14 June 2003.
2 One way to show this theoretically is by introducing political or reputational cost in second-generation models.
3 Such moral-hazard-producing effects are sometimes attributed to the IMF's financing policy (see, for example, Liane and Phillips 2000); but here the focus is solely on national institutions.
4 For various approaches to empirically identify crises, see Abiad (2003).
5 Although the threshold of 2.0 seems somewhat arbitrary, the list of crises obtained by this methodology is in line with the crises described in Arvai and Vincze (2000), Brüggemann *et al.* (2000) and Schardax (2002). Furthermore, the threshold chosen is within the range of thresholds (1.5–3.0) usually used in empirical studies.
6 Observations during crisis months are omitted as the values of economic variables are then subject to erratic fluctuations and may distort the results.
7 Countries that never experienced a crisis in our sample are Lithuania and Slovenia.
8 The real exchange rate was calculated by the nominal exchange rates of local currencies to the euro (ecu for periods prior to 1999) adjusted for relative consumer prices. The trend was specified as, alternatively, log, linear and exponential; the best fit (highest R^2) was then selected on a country-specific basis
9 To remove the sometimes strong volatility of the current account deficit on a monthly basis, the 12-month moving average of the ratio was used.
10 The ratio is also known as the Greenspan–Guidotti rule. According to this, the ratio should not be above 100 per cent.
11 See Bussiere and Fratscher (2002) for a detailed discussion on this topic.
12 Based on the classification of exchange rate regimes used by the IMF since 1999.

13 This does not mean, however, that currency boards can be regarded as invulnerable – as the example of Argentina shows.

14 The IMF classification used in this chapter makes some allowance for the fact that the actual exchange rate regime may differ from the officially announced policy, but it would be interesting to test the early-warning quality of exchange rate indicators based solely on *de facto* policies.

15 As Bussiere and Fratscher (2002) show, the optimal cut-off level increases when the forecast horizon is lengthened. Hence, for the 24-month hybrid model, the cut-off level has been raised to 35 per cent.

16 Results from the GS model are from Bussiere and Frutscher (2002). For GS model specifications, see Ades *et al.* (1998).

References

Abiad, A. (2003) 'Early warning systems: a survey and a regime switching approach', IMF Working Paper 03/32, Washington, D.C.

Ades, A., Masih, R. and Tenengauzer, D. (1998) 'GS-Watch: a new framework for predicting financial crises in emerging markets', Goldman Sachs, December.

Arvai, Z. and Vincze, J. (2000) 'Models of financial crises and the transition economy experience', in Institut für Wirtschaftsforschung Halle (eds), *Financial Crises in Transition Countries – Recent Lessons and Problems Yet to Solve*, Halle: Institute of Economic Research, pp. 7–43.

Brüggemann, A. and Linne, T. (2002) 'Are the Central and Eastern European transition countries still vulnerable to a financial crisis? Results from the Signal Approach', (IWH) Discussion Paper No. 57, Halle.

Brüggemann *et al.* (2000).

Bussiere, M. and Fratscher, M. (2002) 'Towards a new early warning system of financial crises', ECB Working Paper No. 145, Frankfurt.

Castren, O. and Takalo, T. (2000) 'Capital market development, corporate governance and the credibility of exchange rate pegs', in ECB Working Paper No. 34, Frankfurt.

Chai, J. and Johnston, R.B. (2000) 'An incentive approach to identifying financial system vulnerability', IMF Working Paper 00/211, Washington, DC.

Dabrowski, M. (2001) 'The episodes of currency crises in the European transition economies', CASE-Report No. 40.

Demirgüç-Kunt, A. and Detragiache, E. (1998) 'Financial liberalization and financial fragility', IMF Working Paper 98/83, Washington, DC.

Ghosh, A.R., Guide, A.M. and Wolf, H. (2000) 'Currency boards: more than a quick fix?', *Economic Policy* 31: 269–321.

Ghosh, S. and Ghosh, A. (2002) 'Structural vulnerability and currency crises', IMF Working Paper 02/09, Washington, DC.

Goldstein, M., Kaminsky, G.L. and Reinhart, C.M. (2000) *Assessing Financial Vulnerability – An Early Warning System for Emerging Markets*, Washington, DC: Institute for International Economics.

IMF (1997) *World Economic Outlook – IMF* (October), Washington, DC.

Irwin, G. (2001) 'Currency board and currency crises', in University of Oxford, Department of Economics – Discussion Paper Series No. 65, Oxford.

Kaminsky, G., Lizondo, S. and Reinhart, C.M. (1998) 'Leading indicators of currency crises', IMF Staff Paper 45, No. 1: 1–48.

Krkoska, L. (2000) 'Assessing macroeconomic vulnerability in Central Europe', EBRD Working Paper No. 52, London.

Krugman, P. (1979) 'A model of balance of payment crises', *Journal of Money, Credit, and Banking*, 11: 311–325.

Liane, T. and Phillips, S. (2000) 'Does IMF financing result in moral hazard?', IMF Working Paper 00/168.

McKinnon, R. and Pill, H. (1996) 'Credible liberalizations and international capital flows: the overborrowing syndrome', in T. Ito and A.O. Krueger (eds), *Financial Deregulation and Integration in East Asia*, Chicago: University of Chicago Press, pp. 7–24.

McKinnon, R. and Pill, H. (1999) 'Exchange rate regimes for emerging markets: moral hazard and international overborrowing', *Oxford Review of Economic Policy*, 15(3): 19–38.

Mishkin, F.S. (2001) 'Financial policies and the prevention of financial crises in emerging market countries', NBER Working Paper 8087.

Mulder, C., Perrelli, R. and Rocha, M. (2002) 'The role of corporate, legal and macroeconomic balance sheet indicators in crisis detection and prevention', IMF Working Paper 02/59, Washington, DC.

Obstfeld, M. (1996) 'Models of currency crises with self-fulfilling features', *European Economic Review*, 40: 1037–1047.

Pitt, A. (2001) 'Sustaining fixed exchange rates: a model with debt and institutions', IMF Working Paper 01/27, Washington, DC.

Reininger, T., Schardax, F. and Summer, M. (2001) 'The financial system in the Czech Republic, Hungary and Poland after a decade of transition', Deutsche Bundesbank Discussion Paper 16/01, Frankfurt.

Schardax, F. (2002) 'An early warning model for currency crises in Central and Eastern Europe', ONB Focus on Transition 1/2002: 108–124.

Schnatz, B. (1998) 'Makroökonomische Bestimmungsgründe von Währungsturbulenzen in emerging markets', Deutsche Bundesbank Discussion Paper 3/98, Frankfurt.

Zhou, J. (2002) 'Empirical studies on exchange rate policies in transition economies', Aachen, Germany: Shaker.

15 Financial stability and the design of monetary policy[1]

Alicia García Herrero and Pedro del Río[2]

Introduction

The relation between monetary policy and financial stability has been long debated, but there is still no clear consensus on how one affects the other and, in particular, whether there are trade-offs or synergies between them. This issue clearly deserves further attention, since it could help devise arrangements and policy responses to promote both monetary and financial stability.

We look into the role of the monetary policy design, in particular the choice of the central bank objectives and the monetary policy strategy, in fostering financial stability. More specifically, we assess empirically whether countries whose central banks focus narrowly on price stability are less prone to financial instability. In the same vein, we test which monetary policy strategy (exchange-rate based, money or inflation targeting), if any, best contributes to financial stability.

The motivation for focusing on monetary policy design as a potential factor contributing to financial stability stems from the encouraging growth of literature on the role of institutions and policy design. The rationale behind financial stability is that an appropriate policy design should foster a better credit culture and an effective market functioning. The design of monetary policy should be particularly important since the central bank has a natural role in ensuring financial stability, as argued by Padoa-Schioppa (2002)[3] or Schinasi (2003), and has almost always been involved in financial stability, directly or indirectly.[4]

Existing literature

What do we mean by financial stability?

Financial stability is an elusive concept to define, as proven by the fact that practically no explicit definition exists and most often the opposite concept, financial instability, is generally used.[5] The main reason for this difficulty is that 'stability' could, at first sight, be associated with a lack of volatility, while volatility is not necessarily bad for financial markets.[6]

The literature has focused mainly on the extreme realization of financial instability, the occurrence of a financial crisis, in particular a banking crisis. According to Mishkin (1996), a financial crisis is a disruption to financial markets in which adverse selection and moral hazard become much worse, so that financial markets are unable to efficiently channel funds to those who have the most productive investment opportunities. A very different definition of a financial crisis is given by Bordo *et al.* (1995) where a real – as opposed to pseudo – financial crisis is a flight to cash because of the perception that no institution will supply the necessary liquidity. These different definitions reflect the opposing theories concerning the causes of financial crises: asymmetric information in the former and monetary developments in the latter. In any case, both definitions include the danger of a failure of financial and/or non-financial firms.

Apart from the realization of banking crises, there are a number of broader – but also less precise – definitions of financial instability. Bernanke and Gertler (1990) concentrate on financial fragility, as a situation in which potential borrowers have low wealth relative to the size of their projects. Such a low insider's stake increases the agency problems and exacerbates frictions in the credit market (balance sheet channel). Finally, financial instability is sometimes used synonymously to asset price volatility, which takes prices far away from their fundamental level, finally reversing suddenly and producing a 'crash' (Bernanke and Gertler 2000; Crockett 2000). The difficulty with these broader definitions is how to determine when financial fragility or asset price volatility is so large that it creates system-wide instability.

In this chapter, we are interested in the more specific definition of financial instability (banking crisis) since the role of central banks is more widely accepted than for asset price volatility or financial fragility in general.[7] The IMF (1998) has coined a definition that focuses on this: namely, banking crises are situations in which actual or potential bank runs or failures induce banks to suspend the internal convertibility of their liabilities or which compel the government to extend assistance to banks on a large scale. Another more general definition of banking crisis, by Gupta (1996), is a situation in which a significant group of financial institutions have liabilities exceeding the market value of their assets, leading to portfolio shifts or to deposit runs and/or the collapse of financial institutions and/or government intervention. Under such circumstances, an increase in the share of non-performing loans, an increase in financial losses and a decrease in the value of the bank's investments cause solvency problems and may lead to liquidations, mergers and restructuring of the banking system. Both definitions, and others which focus on the banking system, boil down to the description of a banking crisis. However, the complexity of these definitions indicates that no single quantitative indicator can proxy a banking crisis accurately enough. An additional problem is the lack of comparable cross-country data to construct such an indicator (that is, the share of non-performing loans or risk-weighted capital to asset ratios). This is why the empirical literature has opted for identifying banking crises as events, expressed through a binary variable, constructed with the help of cross-country surveys (Lindgreen *et al.* 1996; Caprio and Klingebiel 2003). This will be our approach as well.

Determinants of financial stability

The economic literature has mostly concentrated on the macroeconomic determinants of financial stability and, to a lesser extent, on the financial-sector determinants. Among the former, the main ones are: low growth or recessions (Frankel and Rose 1998); too-high real interest rates (Demirgüç-Kunt and Detragiache 1998), large capital inflows or outflows in the case of emerging countries (Calvo 1997), and shocks to inflation or to the price level (Bordo and Murshid 2000; English 1996; Hardy and Pazarbasioglu 1999). The last one is, in part, related to the way monetary policy is conducted, in so far as monetary policy aims at price stability, and thus it is related to our research objective. Among the latter are: excessive credit growth[8] (Gavin and Hausmann 1996; Sachs *et al.* 1996), low levels of liquidity in the banking system (Calvo 1997), and currency mismatches in emerging countries' banking systems (Chang *et al.* 2000).

Less attention has been paid to the impact of institutional and policy design, with some exceptions; in particular the relevance of a well-functioning legal system (La Porta *et al.* 1998), an explicit and limited deposit insurance scheme (Demirgüç-Kunt and Detragiache 2000), and the risks of financial liberalization if good quality regulation and supervision are not in place (Demirgüç-Kunt and Detragiache 1998).

In this chapter, we focus on the design of monetary policy and, in particular, the central bank objectives and strategy. The existing literature on monetary policy design has concentrated on issues other than financial stability (mainly price stability but also output stabilization). There is some empirical analysis, albeit still scarce, on the reverse issue, namely the impact of financial instability, and in particular of banking crises, on a country's monetary policy. In particular, García Herrero (1997) and Martinez Peria (2000) find empirical evidence that money demand is stable in the long term in countries having experienced systemic banking crises. García Herrero (1997) also reviews seven case studies of the impact of banking crises on monetary policy, including the strategy and instruments. To the best of our knowledge, no study is available on the reverse causality.

The impact of the monetary policy design on financial stability is related to the very much debated question of the relation between price stability and financial stability. The economic literature is divided as to whether there are synergies or a trade-off between them. Among the arguments for a trade-off, Mishkin (1996) argues that a high level of inter-est rates, necessary to control inflation, negatively affects banks' balance sheets and firms' net financial worth, especially if they attract capital inflows, contributing to over-borrowing and increasing credit risk, as well as to currency mismatches if foreign capital flows are converted into domestic-currency denominated loans. Cukierman (1992) states that infla-tion control may require fast and substantial increases in interest rates, which banks cannot pass as quickly to their assets as to their liabilities, increasing the interest rate mismatch and, thus, market risk. Among the arguments for synergies between price and financial stability, Schwartz (1995) states that credibly maintained prices provide the economy with an environment of predictable interest rates, contributing to a lower risk of interest rate mismatches, minimizing the inflation risk premium in long-term interest rates and, thus, contributing to financial soundness. From this view of price stability almost being a sufficient condition for financial stability, some more cautious supporters of the 'synergies' view argue that price stability is a necessary condition for financial stability but not a suffi-cient one (Padoa-Schioppa 2002; Issing 2003).

It is important to note that the focus of this chapter is not so much the relation between the inflation outcome and the occurrence of banking crises but, rather, the importance that the central bank gives to price stability in its objectives, strategy and banking crises. This will obviously depend on how central banks understand the relation between financial and price stability.

Purpose of the study

This chapter builds upon the existing literature on how to foster financial stability, focusing on the role of monetary policy design. In particular, it empirically assesses whether the choice of the central bank objectives and the monetary policy strategy affects financial stability.

Monetary policy design can have important implications for financial stability. Central banks are providers of immediate liquidity and respons-ible for the smooth functioning of the payment system and that of the transmission mechanism. The central bank is also in charge of price stability and, sometimes, output stabilization, both relevant for financial stability, as we shall see later. Monetary policy objectives and strategies are the main tools the central bank has to perform its functions, so they will necessarily influence financial stability, directly or indirectly.[9] In fact, if they lead to a too-lax monetary policy, inflation will tend to be more volatile. Positive inflation surprises redistribute real wealth from lenders to borrowers and negative inflation surprises have the opposite effect. Redis-tribution in either direction – although even more so in the latter case – may provoke bankruptcy, with serious implications for the quality of banks' loans. In addition, a very tight monetary policy leading to very low inflation levels and, thereby, very low interest rates, makes cash holdings more attractive than interest-bearing bank deposits. This may induce dis-intermediation and, thereby, financial instability. On the other hand, if tight monetary policy does not manage to bring down inflation and real interest rates remain high, financial stability might be at risk. Sharp increases in real interest rates may also have adverse effects on the balance sheets of banks and even bring about a credit crunch. While the potential implications of monetary policy design on financial stability are clear from these arguments, the above arguments offer no a priori on which mone-tary policy design is best.

The central bank objectives and the way to achieve them – the mone-tary policy strategy – are crucial elements of the monetary policy design, determining the focus of the central bank and the stance of its monetary policy. We shall, thus, concentrate on these two aspects in our empirical study.

Since their creation, central banks have moved back and forth in the objectives they have targeted. In the last decade, the trend has been towards narrowing down the central bank objectives to a single one, price stability, or at least to a set of objectives considered to be compatible with price stability (see Figure 15.1). However, many other situations still exist: some central banks aim at price stability together with other – in principle non-compatible – objectives; others do not include price stability in their list of objectives or do not have such things as declared objectives.

The trend towards objectives with a greater focus on price stability is explained by the conviction – based on theoretical and empirical liter-ature – that it contributes to price stability while not much is known about

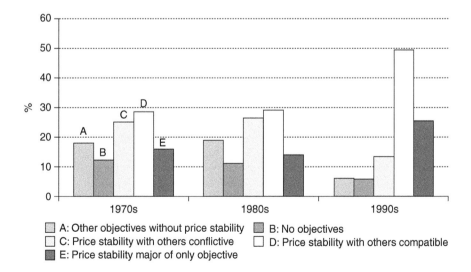

Figure 15.1 Distribution of central bank objectives by decades.

its effect on financial stability. This is partly due to the lack of consensus on whether synergies – or a trade-off – exist between price and financial stability. If synergies exist, a central bank focusing on price stability should also be able to promote financial stability. However, if there is a trade-off, a central bank with multiple objectives should be able to take this trade-off better into account.

As regards the choice of the monetary policy strategy, there is a wealth of literature on the advantages and disadvantages of each strategy for achieving price stability, but hardly any evidence exists on how it affects other potential objectives, such as financial stability. While this might be the right way to choose the strategy – it avoids using one single instrument for too many objectives – it is still interesting to know whether there are spill-overs from the choice of the strategy towards financial stability.

When compared with the central bank objectives, the reasons why the choice of the monetary policy strategy can affect financial stability are less clear-cut. Perhaps the most debated case is the exchange-rate based strategy, but even in this case there is no consensus in the empirical literature (Domaç and Martinez Peria 2000). There is, thus, hardly any a priori on which strategy can better contribute to financial stability.

A historical overview of the monetary policy strategies (based on our data sample) adopted over time shows that the number of central banks with direct inflation targeting strategies has surged from close to zero at the end of the 1980s to over 50 today (see Figure 15.2). The number of central banks targeting a monetary aggregate has also grown albeit less rapidly; they number almost 40 today. On the contrary, central banks with an exchange rate anchor number less than 40 today from over 50 in the mid-1990s. This corresponds to a certain degree of disenchantment with

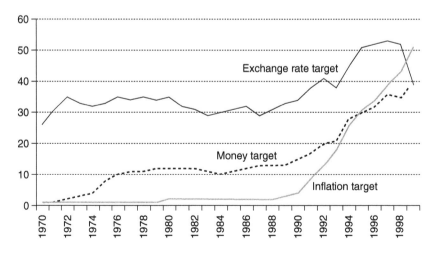

Figure 15.2 Evolution of monetary policy strategies (number of countries).

fixed exchange rates, after the Mexican and Asian crises. The information available also shows that there is a growing number of central banks with more than one target in its monetary policy strategy. This could be understood as a growing preference for a certain degree of flexibility.

Finally, we want to control for the location of regulation and supervision responsibilities. Being a central bank task in several countries, it could influence central bank behaviour, and even the choice of objectives and strategy. As for the objective variables, there is no consensus view on which location (central bank or separate agency) is better to avoid banking crises, although many more efforts have been devoted to this question than to monetary policy design.

Variable definitions and data

We now describe the definitions chosen for our dependent variable, financial instability, and the objective variables (mainly, the central bank objectives and the monetary policy strategy) as well as the source of the data. Finally, the choice of the control variables is also briefly described. A detailed account of the sources and construction of all variables can be found in Appendix 15.1.

Among the different definitions given to financial instability, we concentrate on its extreme realization, namely a crisis event. We choose banking crises, and not currency or twin crises, as banks are the major player in most countries' financial systems and are most directly influenced by the central bank.

To account for banking crises, we use existing different surveys of crisis events and identify periods of systemic and non-systemic crises according to the information and chronology of episodes provided by Caprio and Klingebiel (2003) and Domaç and Martinez Peria (2000). We choose these surveys because they are the most comprehensive and updated ones. We check for potential inconsistencies between the two, and when they exist, we support our choice with other sources (such as IMF staff reports and financial news). We also follow the authors' definition of a systemic banking crisis as the situation when a large part of the banking system is affected by the crisis, in terms of the number of banks, the share of assets or the amount of bank capital lost. Table A15.2 offers a list of crisis events, its classification into systemic and non-systemic episodes and their duration.

We now move to the objective variables, describing the monetary policy design. The first summarizes the type of central bank objectives into an index, which follows the approach of Cukierman *et al.* (1992) although with some transformations following Mahadeva and Sterne (2000). The index takes a larger value the more narrowly the central bank statutory objectives focus on price stability. More specifically, it takes the value of 1 when price (or currency) stability is the only, or the main, goal. It takes the value of 0.75 when the price stability objective is accompanied by – in principle non-conflicting – objectives, such as financial stability. It takes the value of 0.50 when price stability goes together with other – in principle conflicting – objectives, such as economic growth and/or employment creation. In particular, this is the case when objectives such as employment or growth are stated separately without being qualified by statements such as 'without prejudice to monetary or price stability'. Finally, the index takes the value of 0.25 when there are no statutory objectives and 0 when there are statutory objectives but none of the existing goals is price stability.[10] This index is constructed with the information provided by Cukierman *et al.* (1992), Mahadeva and Sterne (2000) and Cukierman *et al.* (2002) in the case of accession countries. The list of objectives for each country is available roughly by decades, so we need to assume the index to be constant during a decade with some exceptions for which more information could be found on changes in central bank objectives, particularly in more recent periods.

The second objective variable is the monetary policy strategy, which consists mainly of the choice of the intermediate variable to achieve the central bank objectives. Strategies are thus classified into exchange rate targeting, monetary and direct inflation targeting. Three dummy variables are created, one for each strategy, which take the value of one when the central bank uses that specific strategy and zero otherwise. It should be noted that these dummies are not mutually excludable since there are countries whose central banks use two different monetary strategies in parallel. One example is that of Spain during the last years of participation in the ERM, when it had both an exchange rate and direct inflation targeting. The euro-zone is also classified as having two strategies (monetary and inflation).

To construct these dummies, we use information on the monetary policy strategies used by 94 central banks from a survey carried out by the Bank of England in 1999 (Mahadeva and Sterne 2000). The survey provides a chronology of the adoption and removal of explicit targets and monitoring ranges for the exchange rate, monetary aggregates and inflation in the 1990s, including strategies adopted before the 1990s and remaining until this decade. Periods with different strategies which ended before 1990 are missing. Since our empirical exercise covers the period 1970 to 1999, we had to complement the data with information from other sources. Regarding the exchange rate strategy, we use existing classifications of exchange rate regimes, namely, Reinhart and Rogoff (2002), Berg *et al.* (2002) and Kuttner and Posen (2001), to extract those countries which had exchange rate anchors during the 30 year period of interest for us. Data for monetary and direct inflation targeting are complemented with information in Kuttner and Posen (2001) and Carare and Stone (2003).

Finally, to control for the location of regulation and supervision, we include a dummy which takes the value of one when the central bank is in charge and zero otherwise. This variable is taken from a survey conducted by the IMF in 1993, found in Tuya and Zamalloa (1994), where all member countries were asked to provide information on which institution was responsible for banking regulation and supervision in their respective countries. Unfortunately, no panel information is available on this issue.

Based on the previously reviewed literature, we include two types of control variables in our estimations, macroeconomic and financial. Among the macroeconomic variables, we take inflation, the real interest rate, the ratio of net capital flows to GDP, the growth of real GDP and the level of real GDP per capita, the last as a proxy of a country's institutional framework. The rationale behind the latter is that poorer countries tend to have more inefficient legal systems, as well as a weaker enforcement of loan contracts and deficient prudential regulations.[11]

While the a priori sign of inflation on the likelihood of banking crisis events is positive, it should be noted that a protracted period of price stability has been argued to be problematic if it leads to an inappropriate discounting of economic risks due to myopic growth expectations in countries which are not used to price stability.[12] As for real interest rates, high levels should hamper financial stability, but too-low levels (namely negative) are also problematic since they reduce banks' margins and discourage savings. Large capital inflows may be detrimental in as far as they are intermediated by the banking system and converted into rapid loan growth. Outflows, on the other hand, can bring about crises by depriving banks of foreign financing and also by heightening the expectation of a meltdown, leading to bank runs. The remaining macroeconomic variables (real economic growth and per capita GDP) have a clearer expected sign. First, higher growth should reduce the likelihood of a banking crisis through lower non-performing loans and higher savings and, thereby, bank deposits. In the same vein, a higher per capita GDP, reflecting better institutions, should reduce banks' uncertainty regarding the operating environment, particularly their right to recover their assets.

A number of financial variables are also included as control variables. In particular, the growth of domestic credit to the private sector, the banks' currency mismatch, measured by the ratio of their foreign liabilities to foreign assets, and the liquidity of the banking system, measured by the ratio of cash to banks assets, to capture the banks' ability to deal with potential deposit runs. From the literature review, the first two variables have a positive a priori sign, and the third has a negative one.

Some stylized facts

Before embarking on the regression analysis, we look at the data properties (see the descriptive statistics and the correlation matrix in Tables A15.3 and A15.4) and show some stylized facts.

Measured by the number of crisis events worldwide, there appears to be a substantial increase in financial instability in the 1980s, when compared

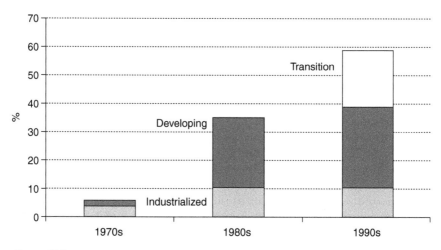

Figure 15.3 Distribution of crises by decades and countries (percentage of total crises).

to the 1970s levels, particularly in emerging countries, a trend which has continued in the 1990s (see Figure 15.3). The latter is due mainly to the larger number of crises that occurred in transition countries in this decade and to the additional, albeit marginal, increase in the number of crises in emerging countries.

In order to assess whether the design of monetary policy can affect the likelihood of banking crisis events, we conduct a few preliminary exercises before embarking on the econometric analysis. We first look at the number of crises which have occurred in the period of study (1970–1999) for different country groups, on the basis of their central bank objectives. Figure 15.4 (light-coloured column) shows that those countries whose central bank objectives do not include price stability experienced the lowest number of crises, followed by those with no statutory objectives and those whose central banks narrowly focus on price stability as the single (or main) objective. On the other hand, those countries with objectives compatible a priori with price stability suffered the largest number of crises.

Since these stylized facts may be biased by the number of observations in each group, we use conditional probabilities to assess under which type of central bank objectives the probability of a banking crisis is higher (Figure 15.4, dark column). As before, those countries whose central bank objectives do not include price stability have the lowest probability that a banking crisis may occur, followed closely by those with no statutory objectives and those who narrowly focus on price stability. The highest probability of crisis is again for those countries whose central banks aim at price stability with other a priori compatible objectives, but followed closely by those with a priori conflictive objectives.

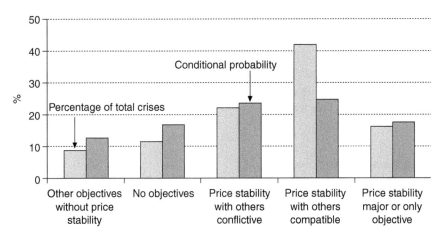

Figure 15.4 Distribution of crises by central bank objectives (percentage of total crises and conditional probability of crises).

We now look at the distribution of countries on the basis of their monetary policy strategies and crisis events during the same period. Figure 15.5 (light column) shows that countries whose central banks target the exchange rate are the ones with the highest percentage of crisis events, followed by those under monetary targeting. However, these stylized facts are clearly biased by the larger number of observations of exchange rate targeting and, to a lower extent, monetary targeting. The conditional probabilities (dark column in Figure 15.5) actually show that the

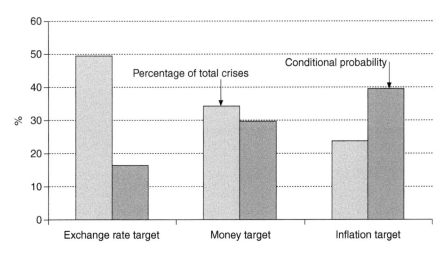

Figure 15.5 Distribution of crises by monetary policy strategies (percentage of total crises and conditional probability of crisis).

probability of a banking crisis event is clearly lower for countries whose central banks target the exchange rate, followed by monetary targeting. The highest probability is for those countries with inflation targeting.

Obviously enough, these stylized facts do not allow us to extract any definitive conclusions, since we do not take into account important factors already identified in the empirical literature as affecting the probability of a banking crisis. This will be the objective of the next section.

Empirical methodology

We apply a binary (logit) model to a panel of yearly data for 79 countries (27 industrial, 32 emerging and 20 transition) over the years 1970–1999. We have an unbalanced panel because of the lack of data for some countries, particularly in the first years included in the sample (see Table A15.1). All in all, we have 1,492 observations.

We estimate the relationship between monetary policy design and financial instability, controlling for other relevant variables. The former is defined in terms of the central bank objectives, and index variable, and the monetary policy strategy (exchange rate, monetary or inflation targeting), which is reflected in three dummies. The latter reflects the occurrence, or not, of a banking crisis, through a dummy, which takes the value of one if a crisis occurs and zero otherwise. The binary nature of the dependent variable explains the choice of a logit model for the estimation.[13]

We use a logistic distribution function to estimate whether, and to what extent, our regressors affect the probability of a banking crisis. The dependent variable equals zero in years and countries where there are no crises and equals one in the country and year where there is a crisis. Given the logistic distribution, the probability of a banking crisis in period t can be expressed as follows:

$$\text{Prob}(Crisis = 1 | X_{t-1}) = \frac{e^{(\beta' X_{t-1})}}{1 + e^{(\beta' X_{t-1})}} \qquad (15.1)$$

Similarly, the probability of no crisis in period t is:

$$\text{Prob}(Crisis = 0 | X_{t-1}) = \frac{1}{1 + e^{(\beta' X_{t-1})}} \qquad (15.2)$$

The ratio of equation (15.1) over equation (15.2) is the odds ratio in favour of a crisis. Taking natural logs of this ratio, it should be clear that it is not only linear in X_{t-1}, but also linear in the parameters β. Given equation (15.3), β measures the change in the log–odds ratio for a unit change in X_{t-1}.[14]

$$\ln \frac{\text{Prob}(Crisis=1|X_{t-1})}{\text{Prob}(Crisis=0|X_{t-1})} = \beta'X_{t-1} \tag{15.3}$$

One of the main challenges we face is the heterogeneity inherent in a study with 79 countries. We exclude the use of a conditional logit (fixed effects) because it would reduced the number of observations to a very low number and, even more importantly, it would have eliminated the information content of some countries that have not experienced any crisis as well as the few countries, especially transition countries, which have been in crisis during their whole sample period. Another problem is the low degree of time variation of the objective variables. In particular, the index of central bank objectives draws mostly from surveys conducted for decades (only for the last decade do we have more frequent data for some countries). We thus need to use random effects, even if it does not take into account the possibility of unobservable individual fixed effects being correlated with the regressors. We also use robust standard errors for our estimation and, finally, in view of the large standard deviation of some control variables, particularly inflation, real interest rates and credit growth (Table A15.3), we substitute the 5 per cent extreme values in the sample for a maximum value close to the ninety-fifth percentile (see the definition of variables in Appendix A15.1). This should avoid outliers determining the results.

Another issue is endogeneity. Once a crisis starts, it is likely to affect the evolution of the macro and financial variables and even our objective variable, the monetary policy regime. This might be true notwithstanding the findings of the empirical literature previously reviewed, that money demand continues to be stable in the long term even after a systemic banking crisis. This should reduce central bankers' interest in changing the design of monetary policy but they could still decide to do so. To reduce the potential endogeneity problem, the empirical literature of banking crises generally eliminates the crisis observations beyond the first year (that is, it only gives the value of one to the starting year of the crisis and loses the rest of the crisis years). We follow the same approach and also lag all regressors by one period.

These adjustments reduce the number of observations to 1,181 from 1,492, and the number of countries to 71 (27 industrial, 31 emerging and 13 transition) instead of the original 79.[15]

Results

With the methodology described above, we conduct one set of regressions, which can be considered the baseline, and five more sets of regressions, as robustness tests. Each set is composed of three specifications. The first includes the index of central bank objectives as the single objective variable and all macroeconomic and financial variables previously described as control variables. The second takes the three dummies for the monetary policy strategy and all control variables, but excludes the index of objectives to avoid interference between the two objective variables.[16] The third takes both the index of central bank objectives and the three strategy dummies, as well as all control variables.

The first set – the baseline – takes all countries in the sample and a narrow definition of banking crisis – which only includes systemic events – as the dependent variable. This should eliminate those crises stemming from one or a few banks' mismanagement and not necessarily from macroeconomic, institutional or policy related issues.

The results show the important role that central bank objectives play in determining the likelihood of a banking crisis in all specifications where it is included. The results for the monetary policy strategy are less clear-cut. As for the control variables, results were as expected: a higher economic growth and higher real GDP per capita – a proxy for the quality of institutions – significantly reduce the probability of a banking crisis in all specifications. Finally, more liquidity in the banks' balance sheets, measured by the share of cash held by banks to bank assets, is found to be beneficial in all specifications.

We move to describing the three baseline specifications in more detail. The first one – with the central bank objectives as single objective variable – yields a highly significant negative impact (at the 1 per cent level) of narrow objectives (focused on price stability) on the probability of a banking crisis (see column 1 of Table 15.1). This result is independent of whether a low inflation environment is actually achieved, since there is a control variable accounting for this and, incidentally, is not found significant. A way to see that the index of central bank objectives is not picking up the effect of the inflation variable is the very low, and even negative, correlation between the objective index and inflation (Table A15.4).

In the second specification, with the monetary policy strategy as a single objective variable, the results yield a negative coefficient for the exchange-rate based strategy at a 10 per cent significance level (column 2 of Table 15.1). In other words, among the three monetary policy strategies included (exchange rate, monetary based and inflation targeting), the former is found superior – albeit marginally significant – as far as financial stability is concerned. It should be recalled that our definition of financial stability focuses on banking crisis events and not on asset prices or currency crises. Finally, in this specification, higher real interest rates appear to contribute to a higher probability of banking crisis at a 10 per cent significance level.

The third and final specification – with all objective variables – confirms the negative coefficient of narrow central bank objectives but not that of the exchange-rate based strategy (column 3 of Table 15.1).

Given that the distinction between systemic and non-systemic crises is

Table 15.1 Logit estimations for systemic banking crises in all countries

Variable	(1)	(2)	(3)
Control variables			
Inflation	−0.0049	−0.0059	−0.0061
	−(0.73)	−(0.90)	−(0.89)
Real interest rate	0.0118	0.0164*	0.0141
	(1.35)	(1.79)	(1.55)
GDP per capita	−0.0003***	−0.0003***	−0.0003***
	−(7.61)	−(7.57)	−(6.78)
Real GDP growth	−0.0616**	−0.0685***	−0.0599**
	−(2.27)	−(2.57)	−(2.19)
Domestic credit growth	0.0065	0.0055	0.0069
	(1.02)	(0.90)	(1.09)
Cash held by banks/bank assets	−2.5173**	−3.5448***	−2.3851**
	−(2.07)	−(2.97)	−(1.97)
Foreign liabilities/foreign assets	−0.0109	−0.0083	−0.0089
	−(0.37)	−(0.30)	−(0.32)
Net capital flows/GDP	−0.1370	−0.1272	−0.1333
	−(0.58)	−(0.63)	−(0.61)
Objective variables			
Central bank focus on price stability	−1.4063***		−1.0740**
	−(3.36)		−(2.27)
Exchange rate target strategy		−0.5361*	−0.3695
		−(1.73)	−(1.14)
Money target strategy		−0.4490	−0.0915
		−(1.15)	−(0.22)
Inflation target strategy		−0.6480	−0.4493
		−(1.33)	−(0.90)
Number of observations	1,181	1,181	1,181
Wald test (p-value)	(0.00)	(0.00)	(0.00)

Notes
Logit estimates with random effects. All variables in first lags. *, ** and *** denote significance at 10 per cent, 5 per cent and 1 per cent, respectively. Tests: z-statistics (in parentheses) robust to heteroskedasticity; Wald test measures the joint significance of all coefficients and it is distributed as a Chi-squared with degrees of freedom equal to the number of coefficients.

not very clear-cut in the available surveys, we carry out the same regressions on a broader crisis definition as a robustness test (see Table 15.2). This includes both systemic and non-systemic crises as events in our binary model. The results hardly change for the central bank objectives and the control variables in the three model specifications. The main difference is that, with this broader definition of crises, the choice of the monetary policy strategy offers clearer results. In fact, an exchange-rate based strategy reduces the likelihood of a crisis to a 1 per cent significance level in all specifications where included. In addition, in the second and third specifications, higher real interest rates increase the probability of a crisis as well as lower inflation, albeit at a lower confidence. This latter result could

Table 15.2 Logit estimations for systemic and non-systemic banking crises in all countries

Variable	(1)	(2)	(3)
Control variables			
Inflation	−0.0076	−0.0106*	−0.0104*
	−(1.22)	−(1.71)	−(1.66)
Real interest rate	0.0129	0.0167**	0.0143*
	(1.59)	(1.99)	(1.74)
GDP per capita	−0.0002***	−0.0002***	−0.0002***
	−(7.21)	−(7.31)	−(6.30)
Real GDP growth	−0.0791***	−0.0763***	−0.0691***
	−(3.22)	−(3.17)	−(2.86)
Domestic credit growth	0.0051	0.0057	0.0066
	(0.90)	(1.02)	(1.16)
Cash held by banks/bank assets	−2.2088**	−2.6255***	−1.6861*
	−(2.18)	−(2.64)	−(1.72)
Foreign liabilities/foreign assets	−0.0137	−0.0120	−0.0123
	−(0.49)	−(0.45)	−(0.47)
Net capital flows/GDP	−0.0241	−0.0706	−0.0546
	−(0.11)	−(0.42)	−(0.30)
Objective variables			
Central bank focus on price stability	−1.1859***		−0.8918***
	−(3.56)		−(2.51)
Exchange rate target strategy		−0.8266***	−0.6951***
		−(3.37)	−(2.79)
Money target strategy		−0.1065	0.0949
		−(0.36)	(0.31)
Inflation target strategy		−0.4666	−0.2106
		−(1.18)	−(0.52)
Number of observations	1,115	1,115	1,115
Wald test (*p*-value)	(0.00)	(0.00)	(0.00)

Notes
Logit estimates with random effects. All variables in first lags. *, ** and *** denote significance at 10 per cent, 5 per cent and 1 per cent respectively. Tests: *z*-statistics (in parentheses) robust to heteroskedasticity; Wald test measures the joint significance of all coefficients and it is distributed as a Chi-squared with degrees of freedom equal to the number of coefficients.

offer some preliminary empirical ground to the recent literature strand which considers very low levels of inflation as the origin of euphoria and potential crises in countries not used to price stability, but it should be recalled that the result is only found for all crises, including non-systemic ones, and is not very robust.

Another important issue which might have a bearing with our empirical analysis is the location of the responsibility for banking regulation and supervision. One could think that central banks in charge of regulation and supervision might have a special interest in reducing the likelihood of a banking crisis, being an additional aim in their portfolio, other than monetary policy. We control for the location of regulation and supervision responsibilities with a dummy variable, which takes the value of one when the central bank is in charge and zero otherwise. The central bank objectives continue to be significant in the first specification – albeit mildly – when all systemic and non-systemic banking crises are included (column 4 of Table 15.3).

As in the previous robustness test, having an exchange-rate based monetary policy strategy significantly reduces the likelihood of suffering from all banking crises, systemic and non-systemic (column 5 of Table 15.3). This is also true when including the central bank objectives as an additional variable (column 6 of Table 15.3). These results, however, do not hold any longer for a stricter definition of banking crises, with systemic events only (column 1, 2 and 3 of Table 15.3).

Finally, an interesting result drawn from this set of regressions is that locating bank regulation and supervision at the central bank significantly reduces the likelihood of a banking crisis in all model specifications. This finding is robust to the dependent variable chosen (only systemic, or all crises). It should be noted, however, that the relevance of this finding is limited by potentially large endogeneity problems. These cannot be minimized as for the other regressors because the dummy variable representing the location of regulation and supervision is time-invariant. In fact, available information does not allow the inclusion of changes in the location of responsibilities for regulation and supervision over time, even if they have taken place, and perhaps even as a consequence of a crisis.

We now split the sample into three groups of countries – industrial, emerging and transition – to check whether the results are robust to the different country groups. As before, in the case of industrial countries, central bank objectives focused on price stability significantly reduce the likelihood of crisis events, in the first specification (column 1 of Table 15.4). However, no monetary policy strategy appears superior to the others as regards the occurrence of a banking crisis (column 2 of Table 15.4). When including all objective variables in the regression, in the third specification, having narrow central bank objectives is still beneficial, but at the 10 per cent significance level. As for the control variables, only the real GDP per capita is found to be significant, with the correct sign, and, in the third specification, high inflation appears to reduce the likelihood of a crisis at a 10 per cent confidence level, as was found for all crises in the full sample.

In the emerging country group, the results are also similar to the baseline (Table 15.5). In the first specification, countries which narrowly focus on price stability tend to suffer from fewer banking crises, other things given. In the second one, no monetary policy strategy seems superior to the others in terms of financial stability. As in the baseline, real GDP per capita and the liquidity held by banks substantially lower the likelihood of a banking crisis and the opposite is true for high real interest rates.

Table 15.3 Logit estimations for banking crises in all countries controlling for central bank supervision of financial system

Variable	Systemic banking crises			Systemic and non-systemic banking crises		
	(1)	(2)	(3)	(4)	(5)	(6)
Control variables						
Inflation	-0.0001	-0.0009	-0.0013	-0.0051	-0.0075	-0.0078
	(0.02)	(0.14)	(0.21)	(0.85)	(1.22)	(1.27)
Real interest rate	0.0135*	0.0155*	0.0144*	0.0136*	0.0155*	0.0139*
	(1.69)	(1.88)	(1.74)	(1.74)	(1.94)	(1.75)
GDP per capita	-0.0003***	-0.0003***	-0.0003***	-0.0002***	-0.0002***	-0.0002***
	(8.12)	(7.97)	(7.34)	(7.45)	(7.42)	(6.63)
Real GDP growth	-0.0521**	-0.0527**	-0.0506*	-0.0702***	-0.0634***	-0.0604**
	(2.02)	(2.01)	(1.91)	(2.88)	(2.63)	(2.49)
Domestic credit growth	0.0061	0.0064	0.0068	0.0059	0.0069	0.0072
	(1.03)	(1.07)	(1.12)	(1.07)	(1.26)	(1.31)
Cash held by banks/bank assets	-2.7822***	-3.0175***	-2.6352**	-2.0940**	-2.1189**	-1.6237*
	(2.52)	(2.85)	(2.33)	(2.16)	(2.28)	(1.72)
Foreign liabilities/foreign assets	-0.0164	-0.0108	-0.0127	-0.0101	-0.0076	-0.0094
	(0.57)	(0.40)	(0.47)	(0.39)	(0.31)	(0.38)
Net capital flows/GDP	-0.1418	-0.1370	-0.1381	-0.0106	-0.0579	-0.0463
	(0.58)	(0.62)	(0.60)	(0.05)	(0.32)	(0.24)
Objective variables						
Central bank focus on price stability	-0.4517			-0.6606*		
	(1.18)			(1.88)		
Exchange rate target strategy		-0.2475	-0.2301		-0.6468***	-0.6008**
		(0.84)	(0.78)		(2.64)	(2.44)
Money target strategy		-0.1586	-0.0629		0.0895	0.1803
		(0.44)	(0.17)		(0.30)	(0.60)

Inflation target strategy		−0.2848	−0.2111		−0.2313	−0.0983
		−(0.63)	−(0.46)		−(0.60)	−(0.25)
Central bank supervision of financial system	−1.1626***	−1.1669***	−1.0980***	−0.7986***	−0.8233***	−0.6960***
	−(4.37)	−(4.46)	−(3.98)	−(3.11)	−(3.39)	−(2.78)
Number of observations	1,181	1,181	1,181	1,115	1,115	1,115
Wald test (*p*-value)	(0.00)	(0.00)	(0.00)	(0.00)	(0.00)	(0.00)

Notes

Logit estimates with random effects. All variables in first lags. *, ** and *** denote significance at 10 per cent, 5 per cent and 1 per cent, respectively. Tests: z-statistics (in parentheses) robust to heteroskedasticity. Wald test measures the joint significance of all coefficients and it is distributed as a Chi-squared with degrees of freedom equal to the number of coefficients.

Table 15.4 Logit estimations for systemic banking crises in industrial countries

Variable	(1)	(2)	(3)
Control variables			
Inflation	−0.0512	−0.0382	−0.0482*
	−(0.71)	−(0.57)	−(0.67)
Real interest rate	0.0855	0.0763	0.0937
	(1.05)	(0.95)	(1.21)
GDP per capita	−0.0002***	−0.0002***	−0.0002***
	−(3.32)	−(3.63)	−(3.12)
Real GDP growth	−0.1495	−0.1730	−0.1574
	−(1.07)	−(1.37)	−(1.15)
Domestic credit growth	0.0008	−0.0007	−0.0013
	(0.03)	−(0.03)	−(0.05)
Cash held by banks/bank assets	−4.5091	−6.3432	−3.9695
	−(0.70)	−(0.90)	−(0.61)
Foreign liabilities/foreign assets	−0.1149	−0.0859	−0.0438
	−(0.34)	−(0.25)	−(0.13)
Net capital flows/GDP	−0.3516	−2.8797	−0.4678
	−(0.05)	−(0.38)	−(0.06)
Objective variables			
Central bank focus on price stability	−1.8625**		−1.7007*
	−(1.95)		−(1.73)
Exchange rate target strategy		−0.4692	−0.2088
		−(0.67)	−(0.28)
Money target strategy		−0.3932	0.0084
		−(0.54)	(0.01)
Inflation target strategy		−35.0796	−34.6788
		(0.00)	(0.00)
Number of observations	613	613	613
Wald test (*p*-value)	(0.00)	(0.00)	(0.00)

Notes
Logit estimates with random effects. All variables in first lags. *, ** and *** denote significance at 10 per cent, 5 per cent and 1 per cent, respectively. Tests: z-statistics (in parentheses) robust to heteroskedasticity; Wald test measures the joint significance of all coefficients and it is distributed as a Chi-squared with degrees of freedom equal to the number of coefficients.

Finally, the same exercise is conducted for transition countries. This is the only case in which having central bank objectives which narrowly focus on price stability does not reduce the probability of banking crises in a significant way. On the other hand, the choice of an exchange-rate based strategy is clearly superior since it significantly reduces the likelihood of a crisis when all specifications were included (column 2 and 3 of Table 15.6). It is interesting to note the marked differences in results for transition economies and the rest of the sample: choosing an exchange rate strategy appears to be more important for them, in terms of financial stability, than focusing on price stability, while the opposite is true for the full sample. Nevertheless, the results for the transition country group

Table 15.5 Logit estimations for systemic banking crises in emerging countries

Variable	(1)	(2)	(3)
Control variables			
Inflation	−0.0008	−0.0014	−0.0025
	−(0.08)	−(0.16)	−(0.27)
Real interest rate	0.0197*	0.0238**	0.0203*
	(1.72)	(2.05)	(1.74)
GDP per capita	−0.0004***	−0.0005***	−0.0004***
	−(3.79)	−(3.93)	−(3.12)
Real GDP growth	−0.0557	−0.0581*	−0.0514
	−(1.52)	−(1.65)	−(1.43)
Domestic credit growth	0.0020	0.0013	0.0023
	(0.22)	(0.15)	(0.26)
Cash held by banks/bank assets	−2.9177**	−3.8944***	−2.8319**
	−(1.96)	−(2.77)	−(1.92)
Foreign liabilities/foreign assets	−0.0036	−0.0012	−0.0030
	−(0.14)	−(0.05)	−(0.12)
Net capital flows/GDP	−0.1083	−0.0916	−0.1053
	−(0.45)	−(0.44)	−(0.46)
Objective variables			
Central bank focus on price stability	−1.1741**		−0.9689
	−(2.10)		−(1.57)
Exchange rate target strategy		−0.3206	−0.2801
		−(0.75)	−(0.63)
Money target strategy		−0.5513	−0.1377
		−(0.95)	−(0.22)
Inflation target strategy		−0.6522	−0.4939
		−(1.12)	−(0.82)
Number of observations	518	518	518
Wald test (*p*-value)	(0.00)	(0.00)	(0.00)

Notes
Logit estimates with random effects. All variables in first lags. *, ** and *** denote significance at 10 per cent, 5 per cent and 1 per cent, respectively. Tests: *z*-statistics (in parentheses) robust to heteroskedasticity; Wald test measures the joint significance of all coefficients and it is distributed as a Chi-squared with degrees of freedom equal to the number of coefficients.

should be taken with care, due to the small number of observations available. The structural break in the early 1990s meant that we could only take them from the early 1990s, rather than from the 1970s as for the rest of the sample.

Conclusions

Building upon the existing empirical literature on the factors behind financial stability, we assess the role of monetary policy design in determining the likelihood of a banking crisis.

With a sample of yearly data for 79 countries for the period 1970 to

Table 15.6 Logit estimations for systemic banking crises in transition countries

Variable	(1)	(2)	(3)
Control variables			
Inflation	0.0013	0.0052	−0.0056
	(0.12)	(0.41)	−(0.34)
Real interest rate	−0.0019	0.0243	0.0367
	−(0.10)	(1.01)	(1.23)
GDP per capita	−0.0001	0.0000	−0.0001
	−(0.64)	(0.09)	−(0.63)
Real GDP growth	0.1456	0.2231	0.2609*
	(1.65)	(1.62)	(1.63)
Domestic credit growth	0.0226*	0.0300**	0.0219*
	(1.75)	(2.30)	(1.66)
Cash held by banks/bank assets	1.6448	0.4500	0.7752
	(0.59)	(0.14)	(0.22)
Foreign liabilities/foreign assets	−0.4312	0.3085	0.2477
	−(0.68)	(0.44)	(0.31)
Net capital flows/GDP	−6.9050	−12.0739	−21.7375**
	−(0.86)	−(1.39)	−(1.93)
Objective variables			
Central bank focus on price stability	−1.7827		5.4542
	−(1.07)		(1.54)
Exchange rate target strategy		−3.2477**	−6.7013**
		−(1.92)	−(2.15)
Money target strategy		−0.5359	−1.5787
		−(0.50)	−(1.22)
Inflation target strategy		−0.7958	−0.2033
		−(0.72)	−(0.17)
Number of observations	50	50	50
Wald test (p-value)	(0.07)	(0.07)	(0.07)

Notes
Logit estimates with random effects. All variables in first lags. *, ** and *** denote significance at 10 per cent, 5 per cent and 1 per cent, respectively. Tests: z-statistics (in parentheses) robust to heteroskedasticity; Wald test measures the joint significance of all coefficients and it is distributed as a Chi-squared with degrees of freedom equal to the number of coefficients.

1999, we find evidence that the choice of the central bank objectives significantly influences the probability that a banking crisis may occur. In particular, having narrow central bank objectives, focused on price stability, reduces the likelihood of a banking crisis, other factors being equal. This result is robust, in general, to broad and narrow definitions of banking crises (systemic and non-systemic, or only systemic) and to different country groups, except for transition countries. The results for this latter group, however, should be taken with care due to the relatively small number of observations on which they are drawn.

As for the monetary policy strategy, exchange rate targeting is found to be beneficial in terms of financial stability when a broad definition of banking crises is chosen and for the group of transition countries, but not for industrial and emerging countries. This finding would support the choice of relatively fixed exchange rate regimes in countries in transition in terms of avoiding banking crises, but the result could change if the definition of financial instability were expanded to currency crises or other asset prices.

We also control for the location of regulatory and supervisory responsibilities and the results do not change for the broad definition of banking crises: focusing the central bank objectives on price stability is still superior. The same is true for an exchange-rate based monetary policy strategy. But the results do not hold for a narrow definition of banking crises. Another interesting result when introducing the location of regulation and supervision is that having the central bank in charge reduces the likelihood of a banking crisis in all model specifications. This is a strong result for an issue which has been long debated in the literature and for which no consensus exists, but it should be taken with caution because of obvious endogeneity problems stemming from the time invariability of this variable.

On the basis of these preliminary, but encouraging, results we intend to improve and extend our analysis in several directions. First, the relation between the central bank monetary policy intentions (in terms of objectives and strategy) and its achievements (the inflation outcome) is worth exploring. This could be achieved by introducing other important aspects of central bank design as the degree of independence but also the rule of law, as recently shown by Eijffinger and Stadhousers (2003). Second, a potentially important determinant of banking crises, financial liberalization, is now absent because of a lack of information for such a large sample of countries. This is particularly unfortunate if we consider that the central bank generally plays an important role in financial liberalization and warrants additional data compilation for an extension of the research reported in this paper. Finally, different angles of financial stability, other than the occurrence of banking crises, would warrant attention. This would imply using broader definitions of financial stability as a dependent variable, measuring the fragility of financial institutions and 'excessive' asset price movements.

Appendix 15.1

Data sources and definitions of variables

Below we list the variables and sources used for this study, as well as the explanation of any changes we have introduced. The data is annual and it covers the period 1970–1999.

Dependent variable

- *Systemic and non-systemic banking crises dummy*: equals one during episodes identified as in Caprio and Klingebiel (2003). They present information on 117 systemic banking crises (defined as much or all of bank capital being exhausted) that have occurred since the late 1970s in 93 countries and 51 smaller non-systemic banking crises in 45 countries during that period. The information on crises is cross-checked with that of Domaç and Martinez Peria (2000) and with IMF staff reports and financial news. (Sources: Caprio and Klingebiel 2003; Domaç and Martinez Peria 2000.)

Objective variables

- *Central bank focus on price stability*: measures to what extent statutory objectives do provide the central bank with a clear focus on price stability, following the approach of Cukierman *et al.* (1992). Statutory monetary objectives may potentially conflict with price stability when objectives such as employment or growth are stated separately without being qualified by statements such as 'without prejudice to monetary or price stability'. Financial stability objectives are not interpreted as potentially conflicting with monetary stability. The classification of objectives differs somewhat from Cukierman's and it is more similar to that of Mahadeva and Sterne (2000). The variable takes the following values: 0 (only goals other than price stability); 0.25 (no statutory objectives); 0.5 (price stability with other conflicting objectives); 0.75 (price stability + financial stability and non-conflicting monetary stability objectives); and 1 (only goal is price, monetary or currency stability).[17] The list of objectives and countries is available by decades, so we have assumed it to be constant through every year of each decade except for the most recent years where the information on some countries has been updated with other sources, mainly Mahadeva and Sterne (2000). (Sources: for the 1970s and the 1980s, Cukierman *et al.* 1992; Cukierman *et al.* 2002. For the 1990s, Mahadeva and Sterne 2000.)
- *Monetary policy strategies*: these three variables (exchange rate target, money target and inflation target) are dummies that equal one during periods in which targets for these variables were used according to the chronology of the Bank of England survey of monetary frameworks, in Mahadeva and Sterne (2000). Since it provides a chronology for the 1990s, we have complemented it with information from other sources for the previous years. Regarding exchange rate arrangements, we use classifications of exchange rate strategies in Reinhart and Rogoff (2002), Kuttner and Posen (2001) and Berg *et al.* (2002) for Latin America countries. Data for monetary and inflation targets were com-

plemented with the information taken from Kuttner and Posen (2001) and Carare and Stone (2003). It should be noted that some judgement has gone into the classification of regimes. (Sources: Mahadeva and Sterne 2000; Reinhart and Rogoff 2002; Kuttner and Posen 2001; Berg *et al.* 2002; Carare and Stone 2003.)

Control variables

MACROECONOMIC VARIABLES

- *Inflation:* percentage change in the GDP deflator. (Since the value for the 95 per cent percentile is 106.3 per cent, but the variance is extremely high due to several cases of hyperinflations, we have substituted all values above 150 per cent for 150 per cent.) (Source: International Monetary Fund, International Financial Statistics, line 99bir.)
- *Real interest rate:* nominal interest rate minus inflation in the same period, calculated as the percentage change in the GDP deflator. (Since the value for the 5 per cent percentile is -30 per cent and for the 95 per cent percentile is 21.2 per cent, but the variance is extremely high, we have substituted all values above 50 per cent for 50 per cent and those below -50 per cent for 50 per cent.) (Source: International Monetary Fund, International Financial Statistics. Where available, money market rate (line 60B); otherwise, the commercial bank deposit interest rate (line 60l); otherwise, a rate charged by the Central Bank to domestic banks such as the discount rate (line 60).)
- *Net Capital Flows to GDP:* capital account plus financial account + net errors and omissions. (Source: International Monetary Fund, International Financial Statistics (lines $(78\text{bcd} + 78\text{bjd} + 78\text{cad})$).)
- *Real GDP per capita in 1995 US dollars:* this variable is expressed in US dollars instead of PPP for reasons of data availability. GDP per capita in PPP was available only for two points in time. (Sources: The World Bank, World Tables; and EBRD, Transition Report, for some transition countries.)
- *Real GDP growth:* percentage change in GDP volume (1995 = 100). (Sources: International Monetary Fund, International Financial Statistics (line 99bvp) where available; otherwise, The World Bank, World Tables; and EBRD, Transition Report, for some transition countries.)

Financial variables

- *Domestic credit growth:* percentage change in domestic credit, claims on private sector. (Since the value for the 95 per cent percentile is 112.2 per cent, but the variance is extremely high, we have substituted all values above 150 per cent for 150 per cent.) (Source: International Monetary Fund, International Financial Statistics (line 32d).)

- *Bank cash to total assets*: reserves of deposit money banks divided by total assets of deposit money banks. (Source: International Monetary Fund, International Financial Statistics (line 20) divided by lines (22a + 22b + 22c + 22d + 22f).)
- *Bank foreign liabilities to foreign assets*: deposit money banks foreign liabilities to foreign assets. (Source: International Monetary Fund, International Financial Statistics (lines (26c + 26cl) divided by line 21).)
- *Central bank supervision of financial system*: this variable is a dummy which takes the value one for countries where the Central Bank is responsible for the supervision of the financial system and takes zero otherwise. This variable is not time-varying; it stems from a survey conducted by the IMF in 1993 where all member countries were asked to inform of which institution was responsible for banking regulation and supervision in their respective countries. The results of the survey are shown in Tuya and Zamalloa (1994). (Source: Tuya and Zamalloa 1994.)

Table A15.1 Countries and years included

Country name	Years	Country name	Years
Industrialized		Honduras	1978–1997
Australia	1971–1999	Indonesia	1981–1999
Austria	1970–1996	Kenya	1975–1999
Belgium	1975–1997	Malaysia	1974–1999
Canada	1970–1999	Malta	1971–1998
Cyprus	1976–1999	Mexico	1982–1999
Denmark	1975–1999	Mongolia	1993–1999
Finland	1975–1998	Nicaragua	1988–1996
France	1975–1997	Nigeria	1977–1999
Germany	1970–1998	Paraguay	1988–1999
Greece	1975–1999	Peru	1977–1999
Hong Kong, China	1991–1999	South Africa	1970–1999
Iceland	1976–1999	Tanzania	1976–1999
Ireland	1974–1998	Thailand	1976–1997
Israel	1979–1999	Turkey	1974–1997
Italy	1970–1998	Uganda	1981–1999
Japan	1977–1999	Uruguay	1978–1999
Korea, Republic	1976–1999	Venezuela, RB	1970–1999
Netherlands	1970–1997	Zambia	1985–1999
New Zealand	1972–1999		
Norway	1975–1999	*Transition*	
Portugal	1975–1999	Albania	1995–1998
Singapore	1972–1999	Armenia	1993–1999
Spain	1975–1997	Bulgaria	1992–1997
Sweden	1970–1999	Kazakhstan	1995–1999
Switzerland	1977–1999	Croatia	1994–1998
United Kingdom	1970–1999	Czech Republic	1994–1997
United States	1970–1999	Estonia	1993–1999
		Georgia	1996–1997
Developing		Hungary	1983–1997
Argentina	1981–1999	Kyrgyz Republic	1996–1998
Bahamas	1985–1995	Latvia	1994–1999
Barbados	1970–1995	Lithuania	1994–1999
Bolivia	1976–1999	Macedonia	1996–1999
Botswana	1976–1999	Moldova	1994–1999
Brazil	1981–1999	Poland	1990–1999
Chile	1977–1999	Romania	1993–1999
China	1985–1999	Russian Federation	1994–1999
Colombia	1970–1999	Slovak Republic	1994–1997
Costa Rica	1970–1999	Slovenia	1993–1999
Ecuador	1975–1999	Ukraine	1994–1998
Egypt, Arab Republic	1976–1999		

Table S15.2 Countries and crises included, 1970–1999

Country name	Systemic	Non-systemic
Industrialized		
Australia		1989–1992
Austria	no crises	no crises
Belgium	no crises	no crises
Canada		1983–1985
Cyprus	not in sample	not in sample
Denmark		1987–1992
Finland	1991–1994	
France		1994–1995
Germany		1978–1979
Greece		1991–1995
Hong Kong, China		1982–1983, 1983–1986, 1998
Iceland		1985–1986, 1993
Ireland	no crises	no crises
Israel	1977–1983	
Italy		1990–1995
Japan	1992–	
Korea, Republic	1997–	
Netherlands	no crises	no crises
New Zealand		1987–1990
Norway	1987–1993	
Portugal	no crises	no crises
Singapore		1982
Spain	1977–1985	
Sweden	1990–1994	
Switzerland	no crises	no crises
United Kingdom		1974–1976, 1984, 1991, 1995
United States	1980–1983	1980–1991
Developing		
Argentina	1980–1982, 1989–1990, 1995	
Bahamas	not in sample	not in sample
Barbados	not in sample	not in sample
Bolivia	1986–1987, 1994–	
Botswana		1994–1995
Brazil	1990, 1994–1999	
Chile	1976, 1981–1987	
China	1990s	
Colombia	1982–1987	
Costa Rica	1987	1994–
Ecuador	1980–1982, 1996–	
Egypt, Arab Republic	1980–1985	1991–1995
Ghana	1982–1989	1997–
Honduras	no crises	no crises
Indonesia	1992–1997, 1997–	
Kenya	1985–1989, 1992, 1993–1995	1996–
Malaysia	1997–	1985–1988
Malta	not in sample	not in sample
Mexico	1981–1982, 1994–1997	

(*continued*)

Table A15.2 Continued

Country name	Systemic	Non-systemic
Mongolia	not in sample	not in sample
Nicaragua	1988–1996	
Nigeria	1990s	1997
Paraguay	1995–1999	
Peru	1983–1990	
South Africa		1977, 1989
Tanzania	1988–	
Thailand	1983–1987, 1997–	
Turkey	1982–1985	1994
Uganda	1994–	
Uruguay	1981–1985	
Venezueta, RB	1994–1999	1978, 1981, 1982, 1985, 1986
Zambia	1995	
Transition		
Albania	1992–	
Armenia	1994–1996	
Bulgaria	1991–1997	
Croatia	1996	
Czech Republic	1997–	
Estonia	1992–1995	1998
Georgia	1991–	
Hungary	1991–1995	
Kazakhstan	not in sample	not in sample
Kyrgyz Republic	1990s	
Latvia	1995–1996, 1998–1999	
Lithuania	1995–1996	
Macedonia	1993–1994	
Moldova	not in sample	not in sample
Poland	1990s	
Romania	1990–	
Russian Federation	1995, 1998–1999	
Slovak Republic	1991–	
Slovenia	1992–1994	
Ukraine	1997–1998	

Note
This table presents the periods of systemic and non-systemic banking crisis based on the information provided by Caprio and Klingebiel (2003) and Domaç and Martinez Peria (2000).

Table A15.3 Descriptive statistics of the regression variables

Variable	No. Obs.	Mean	Std. Deviation	Minimum	Maximum
Crisis dummy	1,492	0.23	0.42	0.00	1.00
Inflation	1,492	72.64	562.01	−4.00	11,750.00
Real interest rate	1,492	8.62	626.98	−11,680.85	14,155.99
Real GDP per capita	1,492	6,925.07	4,976.04	125.20	21,487.30
Real GDP growth	1,492	3.46	4.67	−38.29	52.55
Domestic credit growth	1,492	87.91	800.47	−55.71	18,939.19
Cash held by banks/ bank assets	1,492	0.14	0.17	0.00	1.78
Foreign liabilities/foreign assets	1,492	1.88	4.26	0.00	85.25
Net capital flows/GDP	1,492	0.00	0.71	−12.99	8.07
Central bank focus on price stability	1,492	0.61	0.31	0.00	1.00
Exchange rate target strategy	1,492	0.60	0.49	0.00	1.00
Money target strategy	1,492	0.27	0.44	0.00	1.00
Inflation target strategy	1,492	0.17	0.38	0.00	1.00
Central bank supervision	1,492	0.69	0.46	0.00	1.00

Note
For an explanation on the construction and modification of the variables see main text and the description in this Appendix.

Table A15.4 Correlation matrix of the regression variables

	Crisis	Inflation	Real int	GDP pc	Real GDP	Dom credit	Cash/ assets	Foreign liab	Capital flows	Price stab	Exch target	Money target	Inflation Target
Crisis dummy	1												
Inflation	0.11	1											
Real interest rate	0.05	-0.19	1										
Real GDP per capita	-0.16	-0.11	0.02	1									
Real GDP growth	-0.11	-0.15	0.00	-0.07	1.0								
Domestic credit growth	0.08	0.92	-0.20	-0.09	-0.12	1							
Cash held by banks/ bank assets	0.08	0.10	-0.06	-0.44	0.03	0.07	1						
Foreign liabilities/foreign assets	-0.05	-0.01	-0.01	-0.04	-0.02	0.00	0.03	1					
Net capital flows/GDP	-0.12	-0.01	0.00	0.03	-0.01	-0.01	-0.06	-0.08	1				
Central bank focus on price stability	0.05	-0.05	-0.06	-0.07	-0.01	-0.03	0.01	-0.09	0.00	1			
Exchange rate target strategy	-0.11	-0.08	-0.02	-0.04	0.13	-0.06	-0.04	-0.02	0.05	0.03	1		
Money target strategy	0.09	-0.06	-0.01	0.07	-0.10	-0.04	-0.13	-0.07	0.03	0.10	-0.11	1	
Inflation target strategy	0.19	-0.05	0.00	-0.08	0.01	-0.04	-0.10	-0.01	-0.01	0.19	0.02	0.18	1

Note
For an explanation on the construction and modification of the variables see main text and the description in this Appendix.

Notes

1 This chapter received the Marjolin Prize at the SUERF Colloquium in Tallin, June 2003. It has benefited from comments from Roberto Chang, Martti Randveer and José Viñals. Holger Wolf also offered substantial comments to a very preliminary version. Remaining errors are the authors' responsibility.

2 Both authors are affiliated with Banco de España. However, the opinions expressed are those of the authors and not of the institution they represent.

3 In his words, 'the issue of financial stability was part of the central banks' genetic code'.

4 In the beginning, the stability issue arose because the issuers of banknotes were profit-maximizing commercial banks, who had incentives to print more notes than they could back with holdings of gold and silver, or with deposits of government bonds. This led to 'wildcat banks that heavily engaged in over-issuance' (Gorton 1999). For a description of the role of central banks in financial stability across regimes, see Borio and Lowe (2002).

5 Recently, Padoa-Schioppa (2002) has offered a working definition of financial stability, namely 'a condition where the financial system is able to withstand shocks without giving way to cumulative processes which impairs the allocation of savings to investment opportunities and the processing of payments in the economy'. However, as in the other cases, financial stability is defined in terms of financial instability, rather than explicitly.

6 As Schinasi (2003) explains, even stable markets can have high volatility in asset prices. Issing (2003) goes even further, arguing that large swings in asset prices leading to some failures of financial institutions could even be a sign of stability or of the self-purifying powers of the system. The question is, thus, when is volatility so large that it creates systemic damage to the system and the real economy?

7 See Borio and Lowe (2002) for a review of the trade-offs of monetary authorities reacting to asset price movements and, more generally, to financial imbalances.

8 Lending booms are often seen as the domestic image of large capital inflows (Gourinchas *et al.* 2001).

9 Padoa-Schioppa (2002) argues that financial stability considerations are taken into account when designing the central bank objectives and strategy.

10 We could have used a dummy for each objective, or a non-linear index instead of a linear index. However, our goal here is to examine the importance of narrow objectives, which is a proxy of how much central banks focus on price stability, rather than on the choice among the many different options.

11 While there may be more accurate information on the quality of institutions than the GDP per capita, available surveys do not have a time dimension. The lack of different observations over time makes these – in principle better – institutional indicators inadequate for our empirical analysis. The same is true for other relevant institutional variables, such as the existence of a deposit insurance scheme.

12 Blinder (1999), Crockett (2000), Viñals (2001) and Borio and Lowe (2002).

13 A logit model is preferred to a probit to avoid assuming normality.

14 However, the marginal effect of a regressor on the dependent variable, which is the usual interpretation for coefficients in the ordinary least squares setup, is different from β (although it still depends on it), namely:

$$\frac{\partial \text{Pr } ob(Crisis = 1|X_{t-1})}{\partial X_{t-1}} = \beta * \frac{\exp(\beta' X_{t-1})}{1 + \exp(\beta' X_{t-1})} * \frac{1}{1 + \exp(\beta' X_{t-1})}$$

Note that this expression will vary with X_{t-1}. In practice, the marginal effects are calculated at the means of the regressors.

15 The eight countries lost are transition ones which had experienced crises throughout the period. Given that we take lags, we need at least two observations to keep a country in the sample.

16 Note, however, that we do not expect much interference since the correlations are low. In the most obvious case, between the dummy for the inflation targeting strategy and the index showing how important the price stability objective is, the correlation is only 0.19, and in any case the highest between the two objective variables (Table A15.4).

17 Cukierman's classification distinguishes between 'price stability is the only objective', rated 0.8, and 'price stability is the major or only objective in the charter, and the central bank has the final word in case of conflict with other government objectives', rated 1.

Bibliography

Berg, A., Borensztein, E. and Mauro, P. (2002) 'An evaluation of monetary regime options for Latin America', IMF Working Paper WP/02/211.

Bernanke, B. and Gertler, M. (2000) 'Monetary policy and asset price volatility', NBER Working Paper 7559. National Bureau of Economic Research, Cambridge, MA.

Bernanke, B. and Gertler, M. (1990) 'Financial fragility and economic performance', *Quarterly Journal of Economics*, 105(1): 87–114.

Blinder, A. (1999) 'General discussion: monetary policy and asset price volatility', *Fed of Kansas City Economic Review*, 4th quarter: 139–140.

Bordo, M. (1985) 'Financial crises, banking crises, stock market crashes, and the money supply: some international evidence, 1887–1933', in F. Capie and G. Wood (eds), *Financial Crises and the World Banking System*. New York, NY: St. Martin's.

Bordo, M. and Murshid, A. (2000) 'Are financial crises becoming increasingly more contagious? What is the historical evidence on contagion?', NBER Working Paper 7900. National Bureau of Economic Research, Cambridge, MA.

Bordo, M., Mizrach, B. and Schwartz, A. (1995) 'Real versus pseudo-international systemic risk: some lessons from history', NBER Working Paper 5371. National Bureau of Economic Research, Cambridge, MA.

Borio, C. and Lowe, P. (2002) 'Asset prices, financial and monetary stability: exploring the nexus', BIS Working Papers No. 114.

Calvo, G. (1997) 'Capital flows and macroeconomic management: Tequila lessons', *International Journal of Finance and Economics*, 1(3): 207–223.

Caprio, G. and Klingebiel, D. (2003) 'Episodes of systemic and borderline financial crises', Dataset mimeo, The World Bank.

Carare, A. and Stone, M. (2003) 'Inflation targeting regimes', IMF, Working Paper 03/9.

Crockett, A. (2000) 'In search of anchors for financial and monetary stability', SUERF Colloquium, Vienna, April.

Cukierman, A. (1992) *Central Bank Strategy, Credibility and Independence: Theory and Evidence*. MIT Press.

Cukierman, A., Miller, G.P. and Neyapti, B. (2002) 'Central bank reform, liberalization and inflation in transition economies – an international perspective', *Journal of Monetary Economics*, 49: 237–264.

Cukierman, A., Webb, S.B. and Neyapti, B. (1992) 'Measuring the independence of central banks and its effect on policy outcomes', *The World Bank Economic Review*, 6: 353–398.

Chang, R., Cespedes, L. and Velasco, A. (2000) 'Balance sheets and exchange rate policy', NBER Working Papers 7840. National Bureau of Economic Research, Cambridge, MA.

Demirgüç-Kunt, A. and Detragiache, E. (1998) 'Financial liberalisation and financial fragility', Annual World Bank Conference on Development Economics.

Demirgüç-Kunt, A. and Detragiache, E. (2000) 'Does deposit insurance increase banking system stability?', IMF Working Paper 00/3.

Domaç, I. and Martinez Peria, M.S. (2000) 'Banking crises and exchange rate regimes: is there a link?', The World Bank Working Paper No. 2489.

Eijffinger, S. and Stadhousers, P. (2003) 'Monetary policy and the rule of law', Center for Economic Policy Research, International Macroeconomics, No. 3698.

English, W. (1996) 'Inflation and financial sector size', Finance and Economic Discussion Papers No. 96/16, Board of Governors of the Federal Reserve, Washington, DC.

Frankel, J. and Rose, A. (1998) 'Currency crashes in emerging markets: an empirical treatment', *Journal of International Economics*, 41: 351–366.

García Herrero, A. (1997) 'Monetary impact of a banking crisis and the conduct of monetary policy', IMF Working Paper 97/124.

Gavin, M. and Hausmann, R. (1996) 'The roots of banking crises: the macroeconomic context', mimeo.

Gorton, G. (1999) 'Pricing free bank notes', *Journal of Monetary Economics*, 44: 33–64.

Gourinchas, P.O., Valdés, R. and Landarretche, O. (2001) 'Lending booms: Latin America and the world', *Economia*, 1(2).

Gupta, P. (1996) 'Currency crises, banking crises and twin crises: a comprehensive review of the literature', International Monetary Fund, mimeo.

Hardy, D. and Pazarbasioglu, C. (1999) 'Determinants and leading indicators of banking crises: further evidence', IMF Staff Papers, 46, no. 3.

International Monetary Fund (1998) 'Financial crises: characteristics and indicators of vulnerability', in *World Economic Outlook*, Chapter IV, May.

Issing, O. (2003) 'Monetary and financial stability: is there a trade-off?', Conference on 'Monetary stability, financial stability and the business cycle'. 28–29 March. Bank for International Settlements, Basle.

Kuttner, K.N. and Posen, A.S. (2001) 'Beyond bipolar: a three-dimensional assessment of monetary frameworks', Oesterreichische Nationalbank Working Paper 52.

La Porta, R., Lopez-De-Silanes, F., Shleifer, A. and Vishny, R.W. (1998) 'Law and finance', *Journal of Political Economy*, 106(6): 1113–1151.

Lindgren, C.J., Garcia, G. and Saal, M.I. (eds) (1996) *Bank Soundness and Macroeconomic Policy*, International Monetary Fund.

Mahadeva, L. and Sterne, G. (eds) (2000) *Monetary Policy Frameworks in a Global Context*. London: Routledge.

Martinez Peria, S. (2000) 'The impact of banking crises on money demand and price stability', The World Bank Working Paper 2305.

Mishkin, F. (1996) 'Understanding financial crises: a developing country's perspective', NBER Working Paper 5600. National Bureau of Economic Research, Cambridge, MA.

Padoa-Schioppa, T. (2002) 'Central banks and financial stability: exploring a land in between', Paper presented at the Second ECB Central Banking Conference 'The transformation of the European financial system', Frankfurt am Main, October.

Reinhart, C.M. and Rogoff, K.S. (2002) 'The modern history of exchange rate arrangements: a reinterpretation', NBER Working Paper 8963. National Bureau of Economic Research, Cambridge, MA.

Sachs, J., Velasco, A. and Tornell, A. (1996) 'Financial crises in emerging markets: the lessons from 1995', *Brookings Papers on Economic Activity*, 1: 147–198.

Schinasi, G.J. (2003) 'Responsibility of central banks for stability in financial markets', IMF Working Paper 03/121.

Schwartz, A. (1995) 'Systemic risk and the macroeconomy' in G. Kaufman (ed), *Banking Financial Markets and Systemic Risk*, Research in Financial Services, Private and Public Policy, Vol. 7. Hampton: JAI Press Inc.

Viñals, J. (2001) 'Monetary policy issues in a low inflation environment', in A. Garcia Herrero, V. Gaspar, L. Hoogduin, J. Morgan and B. Winkler (eds), *Why Price Stability?* European Central Bank.

Tuya, J. and Zamalloa, L. (1994) 'Issues on placing banking supervision in the central bank', in T. Baliño and C. Cottarelli (eds), *Frameworks for Monetary Stability: Policy Issues And Country Experiences.* International Monetary Fund.

Subject index

Author index

380 *Author index*

For Product Safety Concerns and Information please contact our EU
representative GPSR@taylorandfrancis.com
Taylor & Francis Verlag GmbH, Kaufingerstraße 24, 80331 München, Germany

www.ingramcontent.com/pod-product-compliance
Ingram Content Group UK Ltd.
Pitfield, Milton Keynes, MK11 3LW, UK
UKHW021115180425
457613UK00005B/95